AN INTRODUCTION TO LEARNING DISABILITIES

Scott, Foresman Series in Special Education
Richard J. Morris, Series Editor

AN INTRODUCTION TO LEARNING DISABILITIES

Howard S. Adelman and Linda Taylor
University of California, Los Angeles

Scott, Foresman and Company
Glenview, Illinois
London

Two young ones playing restaurant:
  "How do you want your steak?"
  "Medium."
  "I'm sorry, we only have large."

To those whose answers make us think.

Library of Congress Cataloging-in-Publication Data

Adelman, Howard S.
  An introduction to learning disabilities.

  Bibliography: p.
  Includes index.
  1. Learning disabilities.   I. Taylor, Linda
(Linda L.)   II. Title.
LC4704.A325   1986   371.9   85-22124
ISBN 0-673-15902-7

Preface

"What can I do to help the children in my class who have learning disabilities?" the teacher asked with a note of despair. Before the speaker could answer, someone shouted, "Why don't we talk about improving schools to keep kids from becoming learning disabled?" It was more a statement than a question, and the feelings accompanying it were strong. Some in the audience nodded their agreement. Others, who see learning disabilities as a neurologically based handicapping condition, called for establishment of more special classes. And so it goes when the topic of *learning disabilities* is discussed.

This book is intended to introduce learning disabilities in a way that clarifies what can be done for the many persons who need help and what can be done to advance the field. In Parts 1 and 2, we explore the basic questions, What is a learning disability? and What is done about learning disabilities? In Part 3, specific methods and materials for working with those with learning disabilities are discussed. Part 4 is a look at underlying dilemmas in the field and new directions taken in practice and research to advance the field, including ways the reader may become involved.

More specifically, Part 1 introduces the learning disabilities (LD) field by

- identifying characteristics of learning disabilities
- defining learning disabilities
- discussing causes, diagnosis, and labeling
- distinguishing learning disabilities from other types of learning problems

Part 2 describes what is generally done to treat learning disabilities, including

- how persons with learning disabilities are screened and placed
- general approaches to treatment
- how treatment decisions are made
- how the field is evolving

Part 3 describes specific methods and materials for working with individuals and groups in personalized and remedial ways. Highlighted is the importance of

- establishing a good match with the learner's motivation and development
- enhancing motivation for learning
- facilitating development of a variety of skills and knowledge

With regard to the remediation of problems that interfere with learning, emphasis is on

- negative attitudes and protective behavior
- basic and prerequisite skill deficiencies
- overcoming handicaps

Part 4 looks to the future. Particular emphasis is given to the importance of increased understanding of social and ethical issues and of accountability. We conclude with an exploration of the role that the student may play in the future of the field—as a consumer, professional, or concerned citizen.

The book has three types of reading material, so that it can be used in different ways:

1. *text*—the main body of the book offers a straightforward presentation of basic information, theory, and issues;
2. *boxes*—the boxed material provides examples of practices, research, issues, and viewpoints; and

v

3. *supplements*—special topic references and activities at the end of chapters and enrichment opportunities or readings following the last chapter of the book.

This format allows the reader to read the text quickly, without looking at the boxed or enrichment material. Many readers will want to intersperse the other materials as they find that the topics cited are of special interest. Also to allow for ease in reading, we have limited within-text references to bare essentials. Fairly extensive special topic reference lists are provided at the end of most chapters, covering key topics that the reader may want to explore in greater depth.

Our intent in introducing the topic of learning disabilities is to provide a broad overview to an exciting field. As we stress in our text for advanced students *(Learning Disabilities in Perspective)*, learning disabilities must be understood in a broad context—as one of several types of learning problems. Thus, we focus on motivational and developmental differences, deficiencies, and dysfunctions, on a variety of causal factors, and on current and evolving approaches to correction. Throughout, we present general concepts and specific examples of practical application.

The reader is going to be introduced to a creative, rapidly developing and changing field, a field focusing on incredibly complex challenges. We want to introduce the field in a way that allows an appreciation of both what has been accomplished and what more needs to be done.

We owe too much to too many to be able to name them all. However, we do want especially to thank the staff and students at the Fernald Laboratory and Clinic for all they have taught us. Also, as we were writing the book, our editor sought reactions from knowledgeable leaders in the field. Although feedback was anonymous when first given, the identity of the reviewers has now been revealed to us, and we want to acknowledge their contribution in reviewing the manuscript in its various stages. The reviewers were Robert Algozzine (University of Florida), Don Deshler (University of Kansas), Anna Gajar (Pennsylvania State University), Noel Gregg (University of Georgia), Richard Morris (University of Arizona), Suzanne Robinson (University of Kansas), and Joseph Wade (University of Wisconsin–Milwaukee).

Overview

Contents

READINGS AND RESOURCES 235

Part I

WHAT IS A LEARNING DISABILITY?

The single most characteristic thing about human beings is that they learn.

Bruner (1966, p. 113)

For you to understand what a learning disability is and what it isn't, it must be separated from other types of learning problems. Not all persons who have learning problems are learning disabled.

Diagnostically separating those with learning disabilities from those with other learning problems will improve understanding and help in planning intervention. The continuing and growing interest in learning disabilities suggests that many people are finding this particular diagnostic label to be useful.

Our intent in Part 1 is to explore (1) the nature of learning disabilities and their relationship to other types of learning problems, (2) the history of the learning disabilities (LD) field and how that history shapes current thinking about learning disabilities, and (3) some basic points about identifying causes.

The main objective in Part 1 is to help you answer the general questions, What is a learning disability? and Who should and shouldn't be diagnosed as learning disabled?

1

Chapter 1

Characteristics and Definition

Someone is in trouble

At school each day the words go by,
    too quickly to make sense.
So attention turns from reading
    to avoidance, pain, pretense.

FOUR PEOPLE IN TROUBLE

Let us introduce you to Bret, Sally, Jan, and Chris. They are composites of persons we have encountered over the past twenty years. We will refer to them many times in the ensuing chapters.

Bret

No doubt about it; it was a tale of horror.

To hear his parents tell the story, the fact that Bret had been diagnosed as learning disabled was almost as bad as if he had been found to have a fatal disease.

Bret entered kindergarten at age five with the same eagerness and cheerfulness his older brother and sister had shown. There was no question in anyone's mind about his future. First there would be kindergarten, a brief hitch in elementary and secondary school, and then on to a good university and a profession.

By the end of second grade, however, expectations were changing. Bret was still a nonreader. He hated school. His teacher described him as her worst behavior problem. He was tested by a school psychologist, who diagnosed him as learning disabled.

What had happened to Bret's eagerness and promise? What convinced the psychologist that he was learning disabled? Could the problem be corrected? What about his future?

Sally

Jackson F. Floyd, M.D.   Feb. 18, 1984
10 Main St.
Bryant, Ariz.   Re: Sally Brown
                                            Born 1/9/76
                                            Age 8 yrs.

Dear Jack:

Thanks for referring Sally for a psychological evaluation.

My full report is attached. By way of summary, I met with her and her
mother on Jan. 5 and 6, 1984. First I interviewed Mrs. Brown who reported
that Sally was suffering from reading and writing difficulties and poor
coordination. The mother thinks Sally is simply lazy but wonders about
the possibility of some sort of disability. Apparently Sally tends to be
argumentative at home, especially with her younger brother. She is described as having a strong personality and as being quite a "stinker" at
times. She also apparently can be quite affectionate.

With regard to past problems, the mother states there were no special
traumas, physical or emotional, except that Sally has appeared to be somewhat upset by her father's frequent business trips. Since you have an
extensive file on her developmental, medical, and family history, there is
no need to review such matters here.

The school history is checkered. She went to preschool at 3 1/2 with no
reported difficulties. In kindergarten, she was in continuous conflict
with her teacher, but in first grade, the teacher apparently worked very
well with Sally. Second grade and now the first half of third grade have
been almost complete disasters. Besides poor academic performance, she
has gotten into frequent fights and often refuses to go to school.

To assess the nature of Sally's problems, I administered a psychological
test battery consisting of the Wechsler intelligence test (WISC-R), the
Wide Range Achievement Test (WRAT), the Illinois Test of Psycholinguistic
Abilities (ITPA), the Bender Visual Motor Gestalt Test, several personality
tests, and I made some observations while interacting informally with her
in the play room. My conclusions are as follows:

Sally is a nice looking, red headed girl of average height and weight.
She entered the test situation somewhat apprehensively, but I was able to
calm her anxiety and get her focused on the tasks with little difficulty.
She performed in the average range on the IQ test with some unevenness in
her performance on both the verbal and nonverbal subtests. Her achievement
scores were all at the first grade level, and it is, therefore, not surprising she is having difficulty at school. The pattern of her performance
on the perceptual motor and psycholinguistic test leads me to a diagnosis
of Learning Disabled and to recommend special remedial help as soon as
possible. In this connection, I have given the mother the names of several
agencies and private tutors. Since Sally also shows signs of emotional
upset and seems to have an intense rivalry with her younger brother, I
also recommended they be separated as much as possible and that family
counseling be pursued.

Sally should have the benefit of retesting in about a year to evaluate
progress.

Thanks again for the referral.

                              Sincerely yours,

                              George P. Blanc

                              George P. Blanc, Ph.D.
                              Licensed Psychologist

Jan

I am 18 years old and learning
disabled. I have had problems along time.
People say I am smart but I lak eng
ability and I am tired of trying.
My parrents tryed to help me,
but I dont deserve there support
or concern, I am just not worth
it. I do not get allong with
people eneywhere and never have been
able to. I am affraid of every one
and hate being told to wake up
or come out of my dreemworld.
I dont know how to deel with
eneything eneywhere.

Chris

We adopted Chris when he was five—a beautiful child, with curly hair and flawless skin. But he clearly had been hurt by the loss of his parents and two years in foster homes. When first approached, he had such a look of fear—like that of a frightened animal.

After a few months, Chris seemed to adjust well to his new home, and we all grew to love each other. While quieter than Jenny, our eight-year-old, he joined in all activities readily and ably.

We enrolled Chris in school when he was six. School brought letters and numbers and a new identity—learning disabled. At first we were shocked. We had seen no signs of learning problems at home. We wondered if it could be an emotional reaction. The tests showed a perceptual-motor problem and other signs of neurological dysfunctioning. We decided we would do everything we could to help him overcome his handicap.

For the next six years, Chris had special tutoring and support at school. It helped, but not enough to let him catch up with the others. Teacher after teacher described him as immature, impulsive, and easily distracted and confused. By the time he got to junior high, he was convinced he couldn't do it. Gradually, the self-doubt led to frustration and then to anger. He lashed out at everyone. Soon he was in trouble with the law—stealing, fighting, hitting a teacher, drugs.

As soon as he was sixteen, Chris dropped out of school. They were glad to see him go.

Chris is twenty now. He works when and where he can. He's worried about his future. So are we.

CHARACTERISTICS OF PEOPLE WITH LEARNING DISABILITIES

If you know anyone like Bret, Sally, Jan, or Chris, or anyone called one of the names cited in Box 1–1, you probably have some thoughts about the characteristics of people with learning disabilities. Obviously, they have trouble learning certain things—but so do people who are not learning disabled. They also may be immature, disorganized, impulsive, distractable, inflexible, and awkward—but so are people who are not learning disabled. They may be hyperactive, emo-

---

Box 1–1

Clinical Example
Someone You Know May Have Been Called by a Special Name

Individuals who have not learned to read very well in spite of apparent ability and opportunity have, for about the last forty years, been assigned a variety of labels in addition to *learning disabled*. The labels referring to these persons and their conditions include

    brain injured
    dyslexic
    educationally handicapped
    hyperactive
    hyperkinetic behavior syndrome
    language disordered
    learning disordered
    minimal brain damaged
    minimal cerebral dysfunctioned
    perceptually impaired (dysfunctioned)
    problem learner
    problem reader

    psycholinguistic disability
    psychoneurological disorder
    reading disability
    slow learner
    Strauss syndrome
    underachiever

Less commonly used names are

    auditory learner
    choreiform child
    developmental aphasia
    developmentally imbalanced
    driven child
    dyssynchronous child
    educationally maladjusted
    interjacent child
    invisibly crippled child
    kinesthetic learner
    organic brain syndrome
    performance disabled (handicapped)
    visual learner

tionally upset, and generally disruptive—but so are many people who have no problem learning. Which characteristics are unique to learning disabilities?

Box 1–2 provides examples of some of the efforts made to pinpoint the characteristics of those who are learning disabled. Also see the special topic references at the end of the chapter.

One characteristic of those in LD pro-

Box 1–2

Clinical and Research Example
Characteristics of People with Learning Disabilities

Perhaps the most frequently cited list of characteristics of individuals who today are diagnosed as learning disabled is that generated by a government-sponsored task force in the 1960s (Clements, 1966). After reviewing the many varied descriptions cited in the literature, the panel of experts identified ten characteristics it viewed as general symptoms:

1. hyperactivity
2. perceptual-motor impairments
3. emotional lability
4. general coordination defects
5. disorders of attention
6. impulsivity
7. disorders of memory and thinking
8. specific learning disabilities
9. disorders of speech and hearing
10. equivocal neurological signs and encephalographic irregularities

There have been many subsequent studies of characteristics and the specific problem behaviors associated with each. Examples of specific behaviors frequently reported include:

1. reversals of letters, words, and numbers (called *strephosymbolia*, which means "twisted symbols")
2. mistakes in identifying left and right
3. not having well-established preferences when using one's hands and feet (often called a laterality or mixed-dominance problem)
4. clumsiness
5. writing illegibly
6. difficulty blending speech sounds
7. leaving out or adding speech sounds
8. difficulty with abstractions
9. high degree of activity or agitation (often called *hyperactivity*)

References to a sample of research reports on characteristics are provided as potential resources at the end of the chapter.

Well-designed, large-scale studies that may clarify which characteristics are *unique* to the learning disabled have not yet been carried out. One problem hindering such research is the disagreement among experts as to what a learning disability is. The term has been used for persons whose learning problems have very different causes and whose remedial needs differ greatly. Programs serving the "learning disabled" often contain people with so many different types of learning and behavior problems that the main thing these people have in common is not performing well in learning situations. In such programs, one can find a little of every characteristic described so far.

To improve understanding, future research will focus on refining the study of characteristics by focusing on persons at specific ages with specified types of learning problems and comparing these persons with those who do not have learning problems. The immediate objective of such research will be to clarify which behaviors are primarily associated with learning disabilities. In the long run, such studies also may help to identify specific causes of learning disabilities.

grams that is not found in non-learning-problem populations is severe academic underachievement. As outlined in federal regulations in the United States, this "characteristic" is the major inclusive criterion for identifying specific learning disabilities.

"A team may determine that a child has a specific learning disability if: (1) the child does not achieve commensurate with his or her age and ability levels in one or more areas [seven of which are specified—oral or written expression, listening comprehension, basic reading skill or comprehension, mathematics calculation or reasoning] when provided with learning experiences appropriate for the child's age and ability levels; and (2) the team finds that a child has a severe discrepancy between achievement and intellectual ability in one or more of [these] areas." *(Federal Register*, 1977, p. 65, 083)

How severe the discrepancy between achievement and intellectual ability must be and how it should be measured are difficult questions. To illustrate, think about two individuals, both one year below grade level in reading as measured by a standard achievement test. If one of them has a very high IQ and the other has a very low IQ, should they both be seen as having a severe discrepancy? What if they both have an average IQ, but one is in the ninth grade and the other is in the second grade?

To deal with the problem of defining a severe discrepancy, a variety of formulas have been proposed. None has found wide acceptance, however, and specific procedures and criteria for determining a severe discrepancy continue to vary from one locale to another (Forness, Sinclair, & Guthrie, 1983).

LEARNING DISABILITIES DEFINED

Ever since the term *learning disabilities* was popularized in the early 1960s (see Box 1–3), there has been controversy over how it should be defined. After several years of

debate, a compromise was worked out by the National Advisory Committee on Handicapped Children. The definition this group proposed in 1968 was given official status throughout the United States when it was incorporated (with very minor modifications) into federal legislation in 1969. As stated in current federal statute (U.S. Public Law 94-142—the Education for All Handicapped Children Act of 1975), individuals with specific learning disabilities are those who have

"a disorder in one or more of the basic psychological processes involved in understanding or in using language, spoken or written, which may manifest itself in an imperfect ability to listen, think, speak, read, write, spell, or to do mathematical calculations. The term includes such conditions as perceptual handicaps, brain injury, minimal brain dysfunction, dyslexia, and developmental aphasia. The term does not include children who have learning problems which are primarily the result of visual, hearing, or motor handicaps, of mental retardation, or emotional disturbance, or of environmental, cultural, or economic disadvantage." *(Federal Register*, 1977, p. 65, 083)

While useful for legislative purposes, this definition has been controversial from the start. As a result, individuals and organizations have proposed new definitions. A recent and prominent example is the proposal of the National Joint Committee for Learning Disabilities (NJCLD).

The NJCLD consists of six major organizations concerned with learning problems: the American Speech-Language-Hearing Association (ASHA), the Association for Children and Adults with Learning Disabilities (ACLD), the Council for Learning Disabilities (CLD), the Division for Children with Communication Disorders (DCCD), the International Reading Association (IRA), and The Orton Dyslexia Society. In 1981, official representatives of the six organizations

Box 1–3

Historical Note
Popularizing "Learning Disabilities"

The problem that the term *learning disabilities* is meant to represent has been of increasing concern to professionals throughout this century. Terms such as "minimal brain damage," "minimal cerebral dysfunction," "perceptual impairment" or "dysfunction," "neurological handicap," "learning disorders," and many more have been used to describe the problem (see Box 1–1). In the 1960s, the term "learning disabilities" began to take the place of these other terms. William Cruickshank (Cruickshank, Bentzen, Ratzeburg, & Tannahauser, 1961) and Samuel Kirk (1962) usually are credited with starting the trend toward widespread use of the term.

As related by Kirk and Gallagher:

"The term *learning disability* became popular when the Association for Children with Learning Disabilities (ACLD) was organized under the name in 1963. During the period just prior to that, parents throughout the United States became concerned because their children who were not learning in school were rejected from special education since they were not mentally retarded, deaf or blind, or otherwise handicapped. Local parent groups were organized. Parent-sponsored schools were initiated. They were called by different names such as schools for the neurologically handicapped, brain injured, aphasoid,

dyslexic, and perceptually handicapped. Parent organizations met in Chicago in 1963 to discuss their mutual problems, one of which was the need for a national organization and an appropriate name.

"Discussing the problem and the difficulties of labels for these children, Kirk (1963) explained that sometimes classification labels block out thinking. It is better, he told the conference, to state that a child has not learned to read than to say the child is dyslexic. He continued that it may be more scientific to say 'a child has not learned to talk' than to say the child is aphasic or brain injured. He advised that a name should be functional and that if the parents were interested in research on the relation of the brain to behavior, they could use a neurologic term. He suggested further that if they were interested in service to their children, it might be preferable to use a term related to teaching or learning and that a term such as learning disability might be preferable to some currently used terms such as *cerebral dysfunction* and brain injured.

"The term *learning disabilities* struck a receptive chord with the parent groups since it implied teaching and learning and since they were interested primarily in service for their children. They selected the name Association for Children with Learning Disabilities, and from that point on, learning disabilities became a new category of exceptional children and crept into federal, state, and local legislation."
Kirk and Gallagher (1979, p. 287)

agreed to propose a new definition of learning disabilities.

"Learning disabilities is a generic term that refers to a heterogeneous group of disorders manifested by significant difficulties in the acquisition and use of listening, speaking, reading, writing, reasoning or mathematical abilities. These disorders are intrinsic to the individual and presumed to be due to central nervous system dysfunction. Even though a

learning disability may occur concomitantly with other handicapping conditions (e.g., sensory impairment, mental retardation, social and emotional disturbance) or environmental influences (e.g., cultural differences, insufficient/inappropriate instruction, psychogenic factors), it is not the direct result of those conditions or influences." (Hammill, Leigh, McNutt, & Larsen, 1981, p. 336)

As Hammill, Leigh, McNutt, and Larsen (1981) indicate, the NJCLD believed that a new definition was needed because of inherent weaknesses in the definition enacted into law in the United States (*Federal Register*, 1977). Among the weaknesses cited are that (1) the term *children*, makes the definition unnecessarily restrictive, (2) the phrase "basic psychological processes" is too closely associated with "mentalistic process" and "perceptual-motor ability" training programs, (3) the list of inclusive "conditions" (e.g., perceptual handicaps, minimal brain dysfunction) is ill-defined, controversial, and confusing, and (4) the "exclusion" clause is ambiguous and has led to widespread misconceptions (i.e., that learning disabilities cannot occur in conjunction with other handicapping conditions or environmental, cultural, or economic disadvantage).

In developing the proposed definition, the NJCLD wanted one that was

"basically a *theoretical statement* specifying the delimiting characteristics of conditions called learning disabilities. These attributes had to be broad enough to include all known examples of learning disabilities, yet narrow enough to permit the distinction of learning disabilties from other conditions. The purpose of the definition was to establish learning disabilities theoretically—not to set up specific operational criteria for identifying individual cases. Important as operational criteria may be to school placement, research subject selection, and funding practices, the theoretical statement must come first, because it serves as a guide for generating actual objective identification procedures. To be practical, the abstract contents of the definition must be implemented in administrative rules and regulations." (Hammill et al., 1981, pp. 338–39)

To minimize misinterpretation of the proposed definiton, Hammill et al. (1981, pp. 339–40) offer the following phrase-by-phrase rationale:

Learning disabilities is a generic term "The Committee felt that *learning disabilities* was a global ('generic') term under which a variety of specific disorders could be reasonably grouped." *that refers to a heterogeneous group of disorders* "The disorders grouped under the learning disability label are thought to be specific and different in kind, i.e., they are 'heterogeneous' in nature. This phrase implies that the specific causes of the disorders are also many and dissimilar."

manifested by significant difficulties "The effects of the disorders on an individual are detrimental to a consequential degree; that is, their presence handicaps and seriously limits the performance of some key ability. Because the NJCLD was concerned that 'learning disabled' is often used as a synonym for 'mildly handicapped,' the Committee wanted to emphasize that the presence of learning disabilities in an individual can be as debilitating as the presence of cerebral palsy, mental defect, blindness, or any other handicapping condition."

in the acquisition and use of listening, speaking, reading, writing, reasoning or mathematical abilities. "To be considered learning disabled, an individual's disorder has to result in serious impairment of one or more of the listed abilities."

These disorders are intrinsic to the individual "This phrase means that the source of the disorder is to be found within the person who is affected. The disability is not imposed on the individual as a consequence of economic deprivation, poor child-rearing practices, faulty school instruction, societal pressures, cultural differences, etc. Where present, such factors may complicate treatment, but they are not considered to be the cause of the learning disability."

and presumed to be due to central nervous system dysfunction. "The cause of the learning disability is a known or presumed dysfunction in the central nervous system. Such dysfunctions may be by-products of traumatic damage to tissues, inherited factors, biochemical insufficiencies or imbalances, or other similar conditions that affect the central nervous system. The phrase is intended to spell out clearly the intent behind the statement that learning disabilities are intrinsic to the individual." (See Box 1–4.)

As can be seen, then, the NJCLD sees the definition adopted by the United States Congress as confusing, ambiguous, and unnecessarily restrictive. Most critics of the legal definition particularly do not like the use of the word *children*. what about older adolescents and adults? The phrase "basic psychological processes" seems too vague to some and concerns others who see it as connected to theories with which they disagree. The "conditions" that are included are seen as implying that central nervous system (CNS) dysfunctions have something to do with learning disabilities. However, the relationship is so unclear that those without CNS dysfunctions can be diagnosed learning disabled as well. Finally, the listing of excluded groups is seen as wrongly implying that individuals in groups such as the economically disadvantaged never have learning disabilities.

So new definitions are frequently proposed. Of course, each proposed definition has its critics as well. Inevitably, any new definition will be criticized. No one definition of learning disabilties can meet all the

---

Box 1–4

Another Proposal for Change

The NJCLD-proposed definition was adopted by six of its seven member organizations. The Board of Directors of the Association for Children and Adults with Learning Disabilities (ACLD) refused to accept the NJCLD definition. Instead, in 1984, they offered their own revision. As reported in the *LD Forum* (Winter 1985), the ACLD-proposed definition and its rationale state:

"Specific Learning Disabilities is a chronic condition of presumed neurological origin which selectively interferes with the development, integration, and/or demonstration of verbal and/or nonverbal abilities.

"Specific Learning Disabilities exists as a distinct handicapping condition in the presence of average to superior intelligence, adequate sensory and motor systems, and adequate learning opportunities. The condition varies in its manifestations and in degree of severity.

"Throughout life, the condition can affect self-esteem, education, vocation, socialization, and/or daily living activities."

Rationale for the ACLD Definition

"*Specific Learning Disabilities:* Specific Learning Disabilities (SLD) was selected to emphasize the fact that this condition has multiple manifestations but is *not* one of a generalized nature. Also, this is the term used in the Education of the Handicappcd Act, thc Education of All Handicappcd

Children Act, and the Rehabilitation Act of 1973, Section 504.

"*Condition:* was made synonomous with SLD because it is a state of being. It is not merely a term nor does it affect only children, which some definitions suggest. For the first time the condition, not the population, is defined.

"*Chronic:* was used to modify 'condition' to define its persistence in spite of the apparent waxing and waning of its manifestations.

"*Neurological origin:* was inserted because early and recent authors of definitions have agreed to a central nervous system basis.

"*Presumed:* was used to modify 'neurological origin' since there are not yet tools to determine origin definitively.

"*Interferes:* is the active verb because the condition does not necessarily destroy or delete function but may variously impair, alter, or redirect functions.

"*Selectively:* was used to qualify the global concept of 'interferes' because the condition differentially affects abilities while leaving others unaffected.

"*Development, integration, and/or demonstration:* this phrase was selected to denote the disruptions the condition creates in developing and using intrinsic abilities.

"*Verbal or non-verbal abilities:* were chose as inclusive terms to emphasize not only receptive and expressive language problems, but also the conceptual and thinking difficulties, the integrating problems and motoric problems. This approach is more descriptive and desirable than the prcvious approach focusing primarily on verbal

needs of professionals in fields as diverse as education, psychology, medicine, and psychiatry (see Box 1–5).

Despite its limitations, the definition enacted into law in the United States has been defended as useful in meeting the educational needs of large numbers of youngsters with severe learning problems. In particular, it is pointed out that the definition has been used effectively to justify funds for programs for many who otherwise might not have received special services.

While it's good to give special help to those who need it, it is not good to ignore the fact that the learning problems of these youngsters undoubtedly were the result of many different causes. As the NJCLD definition suggests, most early leaders in the field intended the term learning disabilities to be used for persons whose learning problems are caused by a CNS dysfunction. That is, in the early stages of the field's development, learning disabilities were widely viewed as the result of minor neurological problems that interfered with effective perceptual or

---

and academic manifestations.

"Distinct: signifies that SLD is separate and different from any other handicap and that any required interventions must be uniquely designed.

"Handicapping: was used because the condition meets the definitional criteria contained in Section 504 of the Rehabilitation Act of 1973 and to emphasize possible eligibility for assistance under all federal legislation for persons with handicaps.

"Intelligence: was inserted to avoid quantitative measurement terminology and to prevent direct translation into 'I.Q. scores.'

"Average to superior: was included because the condition of Specific Learning Disabilities selectively interferes with abilities throughout the range of intelligence. Because of this selective interference, composite scores are inappropriate for use with SLD. Also, it is recognized that appropriate interventions can raise measured scores while a lack of or inappropriate interventions can lead to deterioration, not only on measured scores, but even of the individual.

"Average to superior intelligence: was used to emphasize its co-existence and the potential need for services even among those with very high potential. The condition is not only of generalized low learning ability.

"Adequate sensory and motor systems: was included to clarify the distinction of the condition from other known sensory and motor deficits.

"Adequate learning opportunities: was selected to emphasize that the condition does *not arise* from a lack of exposure to life experiences and/or education typical to the community for the same

age group.

"Varies in its manifestations: was selected to emphasize that SLD does not equate with one or more functional deficits, e.g., reading disability, but is demonstrated in many signs and symptoms.

"Varies: was used to denote its apparent changes in manifestation within the individual and to state that it is not identical across occurrences.

"Degrees of severity: was inserted to clarify further the variance of the condition among the population and the variance in the extent to which it interferes with major life skills.

"Throughout life: was used to emphasize that the condition persists into and throughout adulthood and it begins the sentence to connote its early presence.

"Affect: was the preferred verb rather than disrupts, damages, impairs, interrupts, etc., because the condition may depreciate the function of some abilities while, simultaneously, the person may enhance other abilities through compensation.

"Can: was used to modify the verb 'affect' to allow for differential effects on the areas to follow.

"Self-esteem, education, vocation, socialization, and/or daily living: were used to establish the potential influences of the condition not only on school achievement but also on areas of life such as family life, community living, selection of competitive employment, or even on learning how to drive a car."

(Reproduction of this Definition is granted by ACLD, with the provision that the Definition also be accompanied by the Rationale.)

Box 1–5

Research Findings
Varying Definitions

Researchers studying how the term *learning disability* is defined by various experts have found a variety of definitions currently in use (Tucker, Stevens, & Ysseldyke, 1983). This results in great variations in who is diagnosed as learning disabled (LD).

In one study (Shepard & Smith, 1983), the findings indicate that only 28 percent of those diagnosed and placed in LD programs met a stringent criterion for learning disabilities. Another 15 percent were seen as meeting weak criteria. The remaining 57 percent appeared to be misdiagnosed, e.g., slow learners, persons non-fluent in English, persons with minor behavior problems, or persons with other handicapping conditions.

Even when school districts employ a very specific definition, students not meeting the definition have been declared learning disabled by decision-making teams for administrative reasons (Mirkin, Marston, & Deno, 1982).

The degree of discrepancy between a child's achievement and intellectual potential is seen as an important criterion in diagnosing learning disabilities. The discrepancy is supposed to be severe. Each locale sets its own criteria for how large the discrepancy must be before it is considered severe. Some places have adopted one or another of various discrepancy formulas that have been developed. In a study of eight widely cited discrepancy formulas (Forness, Sinclair, & Guthrie, 1983), the investigators used all eight formulas in diagnosing each individual in a sample of children with learning problems. Findings show the formulas vary greatly in the number of individuals identified as learning disabled. One formula identified 10.9 percent of the children while another identified 37 percent.

Because of varying definitions and criteria, students in one LD program often differ in very important ways from those in another program. This is also true of individuals included in different research studies. This variation hurts the field in many ways. In particular, because research samples have been extremely different from each other, it has been very difficult to arrive at sound conclusions about the causes of learning disabilities and about the characteristics and intervention needs of the learning disabled. In turn, the lack of conclusive research has hurt efforts to improve service programs and to evolve public policy.

Leaders in the field are now calling for consistent reporting of descriptions of individuals in learning disabilities research and service programs as a way of reducing the confusion caused by the varying definitions and criteria (e.g., Keogh, Major-Kingsley, Omori-Gordon, & Reid, 1982). Along with this trend, increasing efforts are being made to identify subtypes among those diagnosed as learning disabled (see McKinney, 1984; also the special topic references at the end of the chapter).

language processing. As the legal definition is applied currently, the label is not restricted to those with such problems.

In recent years, there has been a movement away from tying learning disabilities to neurological dysfunction. That is, some want the term *learning disabilities* applied to learning problems that stem from any factor that produces inefficient learning. They stress that problems arise from such factors as attentional deficits, passive learning, deficiencies in memory processes, or all three (Torgesen & Licht, 1984).

Lack of agreement about the definition and about who should be diagnosed as learning disabled has caused some people to question whether there is such a thing as a learning disability. The thing to remember is that a diagnosis of learning disability is meant to refer to a particular form of learning problem. To help clarify the value of this diagnosis, the next section compares learning disabilities with other types of learning problems.

LEARNING DISABILITIES IN PERSPECTIVE

Although learning is not limited to any one time or place, problems with learning are most often seen in classroom settings. In recent years, an increasing number of students have been identified as having learning and behavior problems due to handicapping conditions such as learning disabilities, emotional disturbance, and mental retardation (see Box 1–6). Unfortunately, in many cases, it is impossible to be *certain* that a learning problem is the result of a handicapping disorder or dysfunction as contrasted to some other causal factor. Nevertheless, it makes good sense to think in terms of learning problems as caused by different factors.

Think about a random sample of students with learning problems but no evident physical defects, e.g., no problems seeing or hearing, no *gross* brain damage. What makes it difficult for them to learn? It is possible that some have a relatively *minor* disorder, dysfunction, or maturational delay that affects how their brain functions. Although the trouble related to their brain function is minor, it is enough to make learning difficult for them even under good teaching circumstances. These are individuals with learning disabilities. To differentiate their learning problems, think of the disabilities as being at one end of a continuum. We'll call them Type III learning problems.

Box 1–6

Concern in the Field
How Many People Are Learning Disabled?

Some experts believe that no more than *1 percent* of the school population are really learning disabled.

Using expert estimates, the U.S. Department of Education uses a *3 percent* figure in making policy decisions.

Sometimes figures as high as *30 percent* of all students are cited.

In a study of expert opinion, estimates of prevalence ranged from zero to 70 percent, most respondents giving figures between zero and 3 percent (Tucker, Stevens, & Ysseldyke, 1983).

Why the different estimates? Mostly it is because different definitions and criteria are used in identifying people as learning disabled.

Although we don't know how many people should be identified as learning disabled, at least we have some reasonable figures about how many currently are labeled as learning disabled.

Not surprisingly, the trend has been for the numbers to increase very rapidly after governmental funding for learning disability became available. Shortly after the passage of federal legislation in 1969, 120,000 students were identified as learning disabled; by 1970, the figure rose to 648,000 (Grant & Lund, 1977); and in 1978, according to U.S. government figures, special services for learning disabilities were provided to 1,135,559 individuals (reported in Strichart & Gottlieb, 1981). Figures reported to the U.S. Department of Education by each state for the 1981–82 school year show that a range of from 1 to 6 percent of school-aged youngsters were served in programs for the learning disabled (reported in Forness et al., 1983). The total figures indicate that the number diagnosed has gone far beyond the incidence figures projected in the 1960s and 1970s. The fact is that in a relatively short period, those diagnosed as learning disabled have become the largest percentage of students currently in special education programs.

At the other end of the continuum are learning problems that arise from causes outside the person. Obviously, individuals may not learn well because the learning situation is not a good one. These problems are primarily the result of deficiencies in the environments in which learning takes place and can be thought of as Type I learning problems.

Finally, there are individuals who do not learn well in learning situations in which their special needs are ignored. In contrast to Type III learning problems, the brains of these individuals are functioning adequately for them to learn under good conditions. However, they may have other types of biological or psychological disorders or dysfunctions or may be just a little too different from their peers. They may need or want special considerations with regard to how much and how fast they can learn at any given time. As a result, they may have

minor difficulty learning even under the best of circumstances and tend to have severe learning problems in situations in which these particular needs are not accommodated. In general, the problems of this group may be seen as resulting from both the specific needs of the individual and the failure of the learning environment to meet their needs. These problems can be thought of as Type II learning problems (see Box 1–7).

SUMMARY

In general, leaders and teachers in the field tend to see learning disabilities as a useful classification and believe they can identify those who are learning disabled. At the same time, these professionals vary in how they define and identify learning disabilities. As a result, there are disagreements among practitioners and researchers about who does

---

Box 1–7

Viewpoint
Warning: This Placement May Be Hazardous to Your Health

Warnings about who is placed in learning disabilities programs are common:

"Our clinical finding over the years since the term *learning disability* has come into vogue is that a large percentage of the boys and girls referred to our own clinical service as learning disabled have been children of apparently quite normal academic potential who simply were overplaced in school. In our opinion, these children are having trouble in school chiefly because they were started too soon—on the basis of their chronological age rather than their behavior age.

"Based on our clinical findings, we would

urge all those involved with the process of education to make absolutely certain that they are not labelling any child as learning disabled who is immature or young for the grade he or she is in and who is thus failing simply because he or she is not ready for the work involved." (Ames, 1983, p.19)

"School districts have identified many children as learning disabled simply because they did not perform at grade level. Many of these children are slow learners, culturally or linguistically disadvantaged, or have had inappropriate instruction. Anyone visiting the programs for learning disabled children will observe that most programs include children who are not the hardcore learning disabled. If this practice continues, the learning disability programs are in danger of becoming dumping grounds for all educational problems." (Kirk & Kirk, 1983, pp. 20–21)

and who doesn't have LD. Viewing learning problems as a continuum and placing learning disabilities on that continuum is one way to understand who should and who shouldn't be diagnosed and treated as learning disabled.

"Learning disabilities" is more than a term used to identify a type of learning problem. It also designates a field of practice and research. To help put the field into perspective, it is useful to understand a bit of its history. This is the focus of Chapter 2.

AN ENRICHMENT ACTIVITY

Do you know anyone who has a learning disability?

If you do, jot down a brief description of what you know about his or her problem. If you don't know such an individual or are uncertain about how to proceed with your description, answer the following questions from general information you have acquired about learning disabilities.

1. Who first identified the problem and on what basis?

2. Does the person have learning problems in all situations or just in certain situations related to specific types of learning?

3. Are there alternative explanations for the person's problems other than that the individual has a *disability?*

4. If not, what is the evidence for the belief that there is a disability?

5. If the individual has behavior or emotional problems as well as a learning problem, are the problems seen as separate or related?

SPECIAL TOPIC REFERENCES

At the end of most chapters, you will find a list of references. These are not meant to be additional reading. Rather, they are offered as a resource for anyone who may want to pursue the particular topic in greater detail, now or in the future, out of personal interest, for a term paper, for an extra-credit assignment, or for any other needs that may arise.

So should you be interested in further information about the *characteristics* identified with learning disabilities, see the following readings.

CRINELLA, F. M. (1973). Identification of brain dysfunction syndromes in children through profile analysis: Patterns associated with so-called "minimal brain dysfunction." *Journal of Abnormal Psychology, 82,* 33–45.

DELOACH, T. F., EARL, J. M., BROWN, B. S., POPLIN, M. S., & WARNER, M. M. (1981). LD teachers' perceptions of severely disabled students. *Learning Disability Quarterly, 4,* 343–58.

DESHLER, D. D. (1978). Psychoeducational aspects of learning-disabled adolescents. In L. Mann & J. L. Wiederholt (Eds.), *Teaching the learning-disabled adolescent.* Boston: Houghton-Mifflin.

DYKMAN, R. A., ACKERMAN, P. T., CLEMENTS, S. D., & PETERS, J. E. (1971). Specific learning disabilities: An attentional deficit syndrome. In H. R. Myklebust (Ed.), *Progress in learning disabilities,* Vol. 2. New York: Grune & Stratton.

KALUGER, G., & KALUGER, M. (1978). Study reported in G. Kaluger and C. J. Kolson, *Reading and learning disabilities,* 2nd ed. Columbus, Ohio: Merrill.

KASS, C. E. (1966). Psycholinguistic abilities of children with reading problems. *Exceptional Children, 32,* 533–39.

OWEN, F. W., ADAMS, P. A., FORREST, T., STOLZ, L. M., & FISHER, S. (1971). Learning disorders in children: Sibling studies. *Monograph of the Society for Research in Child Development, 36,* serial no. 144.

ROUTH, D. K., & ROBERTS, R. D. (1972). Minimal brain dysfunction in children: Failure to find evidence for a behavioral syndrome. *Psychological Reports, 31,* 307–14.

SHEPARD, L. A., SMITH, M. L., & VOJIR, C. P. (1983). Characteristics of pupils identified as learning disabled. *American Educational Research Journal, 20,* 309–31.

VANDE VOORT, L., SENF, G. M., & BENTON, A. L. (1972). Development of audiovisual integration in normal and retarded readers. *Child Development, 43,* 1260–72.

WERRY, J. S. (1972). Organic factors in childhood psychopathology. In H. C. Quay & J. S. Werry (Eds.), *Psychopathological disorders in childhood.* New York: Wiley.

WOLFF, P. H., & HURWITZ, I. (1973). Functional implications of the minimal brain damage syndrome. In S. Walzert & P. H. Wolff (Eds.), *Minimal cerebral dysfunction in children.* New York: Grune & Stratton.

YULE, W., & RUTTER, M. (1976). Epidemiology and social implications of specific reading retardation. In R. M. Knights & D. J. Bakker (Eds.), *The neuropsychology of learning disorders.* Baltimore: University Park Press.

Should you be interested in further information about the ways in which those *diagnosed* as LD *differ* from one other, see the following references.

KEOGH, B. K., MAJOR-KINGSLEY, S., OMORI-GORDON, H., & REID, H. P. (1982). *A system of marker variables for the field of learning disabilities.* Syracuse, N. Y.: Syracuse University Press.

MANN, L., DAVIS, C. H., BOYER, JR., C. W., METZ, C. M., & WOLFORD, B. (1983). LD or not LD, that was the question: A retrospective analysis of Child Service Demonstration Centers' compliance with the federal definition of learning disabilities. *Journal of Learning Disabilities, 16,* 14–17.

SPEECE, D. L., MCKINNEY, J. D., & APPELBAUM, M. I. (1985). Classification and validation of behavioral subtypes of learning-disabled children. *Journal of Educational Psychology, 77,* 67–77.

STRAWSER, S., & WELLER, C. (1985). Use of adaptive behavior and discrepancy criteria to determine learning disabilities severity subtypes. *Journal of Learning Disabilities, 18,* 205–11.

THURLOW, M. L., & YSSELDYKE, J. E. (1982). Teachers' beliefs about LD students (Research Report No. 66). Minneapolis: University of Minnesota, Institute for Research on Learning Disabilties.

WARNER, M. M., ALLEY, G. R., DESHLER, D. D., & SCHUMAKER, J. B. (1980). An epidemiological study of learning disabled adolescents in secondary schools: Classification and discrimination of learning disabled and low-achieving adolescents (Research Report No. 20). Lawrence, Kans: University of Kansas, Institute for Research on Learning Disabilities.

YSSELDYKE, J. E., ALGOZZINE, B., & EPPS, S. (1982). A logical and empirical analysis of current practices in classifying students as handicapped (Research Report No. 92). Minneapolis: University of Minnesota, Institute for Research on Learning Disabilities.

Chapter 2

Historical Perspectives

The term *learning disability* became popular in the 1960s. In the late 1960s, learning disability texts began to appear. In 1968, the first issue of the *Journal of Learning Disabilities* was published. The foundation for the field, however, was laid much earlier. From around the turn of the century, the field evolved through research and practice in clinics and classrooms, through efforts of special interest groups and through political action. That evolution has shaped what is happening today in the LD field and will continue to influence its future.

IN THE CLINIC AND THE CLASSROOM

Although the field of learning disabilities did not exist before the 1960s, the foundation had been laid for over a fifty-year period by influential clinicians and researchers. Their impact is reflected in the extensive emphasis in the early LD texts on perceptual-motor and language/psycholinguistic disabilities and on the use of behavior modification strategies (see Box 2–1).

The Clinical Legacy

During the late nineteenth and early twentieth centuries, studies of brain-damaged adults led to a variety of theories about how the brain functions to produce specific behaviors. Over the first half of the 1900s, clinicians in education, psychology, medicine, and related fields working with clients with brain-damage or severe learning problems, or both, pioneered remedial theories and practices. Their focus was primarily on perceptual-motor and language disabilities. In the 1960s, it was these theories and *therapy-oriented* practices that shaped the field. It was these clinical diagnostic and treatment practices that were presented in textbooks, and thus, it was these practices that were taught to professionals-in-training.

Box 2–1

Historical Note
**Phases in the Development of
the LD Field**

Wiederholt (1974), in his brief historical summary, suggests that three types of disorders shaped most of the development of the field: disorders of spoken language, of written language, and of perceptual and motor processes. Furthermore, he divides the evolution of the LD field into three phases.

Wiederholt describes the first phase of historical development as the *foundation phase* (up to about 1930). This period was characterized by early studies of brain-behavior relationships with brain-damaged adults. Theoretical formulations were proposed regarding the nature and cause of learning disabilities. The prominent pioneers were Goldstein, Strauss, Werner, and Orton.

Second was the *transition phase* (1930–62)

during which attempts were made to translate theoretical formulations into remedial practices. During this phase, the work of Wepman, Myklebust, Kirk, Fernald, Cruickshank, Frostig, and Kephart was prominent.

Third, the *integration phase* (1963 on) is described as reflecting a merging of information into comprehensive diagnostic-remedial practices. During this phase, the number of professionals in the field has grown quickly, and there have been new attempts at theoretical formulations, further proliferation of diagnostic-remedial approaches, and rapid escalation of basic and applied research.

Lerner (1981) proposes that 1980 marked the beginning of a fourth phase, the *contemporary phase*. This emerging phase is seen as characterized by a trend toward broadening the definition of individuals served, provision of services across categories, involvement with students in the mainstream, and increased organizational activity.

Let us briefly introduce you to some of the most prominent pioneers of what has been called the perceptual-motor and language/psycholinguistic approaches to the LD field. (Basic works by each of the individuals presented are listed in the references at the end of the book.)

The Perceptual-Motor Approach. Kurt Goldstein provides a good starting point for discussing perceptual dysfunctioning as a basis of learning disabilities. Working with brain-injured veterans after World War I, he found them to be hyperactive and easily distracted. They had difficulty separating "figure" and "ground," separating the important from the unimportant, dealing with abstractions, and delaying responses to stimuli. Many nineteenth century clinical investigators influenced his work, and in

turn, his clinical research provided a major foundation for several pioneers of the learning disabilities field.

Alfred Strauss and Heinz Werner migrated to America from Germany in 1937. First at the Wayne County Training School and then at the Cove Schools for brain-injured children, they and colleagues who joined them (such as Laura Lehtinen and Newell Kephart) pursued a highly influential line of work. They applied Goldstein's observations to their research differentiating brain-injured from non-brain-injured retarded children. They recommended reducing unessential stimuli and increasing multisensory inputs in teaching.

Strauss and Lehtinen developed additional educational strategies designed to facilitate perceptual organization. These included the use of special materials and teaching strategies to compensate for areas of weakness and to capitalize on strengths. They also stressed the value of analyses of specific task performance as a basis for educational plans.

Kephart's work with Strauss applied the view that motor and perceptual development are the bases for later conceptual learning. Kephart designed techniques to enhance gross motor and perceptual motor functioning of "the slow learner in the classroom." He was particularly concerned with body image, balance, locomotion, perceptual motor coordination, and use of physical sensations as feedback to the learner.

William Cruickshank (e.g., Cruickshank et al., 1961), a student of Strauss and Werner, further refined the educational methods employed by Strauss and Lehtinen. His work focused especially on distractability and hyperactivity in children, including those functioning in the normal range of intelligence. He stressed reduced environmental stimuli and use of multisensory methods and structured educational programming. Many of his students have gone on to play important roles in the development of the field (e.g., Daniel Hallahan and Norris Haring).

Marianne Frostig established the Frostig Center of Educational Therapy where, during the 1950s well into the 1970s, she developed and disseminated the Developmental Test of Visual Perception and a program of workbook materials for training "visual perception." The test and training materials were extremely popular until the mid-1970s, when influential research reviews challenged the validity of the idea of training perceptual processes.

A few others in the perceptual-motor tradition whose remedial ideas subsequently became prominent include Gerald Getman, Ray Barsch, Glen Doman and Carl Delacato, Jean Ayres, and Bryant Cratty.

The Language/Psycholinguistic Approach. Starting a bit earlier than the work of Strauss and his colleagues, two different, but also highly influential, lines of remedial thinking had begun. One line was initiated by Samuel T. Orton, a professor of psychiatry at the University of Iowa; the other was begun by Grace Fernald, a professor of psychology at what is today the University of California, Los Angeles.

From 1928 to 1948, Orton studied the reading processes of brain-injured adults and concluded that the specific location of damage was critical. This led to neurological views about the causes and correction of reading problems, some of which are no longer held. However, his emphasis on reading problems due to language deficits provided a major contrast to the perceptual-motor tradition. He advocated an approach to reading instruction that involved the use of individually paced phonics with kinesthetic aids. This approach is still widely used. His influence also continues to be felt through the Orton Society's conferences and journal.

Fernald established her clinical laboratory in 1921. Her work focused on a variety of remedial approaches for all basic academic skills. She stressed that learning could be improved through enhancing the vividness of stimulus inputs. A major way to do this was through multisensory methods in teaching language, reading, spelling, writing, and math. Also toward this goal, she stressed meaningful content, high-interest activities, and learning as a function of the whole person. Her work is widely cited and used today, and the clinic-laboratory she founded continues to pioneer new approaches.

In the 1950s, the language/psycholinguistic tradition continued to expand with the emergence of two additional remedial approaches. One approach was given special impetus by the work of Samuel A. Kirk; the other approach followed the lead of Helmer R. Myklebust.

Kirk and his colleagues developed the Illinois Test of Psycholinguistic Abilities (ITPA) in the 1950s and 1960s. The test was specifically designed to guide remedial instruction. Despite questions about the validity of training psycholinguistic abilities, specific training programs continue to be developed to correct disabilities identified by the test. Beyond the ITPA, Kirk's work and leadership have influenced a large number of colleagues and policymakers. In the immediate years after the LD label was formally adopted, his students from his years at the University of Illinois played a prominent role in shaping the field.

Myklebust worked initially with deaf children, and this work led to his interest in the development of auditory or receptive language. As interest grew in language-related learning disabilities, his work was seen as particularly promising. Myklebust's strengths as a theorist and researcher provided an important model for the emerging field of learning disabilities.

In the 1960s, Doris Johnson and Myklebust, working at Northwestern University, developed an approach to remediation that advocated specific training procedures designed to strengthen deficit areas and teach through intact sensory modalities. Their comprehensive notions of what was involved in remedying learning disabilities set an influential standard for those who have followed.

As classroom teachers tried to apply the LD practices that had been developed in clinical settings, more often than not, a plaintive cry was heard: "I'm so busy dealing with behavior problems I don't have time to teach." What LD teachers found was that they had been trained to do something about a student's learning problems but had not been prepared adequately to cope with the behavior problems such students often dis-

played. It was logical, therefore, that they now wanted special training in how to control the students long enough to get them to sit down and learn.

The Behavioral Approach

In the 1960s and throughout most of the 1970s, the most frequent answer for teachers asking how to deal with behavior problems in the classroom was to use *behavior modification* techniques. Such procedures had been found useful in controlling certain behaviors of persons diagnosed as emotionally disturbed and retarded. In response to teachers' needs, behavior modification researchers and practitioners designed strategies for use in classroom management. It was not long before these strategies became a major part of training in many programs for learning disability teachers.

As the emphasis on behaviorist principles and techniques spread throughout the LD field, the ideas were applied not only to classroom management but also to practices for remedying problems in learning academic skills. This trend accelerated in the 1970s and in the early 1980s with the adoption of "applied behavioral analysis," "directive instruction," "precision teaching," and "cognitive behavior modification" methods.

Again, we offer a brief introduction to a few of the most prominent names that have come to be associated with the introduction of the behavioral approach into LD classroom programs. (Basic works by each of the individuals presented are cited in the reference list at the end of the book.)

Throughout the 1950s and 1960s, the ideas of Edward Thorndike, B. F. Skinner, and other reinforcement theorists and behaviorists were translated into programs for a wide range of educational and behavior problems (e.g., see Bijou & Baer, 1967; Risley & Baer, 1973). In the field of special education, ideas for classroom application developed by Richard Whelan, Norris Haring, Ogden Lindsley, and Frank Hewett were especially influential and exemplify approaches seen in many current programs for those with learning and behavior problems.

Richard Whelan developed a highly structured behavior modification–oriented classroom program for severely disturbed children in the late 1950s and into the 1960s. The focus was both on improving behavior and on academic remediation. His work provided one of the first comprehensive and sophisticated efforts to apply behavior modification in managing and programming an entire classroom of disturbed children.

Norris Haring, a student of Cruickshank's, also developed a program emphasizing operant conditioning principles and a highly structured environment to improve behavior and academic problems. Working with E. Lakin Phillips in the 1950s and then joining forces with Whelan in 1962, he contributed to the refined use of operant methods in classrooms.

Ogden R. Lindsley, who had studied with Skinner, joined Haring at the University of Kansas in the early 1960s. He brought with him an interest in the problem of precise measurement of behavior for use in planning instruction. The approach he developed and called *precision teaching* involves identifying specific behaviors, counting and charting performance, and using the data to plan subsequent remediation. The system also has been influential in establishing procedures for program evaluation.

Frank Hewett, working at UCLA and in a nearby school district during the early 1960s, designed what he called the "engineered classroom" for emotionally disturbed children. His approach combined behavior modification methods and a developmental sequence of educational goals as a way of "engineering" success. Subsequently, he replaced the concept of "engineering" success

with that of "orchestrating" success. In doing so, he placed greater emphasis on the importance of attitudes, feelings, and self-concepts. His creative approach to remediation and his detailed descriptions of his work resulted in widespread application. Although developed in the context of classrooms for emotionally disturbed children, the breadth and evolving nature of his work has made it of special interest to the LD field.

Contemporary Trends

Hewett's shift from "engineering" to "orchestrating" classroom programs reflects a general shift among behaviorists. In the 1970s, it became evident to many who used behavior modification strategies that M & M's and token reinforcers were useful only for controlling a few behaviors and that for some persons they weren't useful at all. When it came to correcting severe learning and behavior problems, attitudes and emotions kept getting in the way. New strategies were needed to deal with such thoughts and feelings. One immediate response was to modify behavior modification, and thus the field of cognitive behavior modification evolved.

The work of Donald Meichenbaum (1977) is representative of the trend to cognitive behavior modification concepts and methods. To control behavior and improve learning, he stresses teaching children to use self-instruction strategies, which may include simple instructions such as "stop and look" and more complex sets of procedures. The method stresses saying instructions aloud at first and then saying them to oneself in later stages of the approach.

As research and feedback from teachers, students, and parents indicate the need to continue to evolve ideas for correcting learning and related behavior problems, newer directions are being pursued. For example, there is renewed interest in programs that deal directly with social and emotional functioning. In particular, social skills training is being widely discussed (Bryan & Bryan, 1984).

Models of correction that focus on the student's intrinsic motivation, on cognitive strategies, and on how the student interacts with the school environment also are being implemented. Past tendencies to overemphasize students' remedial needs are being countered by an increasing awareness of the importance of enhancing development in nonproblem areas and of providing opportunities for enrichment (Adelman & Taylor, 1983).

As the difficulty of correcting learning disabilities has become clear, there has been increased concern about what is to happen to LD children as they get older. This has become a particularly urgent concern as the movement toward minimum competency testing has spread (Hall & Gallagher, 1984). Where such testing is required for high school graduation or college entrance, steps are advocated for special preparation of LD students and for appropriate modifications in test administration as a way of meeting the special needs of these students.

The concern about the long-range future of the learning disabled also is making career education an important topic. Besides high school vocational programs, new college programs for LD students have been developed to enable them to qualify for a wider and better range of jobs (Mangnum & Strichart, 1985).

All these contemporary trends are explored in subsequent sections of this book.

PARENTS AND PROFESSIONALS ORGANIZE

Also of major importance to the LD field has been the development of special organizations by those concerned about learning disabilities. Two groups have been particularly active.

As has been fairly common in fields involving children's mental health and special education, parents were the first to organize. Starting on a local level in the early 1960s, parents soon banded together to form a national organization. At a conference in Chicago in 1963, it was decided to form the Association for Children with Learning Disabilities (ACLD). The organization rapidly became a major lobbying group and played a key role in creating the new field. In 1979, the group changed its name to the Association for Children and Adults with Learning Disabilities (still ACLD) in recognition that learning disabilities are not just a problem of childhood. The organization also established the Learning-Disabled Adult Committee to focus on adult concerns.

By 1968, professionals had also established a learning disabilities organization. Within the Council for Exceptional Children (CEC), they formed the Division for Children with Learning Disabilities (DCLD). The organization grew rapidly in its first decade and, in 1978, published the first issue of its journal, the *Learning Disability Quarterly*. Like the ACLD, the professional group saw that a name change was in order as part of the group's growing recognition that the field had been paying insufficient attention to learning disabilities among adolescents and adults. Thus, in 1981, it became the Council for Learning Disabilities (CLD). Because of growing dissatisfaction with certain regulations of the governing organization, a voting majority of CLD members decided to withdraw the group from CEC; and on June 30, 1983, CLD became an autonomous organization. On July 1, 1983, CEC approved establishment of the Division for Learning Disabilities (DLD) to replace the now autonomous CLD.

In response to the need for an organization that would bring together major researchers in the field, the International Academy for Research in Learning Disabilites (IARLD) was formed in the latter half of the 1970s. This organization consists of "a rigorously selected group of the world's leaders in learning disabilities" (Cruickshank, 1983, p. 193).

Organizations concerned with learning disabilities, of course, do not exist in a vacuum. They draw from and contribute to the work of all those who are concerned about the rights and needs of special populations. In fact, the effectiveness of such organizations has been largely due to coordinated lobbying that has influenced legislation.

LEGISLATION AND FINANCIAL SUPPORT

The history leading to legislation and funding for programs for persons with learning disabilities is stormy. It is the product of centuries of social reform and judicial decisions in education in general and in the education of exceptional individuals in particular (see the special topic references at the end of the chapter).

The immediate legislative history is the result of a sociopolitical climate that emerged in the United States in the 1960s. During this period, both general and special education became national priorities. This occurred partly out of fear of an apparent shift in the balance of power between the United States and the USSR, partly out of a desire to create a "great society," partly as the result of special-interest lobbying, and partly from litigation in the courts.

The 1960s and 1970s was a time of great change in programs for children, the poor, and the handicapped. In the Congress of the United States and in federal courtrooms, events were taking place that were unprecedented.

As Goodlad (1984) notes, the Eighty-eighth Congress, the "Education Congress," in 1964, enacted such laws as the Equal Opportunities Program of the Civil Rights Act and the Economic Opportunity Act. The new laws provided support for vocational and technical education, teaching the handicapped, prevention of delinquency, desegregation, early learning opportunities for young children in disadvantaged areas, and so much more.

"The 89th Congress extended most of these commitments in the astonishing and unprecedented Elementary and Secondary Education Act of 1965. Title I was designed to assist school districts with their momentous tasks of helping children from low-income families in school and giving them there the kind of education thought to be needed. Title II provided for the purchase of books—in both public and private nonprofit elementary and secondary schools. Titles III and IV provided funds for linking the educational resources of communities and for comprehensive programs of research, development, and dissemination of knowledge through the collaborative efforts of universities, public schools, private nonprofit educational agencies, and state departments of education. Title V put money directly into state departments of education for strengthening their increasingly compelling leadership responsibilities. To effect all of this, the budget of the Office of Education was increased by $1,255,000,000 for fiscal 1966." (pp. 3–4)

It was in 1963 that the Congress of the United States passed Public Law 88-164, which was the first law to provide federal support for educating the handicapped. At that time, however, learning disabilities as a type of handicap were not formally recognized, which is not surprising because the term was just being introduced (review Box 1–3). Still, as has been noted:

"Under P.L. 88-164, the federal government did in fact provide assistance to many pupils we would now consider to be learning disabled, under the mandate to provide support for "crippled or other health impaired." Such children were then typically diagnosed as brain injured, minimally cerebral palsied, aphasic, or perceptually handicapped." (Mann, Cartwright, Kenowitz, Boyer, Metz, & Wolford, 1984).

Along with official legislation came establishment of the National Advisory Committee on Handicapped Children and several task forces, which attempted to clarify the status and needs of certain special education populations (see the special topic references at the end of the chapter). The experts participating in these groups soon concluded that learning disabilities should be included as a category of handicap under the law. Their analyses and recommendations, along with the general climate in the country and the lobbying of parents' organizations, led to congressional action.

Box 2–2

Historical Note
The Changing Sociopolitical Climate

One important sociopolitical factor influencing legislation was a series of judicial decisions. In the courts, parents' and advocacy groups pushed for equality of education during the 1970s. Among the important cases were:

Hobson v. *Hansen*—This was the first major case raising questions about placement of special education students. The court ruled that using test scores to group students into "tracks" was unconstitutional because it discriminated against blacks and the poor.

Diana v. *State Board of Education*—Again, here was a case in which the use of tests to place students was challenged. Diana, a Spanish-speaking student in Monterey County, California, had been placed in a class for mildly mentally retarded students because she had scored low on an IQ test given to her in English. The court ruled that Spanish-speaking children should be retested in their native language to avoid errors in placement.

Mills v. *Board of Education of the District of Columbia*—Seven school-age students had been excluded from school because of handicaps. The school district claimed it did not have the money needed to provide an appropriate education for them. The landmark decision in this case established that handicapped children should be given a free and suitable public education and cannot be excluded for financial reasons.

Pennsylvania Association for Retarded Citizens (PARC) v. *Commonwealth of Pennsylvania*—Like the *Mill's* case, this was a class action suit that declared that all handicapped children have the right to a free and appropriate education.

Larry P. v. *Riles*—Larry P. was a black student in California, and his complaint led to an expansion of the ruling in the *Diana* case. The court ruled that schools are responsible for providing tests that do not discriminate on the basis of race.

Le Banks v. *Spears*—The decision in this case helped to spell out the nature of a suitable or appropriate education for the handicapped.

As Meyen (1982) states:

"Legislation and litigation on the part of parents and advocacy groups can be expected to continue even though the legal base for ensuring equal rights for the handicapped appears to have been achieved. . . . The enactment of legislation . . . does not guarantee that funds required to implement the legislation always will be appropriated at a sufficient level. Nor does legislation guarantee that compliance will be enforced." (p. 9)

In the 1980s, the sociopolitical climate differs from that which produced the type of legislation and litigation described for the 1970s. The current climate is less favorable than that in the recent past for accomplishing what still needs to be done to improve the quality of education for students with problems.

You may want to think a bit about the implications of sociopolitical and economic factors in shaping attitudes toward programs designed to help people with problems.

With passage of the Children with Specific Learning Disabilities Act by Congress in 1969, the concept and the field were given the government's official stamp of approval. The Congress also provided a major economic base of support. And by 1970, learning disabilities were becoming one of the most frequently identified of the official handicapping conditions.

Legislation for the handicapped particularly benefited from the social climate of the 1970s (see Box 2–2 and special topic references at the end of the chapter). Whereas in the 143 years between 1827 and 1970, only 114 federal laws that were passed focused on the handicapped, in the four years between March 1970 and March 1975, sixty-one such laws were enacted (Weintraub, Abeson, Ballard, & La Vor, 1976). The three landmark acts during these four years were (1) Section 504 of the Rehabilitation Act of 1973; (2) Public Law 93-380, the Education of the Handicapped Amendments of 1974; and (3) Public Law 94-142, the Education for All Handicapped Children Act of 1975. The last was intended to guarantee that every child diagnosed as handicapped would receive a free and appropriate education and to strengthen special education programming by specifying procedures to identify and plan instruction for special students and to protect their rights.

As a direct result of federal legislation, universities and colleges in the late 1960s and throughout the 1970s established training programs to prepare professionals to specialize in learning disabilities. Between 1971 and 1980, ninety-seven Child Service Demonstration Centers were established. There was at least one center in every state and one in Puerto Rico. Besides providing services to the learning disabled, these programs aided in training and in program research and development activity. In addition, five Learning Disabilities Research Institutes were funded across the United States in the 1970s to focus on major concerns confronting the field. The work of these institutes has contributed to an increased appreciation of the issues surrounding the field and the directions that need to be pursued (see Box 2–3).

Despite the fact that federal law in the United States provides for educating handicapped individuals from age three to twenty one, the early preoccupation of the field was clearly with children. Throughout the 1970s and 1980s, however, increasing attention has been paid to learning disabilities among adolescents and adults. This has resulted in efforts to provide and improve programs for such persons in secondary schools and colleges and has created renewed interest in career and vocational education to meet the needs of those with learning disabilities.

In the first half of the 1980s, federal involvement in fields such as learning disabilities declined. The immediate impact was a major decrease in support for the types of demonstration, training, and research activities described here. The federal administration's stated intent was that local and state governments and private philanthropy take over important public services where the federal government left off. However, socioeconomic and political conditions worked against such a development.

SUMMARY

The field of learning disabilities is relatively young. It is a field full of controversy. In this chapter, we have highlighted its historical development in the clinic and classroom, through the rise of parents' and professional organizations and through the legislation and related financial support from the government.

The field has evolved rapidly, and major shifts in professional organizations and government support suggest ongoing rapid

Box 2–3

Historical Note
LD Research Institutes

In 1978, concern for improvement in LD research led to the establishment of five federally funded LD research institutes in the United States, located in major universities across the country. Each institute assumed a separate focus:

Focus	Location
Attentional deficits and their correction	University of Virginia
Assessment-identification-placement practices	University of Minnesota
LD adolescents	University of Kansas
Language-reading-social skills	University of Illinois-Chicago Circle
Processing deficits in the 3 Rs	Teachers College, Columbia University

In 1983, summaries of all five LD institutes were published in *Exceptional Education Quarterly.* The abstracts for each summary report provide an overview of institute activity:

"Research at the Chicago institute focused on the social competence of LD children. Studies included competence (e.g., adapting one's style to listeners, conversational skills), reading abilities (oral reading and comprehension), causal attributions of success and failure, and the immediate impression LD children make on naive observers." (Bryan, Pearl, Donahue, Bryan & Pflaum, 1983, p. 1)

"The institute at Teachers College, Columbia University, was organized as five task forces, each of which conducted research in a specific academic skill area. One task force studied memory and study skills of LD children. Two task forces investigated problems in learning basic skills: arithmetic, reading, and spelling. Reading comprehension was studied by two other task forces, one from the perspective of interaction of text and reader and one from the perspective of semantics and application of schemas." (Connor, 1983, p. 23)

"At the Kansas institute, research was concentrated on the problems of LD adolescents.

---

change—but not necessarily progress. To give you a better appreciation of the issues in the field, we discuss views about the causes of learning problems in Chapter 3.

LD field look back on fifty years from now with some dismay and amusement? What seems sound and enduring? What ideas and practices seem likely to be replaced?

AN ENRICHMENT ACTIVITY

Long-established fields of study recount aspects of their history with amusement and sometimes embarrassment. In psychology, for example, it is funny to think that there was a time when personality was assessed by checking the bumps on one's head or the shape of one's body. In medicine, there were the days of bloodletting. In education, people think of one-room school houses and the procedures used in them as quaint relics of the bad old days.

From what you know so far, what may the

SPECIAL TOPIC REFERENCES

Should you be interested in further information about the *history* of the LD field and the *court cases* or about the three major *task forces*, the Child Service Demonstration Centers, and the LD Research Institutes that helped shape the field, see the following readings.

CHALFANT, J. C., & SCHEFFELIN, M. A. (1969). *Central processing dysfunctions in children: A*

Epidemiological studies revealed the unique characteristics of LD in students of high school age. A curriculum comprised of strategy training, social skills, modified materials and instructional procedures was developed. Instructional, motivational, and evaluational components of the curriculum were described." (Schumaker, Deshler, Alley, & Warner, 1983, p. 45)

"The major purpose of the Minnesota institute was to study the assessment of LD children. Included in the scope of the research were investigations of the characteristics of children referred for psychoeducational evaluation, characteristics of those found eligible for placement in special education, methods of planning instructional interventions, evaluations of the extent to which children profited from instruction, and evaluations of the effectiveness of specific instructional programs." (Ysseldyke, Thurlow, Graden, Wesson, Algozzine, & Deno, 1983, p. 75)

"The institute at Virginia focused its efforts on LD children with attentional problems. Emphasis was placed on developing cognitive behavior modification techniques that help children improve their attention to tasks and that provide children an effective strategy for approaching academic tasks. Studies included investigations of metacognition, information processing, self-recording of task-related behavior, and strategy training. Adult-child interactions and psychometric properties of the Woodcock-Johnson battery also were studied." (Hallahan, Hall, Ianna, Kneedler, Lloyd, Loper, & Reeve, 1983, p. 95)

Reviews of the institutes' work are mixed:

"As a group, the five institutes have been highly productive of good quality research that is directly related to the work of teachers and clinicians. It is disappointing to note the lack of longitudinal studies, the low level of cooperation among institutes, the absence of consensus regarding definition and sampling, and the failure to test the replicability and generalizability of findings across the several institutes. Nevertheless, the institutes did yield useful information regarding the nature and complexity of LD, identify important variables in LD pupils' academic and social success, devise and test effective interventions, and lay the groundwork for continuing study." (Keogh, 1983, p. 115)

review of research (Phase III, NINDS Monograph No. 9). Bethesda, Md.: U.S. Dept. of Health, Education, and Welfare.

CHURCH, R. L., & SEDLAK, M. W. (1976). *Education in the United States.* New York: Free Press.

CLEMENTS, S. D. (1966). *Minimal brain dysfunction in children: Teminology and identification* (Phase I of a three-phase project, NINDS Monograph No. 3, U.S. Public Health Service Publication No. 1415). Washington, D.C.: U.S. GPO.

HARING, N. G., & MILLER, C. A. (1969). *Minimal brain dysfunction: Educational, medical, and health related services* (Phase II, N & SDCP Monograph, Public Health Publication No. 2015). Washington, D.C.: U.S. Dept. of Health, Education, and Welfare.

LD RESEARCH INSTITUTES. Each has prepared extensive reports on its research. General summaries are available in the issue of the *Exceptional Education Quarterly* published in spring 1983.

MANN, L., CARTWRIGHT, G. P., BOYER, JR., C. W., METZ, C. M., & WOLFORD, B. (1984). The Child Service Demonstration Centers: A summary report. *Exceptional Children, 50,* 532–40.

ROSS, S. L., DEYOUNG, H. G., & COHEN, J. S. (1971). Confrontation: Special education placement and the law. *Exceptional Children, 38,* 5–12.

SCHMID, R. E., MONEYPENNY, J., & JOHNSTON, R. (1977). *Contemporary issues in special education.* New York: McGraw-Hill.

TAPP, J. L., & LEVINE, F. J. (Eds.) (1977). *Law, justice, and the individual in society: Psychological and legal issues.* New York: Holt, Rinehart & Winston.

WEINTRAUB, F. J., & ABESON, A. (1974). New education policies for the handicapped: The quiet revolution. *Phi Delta Kappa, 55,* 526–29.

WIEDERHOLT, J. L. (1974). Historical perspectives on the education of the learning disabled. In L. Mann & D. Sabatino (Eds.), *The second review of special education.* Philadelphia: JSE Press.

Chapter 3

Causes

Many theories about the causes of learning disabilities focus on how the brain or central nervous system may not be functioning appropriately for specific types of learning. Some of these theories explain the problem as inherited; others see it as acquired. All suggest ways in which the central nervous system is affected in some relatively minor way and, then, how the minor dysfunction disrupts learning in a specific way.

As noted in Chapter 1, there are also theories that do not focus on the neurological bases of learning disabilities; instead, they explore psychological factors that may result in inefficient learning. Such theories point to deficits in perceptual, language, attentional, or memory processes or to problems in learner attitudes or emotional states.

In this chapter, we explore current theories about central nervous system problems and how these disrupt appropriate learning. Then, we discuss factors that may be causing the learning problems of individuals who do not have CNS dysfunctions (see Box 3–1).

FACTORS CAUSING CENTRAL NERVOUS SYSTEM PROBLEMS

When central nervous system problems are discussed in the context of learning disabilities, the emphasis is on minor dysfunctions, as contrasted to major disorders such as cerebral palsy and gross brain damage. Also, the factors discussed in this section do not *always* cause CNS problems, and when they do, the effects may be minimal and may not even result in learning problems.

Factors that may cause CNS problems and lead to learning disabilities may be grouped into four categories: (1) genetic, (2) prenatal (before birth), (3) perinatal (during birth), and (4) postnatal (after birth).

Box 3–1
_____

Student to friend:

"The human brain is amazing. The only time mine stops functioning is when I'm called on in class."

1. *Genetic.* Some genetic syndromes, e.g., neurofibromatosis, Tourette syndrome, appear to have a high probability of leading to learning problems. The transmission of such genetic abnormalities may produce abnormal brain structures, dysfunctional patterns of CNS maturation, biochemical irregularities, or a high risk for diseases that can impair the brain. When any of these occur, learning problems may follow. However, research has not demonstrated that genetic defects are a high-frequency cause of specific learning disabilities (see Box 3–2).

More commonly identified as leading to learning disabilities have been events in the first stages of life (Colletti, 1979; Pasaminick & Knoblock, 1973; Shaywitz, Cohen, & Shaywitz, 1978).

2. *Prenatal (before birth).* Factors suggested as resulting in CNS malfunctioning before birth include

- R-H factor incompatibility
- exposure to disease, such as German measles
- deficiencies in the mother's diet
- illnesses of the mother, such as diabetes, kidney disease, hypothyroidism, emotional stress
- exposure to radiation, such as x-rays
- use of certain drugs and medication by the mother
- excessive use of cigarettes and other substances by the mother that may produce a shortage of oxygen

Because many of these prenatal factors are seen as causing premature birth, premature infants (those less than 5½ pounds) are seen as being especially "at risk" for a variety of illnesses that may affect CNS development.

3. *Perinatal (during birth).* During labor and delivery, a few events can occur that may result in physical damage or oxygen deficiency affecting brain tissue. Perinatal factors, however, are *not* considered as frequent primary causes of learning disabilities. Those perinatal events that may cause problems include

- intracranial hemorrhaging during labor due to prolonged difficulty in passing through the birth canal
- injury from forceps delivery
- deprivation of oxygen when the umbilical cord is wrapped around the infant's throat
- various negative effects from some drugs used to induce labor and control postnatal hemorrhaging.

4. *Postnatal (after birth).* Many factors in subsequent stages of life may instigate CNS malfunctions. To simplify things, they may be categorized as including events or conditions leading to

- destruction or deterioration of brain tissue
- biochemical irregularities that result in development of abnormal brain structures or in malfunctioning of connections between brain cells.

Specific examples of these kinds of events and conditions are head injuries, strokes, tumors, ingestion of toxic substances, poor nutrition (such as vitamin deficiencies), hypoglycemia, severe and chronic emotional stress, glandular disorders (such as

Box 3–2

Viewpoint
Are learning disabilities genetically caused?

When a child with a learning problem has a parent who also has a learning problem, there is a tendency to believe the problem is inherited. This is unfortunate since more often than not similar environmental factors may have caused the problem for both the parent and the child.

The nature of learning experiences and attitudes about learning often are very similar for parents and their children. For example, children often go to schools similar to those their parents attended. Parents often recreate the home environments they experienced as children. If books and reading were not important

in the home where the father and mother grew up, the parents may not make much of an effort to provide books or to encourage their children to spend much time reading.

In general, parents' attitudes and beliefs are "taught" to children in daily encounters. If parents don't like to read or think of themselves as having a learning problem, their children will soon learn the same attitudes. A child may see these attitudes as a "family trait" and may "model" or adopt them. Thus, what is passed on is a *learned behavior* and not a *genetic trait*.

As yet, there is relatively little evidence that genetic transfer of learning problems is a widespread phenomenon (Smith & Pennington, 1983).

---

calcium and thyroid imbalances), and diseases and illnesses, such as meningitis and encephalitis, that cause prolonged high fevers.

HOW THE CENTRAL NERVOUS SYSTEM IS AFFECTED AND LEARNING IS DISRUPTED

It is relatively easy to suggest a variety of ways in which the brain fails to function appropriately and thus causes learning disabilities. Many theories have been offered. However, the more that is learned about CNS functioning, the more some of the theories are seen as too simplistic (see Box 3–3).

Any factor that leads to hormonal, chemical, or blood flow imbalances *may* instigate some degree of CNS trouble. However, only a few factors are likely to have more than a temporary effect. When the effects are more than temporary, they take the form of CNS destruction or deterioration, delayed neurological matura-

tion, development of abnormal brain structures, or malfunctioning of connections between brain cells. (See the special topic references at the end of the chapter.)

Brain Injury and Dysfunctioning

Nerve cells in the brain (neurons) that are destroyed cannot be restored. It is comforting to note, however, that the human brain is estimated to have 12 billion neurons, and that as many as ten thousand die a natural death every day without any apparent negative effect on brain functioning. Therefore, a small amount of damage can occur without severe consequences.

In cases of brain injury, the nature and scope of CNS dysfunction appears to depend, in part, on the amount of tissue damage. For example, as long as enough cells remain undamaged, there are instances where nondamaged cells take over specific functions. Also important in determining the effects of brain injury are its location and the stage of CNS development (see Box 3–4).

Box 3–3

Historical Example
Cerebral Dominance and Mixed Laterality

Causal ideas and remedial approaches based on ideas about the dominance of one side of the brain over the other provide an example of a simplistic theory that was very popular at one time. For most of this century, many believed that a major cause of learning problems was the failure of one hemisphere to develop dominance over the other. The seeds for this idea were planted in the late nineteenth and early twentieth centuries. During that time, it was found that for most people the left hemisphere was primarily responsible for language functioning. This finding led to a widespread view that the left side was the dominant hemisphere and that the right hemisphere was subordinate and somewhat inferior.

The dominant hemisphere also was thought to determine which side of the body would be favored, especially with regard to handedness. Because the right side of the body was seen as controlled by the left hemisphere (viewed as dominant for most people), the fact that most people are right-handed was attributed to left-hemisphere dominance.

Based on these ideas, the theory was proposed that appropriate development of left-hemisphere dominance would be reflected in a consistent preference for the right side of the body with regard to the use of hands, eyes, ears, and feet. Many individuals with learning problems did not show such a consistent pattern. Instead, they had a mixed pattern, such as a preference for right hand and left eye or left hand and right eye. This pattern came to be called *mixed* or *confused dominance* or *mixed laterality* and was seen as the result of the failure to develop cerebral dominance (e.g., see Orton, 1937).

A variation on this theory focused specifically on those who were left-handed. Left-handedness was seen as an indication that the right side of the brain was establishing primacy for language functions. Thus, the learning problems of left-handed persons were seen to be the result of the inability of the nondominant right hemisphere to perform language functions adequately (Delacato, 1966).

Remedial programs based on such ideas were created. The intent was to help individuals develop a dominant cerebral hemisphere through activities designed to establish a consistent (nonmixed) pattern of laterality or left-hemisphere dominance for language.

Remedial programs to establish laterality and dominance lasted quite a while before their validity was seriously questioned. The first evidence that raised concern about these programs was that many *good* learners were noted to have mixed laterality patterns. Then came the finding that handedness is not a good indicator of which hemisphere is dominant. Finally, there was a breakthrough in awareness about areas of right-hemisphere dominance. Currently, it is recognized that both hemispheres have areas of dominance and work together with regard to a variety of functions. In particular, the right hemisphere is seen as having dominance for nonverbal functions and as having the ability to assume dominance for language functions in certain cases.

With the decline of theories about left-hemisphere dominance, there has been a shift in explanations about mixed laterality. It is now suggested that the mistake in looking at laterality as a symptom was in stressing the mixed pattern. Instead, the current view is that problems arise not from mixed laterality and its causes, but from a lack of well-established preference. For example, if a youngster has not established a preference and reliable habits for using one hand over the other because of lack of regular practice with the same hand, she or he is likely to have difficulty performing tasks such as writing and catching a ball. This does not mean that the lack of established preference is causing the learning problem. If learning problems are present, they *and* the failure to establish satisfactory preference both may be due to slow maturation or other CNS problems.

Box 3–4

Research and Theory
Recovery from Brain Damage

Most people have heard of individuals who have lost the ability to speak or read because of stroke, head injury, or surgery. Sometimes these losses are temporary. That is, after the immediate effects of the event wear off, there is spontaneous recovery of lost skills.

For others, the extent of brain damage that occurs is considerable. Thus, there is reason to think the lost functions will not return spontaneously and may be lost forever. There have been instances, however, when a person has been able to regain lost abilities through diligent rehabilitation efforts. In some of the most dramatic instances, significant relearning of lost skills occurred after surgeons had removed an entire section of the brain (e.g., one lobe). As a result of such cases and of research with animals, theories have been proposed about the ability of nondamaged brain cells to take over the functions of damaged neurons. (See the special topic references at the end of the chapter.) For example, in some cases in which the left hemisphere of the brain was damaged, the right hemisphere was able to take over many language functions usually associated with the left side of the brain.

What remains less clear are the factors that make recovery of lost functions possible. Age seems to be one such factor. Adults tend to make a poorer recovery than children. However, just how old one has to be before recovery is impossible has not been established. One reason for children's better recovery may be that their nervous systems are continuing to grow and various areas of their brain have not yet become devoted to established functions. The poorer recovery of adults may be due to a decreased efficiency, associated with age, for establishing new transmission connections between neurons.

Besides age, the nature of rehabilitation efforts also probably is a factor that makes a difference in the degree of recovery. At the same time, clarification of which remedial approaches work and which do not awaits further research.

When learning a particular skill, such as reading, is very uneven, specific areas of the brain are hypothesized to be malfunctioning. For instance, some youngsters readily recognize letters when asked to point them out but have trouble reading them without prompting. Or they may have difficulty understanding that certain groups of letters mean the same thing as the words they speak. In such cases, the reading problem is likely to be seen as caused by a brain malfunction and will be referred to as *dyslexia* by many experts. (To the regret of many, the term *dyslexia* has come to be used widely to designate almost any reading problem, rather than that subset of reading problems caused by CNS dysfunctioning.)

One theory of dyslexia suggests that factors such as oxygen deprivation (anoxia) produce damage to cells in the association centers of the brain, the parietal and parietal-occipital lobes (see Box 3–5). Damage to these areas is believed to result in a specific inability to associate symbols with meaning but is not seen as interfering with the recognition of symbols (Rabinovitz, 1959).

Damaged brain cells can cause malfunctions in the connections necessary for the cells to communicate with each other. Such communication between brain cells is known as *neural impulse transmission*. It is carried out through an electrochemical process and is essential to effective learning and performance.

Impulse-transmission problems occur when a neuron is prevented from communicating with others or when the speed of transmission is inappropriate, e.g., too rapid or too slow. Dysfunctions in neural

Box 3–5

Research and Theory
**Major Areas of the Brain
and Their Functions**

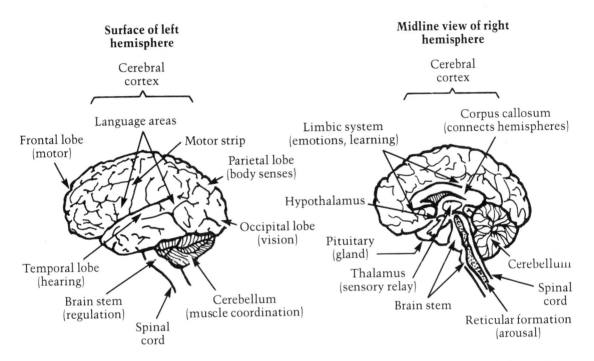

**Surface of left
hemisphere**

**Midline view of right
hemisphere**

Cerebral
cortex

Cerebral
cortex

Language areas

Limbic system
(emotions, learning)

Corpus callosum
(connects hemispheres)

Frontal lobe
(motor)

Motor strip

Parietal lobe
(body senses)

Hypothalamus

Occipital lobe
(vision)

Pituitary
(gland)

Cerebellum

Temporal lobe
(hearing)

Thalamus
(sensory relay)

Spinal
cord

Brain stem
(regulation)

Cerebellum
(muscle coordination)

Brain stem

Reticular formation
(arousal)

Spinal
cord

(Adapted from Timothy J. Teyler, "The Brain Sciences," in EDUCATION AND THE BRAIN, Jeanne S. Chall and Allan F. Mirsky, eds., Chicago, Il., The University of Chicago Press, 1978, p. 10.)

The brain and spinal cord are the two major components of the CNS. Brain activity is determined by the biological structure and electrochemical transmissions of the nervous system.

The brain consists of the brain stem, cerebellum, and cerebral cortex (cerebrum). The functions associated with each are

1. *brain stem*—integrates such functions as heart and breathing rates, regulates motor reflexes, and houses the reticular activating system, which instigates electrical activity in the cerebral cortex;

2. *cerebellum*—coordinates the voluntary muscle system and is involved in controlling balance and coordinated muscle movement;

3. *cerebral cortex*—controls all conscious activity. It consists of two halves, the left and right hemispheres, which have different functions but are almost the same in construction and metabolism. They are connected by the corpus callosum, a large grouping of fibers, which is seen as the channel of communication between the two halves.

Theories about learning disabilities have suggested possible dysfunctions in each of the major parts of the brain. For example, because the reticular formation, or reticular activating system, is seen as filtering stimuli to the cerebrum, it has been suggested that some problems in attending are due to cerebral overstimulation caused by dysfunction in this system.

Box 3–5 continued on p. 34.

Box 3–5 continued from p. 33.

However, because the majority of current theories about learning disabilities are concerned with cerebral cortex dysfunctioning, we will focus our brief discussion on this area of the CNS.

Although the roles of the two hemispheres of the cerebral cortex differ, some functions of the body, such as vision and hearing, are a concern of both sides of the brain. For instance, the left hemisphere receives stimuli from the right visual field of each eye, and the right hemisphere receives stimuli from the left visual field of each eye. Motor movements also are a concern of both sides: movement on the right side of the body is controlled by the left hemisphere and vice versa.

For most people, the left hemisphere is primarily concerned with language functioning and detailed and analytic thought: the right hemisphere is primarily, although not exclusively, concerned with nonverbal functioning and processes information as a whole. Functions related to most fine arts (drawing, music, dance) are seen as associated with the right hemisphere. While the right hemisphere tends to have nonverbal functions, it apparently can assume some language functions in certain cases. For example, if a child is born with a defect in the left hemisphere or if the left side is damaged

before the child gets too old, usually under age twelve, the right hemisphere may take over language functions.

When the left hemisphere is damaged to the point where language is affected, learning and performance are affected, e.g., reading, writing, and communicating ideas verbally. When the damage is in the right hemisphere, the problem is with areas requiring spatial imagery, e.g., understanding math concepts and performing fine and industrial arts.

Besides the distinction between the left and right hemispheres, each hemisphere has (1) four major regions (the temporal, frontal, parietal, and occipital lobes), (2) separators between the regions (e.g., the angular gyrus, the lateral sulcus), and (3) related association areas. Efforts to map out relationships between the brain and specific behaviors have pinpointed areas in the cortex responsible for the performance of certain functions. For example, the parietal lobe is seen as the locale associated with reading and writing, and dysfunctions in specified areas of this lobe are hypothesized to be involved in specific learning disabilities in reading and writing.

References are included at the end of the chapter for readers interested in further information about brain function as related to learning disabilities.

impulse transmission usually are the result of endocrine malfunctions and chemical imbalances.

If brain cells cannot communicate efficiently and effectively with each other, development, learning, and performance will be affected. For example, this may be the case for individuals who appear to have extremely high activity levels and difficulty sustaining attention. One hypothesis suggests that when brain cells are damaged, neurotransmitter chemicals usually are destroyed as well. Thus, there is not enough of the chemical needed to inhibit transmission, and it becomes too rapid (Wender, 1976). Another hypothesis proposes that

overly rapid transmissions occur when the points of connection between neurons (i.e., synapses) are so insensitive to chemical inhibitors that they do not adequately slow down transmission (Kinsbourne & Caplin, 1979).

Maturational Lag

Not all theories about neurological causes focus on CNS *dysfunction*. Because of any of the instigating factors cited, the rate of CNS maturation can be delayed. It is widely hypothesized that persons whose neurological development is disrupted or is comparatively slow will lag behind their peers, especially in the early, formative years. This slow development often is referred to as *maturational* or *developmental lag* (Goldstein & Myers, 1980; Koppitz, 1973). According to this view, children whose neurological development is not the same as that of others their age are not ready to learn the same tasks as the majority of their peers. At school, children who are lagging considerably behind others find that most classrooms cannot wait for them to catch up. It is this fact, not the maturational lag by itself, that is seen as the instigating factor leading to learning problems.

For instance, the first-grade reading curriculum begins with the assumption that all students have a certain level of auditory and visual perceptual capability. Auditory and visual *perception* differ from auditory and visual *acuity*. Acuity is a matter of sharpness and depends on the sensitivity of one's sense organs, e.g., an eye that can clearly see shapes and forms. Perception is the psychological process by which a person organizes and makes sense out of incoming sensory information. A child may have 20/20 vision (perfect acuity) but not be able to discriminate (perceptually distinguish) differences among letters.

If Bret (see Chapter 1) has not yet developed such capabilities at the expected level, chances are he will not be able to handle parts of the reading lessons *at the expected time*. As the teacher moves on to teach the next lesson, he falls further behind. A year or so later, his neurological development will advance to a point where he has the necessary physiological capability. Unfortunately, he will have missed learning important basic skills. In such cases (and in many cases in which CNS malfunctions produce only temporary disruptions in learning), subsequent learning problems are no longer due to the initial CNS factors. They are caused by the fact that the individual is missing certain skills that are prerequisites for subsequent learning.

The sequence of events discussed to this point, beginning with initial instigating factors, is diagrammed in Box 3–6. The sequence of events becomes complicated after a CNS disorder causes learning problems. More often than not, the learning problems themselves cause more problems. Subsequent development, learning, and performance are disrupted. The impact on the individual can extend into all areas of learning and can be responsible for a variety of negative emotions, attitudes, and behaviors.

OTHER INSTIGATING FACTORS

A list of specific instigating factors that could cause the learning problems of individuals who do not have CNS disorders or dysfunctions would fill the rest of this book. As an alternative to listing all these factors, we have attempted to categorize them. We have done so based on an interactional view of the causes of learning problems (see Chapter 4). To provide a perspective, the factors related to CNS disorders and dysfunctions are included.

The table in Box 3–7 shows the broad range of factors besides neurological damage and dysfunction or developmental delay that can instigate an individual's learning problem. Moreover, such problems can be instigated not only by factors within the person but also by environmental factors and by complex interactions between persons and environments.

It is important to keep in mind the full range of possible causes, rather than assume most learning problems are related to neurological troubles. Only from a broad perspective can one appreciate the difficulty of adequately explaining such facts as the overall higher incidence of learning problems among males and low-income minority groups and the underachievement patterns that appear among females in their later schooling (see Box 3–8).

Box 3–6

Sequence of Events Related to Problems in CNS Functioning and Development

The sequence of events related to CNS disorders can be described as beginning with a *primary* instigating factor that produces the disorder (see diagram). In turn, the disorder can produce a handicap. In the case of disrupted learning resulting from a CNS disorder, such a handicap has come to be called a *learning disability*. Such a handicapping disability is seen as disrupting learning in specific areas, e.g., in associating meaning with symbols. As a result, learning problems become evident as the individual has trouble performing in learning set-

tings, such as during reading instruction at school.

Quite commonly, the performance problems and others' reactions to these problems have a negative psychological impact on the individual. These negative psychological effects are often referred to as an *emotional overlay* to the learning problems.

The combination of performance problems and problems stemming from negative psychological effects often cause the learning problems to become worse. That is, these factors become *secondary* instigating factors leading to further handicapping conditions that cause specific learning problems to become wide-range performance and behavior problems.

Instigating Factors	CNS Disorder	Handicap	Problems in Learning Situations
1. genetic abnormality	delayed or abnormal development or malfunctioning	disability disrupting learning in specific areas (e.g., inability to make certain visual perceptual discriminations)	specific performance problems (e.g., letter reversals) → psychological reactions (e.g., emotional overlay)
2. direct CNS damage or deterioration			
3. biochemical irregularities			

BEHAVIORIST PERSPECTIVES ON CAUSE

Not all professionals are concerned about what originally instigated a learning or behavior problem. Many practitioners have adopted the view that initial causes usually cannot be assessed; and even if they could, little could be done about the cause once the problem exists. Furthermore, behaviorists see appropriate remediation procedures as based on assessing current functioning and contributing factors—not on assessment of initial causes. That is, behaviorists view remediation as *solely* focused on (1) helping the individual acquire learning skills and strategies that should have been previously

learned and on (2) eliminating factors that *currently* are contributing to problems.

Because they choose not to worry about initial cause, advocates of a behaviorist perspective tend to argue against defining learning disabilities in terms of causal factors. Many prefer a broad definition that includes anyone of at least average intelligence who is having difficulty learning despite appropriate motivation and adequate instruction.

In stressing the tendency of behavioral practitioners to put aside the matter of initial causes of learning and behavior problems, we do not mean to imply that behaviorist thinking ignores the causes of human behavior. The behaviorist literature pro-

Box 3–7

Factors Instigating Learning Problems

Environment (E)	Person (P)	Interactions and Transactions Between E and P*
1. Insufficient stimuli (e.g., prolonged periods in impoverished environs; deprivation of learning opportunities at home or school such as lack of play and practice situations and poor instruction; inadequate diet) 2. Excessive stimuli (e.g., overly demanding home or school experience, such as overwhelming pressure to achieve and contradictory expectations.) 3. Intrusive and hostile stimuli (e.g., medical practices, especially at birth, leading to physiological impairment; conflict in home or faulty child-rearing practices, such as long-standing abuse and rejection; migratory family; language used in school is a second language; social prejudices related to race, sex, age, physical characteristics and behavior)	1. Physiological "insult" (e.g., cerebral trauma, such as accident or stroke, endocrine dysfunctions and . chemical imbalances; illness affecting brain or sensory functioning) 2. Genetic anomaly (e.g., genes which limit, slow down, or lead to any atypical development) 3. Cognitive activity and affective states experienced by self as deviant (e.g., lack of knowledge or skills such as basic cognitive strategies; lack of ability to cope effectively with emotions, such as low self-esteem) 4. Physical characteristics shaping contact with environment and/or experienced by self as deviant (e.g., visual, auditory, or motoric deficits; excessive or reduced sensitivity to stimuli; easily fatigued; factors such as race, sex, age, unusual appearance which produce stereotypical responses) 5. Deviant actions of the individual (e.g., performance problems, such as excessive errors in reading and speaking; high or low levels of activity)	1. Severe to moderate personal vulnerabilities and environmental defects and differences (e.g., person with extremely slow development in a highly demanding, understaffed classroom, all of which equally and simultaneously instigate the problem) 2. Minor personal vulnerabilities not accommodated by the situation (e.g., person with minimal CNS disorders resulting in auditory perceptual disability enrolled in a reading program based on phonics; very active student assigned to classroom which does not tolerate this level of activity) 3. Minor environmental defects and differences not accommodated by the individual (e.g., student is in the minority racially or culturally and is not participating in many school social activities and class discussions because he or she thinks others may be unreceptive)

*May involve only one (P) and one (E) variable or may involve multiple combinations.

Box 3–8

Concern in the Field
**Why are more boys than girls
diagnosed as learning disabled?**

Estimated ratios of boys to girls diagnosed as learning disabled range from 2:1 to 6:1 (Coleman & Sandhu, 1967; Rubin & Balow, 1971).

Those who believe current diagnoses of learning disabilities are accurate tend to explain the incidence figures in terms of biological differences between the sexes. One set of theories stresses sex differences in neurological development and specialization of the cerebral hemispheres (e.g., see Dalby, 1979). Another explanation suggests that, on the average, males have larger heads at birth than females, and this size increases the probability of difficult births and higher rate of oxygen deprivation causing brain damage.

In contrast, those who believe that a signifi-

cant number of males are misdiagnosed as learning disabled tend to look for explanations outside the CNS. They hypothesize, for instance, that the source of many males' learning problems and of the underachievement patterns of many girls in their later schooling can be traced to differences in cultural expectations. Many boys come to school having had numerous experiences that tend to make them more interested in highly active pursuits, such as social interactions, rather than quiet academic activity. Similarly, as they get older, many girls have been expected (by their family, teachers, friends, and the majority of other people around them) to behave in ways that play down their academic capabilities.

Comparable points about psychological, socioeconomic, cultural, and political factors have been made about understanding the causes for the high incidence of learning problems found among children reared in poverty.

---

vides detailed descriptions of the factors that determine how people learn and act. A considerable body of work explores how environmental events can selectively reinforce and shape actions, thoughts, and feelings. And although some behaviorists disagree about how to describe the determinants of behavior (see Ross, 1985), they agree that the description should be in psychological rather than neurological terms (see Mahoney, 1974; Skinner, 1974). Thus, it is logical that behaviorists would see little reason to be concerned with factors that cause CNS problems.

At the same time, behaviorists are concerned about current factors that interfere with effective learning and performance. For example, the current existence of bad study habits or the absence of particular skills and strategies for learning may be identified as causing an individual's poor attention to a task or failure to remember something that

was apparently learned. In attempting to correct ongoing problems the assumption is that the bad habits can be overcome and the missing skills can be learned. The implication is that if there is a CNS or psychological disorder that is continuing to handicap the individual's efforts to learn, intervention cannot directly correct the underlying disorder. However, the skills and strategies the individual is taught are seen as either counteracting the disorder or helping the individual compensate for the handicap (Kazdin, 1984).

Other contributing factors may be any of the instigating factors indicated in Box 3–7 that continue to have a negative effect on current functioning. For example, a student may be a rather passive learner at school (e.g., not paying adequate attention) because of physical and emotional stress caused by inappropriate child-rearing practices, illness, poor nutrition, and so forth. Obviously, practitioners concur that the presence of such factors should be assessed and corrected whenever feasible.

SUMMARY

What causes learning disabilities? The question is considerably easier to ask than to answer. Some theorists point to CNS problems that can disrupt learning; others stress psychological factors; still others emphasize causes related to environmental influences and complex interactions between person and environmental factors. It will be some time before researchers can provide satisfactory evidence pinpointing the cause of such problems in individual cases.

Whether or not researchers have satisfactory answers, practitioners are called upon each day to identify learning disabilities. The dilemma for practitioners is that a diagnosis of learning disabilities usually implies a cause, e.g., that the learning problem is due to trouble related to CNS or psychological functioning. This brings us to the topic of identifying learning disabilities. In the next chapter, we explore what is involved in diagnosing the kinds of minor neurological damage, dysfunction, or delays in maturation and the types of attentional or memory deficits that are frequently presumed to cause certain learning problems.

SPECIAL TOPIC REFERENCES

Should you be interested in further information about *brain function* as related to learning disabilities, see the following readings.

CAPARULO, D. P., COHEN, D. J., ROTHMAN, S. L., YOUNG, G., KATZ, J. D., SHAYWITZ, S. E., & SHAYWITZ, B. A. (1981). Computed topographic brain scanning in children with developmental neuropsychiatric disorders. *Journal of the American Academy of Child Psychiatry, 20,* 338–57.

CHALL, J. S., & MIRSKY, A. F. (Eds.) (1978). *Education and the brain.* Chicago: National Society for the Study of Education.

CURTIS, B. A., JACOBSON, S., & MARCUS, E. M. (1972). An introduction to the neurosciences. Philadelphia: Saunders.

DENCKLA, M. B. (1979). Childhood learning disabilities. In K. Heilman & E. Valenstein (Eds.), *Clinical neuropsychology.* New York: Oxford University Press.

GADDES, W. H. (1985). *Learning disabilities and brain function: A neuropsychological approach,* 2nd edition. New York: Springer-Verlag.

GESCHWIND, N. (1979). Specializations of the human brain. *Scientific American, 241,* 180–201.

HARTLAGE, L. C., & TELZROW, C. F. (1983). The neuropsychological basis for educational intervention. *Journal of Learning Disabilities, 16,* 521–28.

HISCOCK, M. & KINSBOURNE, M. (1980). Individual differences in cerebral lateralization: Are they relevant to learning disabilities? In W. Cruickshank (Ed.), *Approaches to learning,* Vol. 1, *The best of ACLD.* Syracuse: Syracuse University Press.

HYND, G. W., & COHEN, M. (1983). *Dyslexia: Neuropsychological theory, research, and clinical differentiation.* New York: Grune & Stratton.

HYND, G. W., & OBRZUT, J. E. (Eds.) (1981). *Neuropsychological assessment and the school-age child: Issues and procedures.* New York: Grune & Stratton.

LURIA, A. R., & MAJOVSKI, L. V. (1977). Basic approaches used in American and Soviet clinical neuropsychology. *American Psychologist, 32,* 959–68.

PLAISTAD, J. R., GUSTAVSON, J. L., WILKENING, G. N., & GOLDEN, C. J. (1983). The Luria-Nebraska Neuropsychological Battery—Children's Revision: Theory and current research findings. *Journal of Clinical Child Psychology, 12,* 13–21.

REITAN, R. M., & DAVISON, L. A. (1974). *Clinical neuropsychology: Current status and applications.* New York: Winston-Wiley.

RIE, H. E., & RIE, E. D. (Eds.) (1980). *Handbook of minimal brain dysfunctions: A critical view.* New York: Wiley.

ROURKE, B. P. (1978). Reading, spelling, arithmetic disabilities: A neuropsychological perspective. In H. R. Myklebust (Ed.), *Progress in learning disabilities.* New York: Grune & Stratton.

ROURKE, B. P., BAKKER, D. J., FISK, J. L. & STRANG, J. D. (1983). *Child neuropsychology.* New York: Guilford Press.

SCHAIN, R. J. (1972). *Neurology of childhood learning disorders.* Baltimore: Williams & Wilkins.

SNOW, J. F., HYND, G. W., & HARTLAGE, L. C. (1984). Differences between mildly and severely learning-disabled children on the Luria-Nebraska Neuropsychological Battery—Children's Revision. *Journal of Psychoeducational Assessment, 2,* 23–28.

TARNOPOL, L., & TARNOPOL, M. (Eds.) (1977). *Brain function and reading disabilities.* Baltimore: University Park Press.

TAYLOR, H. G. & FLETCHER, J. (1983). Biological foundations of "Specific Developmental Disorders": Methods, findings, and future directions. *Journal of Clinical Child Psychology, 12,* 46–65.

TEYLER, T. J. (1978). The brain sciences. In J. S. Chall & A. F. Mirsky (Eds.), *Education and the brain.* Chicago: University of Chicago Press.

WENDER, P. H. (1976). Hypothesis for possible biochemical basis of minimal brain dysfunction. In R. M. Knights & D. J. Bakker (Eds.), *The neuropsychology of learning disorders: Theoretical approaches.* Baltimore: University Park Press.

Chapter 4

Identifying Learning Disabilities

Learning disabilities are only one type of learning problem and represent a small proportion of the large number of learning problems. In cases in which determining what has caused a person's learning problem is difficult, it is hard to identify learning disabilities. In this chapter, we look at the problems of identifying cause-effect relationships in general, and of diagnosing learning disabilities in particular.

THE PROBLEM OF COMPELLING CLUES

The story is told about a tribe of South Pacific natives who believed that lice were responsible for keeping a person healthy (Chase, 1956). They had noticed that almost all the healthy people in the tribe had lice, while those who were sick did not have lice. Thus, it seemed to them very reasonable to see the presence of lice as the cause of good health.

A teacher-in-training working with children with learning problems notices that most of them are easily distracted and are much more fidgety when working on their lessons than are students without learning problems. They also are more likely not to listen and not to do assignments well, and they often flit from one thing to another. The teacher concludes that there is something physically wrong with these youngsters that makes them unable to attend properly.

Everyday we puzzle over our experiences and, in trying to make sense of them, arrive at conclusions about what caused them to happen. It is a very basic and useful part of human nature for peole to try to understand cause and effect. Unfortunately, sometimes we are wrong.

The South Pacific natives didn't know that in tropical climates, sick people usually have a high fever; and since lice do not like it that hot, they jump off.

The teacher-in-training is right in thinking that some children with learning problems may have something physically wrong that makes it hard for them to pay attention. However, further training and experience will show that there are a significant number whose attention problems stem from a lack of interest, or from the belief that they really can't do the work, or from any number of other psychological factors.

Errors in Logic

Because it is so compelling to look for causes and because people so often make errors in doing so, logicians and scientists have spent a considerable amount of time discussing the problem. For example, logicians have pointed out the fallacy of assuming (as the natives did) that one event (lice) caused another (good health) for no more logical reason than that the first event preceded the second. We make this type of error every time we *presume* that a person's learning problems are due to a difficult birth, a divorce, poor nutrition, or other factors that preceded the learning problem.

Another kind of logical error occurs when one event may affect another, but only in a minor way, as part of a much more complex set of events. There is a tendency to think people who behave nicely (or not so nicely) have been brought up well (or not so well) by their parents. We all know, however, of specific cases in which parents' actions seem to have very little to do with the child's behavior. This can be especially true of teenagers who are strongly influenced by their friends.

A third logical error can arise when two events repeatedly occur together. After a while, it can become impossible to tell whether one causes the other or whether both are caused by something else. For instance, children with learning problems fre-

quently are found also to have behavior problems. Did the learning problem cause the behavior problem? Did the behavior problem cause the learning problem? Did poor parenting or poor teaching or poor peer models cause both the learning and behavior problems? The longer these problems exist, the harder it is to know.

Causes and Correlates

Scientists talk about the problem of compelling clues in terms of confusion about the difference between *causes* and *correlates*. Correlates are events that have some relation to each other—lice and good health, no lice and sickness, learning and behavior problems. A cause and its effect is a special type of correlation—one in which the nature of the relationship is known.

Some events that occur together, i.e., correlates, fit so well with "common sense" that we are quick to believe they are cause and effect. However, we may overlook other factors that may be important in understanding the actual cause-and-effect connection.

In trying to understand learning problems, researchers and practitioners look for all sorts of clues, or correlates. Some are particularly compelling because they fit with current theories, attitudes, or policies (see Box 4–1).

In general, once a problem is seen as severe enough to require referral for treatment, any other problem or relatively unusual characteristic or circumstance that is present attracts attention. Often, these other problems, characteristics, or circumstances come to be seen as connected in some cause-effect relationship. The more intuitively logical the connection seems, the harder it is to understand that they may *not* be causally related. They are compelling clues, but may be misleading.

Theory and Research
Causal Models

> In the last analysis, we see only what we are ready to see. We eliminate and ignore everything that is not part of our prejudices. Charcot (1857)

Professionals working in the LD field usually have a general view or "model" of what causes learning problems. Some place the cause of learning problems within the person, and others suggest the cause is in the environment.

Two "person models" that have been dis-cussed widely are (1) the disordered or "ill"-person model, or medical model, and (2) the slow maturation model. These have been con-trasted to two other models, (3) the pathological or inadequate environment model and (4) the in-teractional model, which views problems as caused by the way the person and environment interact. Of the four, the two person models have been the most popular explanations of learning problems. We need to learn a great deal more about all the potential causes of learning problems, however. Used appropriately, all four causal models can help guide research and prac-tice.

ASSESSING CAUSE: AN EXAMPLE

Because there are different types of learning problems with different causes and reme-dies, it is important to differentiate among individuals who have one type or another (see Box 4-2). Differential diagnosis is the process by which a person is assigned to a particular diagnostic category. To conclude that an individual should receive one diag-nosis and not another, it is necessary to show the presence of a set of symptoms or signs unique to the diagnostic category.

For example, if a differential diagnosis is meant to identify learning disabilities that are caused by a neurological problem, it is necessary to show that there is a *minor* CNS dysfunction. If there is a severe neurological problem, other diagnoses are more ap-propriate, such as severe brain damage and cerebral palsy. That is, the key in this in-stance is to show that the cause of an in-dividual's learning problem is a CNS that is dysfunctioning in a minor way. Such a dif-ferrential diagnosis requires valid measure-ment of specific indicators of minor neurological dysfunction or immaturity. Unfortunately, although major CNS dys-functions usually are identified with rela-tive ease, this is not the case for minor CNS trouble. To explain why this is so and to fur-ther exemplify the problems of differential diagnosis of cause, we turn to a brief discus-sion of assessing minor neurological dys-functioning in general and the concept of "soft signs" in particular.

Neurological Soft Signs

In medicine, the term *signs* refers to *objec-tive* evidence of disease, such as detection of a specific virus. When a sign is found, the illness can be diagnosed readily.

Since the late 1940s, it has become in-creasingly commonplace for practitioners to diagnose minor neurological dysfunctions by finding "soft signs." This trend has oc-curred because objective signs are not present for minor neurological dysfunc-tions.

What are called *soft signs* or sometimes

Box 4–2

Concern in the Field
Labeling

"What's the use of their having names," the Gnat said, "if they won't answer to them?"

"No use to *them*," said Alice; "but it's useful to people who name them, I suppose. If not, why do things have names at all?" Lewis Carroll, *Through the Looking Glass*

What's in a name?

When it comes to diagnosis, the label assigned may profoundly shape a person's future. The labels attach names to problems. The names often imply what caused a problem and what to do about it. People tend to have strong images associated with specific labels and act upon these images. Sometimes the images are useful generalizations; sometimes they are harmful stereotypes.

Some people think all labeling is a bad thing. They point to many potential negative effects of assigning diagnostic labels such as *learning disabilities:*

"The label stigmatizes the person. People tend to think less of a person who has a diagnostic label; they often avoid and act differently toward them."

"If you tell people they have problems, they often make your words come true."

"When the label is wrong, serious errors in treatment can be made."

These are important concerns. Labeling a person can have negative effects. The possiblity of negative effects is a good reason to be careful about how labels are used, but it is not a good reason to stop diagnostic labeling.

Diagnostic labeling, like all classification activity in science, is essential. It is basic to communication and to efforts to solve problems. We simply cannot hope to correct and prevent learning problems without some form of classification.

The problem, then, is not to do away with labels, but to develop the most useful labels and to minimize the negative effects that arise when they are used. One criterion of a "good" diagnostic label is that it help more than hurt.

Although there is controversy over how the term *learning disabilities* is defined and applied, there seems to be consensus that the label itself is a good one for describing one major type of learning problem. However, some critics point out that as this label is used in daily practice, a very large number of persons may be misidentified. From these critics' perspective, the label should be used only for purposes of research and theory until the diagnosis can be made with fewer errors.

---

equivocal, borderline, or *ambiguous signs* are not signs at all. They are symptoms. Symptoms, such as nausea and dizziness, are *subjective* and may occur along with many types of illness. They may be interpreted differently by different professionals. What professionals do agree about with regard to the behaviors called *soft signs* is that these symptoms resemble those seen in brain-damaged individuals (see Box 4-3).

Neuropsychological Assessment

Assessment of neurological soft signs primarily involves tasks of motor and sensorimotor integration (see end of chapter for references). Findings from this type of assessment can be differentiated from findings that are considered more direct indications of brain status. For example, direct electrophysiological measures, such as the

Box 4–3

Current Practices
Soft Signs

Of the many procedures that may be used in a standard neurological exam, two examples follow.

As one check of oculomotor functioning, the examiner holds a finger in front of the youngster's eyes and then slowly moves it into the peripheral vision area on one side of the head and then on the other. Those tested are instructed to follow the movement only with their eyes and not move their heads. Anyone over the age of five is supposed to be able to do this successfully. Anyone older who persists in moving his or her head is seen as responding abnormally. One such abnormal response is called *nystagmus,* which is a condition in which both eyes slowly drift toward the periphery and then suddenly snap back (Curtis, Jacobson, & Marcus, 1972).

As a check on tactile and kinesthetic perception, those tested are asked to close their eyes. The examiner then touches the child on the left hand, on the right hand and left side of the face, and on the left hand and right side of the face. After each touch, the youngster is asked to identify the place of stimulation. The sequence is repeated four times. Again, those over five are supposed to be able to identify such stimuli with no more than one error out of the twelve touches.

Neurologists, of course, use medical terms in referring to tests for soft signs. For example, the second test described in this box is known as the test for simultanagnosia. Other soft sign tests look for choreiform movements, mild dysphasias, borderline hyperflexia and reflex asymmetrics, finger agnosia, dysdiadochokinesis, graphesthesias, and so forth (Schain, 1972).

In using tests to detect soft signs, neurologists are looking for responses that are

significantly, but not grossly, less than those expected for age. The degree of performance deficit considered a problem, however, is not well established, and there is not yet a set number or pattern of soft signs that must be found before a diagnosis of learning disabilities can be made.

The logic behind the use of soft signs is reflected in a statement by William Gaddes in his 1985 book, *Learning Disabilities and Brain Function: A Neuropsychological Approach:*

"The confusion in defining MBD [Minimal Brain Dysfunction] stems from the common difficulty of identifying any borderline phenomenon. . . . Intense and localized brain damage in specific . . . areas will produce predictable deficits in adult behavior. . . . As we move along the continuum toward normal brain structure and function, however, we pass through a large number of children and adults who are not 'brain damaged' and who, for no known reason, show many behavioral deficits similar to the brain-damaged patients, but in a much less intense way. These behavioral impairments (e.g., visual reversals, poor finger localization, asymmetry of finger tapping, and astereognosis) are the soft signs, and their presence suggests very strongly that the person's brain and central nervous system has some minimal areas of dysfunction, although a standard neurological examination may have turned up nothing." (pp. 84–85)

Reviewers of research on soft signs indicate major problems in using these measures as indicators of minor CNS dysfunctioning (e.g., Taylor & Fletcher, 1983). Current evidence suggests caution when such measures are used to diagnose learning disabilities.

electroencephalogram (EEG), are useful in detecting gross brain dysfunctions. Unfortunately, such direct measures have had limited effectiveness in identifying minimal dysfunctions.

To improve assessment of CNS functioning, neuropsychological test batteries have been developed. These procedures attempt to go beyond assessing motor and sensorimotor integration by including measures of higher-level cognitive skills. With the rise in use of such batteries as standard ways to measure CNS dysfunctioning, there appears to be a tendency not only to expand the number and types of tests but also to expand the number of soft signs.

In general, neuropsychological assessors attempt to measure

1. gross and fine motor coordination, including integrated motor acts (e.g., tying shoes, buttoning, placing one's finger on one's nose);
2. oculomotor functioning (e.g., eye-muscle control, relative diameter of the pupils);
3. postural control, gait, reflexes, and tremors (e.g., walking a straight line on tiptoes without awkwardness);
4. auditory and visual perception and related cognitive skills (e.g., recognition and discrimination of stimuli, reproduction of rhythmic patterns, discrimination of right and left, understanding and following simple commands, ability to make simple generalizations and deductions;
5. tactile and kinesthetic perception (e.g., ability to localize and discriminate sensations, movement detection;
6. speech and language functioning (e.g., articulation, ability to repeat and initiate verbal responses);
7. memory (e.g., immediate recall of verbal

and nonverbal stimuli—with and without interference); and
8. general looks and demeanor (e.g., physical characteristics).

In addition, some degree of effort often is made to assess basic skills in reading, writing, and arithmetic.

What neuropsychological assessors are seeking is any evidence of abnormal CNS functioning, including performance below expected age level. What they are measuring is overt behavior. When the behavior is not up to expectation, the part of the brain that is seen as responsible for such behavior may not be functioning appropriately. Such a conclusion, of course, is likely to be most valid when other reasonable explanations can be ruled out. In particular, it helps if it can be shown that the behavior is not the result of psychological and sociocultural factors, e.g., emotional disturbance or growing up in economically deprived circumstances. Another problem involves age or developmental expectations. That is, for some of the behaviors that are being measured, there are disagreements about the point at which performance falls below what should be minimally expected of young children, especially those under age seven.

MISTAKEN IDENTITY

For the reasons mentioned and others, mistakes can be made in diagnosing learning disabilities. Despite their status as compelling correlates, soft signs and other behaviors that are seen as symptoms of minor brain disorder or other psychological factors often are not sufficient evidence of the cause of an individual's learning problem. The field is still evolving an agreed-upon set of characteristics, symptoms, or signs associated primarily with learning disabilities as contrasted with other types of learning problems (see Chapter 1).

Again, with reference to the example of assessing soft signs, what makes such signs so compelling to diagnosticians is that they are indeed found with significant frequency among individuals whose neurological disorders have been well established. However, researchers have pointed out that the identified behaviors also are found with considerable frequency among persons whose problems are unlikely to be the result of neurological dysfunctioning and even among persons with no significant problems at all.

In short, it is one thing to have a *theory* about the cause of learning disabilities: it is quite another thing to be able to assess the cause of a particular individual's learning problems (see Box 4–4). Theories about specific causes continue to be essential in

---

Box 4–4

Concern in the Field
Edison, Einstein, and Rodin—Were They Learning Disabled?

Did Albert Einstein really see the theory of relativity like this?

Adapted by permission of Hertz International.

This is the claim made in a recent advertisement seen in a publication of a learning disabilities organization. The caption goes on to indicate that

"Albert Einstein was dyslexic. Like many of the world's 7.5 million children with learning disabilities he was thought to be unintelligent by his teachers. . . . Fortunately, his parents placed him in a special school where he was taught in accordance with his disability. Otherwise he might never have gone on to achieve greatness."

In recent years, it has become fashionable to analyze the lives of famous people and to assign them a diagnostic label. Among those posthumously diagnosed as learning disabled have been Thomas Edison, Albert Einstein, and Auguste Rodin.

What makes these particular historical figures likely candidates for posthumous diagnoses is that they had difficulties as children and some did poorly at school. Edison was described in childhood as stupid and mentally defective; Rodin was seen as uneducable; Einstein apparently did not speak until he was three and had some trouble at school. These cases certainly show that learning and schooling problems can plague even those with special genius. But should their problems be diagnosed as learning disabilities?

Take the case of Einstein, for example. Although his biographers agree that he was somewhat delayed in developing speech, there is no satisfactory evidence of a language disability persisting into adulthood as is sometimes cited. In fact, Einstein's reported fluency as an adult in composing German limericks and his acquisition of foreign language can be cited as evidence that he used language without apparent handicap after his earlier problems. Moreover, none of his biographers suggest that he had any difficulty learning to read. Ironically, it is reported by his sister that he did have some minor problems with math computation in his early school years. However, given his genius in the use of math concepts, it seems improbable that he had a learning disability interfering with his ability

Box 4–4 continued on p. 48.

to learn math. Indeed, his math grades were high. If there was any problem, it was probably that he approached mathematics in ways that confounded those who attempted to get him to work with simple addition and multiplication.

The following quotation from one of his biographers certainly argues against the idea that Einstein was learning disabled or dyslexic:

". . . at the age of five he received his first instruction at home. This episode came to an abrupt end when Einstein had a tantrum and threw a chair at the woman who taught him. At about six he entered public school, the Volkschule. He was a reliable, persistent, and slow-working pupil who solved his mathematical problems with self assurance though not without computational errors. He did very well. In August 1886 Pauline wrote to her mother: 'Yesterday Albert received his grades, he was again number one. His report card was brilliant.' . . .

"In October 1888 Albert moved from the Volkschule to the Luipeold Gymnasium, which was to be his school until he was fifteen. In all these years he earned either the highest or the next to highest marks in mathematics and in Latin. But on the whole he disliked those school years; authoritarian teachers, servile students, rote learning—none of these agreed with him. . . .

"There is another story of the Munich days that Einstein himself would occasionally tell with some glee. At the Gymnasium a teacher once said to him that he, the teacher, would be much happier if the boy were not in his class. Einstein replied that he had done nothing wrong. The teacher answered, 'Yes, that is true. But you sit there in the back of the room and smile and that violates the feeling of respect which a teacher needs from his class.'

"The preceding collection of stories about Einstein the young boy demonstrates the remarkable extent to which his most characteristic personal traits were native rather than acquired. The infant who at first was slow to speak, then becomes number one at school (the widespread belief that he was a poor pupil is unfounded) turned into the man whose every scientific triumph was preceded by a long period of quiet gestation." (Pais, 1982, pp. 37–38)

Because professionals often cannot agree about a diagnosis of learning disabilities for individuals they have personally examined, it is not surprising to find controversy about assigning such a diagnosis to someone who died long before the concept of learning disabilities was conceived.

---

studying learning disabilities. Misdiagnoses, however, do continue to be a source of serious ethical and practical concerns for practitioners and researchers.

A great many differential diagnoses of learning disabilities are made every day. Practitioners use the best procedures that are available. (See Reading A and special topic references at the end of Chapter 3 and of this chapter for listings of the types of procedures and instruments frequently used in assessing learning problems.) Despite the best efforts, however, there are errors in diagnosis whether the focus is on neurological dysfunctioning or deficits in attentional or memory processes.

A great many researchers and practitioners are working for the day when mistaken identification will no longer be a major concern.

SUMMARY

Each day individuals are diagnosed as having learning disabilities. When the intent of the diagnosis is to identify those whose current learning problems are caused by CNS or psychological dysfunctioning, then the diagnosis should be based on valid evidence of such dysfunctioning. Unfortunately, despite the compelling nature of the clues, current assessment procedures cannot always be relied upon to provide conclusive evidence of such dysfunctions.

Currently, research is being directed at improving methods to assess neurologically and psychologically based problems, and researchers remain optimistic about a breakthrough. For example, there is optimism about the promise of new devices for studying the brain, especially those that use computer technology such as computerized axial tomography—the CATSCAN (Denckla, LeMay & Chapman, 1985). (CATSCANS are x-rays that scan the brain and map out the absorption of spinal fluid, the white and gray matter, and the blood.)

While we await necessary advances in assessment, efforts to diagnose the causes of learning disabilities can and often must proceed. Current regulations in the United States acknowledge this state of affairs. Thus, in identifying those who should be diagnosed as learning disabled, regulations stress criteria related to severe underachievement and developmental immaturity, rather than focusing on CNS and psychological dysfunctioning. That is, present practices look more at symptoms than at causes in pursuing procedures for screening, placement, and correction. In Part 2, we explore these practices.

AN ENRICHMENT ACTIVITY

The following item was reported in a large metropolitan newspaper:

"St. Louis, Mo. (UPI)—Being neurotic has its advantages.

"A study of 434 white males by Washington University, St. Louis, showed the neurotics among them earned about 23% higher salaries than those diagnosed as well.

"The results of the survey were reported in a recent issue of American Family Physician.

"Researchers also found that the neurotics

had significantly higher ratings for full-time employment, IQs and total years of schooling."

1. Does this report seem to imply causal connections?

2. Are there other, perhaps more logical explanations for the reported outcomes?

3. Which of the following explanations seems most plausible to you?

• High IQ is the cause of more years of schooling, which leads to higher salaries and full employment

• More years of schooling lead to higher scores on IQ tests as well as to higher paying jobs and better employment opportunities

• Being neurotic leads to higher salaries and better employment opportunities.

4. In this context, what do you think about the use of the label *neurotic?* How do you think the researchers were able to determine that the individuals studied were neurotic?

SPECIAL TOPIC REFERENCES

Should you be interested in further information about *soft signs, neuropsychological assessment,* and *differential diagnosis* of learning disabilities, see the following references.

ARTER, J. A., & JENKINS, J. R. (1979). Differential diagnosis-prescriptive teaching: A critical appraisal. *Review of Educational Research, 49,* 517–55.

BARKLEY, R. A. (1983). Neuropsychology: Introduction. *Journal of Clinical Child Psychology, 12,* 3–5.

BENDER, L. (1947). Childhood schizophrenia: Clinical study of one hundred schizophrenic children. *American Journal of Orthopsychiatry, 17,* 40–55.

COLEMAN, J. C., & SANDHU, M. (1967). A descriptive relational study of 364 children referred to a university clinic for learning disorders. *Psychological Reports, 20,* 1091–1105.

COLES, G. (1978). The learning disabilities test battery: Empirical and social issues. *Harvard Educational Review, 48,* 313–40.

GOMEZ, E. H. (1967). Minimal cerebral dysfunction (Maximum neurological confusion). *Clinical Pediatrics, 6,* 589–91.

LURIA, A. R., & MAJOVSKI, L. V. (1977). Basic approaches used in American and Soviet clinical neuropsychology. *American Psychologist, 32,* 959–68.

PLAISTAD, J. R., GUSTAVSON, J. L., WILKENING, G. N., & GOLDEN, C. J. (1983). The Luria-Nebraska Neuropsychological Battery—Children's Revision: Theory and current research findings. *Journal of Clinical Child Psychology, 12,* 13–21.

REITAN, R. M., & DAVISON, L. A. (1974). *Clinical neuropsychology: Current status and applications.* New York: Winston-Wiley.

STRAUSS, A. A., & LEHTINEN, L. E. (1947). *Psychopathology and education of the brain-injured child.* New York: Grune & Stratton.

WINKLER, A., DIXON, J. F., & PARKER, J. B. (1970). Brain function in problem children and controls: Psychometric, neurological, and electroencephalographic comparisons. *American Journal of Psychiatry, 125,* 94–105.

Also see the references at the end of Chapter 3.

Part II

GENERAL APPROACHES TO THE ASSESSMENT AND TREATMENT OF LEARNING DISABILITIES

What the best and wisest parent wants for his own child that must the community want for all of its children. Any other idea for our schools is narrow and unlovely.

Dewey (1889, p. 7)

Much time and effort in the learning disabilities (LD) field is devoted to identifying who is learning disabled and what special services each individual requires. Tests are given, interviews carried out, observations and ratings made. Poor test performance is likely to lead to a diagnostic label and a prescription for treatment, including at times a special placement.

Just as practitioners differ in how they approach the matter of cause, they differ in their orientations to assessment and treatment. In general, two trends have dominated prevailing practices. Consistent with the concern for central nervous system (CNS) disorders and resulting processing disabilities, one trend has focused on procedures to assess and treat presumed underlying disabilities. In contrast, there is a trend that follows the behaviorist view that original causes usually cannot be assessed and treated; this position stresses reliance on assessing and teaching observable skills and behaviors, including cognitive-behavioral strategies to aid functioning. These contrasting approaches to assessment and treatment are illustrated in the following chapters and related readings.

Our specific objectives in Part 2 are to discuss

- how learning disabilities are screened
- how placement and treatment decisions are made
- prevailing approaches to assessment and treatment
- some evolving directions that hold promise for improving current practices

As you proceed, remember the LD field is always trying to find better approaches. You will want to try to understand both what is done and how current practices can be improved. In the long run, it is your understanding of both what is and what may be that is important to the progress of the field.

Chapter 5

Finding the Learning Disabled: Screening, Diagnosis, and Placement

From what you read in Part 1, you know that finding those with learning disabilities is an intriguing detective job. Searches are made for those called *underachievers, school failures, high challenges*, or *individuals at risk*. All who fit these labels do not have learning disabilities, of course. So it seems logical to try to identify those who do have such disabilities in order to provide the specific help they need. And it seems logical that the earlier they are found, the better. Thus, in the years since the creation of the concept of learning disabilities, screening procedures designed to identify the learning disabled, particularly young children, have become extremely popular.

In one form or another, the task of identifying students unable to profit from regular instruction has been pursued throughout this century. Because professionals have been at it for a long time, screening for learning problems has gained widespread acceptance.

Massive screening procedures in health, education, and welfare programs always raise concern. For one thing, large-scale screening programs are very costly. For another, there are always some errors and other negative side effects.

Because massive screening is desirable but also a matter of concern, a brief look at such assessment activities is a good place to start our discussion of finding the learning disabled.

WHY SEARCH FOR PROBLEMS?

Superintendent Brown was less than pleased.

> "We don't need to find any more learning disabled students!"

The school board had just informed her of its decision to go ahead with a screening program for learning disabilities.

"Our learning disabilities programs are already full!" she continued. "We can't afford any more special programs. Why look for more problems?"

One answer to the question Why search for learning disabilities? is that the law requires it. In the United States, legislative pressure for massive screening programs built rapidly in the 1960s and 1970s. The Social Security Act was amended in 1967 to require states to provide screening for all children who were eligible for Medicare. Congressional action during the decade that followed continued to push for screening of special groups of children. Some states have already begun massive "child-find" programs, and within the next ten years, most states will consider such activity.

The hope is to find children and help them before they have too much failure at school. Thus, screening often is referred to as *early identification, early detection, early warning*, and even *prediction*.

Underlying the legal push for screening is a desire to meet the special needs of all individuals with problems, regardless of age. Identifying problems is essential for some forms of prevention and correction. In these instances, screening can be seen as an ethical responsibility (Adelman & Taylor, 1984a).

Obviously, there are very good reasons for searching for problems.

There are, however, also good reasons to be concerned about the effects of searching and the accuracy of the findings. This is especially true of large-scale programs for screening learning and behavior problems. Such programs bring with them errors in identification and a variety of negative side effects. Too often they are not followed up with needed services after problems are identified. Moreover, searching and finding individuals with problems shapes the nature of efforts to correct problems—the focus is on treating people and this results in a

tendency to ignore causal factors in the learning *environment*.

HOW IS IT DONE?

Essentially, individuals are identified as having learning problems or potential problems in at least one of three ways. First, they may see themselves as having a problem or be seen as having learning problems through informal observations made by family, friends, teachers, or colleagues during daily contacts at home, school, or work. Second, learning problems may be noted by physicians and other practitioners as part of regular checkups or treatment for other problems. Third, large numbers of children may be screened as part of formal "child-find" programs. In the first two instances, the person will need to be referred to a diagnostician if a formal diagnosis is seen as necessary (see Box 5–1). In the case of large-scale screening, sound practice also calls for a follow-up individual assessment before anyone is diagnosed formally; this step, however, is sometimes ignored (Hobbs, 1975).

Because child-find programs are probably the most ambitious of all efforts to find learning disabilities, let's look more closely at this type of assessment activity.

Child-Find Procedures

In the United States, Public Law 94-142 (the Education for All Handicapped Children Act) specifies that child-find programs must be developed. Minimally, this means identifying children already in school and, when feasible, finding those about to enter school.

One of the biggest problems in developing appropriate child-find programs for learning disabilities is deciding on the characteristics of the individuals to be found. Development of criteria for use in diagnosing learning

Box 5–1

Concern in the Field
Referral: The Hidden Screening Procedure

Before any formal assessment, there often is an informal screening procedure. That procedure is *referral*. Most children and adolescents are referred for diagnosis and treatment by school and medical personnel and sometimes by the courts.

Teachers, physicians, and judges see many individuals who have problems, but they only refer a small number of these for psychoeducational diagnoses and treatment.

How do they choose who to refer? Sometimes they refer those they think can best profit from treatment; sometimes they choose those they especially like and sometimes those they especially dislike.

There has been a great deal written about the possibility that racial, sexual, and class biases play a major role in referral processes. In general, individuals from nondominant (minority) groups in a society seem more likely than those in the dominant group to be identified and referred to programs for persons seen as "inferior" and "deviant."

The fact that referral processes can be used in a way that hides prejudiced motives makes such processes controversial and of concern (Gerber & Semmel, 1984).

Another bias that affects referral processes is the tendency to see the causes of others' problems in terms of something wrong with the person observed. Referrers may be influenced by this tendency when they observe learning problems. They may assume the causes are due to something wrong inside the person (such as a learning disability) and therefore send the individual for diagnosis and treatment.

In contrast to observers' tendencies, the person involved may tend to see the problem as due to some external factor, such as a poor teaching situation.

As discussed by *attribution* theorists,

". . . there is a pervasive tendency for actors [those observed] to attribute their actions to situational requirements, whereas observers tend to attribute the same actions to stable personal dispositions." (Jones & Nisbett, 1971, p. 80).

PROFESSOR: The reason students have trouble in my class is that they don't spend enough time studying. Some are simply lazy; others are too busy partying: some just don't care.

STUDENT: The reasons I'm having trouble in this class are that the lectures are boring, and the reading is too hard. Also, the professors in my other courses all give so many assignments that I hardly have time to do any of my work very well.

Whose explanation is right? Often, it is impossible to tell without a great deal more information. However, the point of concern in this context isn't who turns out to be right in a specific case. What's important to understand is that referrers may often operate on the basis of this psychological bias and so, in too many instances, may be ignoring environmental causes and "blaming the victim."

Attribution theorists would criticize prevailing referral processes as favoring causal models that see the cause and correction of learning problems *only* in terms of individuals (review Chapter 3). As suggested, such models tend not to pay sufficient attention to the role of environments in causing such problems or to the need for major changes in the environment as a part of efforts to correct learning problems.

disabilities has been discussed in Part 1. As indicated, federal guidelines in the United States specify minimal criteria related to a severe discrepancy between achievement and intellectual ability in various areas of academic performance. States and local school districts may add other criteria if they wish.

Besides specifying criteria, federal guidelines spell out procedures to be followed in applying the criteria and arriving at a diagnosis. The process involves a multidisciplinary team that minimally includes the student's regular teacher (or a qualified substitute), a qualified diagnostic examiner (such as a school psychologist), and a learning disabilities specialist. At least one member of the team, other than the student's regular teacher, is to observe the student's academic performance during class. After assessing the student, the team must prepare a written report clarifying

"(1) whether the child has a specific learning disability

(2) the basis for making the determination

(3) the relevant behavior noted during observation

(4) the relationship of that behavior to the child's academic functioning

(5) the educationally relevant medical findings, if any

(6) whether there is a severe discrepancy between achievement and ability that is not correctable without special education and related services

(7) the determination of the team concerning the effects of environmental, cultural, or economic disadvantage." *(Federal Register,* 1977, p. 65, 083)

What is not specified by the federal guidelines is how students are to be brought to the attention of the multidisciplinary team. That is, the guidelines do not discuss procedures for large-scale screening, and thus, there is great variability in what is done (Gracey, Azzara, & Reinherz, 1984). This is not surprising because good procedures have proved extremely difficult to develop. Hundreds of studies have been reported over the past twenty years. Researchers have struggled with tests, rating scales, and questionnaires (see Readings A and B), used alone and in various combinations. Their goal has been to evolve procedures that can correctly detect a high per-

centage of problems while not making too many false identifications.

At first, the focus was on assessing individuals by referring to a limited range of signs and symptoms of pathology and developmental deficits. This did not prove to be a successful approach. As a result, researchers who stress the importance of the environment and the interaction between a person and an environment have begun to add home and school factors. Their intention has been not only to improve the screening of individuals, but also to shift the focus to identifying and correcting problematic environments.

As indicated in Box 5–2, research findings and clinical observation indicate that youngsters with severe problems usually are identified readily by parents, pediatricians, and teachers without the use of complex and costly screening devices. Therefore, it is not surprising that severe problems related to learning and behavior are also readily identified by screening devices. However, identifying *severe problems* is not the same thing as identifying *learning disabilities.* Some of these severe problems will be learning disabilities, but many will be related to other general psychological and other biological problems.

Large-scale screening procedures for learning disabilities are meant only to be gross, first attempts at identification. As such, they are expected to overidentify, that is, identify some individuals who are not learning disabled and some who don't even have significant learning problems. The errors are to be found later when each person is individually assessed (e.g., by the multidisciplinary team specified by federal guidelines).

Because large-scale screening procedures make many errors, they are never supposed to be used to make specific diagnoses—not even tentative ones. When it comes time to make decisions about whether a person has a learning disability and about placement for treatment, the need is for assessment strategies that have greater diagnostic and prescriptive validity than available screening procedures.

Assessment for Diagnosis

For practitioners, the whole point of screening is to identify a problem so that it can be taken care of. The point of screening specifically for learning disabilities is to treat the learning disabled differently from those with other learning problems. While such *differential treatment* is not always available, the intent is there.

Before differential treatment for learning disabilities can be applied appropriately, a differential diagnosis must be made. In theory, the assessment procedures used in making a differential diagnosis will be keyed to an LD definition and related criteria. When the definition and criteria stress CNS causes and resulting processing disabilities, the assessment will include procedures developed for the purpose of detecting such underlying disabilities. In contrast, because of their view that it is wasteful to consider initial causes, behaviorists have stressed definitions and assessment procedures and criteria that focus on current functional problems and factors that contribute to such problems.

As mentioned in Chapter 4, assessors currently rely on criteria related to exclusionary categories, degree of underachievement, and symptoms of developmental immaturity. In general, in the United States, the current assessment processes used in diagnosing an individual as learning disabled include the following three categories: exclusion data, intelligence and achievement levels, and underlying psychological processes.

Exclusion data. Information is gathered regarding other problems a person may have that may be the primary cause of the learning problem. As listed in federal guidelines (see Chapter 1), a diagnosis of learning disabilities is *not* given if any of the following problems are identified as the primary cause of the learning problem: (a) vision, hearing, and motor handicaps, (b) mental retardation, (c) emotional disturbance, and (d) environmental, cultural, or economic disadvantage.

Information about these matters often can be gathered from existing school, medical, and psychological records. Where such information is inadequate, the data are gathered through interviews, medical exams, and psychological tests.

One major difficulty in interpreting the information gathered is the lack of agreement about how severe any of the "exclusion" problems must be before a diagnosis of learning disabilities is ruled out. For example, how much loss of vision? Some say that to rule out a diagnosis of learning disabilities, visual acuity in the best eye must be poorer than 20/70 with glasses. What should be considered mental retardation rather than a learning disability? Some say that the person's individual intelligence test score (judged as valid by a qualified psychologist) must be 70 or below; others say 80 or below. What about environmental, cultural, and economic disadvantage? The current intent seems to be to avoid labeling as learning disabled those whose learning and performance problems reflect educational programs and testing procedures that have not appropriately considered an individual's background and native language.

Intelligence and achievement levels. Essentially, any of a number of standardized individual tests of intelligence and achievement in reading, math, and language may be administered (see Reading A). All such tests

Box 5–2

Concern in the Field
Screening Procedures

The desire to identify learning problems at an early age is easily understood. Prevention and intervention in the earliest stages of a problem can be more effective and economical than later remediation. Indeed, for some problems, undue delay can make things considerably worse.

In contrast, arguments against screening often are misunderstood. Such arguments are primarily raised in connection with *large-scale* programs aimed at preschoolers and those in their first years in school. Don't make the mistake of thinking that critics of large-scale screening programs are arguing against efforts to prevent and correct problems. They, too, want to help.

One of their main concerns, however, is about the limitations of available procedures, especially for screening mild-moderate problems—which are by far the most numerous. Studies of how screening programs currently are run tend to support this concern. For example, a statewide survey of preschool screening programs in Illinois found that 77 percent of the responding agencies were using standardized but not well-validated instruments, and 23 percent were using locally developed, largely unvalidated procedures (Van Duyne, Gargiulo, & Allen, 1980).

Because so much emphasis has been placed on early-age screening, the conclusions of reviewers of research in this area have special relevance in discussing large-scale screening procedures. In general, reviewers report that the best of the available tests and rating scales are accurate in identifying only a moderate percentage of young (e.g., five- to seven-year-old) children who will have significant learning problems in their later schooling. In addition to missing individuals who will have problems, the procedures identify as having problems individuals who do not. The procedures are most accurate in identifying youngsters who currently have rather severe problems—those who are so obviously experiencing problems that they are readily identified by parents, pediatricians, and teachers through informal observation. Only a small percentage of those who truly have learning disabilities are easily distinguished from others who have problems but are not learning disabled.

From another perspective, it has been suggested that the money spent on screening would be better used to improve preschool, kindergarten, and first-grade programs. Critics stress that a very large proportion of those who may be identified would never become persons with significant learning problems if their early schooling were redesigned. They also stress that commitment to large-scale screening programs tends to take attention away from the need to make system changes (Graden, Casey, & Christensen, 1985).

As stated in the summary report of a major project focused on the classification of exceptional children:

"Every professionally competent report we have on early screening . . . strongly qualifies most assertions concerning the reliability, validity, or applicability of screening procedures . . ., especially for use in the early years of childhood. . . .

"Most serious developmental problems get picked up in routine clinical practice . . . or are identified by parents or other untrained observers; mild and moderate problems (by far the greatest number), however, are difficult to detect and assess even by well-trained professional people administering complete examinations with the best equipment." (Hobbs, 1975, pp. 92–94)

References to a sample of research reports and reviews on screening and placement procedures are provided in the references at the end of the chapter.

have their limitations, especially when given to individuals with learning and behavior problems. In general, scores from the best available instruments are only moderately accurate for individuals from such populations. This is due to problems in test construction and administration, to psychological influences such as test-taking anxiety and motivation, and to other factors that can affect both the performance of the test taker and how assessors interpret subjective test responses (see Kaufman, 1979).

Because of the limitations of standardized psychoeducational tests, assessors and multidisciplinary teams are encouraged to take note of other information, such as how individuals perform in the classroom or on the job, their motivation during testing, and so forth. Decisions regarding the inaccuracy of test findings often are based on judgments about such matters.

Scores on intelligence and achievement tests are used to determine how severe the discrepancy is between an individual's learning potential and current functioning. Although determining this discrepancy may be done in a highly subjective way, many school districts have adopted one of the many discrepancy formulas that have been proposed (see Box 5–3).

Box 5–3

Current Practice
Discrepancy Formulas

The discrepancy formula developed by Myklebust (1968) provides a representative example of such efforts. The formula yields an index of learning potential called a *Learning Quotient (LQ)*. The *LQ* is based on present achievement, called *Achievement Age (AA)*, as compared with expected achievement, called *Expectancy Age (EA)*.

This is expressed as the formula $LQ = \dfrac{AA}{EA}.$

Myklebust proposes that those whose *LQ* scores are 0.89 or below should be diagnosed as learning disabled. Because this figure was established without a great deal of research, use of a higher- or lower-criterion score can rather easily be justified.

To show how the formula works, we can take the example of Chris (see Chapter 1). When he was twelve, in grade 6.5, he was tested and found to have an IQ of 125. His reading test scores indicated a grade level of 5.5.

1. *AA*—To determine present achievement level, or Achievement Age *(AA)*, Myklebust's approach calls for adding 5.2 to Chris's achievement test score (5.5). So Chris's *AA* = 10.7.

2. *EA*—To determine his expected level of achievement, or Expectancy Age *(EA)*, the approach calls for combining mental age *(MA)*, actual or chronological age *(CA)*, and grade age *(GA)* and dividing by three.

The *MA* is computed by multiplying his IQ score (125) by his chronological age (twelve) and dividing by 100. So Chris's *MA* = 15.

The *GA* is computed by adding 5.2 to his present grade level (6.5). So Chris's *GA* = 11.7.

Thus,

$$EA = \frac{MA + CA + GA}{3} = \frac{15 + 12 + 11.7}{3} = 12.9.$$

3. *LQ*—Dividing 10.7 *(AA)* by 12.9 *(EA)* gives a learning potential or *LQ* score of 0.82.

By Myklebust's criterion of 0.89, Chris would qualify for a diagnosis of learning disabled.

Obviously, discrepancy formulas can be used only with children who have learned to read well enough to produce a reasonably valid score on a reading test.

In a 1984 evaluative review of discrepancy formulas, Berk found that nine out of more than a dozen procedures in use, including Myklebust's were statistically flawed in major ways. Only one, as yet relatively untested, approach was viewed as having promise.

Critics of discrepancy formulas say that although the formulas seem objective, they result in as many errors as the subjective procedures they replace. In part, the errors are due to the degree of error associated with any intelligence and achievement test score. Also, an increase in the degree of error has been shown to occur when separate test scores are combined in discrepancy formulas (Berk, 1984).

Underlying psychological processes. Because of the controversies surrounding the assessment and correction of deficits related to underlying psychological processes, federal guidelines do not specify that such processes must be assessed. Nevertheless, tests intended to assess perception and psycholinguistic abilities are administered quite routinely by diagnosticians. We shall have more to say about such tests in Chapter 6. (For now, see Box 5-4.)

WHAT'S NEXT? SERVICE AND PLACEMENT OPTIONS

Once diagnosed as learning disabled, an individual is eligible for services not necessarily available to those with other types of learning problems. For example, for school-aged youngsters, any of the following decisions may be made:

- *Class placement.* The student may be kept in regular classes or placed in a special classroom for all or part of the day.
- *Private remedial school.* If the student needs to go to a special class and the school cannot provide the program, the youngster may leave the public school and attend a private remedial school (funded by public money).
- *Extra help.* If the student is kept in regular classes, a special teacher may be brought in at selected times to provide special in-

struction, or the student may go to a special class for part of the day. After-school tutoring may also be recommended, instead of the other arrangements or in addition to them.

- *Ancillary services.* In addition to the educational services, counseling/psychotherapy or speech therapy may be recommended for the youngster. When physicians and other "medically-related" specialists are involved in making decisions, then recommendations for medication, special diets, vision correction, or various other services may also be made.

For adolescents and adults, options may also include service programs designed to prepare the individual for a vocation or career. These options may include career counseling, job training, and work-study programs that take into account the individual's special needs. Moreover, because few classroom programs are designed for adults with learning disabilities, those who are not enrolled in special college programs often find that their options for remedial instruction are limited to clinic tutorial programs or private tutoring.

Least Intervention Needed

In making general decisions about treatment, most professionals would agree that the least amount of intervention needed should be applied (see Kanfer & Goldstein, 1980). For example, if a youngster can be helped effectively in the regular classroom by the regular teacher, this seems better than putting the individual in a special classroom.

In addition, because special classrooms tend to segregate "handicapped" persons from others, U.S. law requires placement of all handicapped students, including those diagnosed as learning disabled, in the "least restrictive environment." This is meant to

Box 5–4

Current Practices
Testing for Possible Learning Disabilities

As part of the individual assessment necessary to confirm a suspected diagnosis of learning disabilities, a battery of tests often is used. Although there is no standard battery, the following tests have been frequently recommended by authoritative publications for use in a learning disabilities test battery. Most of these tests have been severely criticized by test reviewers, and practitioners with a behaviorist orientation reject those procedures that focus on underlying processes, such as tests of visual perception.

Area Tested	Tests Commonly Used
Intelligence	Wechsler Intelligence Scales (WPPSI, WISC-R, WAIS-R)
	Stanford-Binet Intelligence Test
Achievement (reading, math, mechanics of english, spelling)	Metropolitan Achievement Test
	California Achievement Test
	Wide Range Achievement Test
	Woodcock-Johnson Psycho-Educational Battery
Perceptual-motor abilities	Bender Visual-Motor Gestalt Test
	Developmental Test of Visual Perception
	Lincoln-Oseretsky Motor Development Scale
	Graham-Kendall Memory for Designs
Language	Illinois Test of Psycholinguistic Abilities
	Test of Written Language
	Peabody Picture Vocabulary Test
	Wepman Auditory Discrimination Test
	Goldman-Fristoe Test of Articulation
Social and emotional functioning	Vineland Adaptive Behavior Scales
	Sentence Completion
	Children's or Thematic Apperception Test
	Rorschach
Neurological and psychoneurological functioning	Soft signs (see Chapter 4)

Research on the validity of these procedures in LD differential diagnosis and treatment planning has not been encouraging. Over the last decade, a great deal of research has focused on the relationship of intelligence test performance to valid diagnosis and treatment planning. Most of the investigations have used the Wechsler Intelligence Scale for Children—Revised (see Kaufman, 1981); but in recent years, this type of research has been extended to the Wechsler Adult Intelligence Scale (e.g., Cordoni, O'Donnell, Ramaniah, Kurtz, & Rosenshein, 1981.

The results of such studies raise concerns about two notions that have been widely shared among LD practitioners. One of these notions is that large differences among the scores on separate subtests and overall differences between the combined verbal and the combined performance subtests can validly be used in making a differential diagnosis of learning disabilities. The other notion is that the profile or pattern of strengths and weaknesses implied by the differences in subtest scores is a valid basis for planning educational interventions. Neither notion has been supported by research.

Analyses of the studies lead to the conclusion that the Wechsler scales "are not likely to be very useful in the diagnosis of LD or in its differential diagnosis" (Kaufman, 1981, p. 523). And although the pattern of subtest performance may eventually be found to have some degree of validity for educational planning, this has not yet been demonstrated.

Other formal tests from the large array that have been used with youngsters and adults are listed in Reading A, as are other procedures used for assessment, such as informal tests, observation methods, and interviews and case histories.

---

ensure that they are educated in a regular environment along with students who are not handicapped and in the school they would regularly attend—unless there is a compelling educational reason for not doing so. The idea that handicapped students should be educated as much as is feasible with nonhandicapped youngsters is called *mainstreaming* because the point is to keep these students in the mainstream of public education rather than segregate them in special classes and special institutions (e.g., Biklen, 1985; Ivarie, Hogue, & Brulle, 1984; Turnbull & Schultz, 1979).

The principle of "least intervention needed" and the idea of placement in the "least restrictive environment" are intended to provide a guideline for those who prescribe treatments. The guideline can be stated as, Do not disrupt or restrict a person's opportunity for a normal range of experiences more than is absolutely necessary. The guideline recognizes that treatments that are very disruptive or restrictive tend to narrow an individual's immediate and future options and choices. The negative results can include poor self-concept, social alienation, and loss of career and other life opportunities.

To help use the idea of placing individuals in the least restrictive environment, several professionals have tried to provide lists and models describing a continuum of placements ranging from least to most restrictive. Not surprisingly, the least restrictive placement usually is described as keeping people in normal situations and using special assistance only to the degree needed. Thus, for example, a decision to place a student in a special class for part of a day is seen as somewhat more restrictive than keeping the individual in a regular class, and a full-day placement in a special class is viewed as even more restrictive. The most restrictive placements are considered to be assignments to a special school or institution. Public Law 94-142 requires the availability in schools of a *continuum of alternative placements* for handicapped children.

There has been a great deal of positive support for the principle of least intervention needed and for descriptions of what types of placements are seen as least restrictive. There are, however, some problems. In particular, what is considered the least restrictive setting may be the most restrictive in the long run if it cannot meet the needs of the individual placed there.

Take the case of two students, Jenny and Susan, who are behind in their reading. It is decided to keep them in a regular sixth-grade classroom and provide them with special in-class tutoring for an hour a day. Jenny has a specific learning disability and is reading at no better than the second-grade level; Susan has no disability and is reading at the fifth-grade level. Both respond reasonably well to the tutoring. Susan also begins to perform satisfactorily during other times of the day. Jenny continues to have trouble learning at other times, and she also tends to have a behavior problem.

Clearly, the treatment plan keeps both students in the mainstream.

However, someone is bound to ask,

"Might it not be better to place Jenny temporarily in a special classroom that can be more responsive to her educational needs so that she can overcome her problems and then return to perform successfully in the mainstream?

"After all," the argument continues, "isn't it much *less restrictive* in the long run to get intensive treatment so the problem might be overcome as quickly as possible? In so many cases, what might seem like the less restrictive approach may mean added years of involvement in special treatments, and the results may not even be as good."

"Those are good points," answer opponents of special class placements, "but the evidence suggests that special classrooms are not particularly effective."

"Moreover," they say, "some never do get to go back to mainstream programs after being placed in special schools and institutions."

Placement decisions are difficult!

Regular and Special Education

The matter of mainstreaming goes right to the roots of the difference between regular and special education. One way to look at the difference is to see regular education classes as trying to serve as wide a range of different people as they can. Those people that regular educators cannot serve appropriately need special education in some form (see McCann, Semmel, & Nevin, 1985). The less the regular education pro-

gram can do, the more the need for special education. The unanswered questions are What range of individual differences can regular education programs serve *optimally?* What range of individual differences can regular education programs serve *typically?*

Most regular programs probably could handle a greater range of individuals than they do currently. To do so, however, some changes in these programs are needed. For those who argue that mainstreaming can work well for many exceptional children, a basic assumption is that most regular classroom programs have to be changed before they can be successful with such children. These changes include additional materials, equipment, and procedures and some training for the teacher in how to use them.

Changes also are recommended in staffing patterns and staff-student ratios, so that a teacher has more time to devote to those with special needs. Examples of these changes are team teaching and the addition of aides or tutors (including peer tutors). The right pattern and ratio certainly will vary depending on the number of students with special needs and severe problems. In addition, there is likely to be a call periodically for specialist help in and out of the classroom (e.g., resource teachers, reading and speech specialists to assess student problems and needs). Finally, it may still be necessary for certain students to have some special help outside their classrooms daily.

If regular classrooms are not changed, the potential value of mainstreaming cannot be fairly tested. The longer regular classrooms stay as they are, the more call there will be for placements in special education programs.

Assessment for Placement

Once a person is assessed as learning disabled, there is no question that special help must be provided. The problem is to decide which of the treatment options described are to be pursued.

Let us assume that all options are available to the individual. How is it decided which treatments will be prescribed?

Special class or not? Public or private setting? Stay in the regular class with extra help? These placement decisions are made primarily with information about what options are available. If a satisfactory educational program can be provided in the student's regular class, there is no reason to place the youngster elsewhere. If an appropriate program cannot be provided anywhere in the public school system, then it becomes necessary to seek placement in a private setting.

What is an *appropriate* educational program? For now, an appropriate program is one with an apparently competent teacher who has time to give the type of one-to-one attention that the student requires.

Ancillary services? After the major decisions are made about educational placement, decisions are made about which ancillary services, if any, seem appropriate. Often, the best assessment of the need for such services is made by waiting to see if the educational placement appears to be working and seems to be enough.

At any rate, the ultimate decision that an individual should pursue ancillary treatments is less likely to be based on *valid* assessment than on decision makers' beliefs. For example, if the person making the decision believes that stimulant drugs or special diets or psychotherapy can help a person overcome a learning problem, such treatments are likely to be implemented if at all feasible (see Reading C).

Although no additional assessment data are necessary in making general placement decisions, additional testing may be considered essential to planning the specific program. Current law in the United States, for example, mandates that an individualized educational program (IEP) be formu-

lated either at the time placement decisions are made or at least within thirty days of such decisions. When such specific planning is necessary before placement, a variety of tests and other assessment procedures may be used (see Readings A and B). The IEP and assessment considerations related to its formulation are discussed in Chapter 6.

WHO DECIDES? INFORMED CONSENT FOR SCREENING AND PLACEMENT

Despite Superintendent Brown's concerns, her school board decided the district would give a battery of screening tests to all incoming kindergarteners to find any who have learning disabilities.

> "Easier said than done," complained the superintendent to the board. "You know I'm not the only one who's concerned about the screening program. What will the parents say?"

The decision to test raises the question Should parents be asked whether their children can be tested?

> "And what will the kids say?"

The decision to test also raises the question Should each child be given a choice about whether to take the tests?

Despite Superintendent Brown's complaints and concerns, the screening program was carried out. Based on the test findings, Jan's parents are told a special class placement is needed.

At this point, additional questions arise: Does the school have the right to place Jan in such a class even if the parents don't want it? Does Jan have any say in what happens?

There are no simple answers to these questions. Each answer has major legal and ethical implications related to the topic of *informed consent*.

There was a time not so long ago when

assigning students with problems to special programs was done matter-of-factly. Most professionals believed they knew who needed help and what help was needed. It was a relatively simple matter to inform those involved that a problem existed and what was to be done.

Growing awareness of rights and of the potentially harmful effects of treatment led to safeguards. Currently, informed consent is not taken for granted (Biklen, 1978). For example, parent and student involvement have become very important concerns in the screening, diagnosis, and placement for learning disabilities.

Increasingly, parents' groups and child advocates have insisted that parents be involved in any decision that might have a profound effect on the course of a child's life. With regard to handicapped children, this fact is reflected in the "procedural safeguards" associated with the passage of U.S. Public Law 94-142 (see Box 5–5).

Children's involvement is only beginning to be discussed seriously. Interest in civil rights in the late 1960s and related advocacy of minors' rights in education and mental health have led to greater consideration of the rights of children and adolescents to be involved in making decisions that affect them. Along with such consideration, long-standing controversies have reemerged about the risks and benefits of young people's involvement in decision making and their competence to make appropriate decisions (see Box 5–6).

Box 5–5

Current Practices
Parental Consent and Due Process in Screening and Placement

In the United States, due process is a legal safeguard established in the Fourteenth Amendment to the Constitution. Due process is stressed in Public Law 94-142 because of its importance for services for handicapped children. Due process is the way in which people's rights are protected, and it is meant to help guarantee that everyone is treated fairly.

Due process is necessary to ensure that parents are involved in school screening and placement and that they consent to all related actions that may profoundly affect their child. Listed here are some of the safeguards that have been found important enough to specify legally:

1. Parents must be notified whenever the school plans to conduct a special evaluation of their child.

2. Parents have the right to refuse consent for such an evaluation. (However, the school district has the right to a legal hearing to prove the need for such an evaluation. Should parents want a special evaluation and the school refuse, the parents can seek a legal hearing.)

3. Parents have the right to

- review the procedures and instruments to be used in any evaluation

- be informed of the results and review all records

- obtain an independent educational evaluation to be considered in any decisions

4. Parents must be notified whenever the school wants to change their child's educational placement, and they have the right to refuse consent for such placement. (Again, the school district can ask for a legal hearing to overrule the parents' decision; and parents who are unable to convince the school to provide the special placement they want can also seek such a hearing.)

All notifications and explanations are to be given in the parents' primary language or other primary mode of communication.

From another perspective, obtaining consent is seen as potentially having major benefits. Giving consent is making a choice. Individuals who feel they have chosen an activity can be expected to have higher levels of commitment and motivation for pursuing the activity than those who feel they didn't have a choice. Thus, consent can be seen as an important prerequisite to positive participation in treatment. Moreover, if competence to make decisions increases with experience and learning, then the experience of participating in treatment decisions should help to increase competence to make future decisions (Adelman, Kaser-Boyd, & Taylor, 1984).

Box 5–6

Concern in the Field
Are children diagnosed as learning disabled competent enough to participate in making treatment decisions?

There are two related concerns that arise in the context of discussions about children's participation in consent procedures. One can be described as the question of *competence*; the other is the problem of *paternalism*.

Stated directly, the question of competence asks: To what degree is an individual capable of understanding the factors that go into making an appropriate treatment decision? There is very little satisfactory research on the degree to which individuals at various ages and with various problems have such capabilities. Current findings suggest that minors, including those diagnosed as learning disabled, may be able to participate in treatment placement decisions considerably before late adolescence—the earliest age most professionals have accepted for encouraging such participation. However, the age at which minors clearly are able to decide for themselves remains to be established (see Melton, Koocher, & Saks, 1983; Taylor, Adelman, & Kaser-Boyd, 1984, 1985).

The problem of paternalism reflects the fact that parents, professionals, and various representatives of the society have special responsibilities for minors. In carrying out such responsibilities, they must have the right to make certain decisions for minors. When these paternalistic decisions produce little complaint or reaction from children or when major health and safety matters are at stake, paternalism is unlikely to be much of a problem.

However, suppose a fourteen-year-old does not want to be placed in a special class. Should the student be compelled?

Currently, students have no legal say until they are eighteen. Only the parents (or a special advocate) can argue for or against the placement.

Are eighteen-year-olds more competent to decide than fourteen-year-olds? Maybe. But an eighteen-year-old may also be as incompetent as a fourteen-year-old to make such a decision. And, of course, it is also possible that by age fourteen, some individuals have developed the competence to decide such matters for themselves.

Legal age aside, there is little agreement about how to determine competence for decision making or about whether a competent minor should be able to overturn any paternalistic decision.

In general, then, when the interests of a minor are the same as the interests of those having responsibility for the minor, such as parents and teachers, there is unlikely to be much concern about who makes decisions. When interests are in conflict, however, who decides becomes a critical matter. In most situations, control of decision making is kept by those with the most authority and power. In this sense, placement decisions involve more than treatment considerations: they are sociopolitical decisions.

In contrast, not participating in decision making may undermine motivation and competence.

We have more to say about these matters in Parts 3 and 4.

SUMMARY

Screening, diagnosis, and placement must be and are done every day. Whatever screening procedures are used, additional assessment and consultation must be done before a diagnosis of learning disabilities is made. Current criteria emphasize exclusionary factors, degree of underachievement, and symptoms of developmental immaturity.

In public schools in the United States, the diagnosis of learning disabilities means that an individual between the ages of three and twenty-one has the right to services, such as extra help and special teachers, that are not necessarily available to those with other types of learning problems. Decisions about what services should be provided are made on the basis of what is available and what seems most appropriate to those who are asked to make the decisions.

In keeping with the principle of providing the least intervention needed, the idea has been set forth that educational placements should be made in the "least restrictive environment." The intent is to keep handicapped students, including those diagnosed as learning disabled, in the "mainstream" of public education. This appealing idea has been easy to accept in principle, but the implications for practice have proven to be rather difficult to turn into specific prescriptions for individuals.

Finally, there is an increasing awareness that screening and placement decisions can be biased. There also is continuing concern that such decisions can have a profound effect on an individual's future. Such awareness and concern have given an added push to the move to involve parents and their youngsters in screening and placement decisions.

Once found and placed, what happens to those who have been diagnosed as learning disabled? We turn to this question now.

SPECIAL TOPIC REFERENCES

Should you be interested in further information about *screening* and *placement* procedures for learning disabilities, see the following readings.

ADELMAN, H. S. (1982). Identifying learning problems at an early age: A critical appraisal. *Journal of Clinical Child Psychology, 11*, 255–61.

ADELMAN, H. S., & TAYLOR, L. (1983). *Learning disabilities in perspective.* Glenview, Ill.: Scott, Foresman.

BADIAN, N. (1976). Early prediction of academic underachievement: Paper presented at the meeting of the 54th Annual International Convention of the Council for Exceptional Children, Chicago. (ERIC Document Reproduction Service No. ED 122 500.)

BERK, R. A. (1984). An evaluation of procedures for computing an ability-achievement discrepancy score. *Journal of Learning Disabilities, 17*, 262–66.

FREUND, J. H., BRADLEY, R. H., & CALDWELL, B. M. (1979). The home environment in the assessment of learning disabilities. *Learning Disability Quarterly, 2*, 39–51.

GALLAGHER, J. J., & BRADLEY, R. H. (1972). Early identification of developmental difficulties. In I. J. Gordon (Ed.), *Early childhood education.* Chicago: University of Chicago Press.

GERBER, M. M., & SEMMEL, M. I. (1984). Teacher as imperfect test: Reconceptualizing the referral process. *Educational Psychologist, 19*, 137–48.

HOBBS, N. (1975). *The futures of children: Categories, labels, and their consequences.* San Francisco: Jossey-Bass.

ILLICH, I. (1976). *Medical nemesis.* New York: Pantheon.

KARNES, M. B., & STONEBURNER, R. L. (1984). Prevention of learning disabilities: Preschool assessment and intervention. In J. D. McKinney & L.

Feagans (Eds.), *Current topics in learning disabilities*, Vol. 1 Norwood, N.J.: Ablex Publishing Co.

KEOGH, B. K., & BECKER, L. D. (1973). Early detection of learning problems: Questions, cautions, and guidelines. *Exceptional Children, 40*, 5–11.

MELTON, G. B., KOOCHER, G. P., & SAKS, M. (Eds.) (1983). *Children's competence to consent.* New York: Plenum.

MERCER, J. R. (1979). *System of multicultural pluralistic assessment: Technical manual.* New York: Psychological Corporation.

REINHERZ, H., GORDON, A. L., MORRIS, K. M. & ANASTAS, J. W. (1983). Who shall be served? Issues in screening for emotional and behavioral problems in school. *Journal of Primary Prevention, 4*, 803–24.

SATZ, P., & FLETCHER, J. (1979). Early screening tests: Some uses and abuses. *Journal of Learning Disabilities, 12*, 56–60.

SCHAER, H. F., & CRUMP, W. D. (1976). Teacher involvement and early identification of children with learning disabilities. *Journal of Learning Disabilities, 9*, 91–95.

SCHRAG, P., & DIVOKY, D. (1975). *The myth of the hyperactive child and other means of behavioral control.* New York: Pantheon.

Chapter 6

Prevailing Treatment Approaches

When her parents were told that Diana should be placed in a special class, they were not surprised. They had noticed some distressing things at home and had been told about other problems by her teachers.

While not surprised, they were concerned. And they were in disagreement about what to do:

Mother: I want Diana to stay in regular classes so she won't feel different from her friends.

Father: But she already feels different. She knows she can't do things as well as the others. She says she feels dumb.

Mother: She might feel worse in a special class. And besides, she'll miss out on a lot of information and experiences that her friends will get.

Father: That might be true, but what if keeping her in the regular program prevents her from overcoming her problems or makes them worse? This is the time to help her. We can't afford to waste any time.

Mother: I see that, but what will they do in a special class that can't be done in the regular one? Aren't there other treatments?

Father: The special teachers have learned special ways to teach children with learning disabilities. Other treatments may help, but the school says she will still need special instruction.

What are the special approaches currently used by most learning disabilities teachers? How is it decided which approaches to use? How about the other treatments? And how effective are any of them? What about negative side effects?

These and other matters related to prevailing treatment approaches are explored in this chapter.

THE PREVAILING CHOICES

What are the decisions to be made if someone has a learning disability? One set of
decisions involves *general* matters such as
what type of service, where the treatment
should take place, and who should do the
treating.

Another *set* of decisions focuses on what
specific things should be done to treat the
problem. This involves making a specific
treatment plan for how to approach the
problem and what to do on a daily basis.

Placements and Resources

Service and placement options were explored
in Chapter 5. As we have indicated, the intention in making service decisions is to
choose the least intervention needed and
place the individual in the least restrictive
environment. To help serve this end, educational placements have been described in
terms of a continuum ranging from least to
most restrictive:

LEAST
RESTRICTIVE

- regular class—consulta-
  tion for teacher provided
  as needed (mainstream-
  ing)
- regular class—resources
  added (e.g., materials,
  aides, tutors, specialist
  help on a regular basis)
- special class—partial
  day (e.g., LD specialist,
  resource room)
- special learning disabilities class—entire day
- special learning disabilities school (public/pri-
  vate)
- special institutions (resi-
  dential homes, hospital
  programs)

MOST
RESTRICTIVE

In general, the relatively small number of individuals with severe problems are the most
likely candidates for the more restrictive
placements (see Schworm, 1976).

It is assumed that placement will be in
the least restrictive environment that is also
the most effective. A short stay in a more
restrictive placement may be more effective
than a long stay in a minimally restrictive
but less effective program.

Besides the least-restrictive-environment
guideline, factors such as financial support
and program availability can be major factors in deciding school placements. Indeed,
there is a trend toward approaching educational placements as an administrative
rather than a treatment arrangement. For
example, efforts to return students from
special schools and classes to regular programs (mainstreaming) generally have not
been paired with improvements in the ability of regular programs to serve the special
needs of such students. Thus, students have
been shifted from one setting to another
without significant attention to whether the
new setting contains adequate resources for
providing appropriate treatment.

One final note about placement: it is
widely recognized that all decisions to place
individuals in special settings need to be
reviewed regularly to detect placement errors and to determine how effective treatment is.

Contrasting Orientations to Treatment

Picture yourself as Diana's parents. If Diana
is to go to a special class, you want to know
more about what will happen there. At first
glance, you may be overwhelmed by the
variety of different teaching models and of
specific strategies and techniques used in
special programs. Despite the variety, however, two major orientations have dominated

the field of learning disabilities for some time. What are they, how do they differ, and how are they evolving?

Reflecting a concern for possible CNS causes, one orientation proposes that the learning disabled lack certain "abilities" necessary for processing what is to be learned. Those who believe this use *underlying-abilities* approaches which focus on improving psychological processes, if possible, or on helping a person overcome handicaps by learning ways to compensate for deficient abilities.

The roots of this orientation are found in medical, psychotherapeutic, and educational concepts. Thus, the approach stresses that specific treatments be based on diagnostic testing designed to analyze psychoneurological (and sometimes psychodynamic) functioning. Treatment processes draw upon traditional learning principles (such as reinforcement theory) and psychotherapeutic concepts (such as rapport building).

If you observed a teacher using the underlying-abilities approach, you would see a range of *therapy*-oriented strategies designed to improve underlying abilities, to teach ways to compensate for ability deficits, or both. You probably would also see considerable attention paid to establishing a therapeutic relationship as a way of reducing anxiety and increasing positive involvement.

In contrast to underlying-abilities approaches are *observable-skills* approaches. These approaches assume that anyone with a learning problem simply hasn't learned certain "skills" as yet. Those who hold this view stress the teaching, directly and systematically, of all missing skills used in school and in daily living.

The roots of this orientation are in behavior modification concepts, particularly those associated with operant conditioning and cognitive behavior modification. Thus, in observing a program that uses an observable-skills approach, you would see a variety of *behavior change* strategies.

In general, specific treatment plans are based on ongoing analysis not only of skills but also of interfering behaviors. Treatment procedures draw upon such behavior change principles as scheduling reinforcers, deprivation, and satiation. The intent is to elicit and reinforce specific responses so that skills are learned, positive behavior is increased, and undesired responses are decreased. In this last regard, the focus is on eliminating any behaviors interfering with classroom learning, such as a student's tendencies to be inattentive or argue about doing tasks.

Because of the degree to which these two orientations have dominated the field, let's look at each in a bit more detail.

Underlying-abilities approaches. Practitioners of underlying-abilities approaches assume that those who are diagnosed as learning disabled have a central nervous system that is not functioning appropriately. The CNS problem is seen as affecting one or more basic abilities involved in receiving or processing stimuli or in responding. The areas of psychological functioning affected include perception, psycholinguistic abilities, and cognition. Practitioners following this orientation believe that learning problems will continue unless something is done to help the individual improve in whatever basic psychological process has been affected. Therefore, they pursue treatments assumed to develop weak abilities or seen as enabling an individual to compensate for areas of weakness.

Treatment approaches based on ideas about weak underlying functioning include educational, psychological, and even some medically-related strategies. Some examples of psychoeducational treatment approaches and prominent names associated with them follow. (Major medically-related approaches and some controversies surrounding them are explored in Reading C.)

Perception and related motor functioning. There is a long history of theory, treatment, and research in the learning disabilities field based on the belief that underlying some learning problems, such as in reading and writing, are deficits in the ability to recognize and interpret sensory stimuli or in the ability to integrate such stimuli with motor activity. Kurt Goldstein, Alfred Strauss, and Heinz Werner are recognized as pioneers in working with such ideas. Later, Laura Lehtinen, Newell Kephart, William Cruickshank, and Marianne Frostig continued to emphasize this line of thinking; they developed treatment approaches that became widely used in the 1950s and 1960s.

For instance, for cases in which learning problems seem to be due to CNS trouble that has caused difficulties with perception of body parts and functions, Cruickshank (1961), Kephart (1960), and others have advocated exercises to improve sense of body awareness and coordination. Such exercises start with simple tasks, e.g., identifying body parts in response to verbal cues; then they move on to more demanding tasks, e.g., catching, throwing, and walking special routes as directed, which require controlled use of the body.

The types of perceptual and related motor functions for which exercises have been developed include

- laterality & directionality
- balance & posture
- gross & fine motor coordination
- figure-ground perception
- position in space
- perceptual motor coordination
- multisensory integration
- rhythm
- strength, endurance, & flexibility
- body image & differentiation
- locomotion
- ocular control
- constancy of shape
- spatial relationships

- auditory & visual integration
- tactile & kinesthetic integration
- agility

Because the exercises usually are designed for young children, practice is encouraged through the use of gamelike activities, such as Simon-says, duck-, crab-, and elephant-walks, rabbit hops, hopscotch, making angels in the snow, jumping rope, walking on balance boards, skating, copying, drawing, coloring, paper cutting and folding, and rhyming games.

Psycholinguistic and related abilities underlying language functioning. Here, as with perceptual-motor functioning, there is a long history of concern about underlying deficits interfering with reading, writing, and speaking. Treatment approaches developed by Samuel Orton and Grace Fernald in the 1920s often are mentioned as pioneer examples of underlying-abilities approaches to learning disabilities that are related to reading and related language functions. However, major concern over underlying processes negatively affecting language development and learning didn't arise until the late 1950s and 1960s. During those years, Joseph Wepman, Samuel Kirk and his colleagues, and Helmut Myklebust and his colleague Doris Johnson focused attention on treatment approaches for disabilities underlying language learning problems.

For instance, there has been tremendous emphasis on the notion that CNS trouble may interfere with the processes by which information from one or more senses is received and understood. These processes are described as sensory "modalities." Thus, when a youngster diagnosed as learning disabled has a reading problem, the possibility of a weak auditory or visual modality is often considered. When a weak modality is found, exercises are advocated to try to strengthen the weakness, if possible, and reading instruction is changed to place greater reliance on strong modalities or combinations of modalities, including use of kinesthetic and tactile senses.

The types of psycholinguistic and related abilities underlying language function for which exercises have been developed include

- reception—auditory & visual
- closure—auditory & visual
- sound-symbol association
- association—auditory & visual
- sequential memory—auditory & visual

Although these two examples cannot do justice to the thinking behind underlying-abilities approaches, they do provide a basis for understanding two basic assumptions of the orientation:

- If there is a learning disability, the CNS trouble is likely to have affected underlying psychological processes, such as perception and psycholinguistic abilities.
- Deficits in underlying abilities must be corrected or compensated for before the learning problems of individuals with learning disabilities can be overcome.

Observable-skills approaches. Practitioners of observable-skills approaches assume that even if a person has a learning disability, the only thing that can be done from a teaching perspective is to teach the skills the individual is to learn. Moreover, those who hold this view also tend to have been influenced by behaviorist models of instruction and so view skill instruction in terms of strategies for behavior change.

Skills are seen as built on one another. Some are *general prerequisites* for a great deal of school learning. These include skills such as learning to attend and to follow directions. Lists of skills, called *skill hierarchies*, have been developed in areas such

as reading and math to identify which skills should be learned first, second, and so forth.

Treatment approaches based on an observable-skills orientation stress classroom use of operant conditioning and cognitive behavior modification strategies, programmed and criterion-referenced instruction, precision teaching, and direct instruction of skills. Besides reading and other school subjects, observable-skills approaches focus on these areas:

- impulse control
- sustained attention & follow-through
- selective attention
- perseverance
- frustration tolerance
- appropriate interpersonal interactions

Some examples of observable skills treatment approaches for learning disabilities and prominent names associated with them follow:

Behaviorist classroom programs. During the 1950s and 1960s, Richard Whelan, Norris Haring, E. Lakin Phillips, and Frank Hewett established classroom models based on behaviorist ideas of learning. In the 1960s and 1970s, an increasing number of learning disabilities programs adopted these models. Such programs strongly emphasize establishment of environments in which desired behavior (observable skills appropriate to the student's level of functioning) can be elicited and then reinforced in a consistent way.

For instance, first a student's most basic missing skills are identified; then relatively short tasks and exercises are provided to help the student acquire each skill. The student is told that he or she can earn rewards for working in a specified way. Thus, after perhaps fifteen minutes of work, a student's efforts and accomplishments are evaluated and checkmarks or some other "reinforcer" are given. Checkmarks are turned in at a specified time for a prize, a special activity, or for free time. If the student does not cooperate or misbehaves, he or she may lose a privilege. In general, reinforcements are seen as the positive and negative consequences students experience for their behavior. Reinforcements have been described as (a) giving students something they want, (b) taking away something they want, (c) giving them something they don't want, and (d) taking away something they don't want (Hewett & Taylor, 1980).

Cognitive behavior modification ideas have been added to such programs in recent years (e.g., Douglas, 1972; Meichenbaum, 1977). The cognitive behaviorist approach stresses the importance of students giving themselves directive messages and monitoring and evaluating their own progress. For instance, to teach students to attend more carefully in learning situations, they are instructed to tell themselves to "stop, look, and listen." More generally, the intention is to have them learn to define what has to be done, attend to the relevant parts of a task, reinforce themselves as they proceed, and evaluate their accomplishments.

To teach such "cognitive strategies," (a) the teacher models the process by talking through the steps while doing a task, (b) the student does the task, with the teacher directing and talking through each step, (c) the student then repeats the task with self-directions, saying the steps aloud and eventually only whispering them, and finally (d) the student does the task without saying the directions aloud. What the student says may sound like this:

"Okay, what is it I have to do? Copy this picture. I should do it slowly so I won't make mistakes.

"Draw the line down—good—then to the right—that's it, now down. I'm doing fine so far. Remember to go slowly. Oh, Oh. I was sup-

posed to go down. That's O.K. Just erase the line. Good. Even if I make a mistake I can go on. I have to draw a circle now.

"Finished. I did it!"

Skill hierarchies, behavioral objectives, and skill monitoring. Observable-skills approaches particularly stress the importance of (a) understanding the developmental scope and sequence of skills to be learned, (b) specifying intended outcomes (objectives) in highly concrete behavioral terms, and (c) carefully monitoring to see if appropriate steps are being followed and to evaluate what has been learned as a basis for planning the next steps for instruction. This emphasis can be found in programmed materials such as DISTAR (e.g., Englemann & Bruner, 1969) and in other "criterion-referenced" strategies, such as Meyen's Instructional Based Appraisal System (IBAS) and Hewett's hierarchy of learning competence; in the ideas for precision teaching formulated by Lindsley and developed as applied behavioral analysis by colleagues such as Lovitt (1975a, 1975b; also see Alberto & Troutman, 1982); and in the directive teaching strategies of Stephens (1977).

Meyen's (1976) system, for instance, is designed to provide special education teachers with a ready-made package for planning and implementing instruction and evaluation. It encompasses six activities ranging from diagnostic worksheets through evaluation and reference formats. Each activity has a printed format and several information banks containing lists of sequential behavioral objectives and evaluation procedures; e.g., there are a total of seventy-three objectives for reading and one hundred for math.

The focus in observable-skills approaches on skill hierarchies, behavioral objectives, and skill monitoring has been appealing to program planners and evaluators. Thus, when U.S. law called for detailed individual education planning (IEPs), the trend was toward using these strategies. For instance, it has been proposed that each skill to be taught should be stated in terms of the behavior to be learned and the criteria for success:

> Joe will decode unfamiliar vocabulary words from fourth-grade texts with 85 percent accuracy.

Again, because brief examples cannot do justice to observable-skills approaches, our only intent here is to provide a basis for understanding two basic assumptions of these approaches:

- Even if an individual has a learning disability, the individual still has skills that can be learned, and the processes by which learning occurs remain the same.
- Learning problems can be overcome by directly teaching missing skills, including prerequisites (see Box 6–1).

For many years, the underlying-abilities orientation dominated the field. As more practitioners adopted behaviorist ideas, observable-skills approaches gained in popularity. However, despite the great emphasis on observable skills in recent years, underlying-abilities approaches continue to be widely advocated. For instance, in a 1982 issue of a special education journal, "an assortment of great teaching ideas" were presented *(Academic Therapy,* May, 1982); of the thirteen ideas covered, ten reflected an underlying-abilities orientation.

In the 1970s and 1980s, the renewed interest in cognitive psychology has given rise to what some have called *learning strategies* approaches. With their emphasis on psychological functioning, these approaches have strong ties to the underlying-abilities tradition. In the form they usually are applied, however, they appear more akin to the observable-skills orientation. Rather than viewing individuals as lacking in basic abilities to learn, the learning-strategies orientation assumes that not only has someone not learned specific skills, but also the individual has not learned to use general learning strategies efficiently.

What are learning strategies? As discussed by Alley and Deshler (1979), "Learning strategies are defined as techniques,

---

Box 6–1

Current Practices
Contrasting Orientations

To illustrate one basic difference between the two approaches, let's assume that Diana has been having trouble learning some beginning math skills. She is the only one in her class who can't count and group objects.

Underlying-abilities approaches would try to determine whether her learning problems were caused by a basic psychological processing deficit, such as poor abilities related to visual and auditory "sequential memory." If such deficits are identified through testing, remediation is likely to include exercises to improve short-term memory and sequencing ability by having Diana do such things as repeat numbers, letters, words, and tapped patterns.

Those pursuing observable-skills approaches would not be especially concerned with why Diana had not learned to count. They would assume that she could learn the skills if a good teaching approach was now used. Such an approach would need to account not only for the math skills currently troubling Diana but also for any related *observable* skills that might be important prerequisites. Diana would then be directly taught all identified missing skills. Exercises might include, for instance, games to help her memorize and recite the numbers one to ten, eleven to twenty, and so forth.

principles, or rules that will facilitate the acquisition, manipulation, integration, storage, and retrieval of information across situations and settings" (p. 13).

One example is seen in the type of study-skills strategies most of us were taught throughout our schooling. Another example involves the memory strategies some people use in recalling names, addresses, and material for tests (Mastropieri, Scruggs, & Levin, 1985). Such strategies tend to emphasize using visual or verbal mental images, systematic sequences of steps, and so forth. Learning strategies vary in their complexity, the more complex ones designed primarily for use in programs for adolescents and adults (Deshler, Schumaker, & Lenz, 1984).

DECIDING WHAT TO DO

Given the various options about placements and services, the decision as to what is best can be confusing. Contrasting orientations to treatment can add to the confusion.

Because of their training and experience, those who have worked with individuals labeled *learning disabled* tend to have views about what is best. The reasons they have for why one choice is better than another is their *rationale.*

At times, decisions can be made rationally without any concern for practical matters such as money, legal requirements, and political clout. Most of the time, *practical considerations* play a very big role.

Ultimately, whatever the rationale and whatever the practical concerns, the question of what the course of treatment should be on any particular day is based on an *assessment* of specific treatment needs.

In general, then, decisions about treatment involve

- decision makers' rationales
- practical considerations

- assessment for planning specific interventions

Let's take a brief look at each of these.

Rationales

Most of us like to think we make decisions on the basis of a thorough understanding of the situation—what's known about the problem and about solutions, what the choices are, what the most effective and efficient alternative would be. This understanding implies sound knowledge and good information. The better the quality of knowledge and information, the sounder the rationale.

Rationales, however, include more than facts. Part of our knowledge reflects the theories that appeal to us; another part involves philosophies we have adopted. We often give a piece of information or an experience more weight than others if it fits with our theoretical and philosophical ideas (Adelman & Taylor, 1985).

When experts in the field of learning disabilities recommend services, placements, and treatment approaches, they have a rationale for doing so. The fact that different professionals recommend different approaches reflects both that the available knowledge and information in the field is still rather limited and that they have judged the appropriateness of what is available in keeping with their rationale.

The poorer the quality of available knowledge and information in a field, the more it is possible for different theories and approaches to be maintained. In particular, not enough is known about the specific causes of learning disabilities and how to identify them. With regard to treatment, not enough is known about what works for those who have learning disabilities.

Unfortunately, the knowledge gap is likely to be filled slowly. There are several reasons for this:

First, it is very difficult to accurately separate learning disabilities from other types of learning problems. This keeps us from knowing what is likely to work best for each type of problem.

Second, most programs don't use just one procedure; they combine methods in ways that make it impossible to know what specific procedure was effective in successfully overcoming a problem. The lack of research focused on different combinations of procedures keeps us from knowing what combination may work best.

Third, measuring progress is most easily done by reference to simple behavioral outcomes and short-term progress; long-term gains in skills and major changes in attitude are seldom evaluated (see Box 6–2). The lack of comprehensive evaluation research keeps us from knowing whether anything makes a major, long-term difference in improving the life situation of those with learning disabilities.

The difficulty of separating learning disabilities from other types of learning problems is particularly troublesome for those tempted to take one side or the other in the debate between advocates of the underlying-abilities and observable-skills approaches. In the 1970s, critics of the underlying-abilities

---

Box 6–2

Research Example
Long-term Evaluations of Treatment Outcomes

Compared to the large number of studies that have looked at the effectiveness of treatment, follow-up research is relatively rare. In making a brief review of work published between 1965 and 1980, we found about thirty titles that seemed potentially relevant. Thirteen of these had sufficient data and procedures to make it worth reviewing them.

Three studies reported positive results that are statistically significant, finding that the majority of individuals were performing satisfactorily in subsequent schooling and that older students had completed high school.

Two studies reported mixed results, finding satisfactory school progress, but some psychological problems. The remaining eight studies indicated negative results.

Each of the follow-up studies had serious methodological flaws. These include overreliance on parent interview data, failure to identify other major factors that might have produced positive and negative outcomes, lack of control and contrast groups, and so forth.

None of this is very surprising. The small amount of long-term follow-up research and the problems with the research that has been done simply reflect the extreme cost and difficulty of doing such studies (see reviews by Horn, O'Donnell, & Vitulano, 1983; Tindal, 1985).

It clearly is not possible to be sure about the long-term effectiveness of current treatment approaches. If any conclusion is to be drawn, it cannot be an overly optimistic one.

In general, we suspect that in cases in which a particular approach is found to be reasonably effective, it is because the individuals treated have other types of learning problems. When persons are found to be rather unresponsive to the approach, it may be because the individuals truly have learning disabilities.

It is important to understand that

• Because so many persons are mislabeled, it is easy to make the mistake of thinking that a successful outcome is due to the specific treatment when, in fact, any treatment designed to produce the same outcome may have been effective.

• It is easy to make the mistake of thinking that such successes are evidence that learning disabilities have been overcome when, in fact, success may be occurring only with those who are not learning disabled.

orientation pointed to research suggesting that such abilities could not be improved and that it was unnecessary to improve such abilities before working directly to improve skills (e.g., Hammill, Goodman, & Wiederholt, 1974; Arter & Jenkins, 1979). The research cited, however, included a wide variety of learning problems. Thus, proponents of the underlying-abilities orientation argue it is not fair to use such findings to claim that underlying-abilities approaches will never be helpful in some of these cases or to claim that the observable-skills orientation would be sufficient for those who truly have learning disabilities.

Because of the relatively poor knowledge and information available to those who work with learning disabilities, there has been a tendency for practitioners to pick and choose from underlying-abilities and observable-skill approaches. This tendency to take something from any available procedures usually is called an *eclectic* approach. Treatment rationales given by those who use an eclectic approach vary from statements of naive beliefs and assumptions to sophisticated and scholarly systems for intervention (see Box 6–3).

Practical Considerations

Ask anyone about why she or he chose one approach or another; you will find that many practical constraints affected the decision. Clients tend to seek help from the professional who is most accessible to them. For parents, this is most likely to be a pediatrician or teacher. Teachers are constrained by the policies and resources of the school in which they teach. Multidisciplinary teams make placement and treatment plans within the guidelines of federal, state, and local policies. Treatment plans are carried out within the constraints of available services, materials, and intervener competence.

Sometimes practical constraints are so great that they interfere with efforts to carry out a treatment in keeping with its rationale. And sometimes practical considerations force practitioners to operate on a rationale that conflicts with their own.

An example of the latter situation arises when government guidelines reflect a specific orientation to treatment. In the United States, for instance, federal guidelines increasingly have reflected an observable-skills orientation to treatment for learning disabilities. This seems to have happened because (1) underlying-abilities approaches have not been proved effective and (2) observable-skills ideas make it relatively easy to plan treatment and evaluation and measure immediate outcomes. In order to qualify for federal support, many practitioners with rationales that conflict with an observable-skills orientation find themselves forced to incorporate procedures they do not believe in and which sometimes undermine the intent of their approaches. This is unfortunate because the approaches reflected in federal guidelines have been advocated without sound evidence of their effectiveness and thus may be no better than the procedures they replace (See Box 6–4).

Assessment for Planning Specific Treatment

When it comes time to plan the *specifics* of a program, formal and informal assessment are essential. Assessment procedures include tests, observations, interviews, trial teaching, and so forth (see Reading A). Prevailing assessment procedures in the field of learning disabilities have been shaped by the two dominant, contrasting orientations to treatment.

Those who follow underlying-abilities approaches are concerned with developmental deficits in such areas as perception, memory, and linguistic and motor functioning. Thus, they are interested in assessing these areas when making treatment plans. The

Box 6–3

Viewpoint
Eclecticism

> "What's your orientation?"
> "Whatever works."

Increasingly, when asked their orientation, professionals in education and psychology seem to be answering "I am eclectic."

Eclecticism can be a very healthy thing, especially in a field like learning disabilities, which has so much to learn that it can't afford to be dogmatic. But eclecticism takes many forms. We distinguish three:

Naive eclecticism. There is a tendency among many practitioners simply to keep their eyes open for every new idea that pops up. If it appeals to them, they adopt it without any concern for whether it is valid or consistent with other practices they use. It is this casual and undiscriminating approach that results in the negative reaction against eclecticism.

Applied eclecticism. After years of practice, professionals find that certain practices don't work and should be avoided and others are found useful in certain situations but not others. They also come to identify a large number of procedures that fit their philosophy and orientation.

Scholarly eclecticism. Through systematic theoretical and philosophical analyses and research, some professionals evolve a set of procedures that is comprehensive, integrated, and consistent.

Experienced practitioners who pursue "clinical teaching" tend to be eclectic. *Clinical teaching* is a term used to describe the cyclical, day-by-day process followed by most remedial teachers. The cycle involves (1) assessment to make a specific plan for the day's work, (2) actual planning, (3) carrying out the plan (flexibly), and then (4) evaluating the effects (positive and negative). The evaluation provides some of the assessment data for planning the next session. The evaluation findings are supplemented with additional assessment procedures for specific planning, and the cycle has begun again. It is not the cycle alone that makes experienced clinical teachers eclectic, however; it is the fact that they have acquired at least an applied and sometimes a scholarly understanding of what is likely to work or will not work with a specific individual.

---

assessment usually relies heavily on available tests. For example, among the most popular assessment procedures used with youngsters have been the

- Developmental Test of Visual Perception (the "Frostig")
- Developmental Test of Motor Integration (the "Beery-Buktenica")
- Illinois Test of Psycholinguistic Abilities (ITPA)
- Wechsler Intelligence Scale for Children— Revised (WISC-R)
- Wepman Auditory Discrimination Test (the "Wepman")

In addition, standardized achievement tests, case histories, interviews, and observations are usually part of the assessment (see Reading A for references).

Available research and logical analyses both suggest that devices currently used to assess such areas are inadequate, especially for assessing problem populations. This does not mean, however, that such tests won't be improved or that others won't be developed (see Snart, 1985). And the poor validity of a given test says nothing about the theory upon which it is based. The ultimate value of theories about how underlying deficits affect learning is yet to be determined. Thus, it is well to be aware of the nature of assess-

Box 6-4

Concern in the Field
The IEP

To improve treatment planning and evaluation, guidelines connected to Public Law 94–142 call for preparation of a written individualized education plan (an IEP) for each student diagnosed as handicapped. The idea of writing out a specific plan is not very controversial. Most practitioners feel that although this is a bit of a bother, it is reasonable for professionals to be open and accountable for their actions (Dudley-Marling, 1985).

What has become controversial is the manner in which government guidelines have tried to shape treatment rationales by stressing how intended outcomes should specifically be stated (Popham, Eisner, Sullivan, & Tyler, 1969).

The emphasis in current guidelines reflects the observable-skills orientation toward writing *all* intended outcomes in the form of very specific statements of behavior known as *behavioral or criterion-referenced objectives.* Following behaviorist thinking, such an approach assumes that any long-range aim or goal (which can be a very comprehensive and abstract outcome) is best achieved by listing each behavior or skill to be learned and then proceeding to teach it.

For instance, one long-range aim of schooling is to facilitate the development of children in a manner that prepares them to be effective citizens. A long-range goal related to this aim is to teach each child to read and write at a level adequate to participate in society, e.g., at a level where they can hold a job. A great variety of objectives can be stated with regard to such a goal. One behavioral or criterion-referenced objective may be that "the student will learn to recognize 85 percent of a basic vocabulary list and correctly spell 60 percent of the words."

Alone, objectives expressed in behavioral terms and including criteria for evaluation tend to look like a promising aid in planning and evaluating treatment. Critics concede that aspects of treatment can and should be spelled out in very concrete ways. However, they also point out that students with a range of motivational, learning, emotional, and social problems are likely to require outcomes that cannot appropriately be translated into a set of simple behaviors and skills. Included are the many abstract outcomes of developing and changing attitudes and overcoming emotional blocks and other problems that may be interfering with learning. Attempts to state such outcomes as simple behaviors can end up as a list of objectives that have little connection with the treatment's intended long-range outcomes (Adelman & Taylor, 1983).

Many concerned theorists have cautioned that limiting programs to such simplistic objectives is, at best, irrelevant and, at worst, a cruel hoax.

---

ment and treatment procedures based on such theory (see Box 6–5).

Those who follow observable-skills approaches are concerned with specific knowledge and skills that have not been learned as yet by the individual. Thus, skill-oriented assessments use such procedures as standardized achievement tests, unstructured, informal skill diagnostic tests, observation of daily performance, and criterion-referenced evaluations.

No one skills-assessment instrument is mentioned in the literature more than others; Reading A provides a listing of representative examples. However, the process called *applied behavior analysis* especially should be mentioned. It represents one of the most highly structured and ambitious forms of skills assessment developed yet. This system involves simultaneous, direct, continuous, and discrete measurement of several designated behaviors, treatment procedures, or environmental factors. Because of the complexity of the process,

Box 6–5

Current Practices
Assessment for Planning Specific Treatment: Underlying-Abilities Approaches

To provide an example, let's look at a widely used test of visual perception—the Developmental Test of Visual Perception (Frostig, Maslow, Lefever, & Whittlesey, 1964; Frostig, Lefever, & Whittlesey, 1961). It is individually or group administered and takes about forty minutes. There are five subtests, described as follows:

1. Eye-Hand Coordination—items require drawing various continuous lines within boundaries and from point to point
2. Figure-Ground Perception—items require distinguishing figures from increasingly complex backgrounds and separating out intersecting and hidden geometric figures
3. Form Constancy—items require recognizing various geometric shapes regardless of size or orientation
4. Position in Space—items require discrimination of reversals and rotations of figures in a series
5. Spatial Relations—items require copying patterns using dots as guide points

Although not an actual item, the following is a close copy of the type of item included in the Position in Space subtest:

Type of instructions used:

Look at the first stick figure—the one in the box. Now look at the row of stick figures. One figure is the same as the one in the box.

Put your finger on the one in the box, and then find the one that is just like the one in the box. Now take your pencil and mark it.

Poor performance on a set of subtest items is seen as indicating that training is needed to help develop the ability to make accurate perceptions. Frostig and her colleagues have developed practice worksheets similar to the content of each subtest. Thus, individuals who do poorly on items such as the stick figure often are given exercises intended to improve their discrimination of reversed and rotated figures. The assumption is that the exercises develop deficient underlying abilities and enable the individual to successfully discriminate letters (*b* from *d*) and numbers (6 from 9).

Test reviewers point out many concerns. For one, the test has not proved very reliable, e.g., does not yield consistent scores from one administration to another. For another, it has questionable validity, e.g., the five areas do not assess five different functions; whatever the subtests are measuring, there is considerable overlap among them. As a result, it is unsafe to assume that a low score is accurate or really reflects visual perceptual deficits (Salvia & Ysseldyke, 1981). Thus, it is not safe to base an instructional prescription on the test's findings.

With regard to exercises designed to teach basic perceptual discriminations, there is little argument about teaching individuals to discriminate among stimuli. There is, however, considerable debate about what the exercises are meant to do and what the content of practice materials should be.

Critics say: Individuals trained on visual perception worksheets simply learn to discriminate what they are exposed to and, at best, there is a small degree of generalization to similar tasks. Furthermore, critics suggest that if the intention is to help the individual learn to discriminate letters and numbers, training materials that emphasize letters and numbers would be better to use than pictures, patterns, and forms (see Arter & Jenkins, 1979).

Box 6–6

Current Practices
**Assessment for Planning Specific
Treatment: Observable-Skills Approaches**

An example of an observable-skills approach is provided by *Criterion Reading* (Hackett, 1971). Administration time varies depending on the reading level of the person tested, but it can take several hours or more. The content is based on a hierarchy of 450 skills, divided into five levels across the following eight areas:

- Motor Skills—items require motor behavior such as holding a pencil, tying a shoelace, walking a balance beam

- Visual Input-Motor Response—items require matching symbols, objects, and colors

- Auditory Input-Motor Response—items require matching beginning sounds and repeating initial consonants

- Phonology—items require identifying, classifying, using, and producing alphabet-letter names, consonants, vowels, and their combinations

- Structural Analysis—items require classifying singular possessive nouns, using rules for forming singulars and plurals, and using rules to divide words into syllables

- Verbal Information—items require identification, classification, use, and production of concepts and facts

- Syntax—items require classification of verbs, subject-predicate function, and the use of rules for sentence punctuation

- Comprehension—items require analysis, synthesis, and evaluation of language

Note: The first three areas are for students in kindergarten and first grade.

To provide a sample item, let's look at one test of consonant skill from the phonology area. The student is presented with rows of consonants. Instructions tell the student to identify initial single-consonant sounds. Criterion for success is listed as 95 percent accuracy.

Individuals expected to know initial consonants but who fall below criterion are seen as needing instruction and practice to develop this skill until they can reach the criterion. The system provides workbooks with specific objectives and exercises designed to help the student achieve criterion. The assumptions are that there is no reason why the individual cannot learn such consonants and that such direct instruction is the best way to learn them.

There is little in the way of adequate research to judge the worth of the *Criterion Reading* diagnostic system. We may, however, reasonably generalize given what is known about the limitations of all such systems. For one, the tests tend to yield inconsistent findings from one administration to another. For another, there is considerable controversy over what skills should be included in such tests and programs. As a result, skills identified as missing may have been learned but not performed on the test because of anxiety, lack of motivation, and so forth. Even if they haven't yet been learned, they may not be the ones that should be taught.

Critics say: Not all skills require formal instruction; many are learned informally—in the course of daily experiences or while learning other things. Spoken language is frequently noted as an example of this informal learning. Moreover, factors that may be interfering with skill learning, such as avoidance motivation, must be dealt with before the student will attend to learning and applying skills (see Adelman & Taylor, 1983).

---

machine processing of the data often is needed.

Although practitioners could make such assessments by daily observation of performance, diagnostic skill tests are used to provide the information quickly and easily. As with underlying-abilities tests, diagnostic skill tests have their limitations, especially in assessing problem populations (see Box 6–6).

In general, tests used for underlying-abilities assessment have been more severely criticized than skills tests. They are seen as not really measuring the underlying abilities specified by the test developers.

More generally, *all* tests used to assess and prescribe specific treatment plans raise some general concerns (Ysseldyke & Mirkin, 1981). For one, many experts suggest that among problem populations a person's poor test performance often is due to low motivation or high anxiety. When this is the case, the findings are "contaminated." Under such circumstances, it is impossible to know whether failure to demonstrate an ability or skill represents a real deficiency in a particular area of development. Under such circumstances, it is easy to misprescribe treatment. It is easy, for example, to make the mistake of planning to teach skills that a person has already acquired—instead of helping the individual overcome psychological problems interfering with the demonstration of what she or he knows and can do. Also, concern has been raised that the focus of prevailing assessment procedures is on too narrow a range of factors. That is, comprehensive treatment plans must go beyond the types of things that can be readily assessed by dominant practices, and assessment practices must be viewed as only one facet of making intervention decisions. (See Box 6–7; more on this in Chapter 7.)

NO MAGIC BULLETS

Medical researchers warn that it is a mistake to think about medication as if it worked like a magic bullet. They say many people tend to think that, once administered, a drug speeds directly to its target and cures the problem. That is, the medication is imagined to disappear upon entering the body and to reappear magically at its goal where it performs its work and again disappears. This belief causes a tendency to ignore such facts as (1) drugs can cause damage as they go through the body and (2) drugs don't necessarily stop having effects as soon as they have done the work they are intended to do (Lennard, Epstein, Bernstein, & Ransom, 1970).

We all dream of miracle cures, but most of us recognize that quick and easy treatments are rare. Still, when we are involved with a problem, the hope for a miracle is strong. This makes us a bit too receptive to anyone who claims to have an effective answer (see Reading O) and a bit too ready to ignore the possible harmful effects of treatments.

There are no magic bullets in treating learning disabilities. All approaches can do harm as well as good.

It's customary to speak of the unwanted consequences arising from treatment as "negative side effects." This term may make the harmful effects caused by treatment sound inconsequential. Negative consequences may be trivial, but they also may be life-shaping—physically, psychologically, economically, and socially.

Commonly discussed potential negative consequences of assessing and treating learning disabilities include

- invasion of privacy
- errors in identification
- stigmatization
- segregation and social isolation
- limitation of current and future opportunities
- overdependence on others
- creation of self-fulfilling prophecies
- burdensome financial costs

Ethical practitioners, of course, try to minimize negative consequences and try to ensure that benefits outweigh harm. Controversy arises when there is a disagreement about whether a given negative consequence should be tolerated at all and whether benefits outweigh harm (see Box 6–8).

Box 6–7

Assessment Processes and Purposes

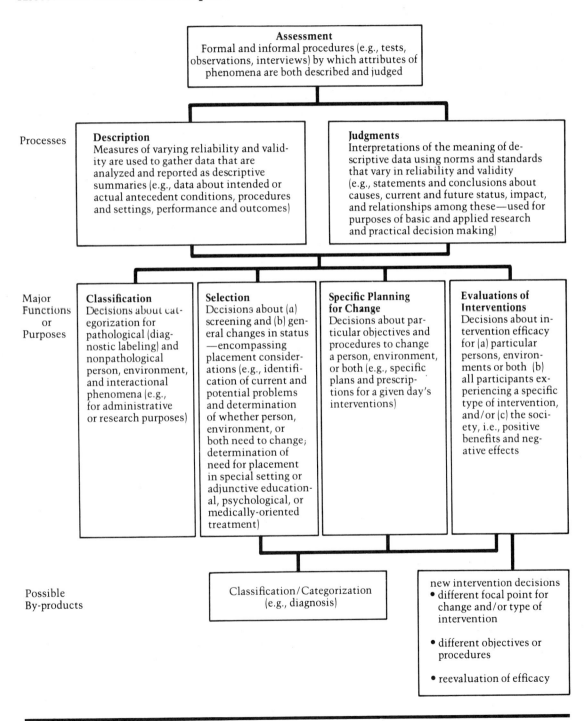

Assessment
Formal and informal procedures (e.g., tests, observations, interviews) by which attributes of phenomena are both described and judged

Processes

Description
Measures of varying reliability and validity are used to gather data that are analyzed and reported as descriptive summaries (e.g., data about intended or actual antecedent conditions, procedures and settings, performance and outcomes)

Judgments
Interpretations of the meaning of descriptive data using norms and standards that vary in reliability and validity (e.g., statements and conclusions about causes, current and future status, impact, and relationships among these—used for purposes of basic and applied research and practical decision making)

Major Functions or Purposes

Classification
Decisions about categorization for pathological (diagnostic labeling) and nonpathological person, environment, and interactional phenomena (e.g., for administrative or research purposes)

Selection
Decisions about (a) screening and (b) general changes in status —encompassing placement considerations (e.g., identification of current and potential problems and determination of whether person, environment, or both need to change; determination of need for placement in special setting or adjunctive educational, psychological, or medically-oriented treatment)

Specific Planning for Change
Decisions about particular objectives and procedures to change a person, environment, or both (e.g., specific plans and prescriptions for a given day's interventions)

Evaluations of Interventions
Decisions about intervention efficacy for (a) particular persons, environments or both (b) all participants experiencing a specific type of intervention, and/or (c) the society, i.e., positive benefits and negative effects

Possible By-products

Classification/Categorization (e.g., diagnosis)

new intervention decisions
• different focal point for change and/or type of intervention

• different objectives or procedures

• reevaluation of efficacy

Box 6–8

Concern in the Field
Possible Harmful Effects of
Medically-related Treatments

When new treatments are suggested for bothersome problems that have no proven cure, most of us are tempted to give them a try. This is especially the case when the treatment is intuitively appealing and advocated by someone who seems to have some expertise. The attitude of "What harm can it do?" operates whenever the possible harm is not obvious or well publicized.

The use of diets and megavitamins for those diagnosed as learning disabled and hyperactive seem, to many people, to have no potential harmful effects. Indeed, advocates of such treatments generally claim this is the case.

Concerned physicians, however, have raised cautions (Sieben, 1977):
Special diets may

- cause a person to feel different from others
- cause family conflict when parents must insist that a youngster follow the prescribed diet
- cause elimination of foods that have positive effects, e.g., antioxidant preservatives have been cited as inhibiting carcinogens
- cause a person to use failure to follow the diet as an excuse for ongoing problems
- cause other, potentially more effective actions to be ignored

Megavitamins may cause

- edema (watery swelling) of the brain (large doses of vitamin A)
- kidney stones (massive doses of vitamin C)
- liver damage (vitamin B_6 and nicotinic acid)

As with the positive effects of diet and megavitamin treatments, the evidence of harmful effects has not been adequately studied. Without adequate evidence, the concerns remain simply concerns, just as the promises of such approaches remain simply promises.

Even treatments that have fairly well-publicized, potential harmful effects may produce some surprising negative outcomes. For example, those who prescribe stimulant medication usually point out that concerns have been raised about possible appetite loss, sleeplessness, irritability, retardation of physical growth, and so forth. However, they are unlikely to think that such medication could lead to Tourette's syndrome. This hereditary syndrome is characterized by multiple repetitive tics and uncontrollable verbalizations that often, but not always, include cursing. The March 1983 issue of *The Journal of the American Medical Association* published a report of research at Yale University suggesting that about 15 percent of children with Tourette's syndrome might not have developed the disease if stimulant drugs had not been used to treat hyperactivity and attention problems. The implication is that those with a family history of Tourette's may be particularly at risk when stimulant medication is prescribed. Further study, of course, is needed, but the point is clear.

Besides surprising harmful effects, some negative consequences are so subtle and pervasive that they creep into our lives without our awareness. Critics of institutionalized professional activity such as Ivan Illich, R. D. Laing, Irving Goffman, and Thomas Szasz have warned about such hidden consequences. In a major attack on the drug companies, journalists Peter Schrag and Diane Divoky (1975) warn that:

"It is nearly impossible to overestimate the role of the pharmaceutical houses in shaping medical and lay opinion about learning-disabled children. We are not talking here about their campaigns to convince practitioners and parents that medication—usually stimulant drugs—is the answer to problems in learning and behavior . . . but primarily about their part in creating the idea that any number of common childhood quirks are medical problems in the first place. The promotion of drugs to cure learning disabilities and related syndromes—particularly MBD and hyperkinesia—is quite obviously related to the promotion of the ailments themselves. . . ." (pp. 56–57)

The concern is that society's whole way of thinking about learning problems is shaped by professional activity. The public is led to think about individual differences ("quirks") as problems; problems are thought of as disorders within people rather than as trouble with the way society functions. Such thinking leads to treatments focused on changing people rather than institutions and to overreliance on medi-

cal, psychological, and educational professionals for answers (Illich, 1976).)

Harmful effects have a way of coming back to haunt professionals. Professionals who downplay negative consequences of treatment and professions that allow the public to become overdependent on them may be pleased at first. However, there often is a backlash when the public becomes disappointed and disenchanted because of the repeated failure of the professionals to live up to their expert images. Such backlash is seen in the increasing malpractice suits in medicine and psychology and in the rising demands for accountability and excellence in education.

SUMMARY

Diana's parents have been confronted with a dilemma. Diana seems to need special help to succeed at school. There are decisions to be made—some by the family, some by those who provide special help.

One set of options involves deciding about services, places where treatment will be carried out, and who should do the treating. The choice may be to pursue special education services in or out of special classrooms and schools; medically-related and psychotherapeutic treatments also may be chosen. In all cases, decisions are guided by the intention of choosing the least intervention needed, e.g., the least restrictive environment. But Diana's parents find this is not an easy guideline to use.

The other set of decisions involves the form that help should take each day. For example, two contrasting treatment orientations—underlying-abilities and observable-skills approaches—have dominated programming for those diagnosed as learning disabled. Each orientation is based on different assumptions about what must be done to help students like Diana.

Despite controversies surrounding service, placement, and treatment decisions, rational choices can be made. Any of us may combine theory, philosophy, research, and practical experiences into a rationale to help us make such decisions.

Once a general orientation to treatment is decided upon, formal and informal assessment procedures are used in deciding what to do each day. Assessment practices differ markedly, of course, depending on the intervener's orientation to treatment.

In general, what should be clear by this point is that prevailing treatment approaches can be rather complex and controversial. Yet, despite complexities and controversies, each day professionals are called upon to screen, diagnose, place, and treat learning disabled individuals. It is one of the ironies of the field that in some cases, those of us in practice are often called upon to do more than we can know, and at other times we know more than we can do.

Yet, do we must. Decisions must be made and treatments carried out. There may be major concerns about specific practices, but persons with problems can and must be helped.

Fortunately, the help does not need to be limited to the ideas reflected in prevailing treatment approaches. Interveners can readily build on such approaches and go beyond them. To do this, it is important to understand other ideas besides those that have shaped the field so far. Chapter 7 discusses some evolving trends that seem to hold special promise for the future.

ENRICHMENT ACTIVITIES

1. We strongly recommend that you read more about issues related to prevailing assessment and treatment approaches. See the following readings.

ARTER, J. A., & JENKINS, J. R. (1979). Differential diagnosis-prescriptive teaching: A critical appraisal. *Review of Educational Research, 49,* 517–55.

COLES, G. (1978). The learning disabilities test battery: Empirical and social issues. *Harvard Educational Review, 48,* 313–40.

SCHRAG, P., & DIVOKY, D. (1975). *The myth of the hyperactive child and other means of child control.* New York: Pantheon Books.

2. What treatment approach do you tend to favor and why?

You may want to think a bit more about how your preference fits in with the range of prevailing approaches. In doing so, you may want to look over the readings listed in the special topic references for this chapter.

SPECIAL TOPIC REFERENCES

Should you be interested in further information about *prevailing assessment* and *treatment* approaches, see the following readings.

ALLEY, G., & DESHLER, D. D. (1979). *Teaching the learning disabled adolescent: Strategies and methods.* Denver: Love Publications Co.

FERNALD, G. (1943). *Remedial techniques in basic school subjects.* New York: McGraw-Hill.

HAMMILL, D. D., & BARTEL, N. R. (1982). *Teaching children with learning and behavior problems,* 3rd ed. Boston: Allyn & Bacon.

KIRK, S. A., & CHALFANT, J. C. (1984). *Academic and developmental learning disabilities.* Denver: Love Publications Co.

LERNER, J. W. (1984). *Learning disabilities: Theories, diagnosis, and teaching strategies,* 4th ed. Boston: Houghton-Mifflin.

SABATINO, D. A., MILLER, T. L., & SCHMIDT, C. R. (1981). *Learning disabilities: Systemizing teaching and service delivery.* Rockville, Md.: Aspen.

SALVIA, J., & YSSELDYKE, J. E. (1981). *Assessment in special and remedial education,* 2nd ed. Boston: Houghton-Mifflin.

SMITH, C. R. (1983). *Learning disabilities: The interaction of learner, task, and setting.* Boston: Little, Brown.

SMITH, D. D. (1981). *Teaching the learning disabled.* Englewood Cliffs, N.J.: Prentice-Hall.

Chapter 7

Emerging Trends: The LD Field Moves Ahead

A CHAIN OF IDEAS

Solutions to complex problems emerge slowly from a great deal of exploration and problem solving. One experience may suggest an idea. One idea may lead to another. Gradually, ideas that complement each other are linked together into new approaches and systems.

Many professionals concerned with learning disabilities and related problems have suggested ideas for evolving the field. In this chapter, we present an overview of these emerging trends to illustrate some of the ways the LD field is moving ahead (see Box 7–1).

A CHAIN OF IDEAS

Research and theory in the learning disability field clearly are evolving beyond the ideas that have dominated practice over the last twenty years (see McKinney & Feagans, 1984). There is a growing appreciation that the field must be based on a complex and systematically linked set of ideas about learning and problems in learning (Adelman & Taylor, 1985).

Linking Ideas Together

An adequate intervention program is unlikely to be a one step process. Take, for example, assessment related to screening,

Box 7–1

Theory and Practice
Moving Ahead

Do not follow where
the path may lead.
Go, instead, where
there is no path
and leave a trail.

Anonymous

placement, and specific intervention planning. It would be handy to do all the assessment at once. However, this is probably not the best approach. After screening has identified a potential problem, subsequent steps must be taken to confirm or disconfirm the problem. Only then can *initial* placement considerations and *preliminary* specific program plans be considered. And, only after specific treatment plans are initiated can the appropriateness of the placement decisions and specific intervention plans be determined through daily assessment (see Box 7–2). In general, *sequential* assessments

have been recommended as one way to work on improving decision accuracy.

As another example of the ways thinking may be expanded by considering steps and sequences, let's look at remedial strategies. Those who pursue underlying-abilities and observable-skills orientations have recognized the value of sequential strategies in their discussions of how to analyze and correct problems. For instance, Hewett (Hewett and Taylor, 1980) sees the competence to learn as developing through six hierarchical levels. The hierarchy begins with the individual developing the ability to attend, go-

---

Box 7–2

Screening, Placement, and Specific Planning as a Complex Sequence

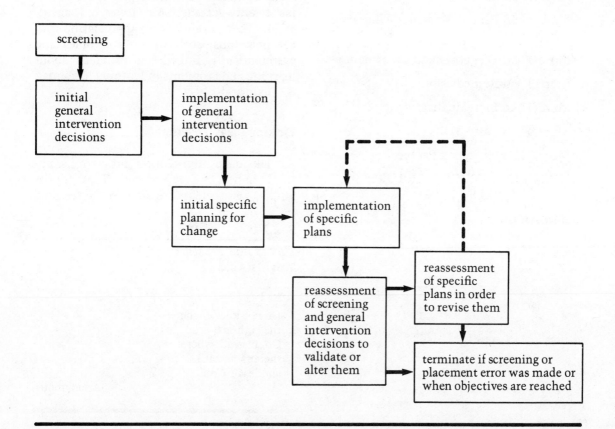

ing on to develop the ability to respond, order stimuli, explore, interact socially, and finally arriving at the ability to master complex skills and ideas (such as those found in academic learning). Based on such hierarchical views of development, lists of skills have been outlined to guide assessment for missing skills and to provide teachers with specific objectives.

Thinking in terms of steps, sequences, and levels requires practice and care. Sometimes steps can be taken one at a time in a straightforward sequence. More often, however, implementation involves jumping around—skipping a step, repeating another, and so forth. Sometimes new steps must be added and old steps deleted. The order in which skills are listed is not necessarily the order in which they are best learned. And, of course, some skills can be acquired without formal instruction.

Obviously, thinking in these terms requires some mental juggling and flexibility. Nevertheless, such thinking has the potential to advance the field in promising directions.

In general, what we are talking about is the value of building and expanding models and theories to guide the field. And we are talking about more than theories about CNS dysfunctioning and about the causes of learning problems. Just as important are efforts to connect ideas (i.e., build theory) about instruction, remediation, therapy, or intervention, in general. To this end, steps, sequences, hierarchies, and various other system components are important building blocks. Their importance is further illustrated later in this chapter and in Part 3 (also see Kavale & Forness, 1985).

Experimenting and Problem Solving

Efforts to develop new ideas and link them together involve a great deal of research. Unfortunately, the term *research* has come to convey such abstract activities that it seems irrelevant to many practitioners. This is unfortunate because the energy, experience, and insight of practitioners are too valuable to lose as resources for research.

Perhaps it would help to think about research as involving primarily exploration and problem solving. Practitioners do both these things in their daily work. For instance, teachers, remedial specialists, and therapists and other clinicians begin with their best estimate of what will be effective in working with an individual's learning problem. If they are not effective, they appraise what they have done, looking for why it didn't work and for clues to what to attempt next. This exploratory and problem-solving process of *experimentation* or *trial and appraisal* is pursued until the problem is resolved or until there are no new ideas for working on it (see Box 7–3). Whether or not the practitioner realizes it, this is the essence of research activity.

A great deal of important data on what works and what doesn't is discovered through daily exploration and problem solving in the classroom and the clinic. What makes the data more than an interesting set of anecdotes is the care with which the intervention is carried out and described and the systematic way in which positive and negative findings are sought and reported. Systematic and cautious reports of case results—positive and negative—help a field advance.

CONNECTING LINKS

Practitioners are becoming increasingly aware of many ideas that cannot be ignored if we are to do a better job helping those with learning disabilities. In general, it is becoming clearer that the focus in the field has been a bit too narrow.

As a result, the tendency to ignore adolescents and adults with learning disabilities is being countered. Broader models are being advocated for understanding the patterns of

Box 7–3

Key Steps and Tasks in Problem-Solving Intervention

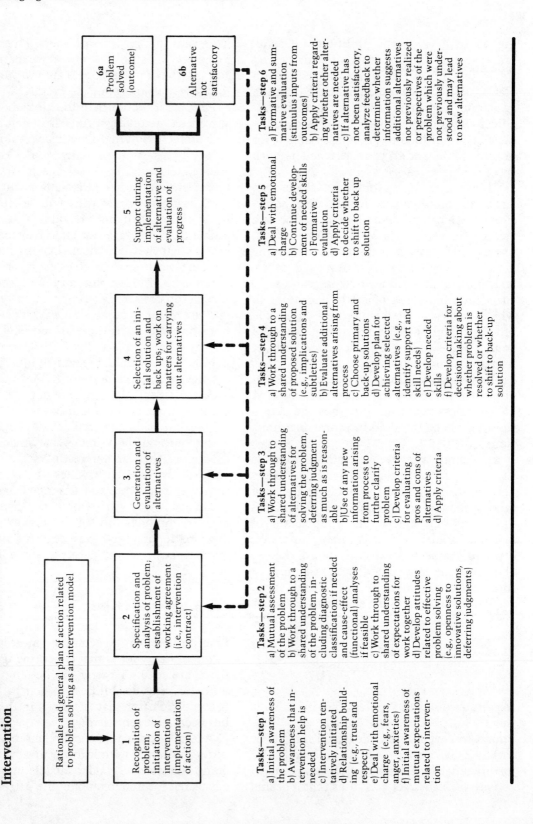

Rationale and general plan of action related to problem solving as an intervention model

1 Recognition of problem; initiation of intervention (implementation of action)

2 Specification and analysis of problem; establishment of working agreement (i.e., intervention contract)

3 Generation and evaluation of alternatives

4 Selection of an initial solution and back ups; work on matters for carrying out alternatives

5 Support during implementation of alternative and evaluation of progress

6a Problem solved (outcome)

6b Alternative not satisfactory

Tasks—step 1
a) Initial awareness of the problem
b) Awareness that intervention help is needed
c) Intervention tentatively initiated
d) Relationship building (e.g., trust and respect)
e) Deal with emotional charge (e.g., fears, anger, anxieties)
f) Initial awareness of mutual expectations related to intervention

Tasks—step 2
a) Mutual assessment of the problem
b) Work through to a shared understanding of the problem, including diagnostic classification if needed and cause-effect (functional) analyses if feasible
c) Work through to shared understanding of expectations for work together
d) Develop attitudes related to effective problem solving (e.g., openness to innovative solutions, deferring judgments)

Tasks—step 3
a) Work through to shared understanding of alternatives for solving the problem, deferring judgment as much as is reasonable
b) Use of any new information arising from process to further clarify problem
c) Develop criteria for evaluating pros and cons of alternatives
d) Apply criteria

Tasks—step 4
a) Work through to a shared understanding of proposed solution (e.g., implications and subtleties)
b) Evaluate additional alternatives arising from process
c) Choose primary and back-up solutions
d) Develop plan for achieving selected alternatives (e.g., identify support and skill needs)
e) Develop needed skills
f) Develop criteria for decision making about whether problem is resolved or whether to shift to back-up solution

Tasks—step 5
a) Deal with emotional charge
b) Continue development of needed skills
c) Formative evaluation
d) Apply criteria to decide whether to shift to back up solution

Tasks—step 6
a) Formative and summative evaluation (stimulus inputs from outcomes)
b) Apply criteria regarding whether other alternatives are needed
c) If alternative has not been satisfactory, analyze feedback to determine whether information suggests additional alternatives not previously realized or perspectives of the problem which were not previously understood and may lead to new alternatives

behavior and learning seen in LD programs. The need to go beyond the concepts of diagnosis, treatment, remediation, and individualized instruction has been stressed. The importance of expanding prevailing views of basic skills has been emphasized. And we are learning that more is needed than strategies designed to change people.

More Than Children

In its formative phases, the LD field focused on children. This bias is reflected in the nature of early legislation, professional and parent organizations, and training and intervention programs.

Over time, there has been an increased consciousness of the fact that learning disabilities remain a problem for many adolescents and adults. Often despite the best efforts of professionals and parents, the learning problems do not disappear as the youngster gets older. Thus, it has become imperative for the field to reformulate organizations, ideas, and services in ways that do not ignore or discriminate against older individuals. In addition, new programs have been developed. For example, as highlighted in Chapter 13, much greater attention is being paid to postsecondary education and career/vocational programs.

More Than Person Models to Understand Behavior

As discussed in Chapter 4 (see Box 4–1), the previous trend has been to view learning problems in terms of (1) the disordered or "ill"-person model, or medical model, and (2) the slow-maturation model. Behaviorist and ecological thinking has helped to stress an alternative to such "person" models. The result has been an increased recognition that significant numbers of learning problems do not arise from factors within the individual;

rather, many problems are seen to stem from a pathological or inadequate environment.

Interactional and transactional ways of understanding human behavior have offered an even broader way to view the range of learning problems confronting us daily. Such models (or general paradigms) recognize that problems may be due primarily to something within the individual *or* something in the environment *or* something related to the unique way the person and the environment interact (see Box 7–4).

Increasingly, environmental and interactional models for understanding human behavior and learning are influencing thinking about assessment and corrective interventions for those in LD programs. As discussed in the following sections and in Part 3, the implications of such models are far reaching.

More Than Diagnosis and Treatment

Concerns about prevailing practices for diagnosis and treatment have helped clarify that there is more to assessment than objective diagnosis and that there is more to treatment than the day-by-day activity of a teacher or therapist. Such activity is only part of a broader set of intervention *tasks*. These major, programmatic tasks are interrelated, and each requires a rationale and formulation of planning, implementation, and evaluation *phases* (see Box 7–5).

To show what we mean, let's take up the case of Bret again. By the third grade, it was clear that something should be done. But what? He was sent to a psychologist who gave him a battery of tests. Using the results of the tests, the psychologist decided that Bret was learning disabled and prescribed perceptual motor training and placement in a special class. In keeping with the practices of the day, Bret had been diagnosed, and treatment was prescribed; all that had to

Box 7–4

Theory
**An Interactional View of
Learning Problems**

From an interactional perspective, learning and problems in learning are a product of (1) what the individual brings to a situation, such as interests and abilities, and (2) what the environment confronts the individual with, such as opportunities and demands. Sometimes an individual's lack of capability is so great that she or he cannot meet the opportunities and demands of any environment. Such an individual clearly has a handicapping disability. Sometimes an environment is so demanding or lacking in opportunities that almost anyone may have trouble doing well.

> Think about trying to learn calculus on your own or from a teacher who hates math, has never been taught how to teach it, and who is angry because she has been assigned to the course against her will.

Sometimes neither the environment nor the individual is quite up to the tasks of teaching and learning.

> Think about a course in which you weren't particularly interested in the topic or didn't have the necessary background, and the instructor wasn't very well organized or particularly interested in teaching the class.

Whenever a student and a school environment mesh well together, we say there is a good *match* between them, and we do not expect problems to arise. When there is a bad match, we expect the worst. Formally stated:

"A given student's success or failure in school is a function of the interaction between the individual's motivational and developmental status—such as interests, expectations, strengths, and limitation—and specific classroom situational factors encountered—such as individual differences among teachers and differing approaches to instruction." (Adelman, 1971; Adelman & Taylor, 1983)

Establishing a good match is not easy. Even if there is only one student, it is hard to provide a wide range of opportunities that both maintains interest and keeps the right pace with developing abilities. When there is a whole classroom of individuals, the problem of facilitating a good match becomes quite a bit harder.

An interactional view of school success and failure suggests that the better the match between what the student brings to the classroom and what the classroom confronts the student with, the greater the likelihood of school success; in contrast, the poorer the match, the greater the likelihood of poor school performance.

This in no way argues against learning problems that result from CNS trouble (learning disabilities). We recognize that the greater the disorder and handicap that the individual brings to the situation, the more difficult it is likely to be to establish a good match.

In terms of all types of learning and behavior, however, an interactional view suggests that the more a school uses "personalized" approaches to increase the likelihood of facilitating a good match, the fewer students it will have who develop patterns of learning and behavior problems; in contrast, the less a school uses personalized approaches, the more students with learning and behavior problems it will have.

happen was for the teacher to carry out the prescription. There is, however, much more to pursuing effective change than that.

Assessment activity provides an example of how much more is required. Although it is not always clear from the way practices currently are carried out, assessment is meant to be only an *aid* in making decisions. The decisions can be grouped into four major types:

Box 7–5

Major Programmatic Intervention Tasks

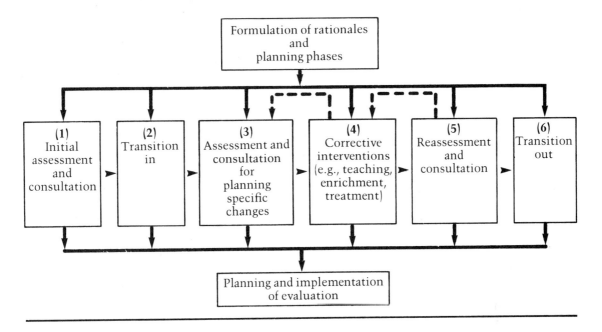

Phases of Intervention Tasks

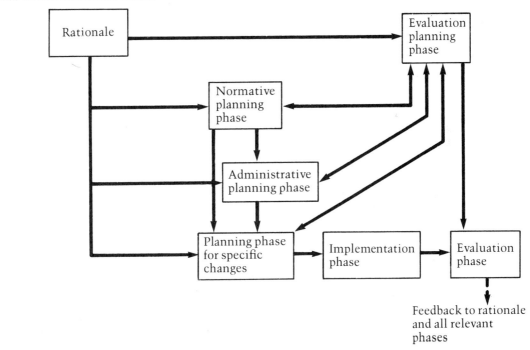

- classification (including diagnostic labeling)
- selection (including screening and placement)
- specific planning for change
- evaluation of intervention (review Box 6–8)

It would be nice if decisions about these matters could be made in objective ways, but assessment and decision-making processes are prone to many subjective influences. For instance, the meaning of assessment data must be *interpreted*, and *judgments* must be made about whether something is good or bad, above or below norm, pathological or not. Even the fact that the focus for assessment usually is presumed to be an individual's deficiencies reflects several biases in decision making.

Because decisions involve much more than the data gathered, processes related to all four types of decisions have come under criticism. To build some safeguards into the processes, one strategy has been to warn of the fallibility of test findings; another approach has been to encourage a more active decision-making role for parents, youngsters, and adult clients. This latter trend changes the professional's role in decision making from prescribing to offering *consultation*.

This brings us back to Bret. Based on a broad understanding of the functions and limitations of assessment, three major *assessment and consultation* tasks can be seen as essential in any comprehensive program to help him overcome his learning problems. Because each task has an extensive rationale, we can only describe the essence of each here.

Initial assessment and consultation. The first thing needed is consultation to decide generally what to do. Transfer to a special remedial program at school? Seek after-

school tutoring? Look into medically-related services? At this stage, there is no particular need for decisions detailing specific daily programming. And a diagnostic label probably would be necessary only if program admission required it. The task at this stage is to gather and generate data on the severity of the problem and, if possible, its cause, to provide information about what options are available, and to assist the family in making a decision about which option is most appropriate and feasible.

Assessment and consultation for planning specific changes. The task here is to guide each specific intervention action so that intended outcomes are achieved efficiently. Corrective interventions are shaped by *ongoing* assessment and decision-making processes. In Bret's case, these processes would have been best initiated at the time he began a particular program. When specific plans are prescribed ahead of placement, they often are of little use because they are not up-to-date or because the program has an orientation different from the one reflected in the prescription.

Reassessment and consultation. After corrective interventions have gone beyond an appropriate "transition-in" period, there must be regular consideration of how things are proceeding. Was the initial decision to pursue this type of service a good one? Is anything interfering with progress? Is it time to stop, and if so, what's the next step? (The ongoing assessment data gathered for specific planning often is sufficient to help in consulting about such decisions.)

As can be seen, then, assessment and consultation involve much more than diagnostic testing. Similarly, corrective intervention involves much more than treatment.

Corrective intervention. Although corrective interventions for learning disabilities usually are discussed as treatments, they generally involve treatment, teaching, and enrichment activities. The complex task here, then, is to implement all the specific intervention actions that have been planned

When decisions are made to pursue corrective interventions, the task of transition-in becomes a concern; similarly, when a corrective intervention is completed, the task of transition-out arises. Briefly, these two tasks can be described as follows:

Transition into corrective interventions. Decisions about what service is appropriate are no guarantee that the service will be pursued. Many practical and psychological barriers (e.g., funds and anxiety) can prevent follow-through. In the case of Bret and his family, once decisions were made, the task became one of helping them deal with such barriers. The goal is to introduce procedures to ensure that corrective interventions are begun effectively.

Transition from the intervention. Once it is decided to stop a service, there is the task of dealing with the practical and psychological barriers that may arise. For example, Bret may need help overcoming anxiety when the time comes for him to leave the special class program; moreover, he may need to learn specific "survival skills" if he is to succeed in mainstream programs.

More Than Remediation

Special interventions for special problems are usually referred to as *treatment, therapy,* or *remediation.* When remediation is needed, it should be pursued. However, concern has been raised about the danger of allowing the *entire* emphasis in working with an individual to be on remedying the referral problem. Programs that stress only problem remediation can deprive a person of other important experiences and can become overwhelmingly tedious and disheartening (see Box 7–6).

Schools, for example, have the responsibility not only to help youngsters overcome learning and behavior problems but also to facilitate ongoing development and provide opportunities for creative growth. The fact that a youngster has a problem learning to read doesn't alter the fact that he or she can and probably wants to learn a variety of other things (Swift & Lewis, 1985). To find the time for remediation, it may be tempting to set aside other learning opportunities; to do so, however, deprives youngsters of other experiences and may also negatively affect their attitude toward the school, toward the teacher, and toward overcoming their problems. The strong emphasis on mainstreaming handicapped students is one prominent manifestation of the effort to minimize such negative effects.

More Than Individualization

Ask what's wrong with putting Jan into a regular classroom and probably the answer will be that the program will not be "individualized" enough.

Ask: "What does Sally need?" Chances are the answer will be "individualized instruction."

Chris? Bret? "Individualized instruction!"

Individualized instruction has become the norm for those with learning disabilities and other problems. This is a major improvement over the days when few serious attempts were made to treat learners as individuals. There are, however, tremendous differences among individualized programs, and almost all of them ignore some very important individual differences.

Individualized programs propose to "meet learners where they are at." This generally means activities are planned with reference to an individual's current developmental level. For example, if a fifth grader is reading at a second-grade level, functioning in math at a fourth-grade level, and so forth,

Box 7–6

Clinical Example
More Than Remediation

There seems to be a growing appreciation for the importance of providing students diagnosed as learning disabled with opportunities to work in areas of special strength and interest. Baum and Kirschenbaum (1984) report the case of Neil in answering the question "What happens when all the needs of the child are not addressed, due to a preoccupation with academic deficit?"

"Neil, a junior in high school, was failing all his subjects. He was disgusted with school and was exhibiting symptoms of depression requiring weekly visits to a psychologist. His teachers described him as lazy, claiming he could do better if only he would apply himself. A typical comment was, 'When I talk to Neil, he has so much to offer. However, he just doesn't produce.'"

"On his own, Neil had acquired a wealth of knowledge about music, religion, psychology, and photography. He pursued his extracurricular interests with enthusiasm and persistence. His major interest during this time was photography."

"He had not received much praise for his creativity. Instead, he had been regularly criticized for poor academic work."

The school did try to capitalize on his interest in photography—but at first did so in a manipulative way.

"When Neil's school tried to incorporate his interest in photography into academic assignments, he rebelled to the extent of temporarily abandoning photography. Instead of attracting him to academics, Neil was 'turned off' to photography for months. He wanted to enjoy his photographic ability unfettered by the expectations of the school."

The one major success for Neil in high school apparently occurred when he was finally given the opportunity to pursue his interest in photography at school—in ways he defined for himself.

"Once Neil had defined a personally chosen task, he became alive and motivated. He became an investigator of a problem real to him, and the product that resulted has indeed had an impact on others."

Unfortunately, this experience appears to have been the exception rather than the rule.

"Neil finished high school, but decided not to go to college. Four months after graduation, he said, 'Now that school is out, I finally have time to learn.' He talked about several contemporary history books he was reading, even though he had hated history in school.

"Neil's experiences dramatically illustrate the importance of considering the whole child. It can be profoundly destructive to a student's self-esteem to be labeled and treated only in terms of a learning disability when, in addition, a student may be exhibiting gifted behaviors that are equally worthy of attention."

"Within the school setting, with its fixed time periods, predetermined curricula, isolated subject areas, and teacher accountability with regard to students' minimal competencies, gifted behaviors often go unrecognized.

"What is needed, then, is *information* about the talents and strengths of these children. Usually, the folders of learning disabled students are filled with notations concerning the things they *can't* do in school. Their strengths are overshadowed by problematic weaknesses that consume the school's well intentioned energies and attention."

"Attention needs to be given to strengths (in their own right) as well as weaknesses, rather than simply working *through* strengths to get to weaknesses." (pp. 92–98)

the program should be designed to take these different levels into account. Moreover, if youngsters with the same level of skill learn at different rates, the program also should allow for this. Increasingly, it is being stressed that differences in *motivation* also ought to be accounted for in a highly systematic way. Because the term *individualization* has become so identified with accommodating individual developmental differences, the term *personalization* has been proposed to encompass attempts to meet learners where they are at—developmentally and *motivationally*.

More Than Basic Skills

The three Rs certainly are a basic focus of any program for learning disabilities. But they are not the only *basic* skills, nor are basic *skills* a sufficient focus for such programs.

Besides reading, writing, and arithmetic, the abilities to "problem solve" and make appropriate decisions are increasingly recognized as essential skills. These areas of basic human functioning require the ability to analyze problems, weigh alternatives, and figure out how to accomplish daily tasks and deal effectively with other people.

Even expanding the definition of basic skills, however, does not result in a broad enough focus. We all have skills we choose not to use in certain circumstances. We all could acquire other useful skills, but choose not to do so. What we do is influenced strongly by our *attitudes.*

Two big problems with the "Back to Basics" movement have always been that the advocates define basics in terms of a limited range of skills (i.e., the three Rs) and approach the learning of skills without sufficient appreciation for the role of attitudes in learning. An expanded view, including other

basic skills and a strong emphasis on intrinsic motivation for learning, suggests not going backwards but going "Forward to Basics."

More Than Changing People

It is easy to fall into the trap of thinking that corrective interventions for learning problems always should be directed at a specific individual. In some ways, we have done just that in the way we have discussed many of the preceding points. Adopting an interactional view, however, points to an expanded set of options regarding who or what should be the object of change (see Box 7–7).

Currently, when a person is identified as having problems, efforts are made, directly or indirectly, to produce changes in the individual. Direct efforts include remediation, psychotherapy, and medically-related approaches. Indirect efforts include changing the way parents and teachers interact with youngsters.

Interventions designed to change the individual may be the most appropriate choice in any given case. Sometimes, however, the *environment* needs to change in ways that attempt to *accommodate* rather than modify individual differences. Such environmental changes are *not* the same as modifying the environment as an indirect way of changing the individual.

Instructing parents and teachers to be more discriminating in their use of reinforcement contingencies is meant to be an indirect way of changing the child. It is not a strategy for teaching parents and teachers the value of offering additional options whenever appropriate and feasible—such as increasing the range of choices about what a child is allowed to do and how the child is allowed to pursue a chosen option. It also is not the same as helping them and others in the society to understand the impact of appropriately changing their expectations about what is acceptable behavior, performance, and progress.

The implications of an expanded focal point for intervention are immense. For one, environments and the interactions between persons and environments become primary concerns for assessment activity and correc-

Box 7–7

**Options Related to Focal Point
of Intervention**

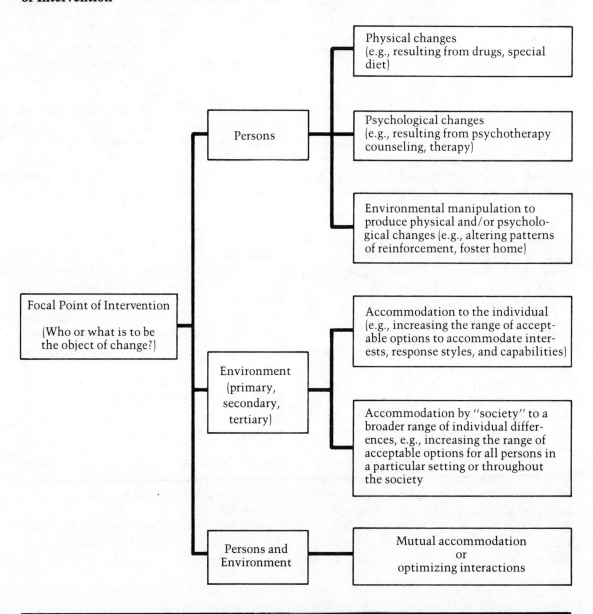

tive interventions. Problem prevention efforts expand to include programs that encourage accommodation of a wider range of individual differences in schools and society. And the broadened perspective works against presumptions about dysfunctions within people as the source of most learning problems.

FINDING DIAGNOSTIC ERRORS: THE WEAKEST LINK

Sally's family was delighted to have her diagnosed as learning disabled. Joseph, a high school senior, wasn't quite so pleased, but he thought he could turn it to his benefit.

We have probably known as many individuals who were content with the label as those who were upset by it.

For Sally, the label provided the family with public funds to help them pay for special programs. Many people would never be able to afford special help without such funds. Ask those who have been in similar circumstances, and they usually say they would have suffered considerably more without the label than they have with it.

Joseph plans to use the label to explain to college admission's officers why his reading and writing skills and some grades and admission test scores are so poor. He knows he is entitled to certain special considerations because those diagnosed as learning disabled are officially recognized as handicapped. Those who simply have learning *problems* receive no exceptions to admission criteria nor are they usually offered individual remedial help and other special considerations after admission.

Despite the advantages people like Sally and Joseph found in being diagnosed as learning disabled, they may be among those who have been misdiagnosed. One of the most difficult problems confronting those who are trying to evolve the LD field is that of identifying individuals erroneously labeled as learning disabled. The importance

of finding the errors cannot be stressed enough—neither can ideas about how to do so.

Those who argue that the errors must be identified don't want to deprive anyone of opportunities for help. Anyone who has a learning problem deserves as much help as possible.

But there is more at stake than whether some individuals will qualify for special considerations. The large number of individuals misdiagnosed as learning disabled combined with the lack of procedures to find these errors represents such a weak link in the LD field's chain of knowledge that it threatens the very existence of the field.

To be more specific, at this time, the primary value of having a field devoted to learning disabilities is to lobby for the learning disabled and to help distinguish who does and who doesn't have learning disabilities. (The many learning disabilities programs are seen as a result of the lobbying.) The next major advances in knowledge about learning disabilities await the time when the learning disabled can be isolated as a unique group among all those who have learning problems. As more and more persons are indiscriminately declared learning disabled, the public and its policymakers will become tired of the drain on special resources and will cut back on support. Without support, the LD field cannot live up to its promise.

Cutting down on the number of errors in identification also is an important key to preventing the learning problems of such individuals. For instance, if many persons labeled as learning disabled can be shown to learn effectively in optimal, but nonremedial, learning environments, it becomes reasonable to argue that (1) these individuals were not actually learning disabled and (2) similar individuals need not become learning problems if such optimal environments replace current classroom programs. Moreover, such programs may go far toward minimizing the emotional overlay that accompanies learning disabilities and other problems.

Several researchers have suggested some type of sequential filtering system for separating out those whose learning problems are due to CNS trouble (Adelman, 1971; Wissink, Kass, & Ferrell, 1975; Lindsay & Wedell, 1982; Wedell, 1970). Such approaches eventually may lead to improvements in the diagnosis of learning disabilities and may even help distinguish several other significant subgroups within that category of handicap. At the very least, these strategies hold promise for reducing the number of persons wrongly diagnosed as learning disabled.

SUMMARY

Efforts to advance knowledge in the field of learning disabilities require taking ideas that currently dominate the field and connecting them with new ideas. In making such connections, it is helpful to think in terms of sequences of steps and hierarchical strategies and other ways of building models and theories. Thinking in such comprehensive and systematic ways guides exploration of new directions and improves problem solving.

A review of evolving trends suggests the field is moving toward

- learning disabilities programs that address the problems of adolescents and adults as well as children
- environmental and interactional models of human behavior and learning that provide a broader framework for understanding important implications for intervention practices and research
- an expanded and systematically integrated set of intervention tasks and phases
- greater emphasis on facilitating ongoing development and providing opportunities for creative growth in addition to the remedial focus

- personalization as a process that goes beyond individualization to meet learners where they are at developmentally *and* motivationally
- a focus on basics that goes beyond the three Rs and beyond skills to include problem solving, decision making, and basic attitudes
- expanding the range of intervention focus beyond individuals to include changing the environment to accommodate rather than modify individual differences and, where appropriate, simultaneously pursuing changes in both the environment and the individual

Along with these evolving trends, workers in the learning disabilities field continue to investigate ways to uncover the increasing number of individuals misdiagnosed as learning disabled. The errors in diagnosis are seen as an increasing threat to the field's progress. Sequential strategies for identifying errors have been proposed as one step for dealing with the problem.

The steps in working with learning disabilities discussed in Part 3 reflect integration of prevailing approaches with the evolving trends highlighted in this chapter.

An Enrichment Activity

In study courses, a sequential strategy often taught is the SQ3R, or Survey Q 3R method. The procedure involves use of the following five steps in reading textbook material:

1. Survey
2. Question
3. Read
4. Recite
5. Review

Briefly, the steps involve the following activity:

1. Surveying means intially taking a quick but meaningful look at a book's preface and table of contents to find out what the book covers. Then, you are to leaf through it, page by page, to get a sense of how it's laid out and what it contains. In particular, you should read headings and summaries and look at pictures and graphs and read their captions.

When it comes time to read a particular assignment, you are again to survey the assigned material, but more thoroughly than before. Special attention is to be paid to headings so you can see how the material is outlined and organized. (What are the main topics and subtopics?)

Surveying provides a roadmap showing what the important points of interest are.

2. Questions are basic to learning. They direct, guide, and help bring meaning to the process. There are two major sources of questions related to textbook material. (Ask yourself: What are the two major sources of questions?)

If a teacher has assigned questions or the text contains questions (e.g., at the end of the chapter), read them carefully and think about them before reading the chapter. Whether or not there are assigned questions, you should make up your own. You can do this by asking questions about each heading before reading a chapter and again before reading the specific section. You can also do so when key statements are made (as we demonstrated already). As you approach Chapter 8, notice it is entitled "Matching Motivation and Development." You might ask: What does matching mean? Why is it worth doing? etc.

Before reading, you may have some ideas about the answers for some of the questions. As you read, you can compare your ideas with those presented.

3. Reading is an obvious step. Or is it? Reading should be done actively. (Remember all the times you have gotten to the end of a page and wondered what you had just read! That's passive reading.) As you read, you should be answering the questions you have identified.

4. Recitation helps to keep you reading actively. Stop regularly (after each paragraph for a while if necessary) and try to answer the relevant question(s) you have identified for the section. If you don't have a question, simply recite the important points covered in the material you just read. If you can't recite, it's time to formulate a question and reread the material.

5. Reviewing means taking another look at what you've read. As you skim over the headings once more, think through the questions and recite the answers. It rapidly becomes clear what you remember and what you don't.

Reviews should be done regularly—beginning as soon as you've finished a chapter. Rereading then is done whenever you find you remember too little of the material. Several reviews are recommended at spaced intervals before an exam rather than one long cram-session.

Try the SQ3R strategy as you approach the next chapter.

Afterwards evaluate whether it improved your learning.

When you finish the book, evaluate whether you continued to use the strategy related to this book and other texts.

If you did continue to use it, think about the reasons you did so.

If you didn't, think about why not.

Part III

SPECIFIC CONCEPTS AND STEPS FOR WORKING WITH LEARNING PROBLEMS

"Let the main object . . . be as follows: To seek and to find a method of instruction, by which teachers may teach less, but learners learn more; by which schools may be the scene of less noise, aversion, and useless labour, but of more leisure, enjoyment, and solid progress. . . .

Comenius, 1632

In Part 2, you read about general considerations and evolving trends in working with learning disabilities. New ideas are merging with established practices. The field is broadening its scope and clarifying how its special approaches blend with those designed for nonproblem learners. In this connection, the principle of least intervention needed provides a useful guideline. Based on this principle, intervention guidelines for those with learning disabilities can be organized into five sets of sequential steps:

First ---------➤ *Only if necessary*

- Provide an appropriate match between the learner and the learning environment ------➤ • Remedy individual problems

- Try general, enriched, and least disruptive solutions -----------➤ • Try specialized treatments and settings, maintaining them only as long as needed

- Use assessment and consultation to screen, place, plan, and evaluate---➤ • Use assessment to diagnose and then to find diagnostic errors

- Make decisions and plans with those involved using careful analysis of alternatives---➤ • Proceed temporarily without their participation until they can or will decide

- Look for simpler explanations before assuming there is a learning disability ---------→
- Look for disorders after simpler explanations have been systematically ruled out

With such guidelines in mind, our objective in Chapter 8 is to discuss "matching" motivation and development and personalizing interventions in and out of classroom settings. Then, in Chapters 9, 10, and 11, we focus on teaching and remediation for individuals with learning problems. The discussion emphasizes the importance of a comprehensive curriculum, motivation as an initial focus in improving the match, personalizing classrooms to teach basics, and sequential steps in remedying learning disabilities.

Throughout Part 3, a variety of concepts and specific steps and procedures are explored. It remains for research to tell us just how good any of these are. Because evaluation plays a key role in studying interventions for learning disabilities, Part 3 ends with a brief presentation of current approaches and findings related to evaluating programs.

Chapter 8

Matching Motivation and Development

"I hate reading!" Sally is having lots of trouble learning to read, and she's not about to spend any more time doing it than she has to.

What came first—the learning problem or her negative attitude? It's hard to be sure. But it isn't hard to understand that Sally's present efforts in the classroom and on tests are influenced both by her poor skills and by her negative attitude.

Does she have a learning disability? We don't want to make a mistake in answering this question, and we want to help her learn to read. So our first step is to find a situation in which Sally will really try to learn. If she's so angry or scared that she holds back or just goes through the motions, we won't see what she *can do;* we'll only see the abilities she *wants* to show us. The less she shows of what she can do and the less effort she puts into learning, the more we are likely to see false symptoms. Because the information available is not good data for arriving at a diagnosis, one may prematurely conclude that someone like Sally has a learning disability (see Box 8–1). She may or may not. One of the tasks in working with her will be to help clarify the matter.

A big part of the job, then, is to provide a program in which Sally will want to learn. This will help us to see what type of learning problem she has, and it will help her take a big step toward overcoming her problem.

Of course, the environment must do more than affect Sally's attitudes toward learning. It must also be a good match for her current levels of competence and style of performance.

Thus, the first step in working with Sally and other students with learning problems is to meet them where they are at—motivationally and developmentally. How to accomplish the first step requires understanding the interactions between learners and learning environments.

Box 8–1

Parent: "Well, Sally, how do you like school?"
Sally: "Closed!"

_____

INTERACTION OF THE LEARNER WITH THE ENVIRONMENT

When asked to do course evaluations, students in the introductory learning disabilities class we teach have a lot to say. Some tell us the course is too demanding, others say it's easy; some think it is too loosely organized, others see it as highly structured; some enjoy the amount of class discussion, others see student interchanges as a waste of time.

Why the differences?

A common-sense answer suggests that each student brings something different to the situation and therefore experiences it differently. And that's a pretty good answer—as far as it goes. What gets lost in this simple response is the fact that each student is continuously changing and so is the situation, and the changes influence each other. The transactions can be described as follows:

What the learner brings to the situation are *capacities and attitudes* accumulated over time and *current states of being and behaving.*	◄ interacts ► with	Besides the specific *instructional processes and content*, the learning environment consists of the *physical and social context.*
These factors interact with each other and with the learning environment.		These factors interact with each other and with the learner.

The outcome of all these interactions may be positive learning or learning problems. Because the nature of the interactions can vary considerably, the outcomes can vary dramatically. In general, the types of outcomes can be described as

- deviant learning—capacities and attitudes change and expand but not in desirable ways
- disrupted learning—interference with learning and possibly a decrease in capacities
- delayed and arrested learning—little change in capacities
- enhanced learning—capacities and attitudes change and expand in desirable ways

Let's look a bit more closely at the learner and the environment and how they interact to produce a good or bad match for learning.

The Learner

Sally comes to every learning situation with certain accumulated capacities and attitudes. She also is affected by her current physiological and psychological states.

With her *innate* qualities providing a foundation to build on, Sally has *acquired* a variety of abilities, expectations, and values over the years. These accumulated capacities and attitudes, in turn, provide the foundation upon which all subsequent learning is built.

Although her capacities and attitudes establish a foundation for Sally's learning, she does not enter the classroom in the same condition or state each day. She may be well rested or tired, well nourished or hungry, ready to listen or preoccupied with thoughts of what happened earlier or with plans for later in the day. She may feel happy, sad, or angry.

Stop reading for a minute and tune in to your own experience. You may be tired or hungry, bored or preoccupied, or distracted by what's going on in the room. It's easy to see that your current physiological and psychological state affects your concentration and learning.

The concern in the LD field about poor diet and health habits, allergic reactions to foodstuffs, frequent illnesses, and arousal and orienting responses reflects an appreciation of the importance of the current physiological state of the learner (e.g., Dykman, Ackerman, Holcomb, & Boudreau, 1983). Similarly, concern about fear of failure, high levels of anxiety, and anger toward teachers and school reflects an awareness of the importance of the learner's psychological state.

Somewhat less obvious is the fact that people appear to be influenced by their own actions, which then further influence the way they think and feel (see Bandura, 1978). If you notice that you are fidgeting or are having trouble keeping your eyes open in class, you try to understand why. If it is a hot day and the lecture is dull, you may conclude that the temperature in the room is too high or that you are bored. And, of course, your actions produce changes in the learning environment; if you nod off, the teacher is likely to react.

Given that Sally's background is similar to that of some individuals and differs from that of others, we can make some general assumptions about why she is having trouble learning. Like all generalities, however, they may be wrong in her particular case. To go beyond assumptions, tests may be administered in an attempt to measure her accumulated capacities and attitudes and current states. Because of the limitations of available tests, additional assessment strategies are constantly being evolved as part of ongoing learning programs. As discussed in the following chapters, these strategies include ongoing analyses of a learner's direct statements, actions, and performance under conditions of high intrinsic motivation to learn.

The Environment

When you think about the learning environment, your tendency may be to think first about features directly associated with *instructional processes and content*, especially materials, personnel, activities, and equipment. The context of instruction may also strongly influence learning (see Box 8–2).

Before going on, look around you and decide how well the environment you're in lends itself to reading this text. If it's less than optimal, what changes may make it better? (See Box 8–3.)

Available research indicates the important role that the *physical* context plays in learning. The ease with which a student can see the chalkboard, the comfort of the furniture, the spaciousness or crowding, and the temperature in the room are only a few of the physical features that may influence learning.

Perhaps more influential is the *social* context. For a school-age youngster, the teacher and other adults in the school are extremely vivid features of the environment. Competition for attention, fear of embarrassment, desire to be praised, interest in what others are doing—all are part of the social experience in a classroom and affect learning.

Besides the physical and social context are the instructional processes and content presented to the learner. As discussed in Chapter 7, the intent in many programs is to individualize instruction to match aspects of the learner's accumulated capacities. Additional steps to match instructional processes and content to the motivation of the person also play an important role in learning.

Box 8-2

Theory
**The Many Contexts of Learning
and Instruction**

When we talk about the learning environment, it would be a mistake to think only about classrooms and schools. It would also be a mistake to think of each environment as a distinct and separate place.

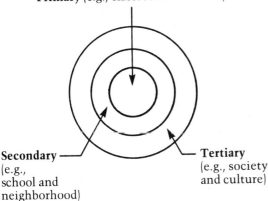

Primary (e.g., classroom and home)

Secondary (e.g., school and neighborhood)

Tertiary (e.g., society and culture)

There are layers of environments that interact with one other and with learners. For convenience, we think about them as follows:

To clarify the point further, the learner in the classroom obviously experiences the physical and social climate created by the teacher and other students, the materials, equipment, furniture, lighting, and general decor (the primary environment).

At the same time, there is bound to be an effect generated by such factors as the size, general condition, and decor of the school, the composition and values of the student body, and the socioeconomic level, racial composition, and general values of those living in the surrounding neighborhood (the secondary environment).

There are also the effects of the values, beliefs, standards, customs, and political policies of the society and culture (city, state, and nation). This tertiary level of environment may seem far removed from the daily classroom learning environment. The reality, however, is that factors such as political policies are some of the most powerful determinants of the type of resources and services made available to problem and nonproblem learners alike.

Although many of the features of instruction and its physical and social context are easy to measure, the key aspect—the learner's perception of the situation—is difficult to assess (see Moos, 1979).

The Interaction and the Match

Poor learning environments are ones in which the interaction between learner and environment produces undesirable outcomes. When this occurs, there is a bad match between the learner and the environment. There are three different forms that a bad match may take—unchallenging, overdemanding, and overwhelming.

Some environments seem to offer little or no challenge to the learner. No new learning

takes place when a person can consistently use already acquired capacities in responding to a learning environment. If this situation continues for any significant length of time, important areas of learning will not expand.

In contrast, a rather common situation is one in which the learner perceives the environment as demanding more than she or he can or wants to give in terms of ability and effort. Under such circumstances, learning may occur, but not usually the type that is desired. When asked to practice her reading, Sally doesn't always argue about the matter. There are times when her transactions with the environment are attempts to find other ways of getting around the demand. In her search for ways to avoid assignments, she learns a great many new ways to manipulate and distract others. Thus, her learning is enhanced, and she is learning new skills all the time—but probably not those most of us view as desirable. What she is learning is sometimes called *deviant behavior.*

Sometimes, individuals find themselves in environments where the demands are so great that they cannot find any way to deal with the situation. If they must stay in this demanding environment for a long time, they not only stop functioning, they may

Box 8–3

Environmental Variables that Can Influence Learning

I. Setting and context characteristics
   A. Organizational format
      (e.g., personnel patterns, client/student groupings)
   B. Locale, nature, and scope
      (e.g., geographic context, architectural features, availability and use of materials and furnishings, population "density")
   C. Climate
      (e.g., perceptions of physical, social, intellectual, political, and moral atmosphere)
II. Characteristics of the participants
   A. Formal role identification
      (e.g., intervener, client, student, parent, societal agent, and/or association with specific organizations)
   B. Demographics
      (e.g., urban/rural, ethnicity, socioeconomic status, sex and age distribution, association with specific groups)
   C. Individual differences in current motivation and development
      (e.g., competence, commitment, perceptions of self and others)
   D. Criteria and standards used in judging person characteristics
      (e.g., absolute or relative standards about good-bad, normal-abnormal, success-failure; psychological, socioeconomic-political criteria; cutoff points altering the number of false-negatives and false-positives)

III. Task-process-outcome characteristics
   A. General features
      1. Quantitative
         (e.g., amount to be accomplished; sequencing, duration, pacing, and rate; number of persons required or involved)
      2. Qualitative
         (e.g., underlying rationale; intrinsic and extrinsic value; cooperative or competitive; actual and perceived difficulty)
   B. Specific types, areas, and levels of tasks and outcomes
      (e.g., current system tasks; prerequisites needed to perform current tasks; remediation; development; enrichment)
   C. Specific processes
      1. Procedural methods and models
         (e.g., helping or socialization; mechanistic-behavioral, industrial, humanistic; role of participants; nature of structure)
      2. Tools (actions/experiences/materials)
         (e.g., communication, practice, learning; printed material such as texts and workbooks; audiovisual—including computer—presentations; games)
      3. Techniques
         (e.g., variations in the characteristics of a tool or the way it is applied, such as varying intensity, duration, patterning, and cuing; systematic or unsystematic feedback, rewards, punishments)

Note: While primary, secondary, and tertiary environments might each be the focus of change, the examples here emphasize variables in the primary environment.

also start to decompensate, e.g., experience a decrease in their accumulated capacities. For instance, because of his learning problems, Chris increasingly experienced strong feelings of anxiety and embarrassment each day at school; he felt socially isolated from other students and criticized. Whenever something new was to be learned, he knew he would have trouble. He tried to hide within himself. Not only couldn't he cope with the new tasks, he also became uncertain about what he had learned in the past. He became uncertain of words he once could read and spell, and he no longer risked reading them aloud or writing them. Soon his progress was entirely disrupted.

Given a reasonably adequate learning environment, most of us readily learn what is minimally expected. In such instances, the interaction between the environment and the learner has produced a desirable, if not always optimal, outcome (see Box 8-4).

In theory, optimal learning occurs when the match between learner and environment results in an interaction in which the learner wants to and is able to make full use of accumulated capacities. That is, the learning environment and the individual's developmental *and* motivational capacities differ just enough that the learner sees the task as a challenge that can be achieved and that is worth pursuing.

Remember the last time when some abstract idea a teacher was trying to help you understand suddenly became clear? Or you finally saw how to solve a problem or puzzle you had been struggling to figure out? These magical moments of insight and learning occur when the learner-environment match is probably optimal or close to it. Such moments don't have to be infrequent or accidental. The more we understand about creating a learning environment that matches an individual's motivation and development, the more that appropriate learning will occur.

MATCHING MOTIVATION

Sally doesn't want to work on improving her reading. Not only is her *motivational readiness* for learning in this area low, but she also has a fairly high level of *avoidance motivation* for reading.

In contrast, Bret is motivationally ready to improve reading skills, but he has very little motivation to do so in the ways his teacher proposes. He has high motivation for the *outcome* but low motivation for the *processes* prescribed for getting there.

Jan often gets very motivated to do whatever is prescribed to help her learn to read better, but her motivation starts to disappear after a few weeks of hard work. She has trouble maintaining a sufficient amount of ongoing or *continuing motivation*.

Chris appeared motivated to learn and did learn many new vocabulary words and improved his reading comprehension on several occasions over the years he was in special school programs. His motivation to read after school, however, has never increased. It was assumed that as his skills improved, his attitude toward reading would too. But it never has.

Motivation and Learning

What the preceding examples show is that

- motivation is a prerequisite to learning, and its absence may be a cause of learning problems, a factor maintaining such problems, or both
- individuals may be motivated toward the idea of obtaining a certain learning outcome but may not be motivated to pursue certain learning processes
- individuals may be motivated to start to work on overcoming their learning problem but may not maintain their motivation

Box 8–4

Learning as a Function of Person-and-Environment Transactions

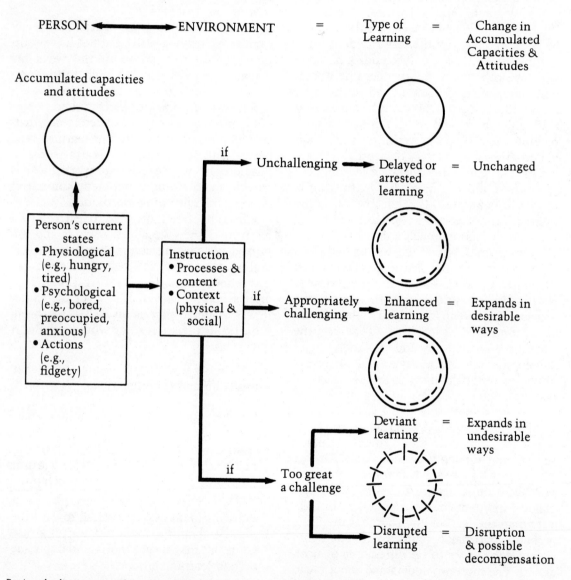

Review the discussion in Chapter 3 and Boxes 3–6 and 3–7 for examples of person, environmental and interactional factors that lead to learning problems.

- individuals may be motivated to learn basic skills but maintain a negative attitude about the area of functioning and thus never use the skills except when they have to

Obviously, motivation must be considered in matching a learner with a learning environment. What's required is

- developing a high level of motivational *readiness* for overcoming the learning problem (including reduction of avoidance motivation)
- establishing *processes* that elicit, enhance, and maintain motivation for overcoming the problem
- enhancing motivation as an *outcome* so that the desire to pursue a particular area, such as reading, increasingly becomes a positive intrinsic attitude

An increased understanding of motivation clarifies how essential it is to avoid processes that make students feel controlled and coerced, that limit the range of options with regard to materials, and that limit the focus to a day-in, day-out emphasis on the problem to be remedied. From a motivational perspective, such processes are seen as likely to produce avoidance reactions among students and thus reduce opportunities for positive learning and for development of positive attitudes (Adelman, 1978; Adelman & Taylor, 1983; Ruble & Boggiano, 1980; Stinsen, 1984; Weiner, 1979).

Two Key Components of Motivation: Valuing and Expectations

Two common reasons people give for not bothering to learn something are "It's not worth it" and "I know I won't be able to do it." In general, the amount of time and energy spent on an activity seems dependent on how much the activity is valued by the person and on the person's expectation that what is valued will be attained without too much cost (see Weiner, 1980).

Valuing. What makes something worth doing? Prizes? Money? Merit awards? Praise? Certainly!

We all do a great many things, some of which we don't even like to do, because the activity leads to a desired reward. Similarly, we often do things to escape punishment or other negative consequences that we prefer to avoid.

Rewards and punishments may be material or social. For those with learning problems, there has been widespread use of such "incentives." Rewards often have taken the form of systematic awarding of points or tokens that can be exchanged for candy, prizes, praise, free time, or social interactions. Punishments have included loss of free time and other privileges, added work, fines, isolation, censure, spanking, and suspension. Grades have been used both as rewards and punishments.

Because people will do things to obtain rewards or avoid punishment, rewards and punishment often are called *reinforcers*. Because they generally come from sources outside the person, they often are called *extrinsics*.

Extrinsic reinforcers are easy to use and can have some powerful immediate effects on behavior. Therefore, they have been widely adopted in the fields of special education and psychology. Unfortunately, the immediate effects are usually limited to very specific behaviors and often are short-term. Moreover, as discussed in the next section, extensive use of extrinsics seems to have some undesired effects. And sometimes the available extrinsics simply aren't powerful enough to get the desired results (see Box 8–5).

Although the source of extrinsic reinforcers is outside the person, the meaning or value attached to them comes from inside. What makes some extrinsic factor rewarding to you is the fact that you experience it as a reward. And what makes it a highly valued reward is that you highly value it. If you don't like candy, there is not much point in our offering it to you as a reward.

Furthermore, because the use of extrinsics has limits, it's fortunate that we sometimes do things even without apparent extrinsic reason. In fact, a lot of what we learn and spend time doing is done for *intrinsic* reasons. Curiosity is a good example. Our curiosity leads us to learn a great deal. Curiosity seems to be an innate quality that leads all of us to seek stimulation and avoid boredom.

We also pursue some things because of what has been described as an innate striving for competence; people seem to value feeling competent. We try to conquer some challenges, and if none are around, we usually seek one out. Of course, as we discuss in the next section, if the challenges confronting us seem unconquerable or make us too uncomfortable (e.g., too anxious or exhausted), we try to put them aside and move on to something more promising.

Box 8–5

Viewpoint
Extrinsics Are Limited

"External reinforcement may indeed get a particular act going and may lead to its repetition, but it does not nourish, reliably, the long course of learning by which [one] slowly builds in [one's] own way a serviceable model of what the world is and what it can be." (Bruner, 1966, p. 128)

Another important intrinsic motivator appears to be an internal push toward self-determination. People seem to value feeling and thinking that they have some degree of choice and freedom in deciding what to do.

Expectations. We may value something a great deal; but if we believe we can't obtain it without paying too great a personal price, we are likely to look for other valued activities and outcomes to pursue. Expectations about these matters are influenced by previous experiences.

Areas where we have been unsuccessful tend to be seen as unlikely paths to valued extrinsic rewards or intrinsic satisfactions (Harackiewicz, Sansone, & Manderlink, 1985). We may perceive failure as the result of our lack of ability; or we may believe that more effort was required than we were willing to give. We may also feel that the help we needed to succeed was not available. If our perception is that very little has changed with regard to these factors, our expectation of succeeding at this time will be rather low.

Learning environments that provide a good match increase expectations of success by providing a learner with the support and guidance he or she wants and needs (Koestner, Ryan, Bernieri, & Holt, 1984).

In general, then, what we value interacts with our expectations, and motivation is one product of this interaction. Within some limits (which we need not discuss here), high valuing and high expectations produce high motivation, while high valuing and low expectations produce relatively weak motivation.

Bret greatly values the idea of improving his reading. He is unhappy with his limited skills and knows he would feel a lot better about himself if he could read. But, as far as he is concerned, everything his reading teacher asks him to do is a waste of time. He's done it all before, and he *still* has a reading problem.

Sometimes he will do the exercises, but just to earn points to go on a field trip and to avoid the consequences of not cooperating. Often, however, he tries to get out of doing his work by distracting the teacher. After all, why should he do things he is certain won't help him read any better.

High expectations paired with low valuing also yield low approach motivation. Thus, the oft-cited remedial strategy of guaranteeing success by designing tasks to be very easy is not as simple a recipe as it sounds. Indeed, the approach is likely to fail if the outcome (e.g., improved reading) is not valued or if the tasks are experienced as too boring or if doing them is seen as too embarrassing. In such cases, a strong negative value is attached to the activities, and this contributes to avoidance motivation.

Throughout this discussion of valuing and expectations, the emphasis has been on the fact that motivation is not something that can be determined solely by forces outside the individual. Others can plan activities and outcomes to influence motivation and learning; however, how the activities and outcomes are experienced determines whether they are pursued (or avoided) with a little or a lot of effort and ability. Appropriate appreciation of this fact is necessary in designing a match for optimal learning (see Box 8-6).

Overreliance on Extrinsics: A Bad Match

A growing appreciation of the importance of a learner's perceptions has led researchers to a very important set of findings about some

---

Box 8-6

Fable
Is It Worth It?

In a small town, there were a few youngsters who were labeled as handicapped. Over the years, a local bully had taken it upon himself to persecute them. In one recent incident, he sent a gang of young ragamuffins to harrass one of his classmates who had just been diagnosed as learning disabled. He told the youngsters that the boy was retarded, and they could have some fun calling him a "retard."

Day after day in the schoolyard the gang sought the boy out.

"Retard! Retard!" they hooted at him.

The situation became serious. The boy took the matter so much to heart that he began to brood and spent sleepless nights over it. Finally, out of desperation, he told his teacher about the problem, and together they evolved a plan.

The following day, when the little ones came to jeer at him, he confronted them saying, "From today on I'll give any of you who calls me a 'retard' a quarter." Then he put his hand in his pocket and, indeed, gave each boy a quarter.

Well, delighted with their booty, the youngsters, of course, sought him out the following day and began to shrill, "Retard! Retard!"

The boy looked at them—smiling. He put his hand in his pocket and gave each of them a dime, saying, "A quarter is too much—I can only afford a dime today." Well, the boys went away satisfied because, after all, a dime was money, too.

However, when they came the next day to hoot, the boy gave them only a penny each.

"Why do we get only a penny today?" they yelled.

"That's all I can afford."

"But two days ago you gave us a quarter, and yesterday we got a dime. It's not fair!"

"Take it or leave it. That's all you're going to get."

"Do you think we're going to call you a "retard" for one lousy penny?"

"So don't."

And they didn't.

(Adapted from a fable presented by Ausubel, 1948)

undesired effects resulting from overreliance on extrinsics.

Would our offering you a reward for learning about learning disabilities make you more highly motivated? Maybe. But a reward might also reduce your motivation for pursuing the topic in the future.

Why might this happen?

You might perceive the proposed reward as an effort to control your behavior. Or you may see it as an indication that the activity needs to be rewarded to get you to do it. Such perceptions may start you thinking and feeling differently about what you have been doing. For example, you may start to resent the effort to control or bribe you. Or you may begin to think there must be something wrong with the activity if we have to offer a reward for doing it. Also, once the course is over, you may come to feel that the topic is not worth pursuing any longer because we are no longer going to reward you.

Any of these thoughts and feelings may cause you to shift the intrinsic value you originally placed on learning about learning disabilities. The point is that extrinsic rewards can undermine intrinsic reasons for doing things (see Lepper & Greene, 1978). Although this may not always be a bad thing, it is an important consideration to think about in deciding to rely on extrinsic reinforcers (see Box 8–7).

You might want to think about how grades affect your motivation.

Do good grades increase your motivation? Do poor grades?

Do you feel that you're working for a grade or to learn?

Box 8–7

Theory and Practice
Rewards — To Control or Inform?

"Rewards are generally used to control behavior. Children are sometimes rewarded with candy when they do what adults expect of them. Workers are rewarded with pay for doing what their supervisors want. People are rewarded with social approval or positive feedback for fitting into their social reference group. In all these situations, the aim of the reward is to control the person's behavior — to make him continue to engage in acceptable behaviors. And rewards often do work quite effectively as controllers. Further, whether it works or not, each reward has a controlling aspect. Therefore, the first aspect to every reward (including feedback) is a controlling aspect.

"However, rewards also provide information to the person about his effectiveness in various situations. When Eric received a bonus for outstanding performance on his job, the reward provided him with information that he was competent and self-determining in relation to his job. When David did well at school, his mother told him she was proud of him, and when Amanda learned to ride a bike, she was given a brand new two-wheeler. David and Amanda knew from the praise and bicycle that they were competent and self-determining in relation to school and bicycling. The second aspect of every reward is the information it provides a person about his competence and self-determination.

"When the controlling aspect of the reward is very salient, such as in the case of money or the avoidance of punishment, [a] change in perceived locus of causality . . . will occur. The person is 'controlled' by the reward and he perceives that the locus of causality is external." (Deci, 1975, pp. 141–42)

If you took a course on a pass/fail basis, instead of for a grade, do you think it would affect your motivation?

Because of the prominent role they play in school programs, grading and other performance evaluations are a special concern in any discussion of the overreliance on extrinsics as a way to reinforce positive learning. Although grades often are discussed as simply providing information about how well a student is doing, many, if not most, students perceive each grade as a reward or a punishment. Certainly, many teachers use grades to try to control behavior—to reward those who do assignments well and to punish those who don't. Sometimes parents add to a student's perception of grades as extrinsic reinforcers by giving a reward for good report cards. (For one of the authors, it was a nickel for a B and a dime for each A, but that was thirty years ago; the going rate today has to be much higher to be highly valued as a reward.)

We all have our own horror stories about the negative impact of grades on ourselves and others. In general, grades have a way of reshaping what students do with their learning opportunities. In choosing what to study, students strongly consider what grades they are likely to receive. As deadlines for assignments and tests get closer, interest in the topic gives way to interest in maximizing one's grade. Discussion of interesting issues and problems related to the area of study gives way to questions about how long a paper should be and what will be on the test. None of this is surprising given that poor grades can result in having to repeat a course or being denied certain immediate and long-range opportunities. It is simply a good example of how systems that overemphasize extrinsics may have a serious negative impact on intrinsic motivation for learning.

And if the impact of current practices is harmful to those who are able learners, im-

agine the impact on students with learning problems!

The point, then, is that learning involves matching motivation. Matching motivation requires an appreciation of the importance of a learner's perceptions in determining the right mix of intrinsic and extrinsic reasons for learning. It also requires understanding the key role played by expectations of success.

When a good match is achieved, negative attitudes and behaviors tend to decrease. They are replaced by an expanding interest in learning, new feelings of competence and self-determination, and an increase in the amount of risk taken in efforts to learn.

Specific intervention strategies for matching motivation are discussed in Chapter 9.

MATCHING DEVELOPMENT

Matching motivation is a first objective in creating an optimal match for learning. However, matching motivation is difficult without simultaneously matching the learner's level of development. This point may already be clear from our discussion of expectations and the key role they play in determining motivation. If Sally can't do the learning activities, she has little motivation to proceed.

Let's consider the matter of matching the learning environment to development (see Box 8–8). To understand some of the complexities, it is important to appreciate the variability of development. Therefore, we begin by discussing variations in developmental patterns. Then, we turn to the topic of key performance dimensions used to measure individual differences in development.

Variations in Developmental Patterns

As outlined in Chapters 2 and 6, the primary historical emphasis in the LD field has been

Box 8–8

Current Practices
Matching Development and Instruction

The literature on learning and learning problems offers a range of discussions on how to provide instruction to meet developmental deficits and differences. Here are three major examples:

1. Modifying learners to match instruction. Education has had a tradition of working with learners to prepare them for what the learning environment expects of them. Early education, kindergarten, and first-grade programs are devoted in great measure to teaching school-readiness skills.

A recent trend in the learning disabilities field exemplifies this tradition. The focus of this trend has been to teach students strategies and skills for coping with assigned tasks and social situations at school. Although different strategies have been developed, probably the most popular are cognitive behavior modification techniques. For instance, there are approaches that stress teaching students "cognitive strategies" in efforts to enhance their attention and organize their thinking related to tasks such as reading (see examples in Chapter 6).

2. Modifying instruction to match learners. There has been a growing emphasis on the importance of efforts to match teaching to the current level of development of the learner. Sometimes the focus is on matching specific observable skill levels, sometimes it is on pervasive "aptitudes."

For example, since learners differ in their ability to conceptualize, it has been proposed that those with a low conceptual level be given tests with a high degree of structure, while those with a high conceptual level be allowed to work with a low or intermediate level of structure (Hunt & Sullivan, 1974).

A comprehensive approach to matching learning tasks and settings to the skills of individuals diagnosed as learning disabled is presented by Corrine Smith (1983). In particular, she stresses matching tasks and instructions to the student's attention, speed of processing information, need for practice, strongest modalities, cognitive style, and learning strategies. To match such developmental differences among students, Smith proposes that teachers replace current analyses of the order in which skills should be taught with analyses of learning tasks that reflect a variety of learner dimensions she identifies as critical.

3. Modifying environments, persons, or both. The approach to establishing a good match for learning outlined in this chapter does *not* presume that the learning environment is essentially fixed or that the goal of instruction at each stage is to prepare the learner for the next level of development. The approach does emphasize modifying instruction and the learning environment. But, in doing so, it looks beyond levels of development to consider learner's motivation. Moreover, because learning is understood to result from the ongoing transactions between the learner and the learning environment, it is recognized that a change in either or both may be appropriate at any given time.

on problems in *perceptual, motor,* and *language* and related *cognitive* development. Problems in *social* and *emotional* development, for the most part, were seen as secondary concerns until recently. Currently, it is recognized that persons with learning disabilities and other learning problems may have difficulty functioning in any one or more of these six areas.

Difficulties in developmental functioning may be caused by CNS trouble, but failure to account properly for individual differences can also cause such difficulties. This occurs when others' expectations result in demands that go beyond a person's stage of development.

Difficulties caused by CNS dysfunctions aside, there are very important differences in the way people develop. Although most of us finally reach at least some minimal level of competence in each area of development, we do so at different rates. For example, it has been widely noted that, on the average, girls develop verbal abilities earlier than boys. Among both sexes, in the years when youngsters are first learning to read, there appear to be relatively large individual differences in a number of areas of development. This is the case, for example, with regard to the minimal level of visual perceptual ability needed for discriminating among letters and words. Again we stress that such natural differences are only problems when situations and events make demands on individuals to do things that are beyond their current level of development (see Dalby, 1979).

Whatever the reason, it is clear that individuals vary with regard to developmental patterns. In facilitating learning, efforts must be made to match a person's current capacities in all areas of development. This means accounting for areas in which development clearly is lagging and for areas in which development has kept up with or surpassed the norm (e.g., Miller, 1981).

In first grade, Bret's visual perception and language functioning developed more slowly than that of most of the others in his class. However, he was a very sociable and bright youngster who related well to children and adults. If the teacher had replaced his group participation activities with individual remedial exercises, he would have been cut off from the few times during the school day when he could demonstrate his competence and experience school as an enjoyable place (see Box 8–9).

In general, although it is useful to discuss specific areas of development, it is the overall *pattern* that must be considered in creating a good match. And the pattern, as it

---

Box 8–9

Concern in the Field
Strengths and Weaknesses

Sometimes the problem of matching a learner's pattern of development is equated with focusing on strengths and weaknesses. This is understandable since both topics deal with differences in developmental functioning—areas that are well developed and those that are not. However, the two matters are not the same.

The issue of whether to focus on strengths or weaknesses initially arose as part of the underlying-abilities orientation. The argument centers on whether remedial approaches should (1) attempt to build up weak areas of development (underlying abilities) or (2) teach students to compensate for deficits by relying on areas of strength.

Those who advocate building up deficiencies in underlying abilities assume that underlying-ability deficits are interfering with the learning of basic school subjects; they also assume they can accurately identify and facilitate the development of such deficiencies in ways that improve overall learning. Those who advocate relying on strengths assume that basic school subjects, such as reading, can be learned even though use of major facets of human functioning (identified as the weak underlying abilities) are ignored.

Some practitioners have tried to settle the issue by advocating a strategy that combines both approaches. While this may appear to be a pragmatic solution, the combined strategy has been criticized as ignoring the fact that the assumptions of the two approaches are in conflict.

Whether or not weak areas of development reflect underlying-ability deficits, they must be accounted for in efforts to personalize learning. Similarly, strong areas of development must be accounted for both to facilitate continuing development and to maintain and enhance motivation.

can be observed, reflects both accumulated capacities and attitudes.

Key Performance Dimensions

Psychologists and educators interested in individual differences have found it useful to stress four key performance dimensions when measuring the pattern of human functioning (Gagné, 1967). These are

- rate—the pace at which the person performs, e.g., given three second-graders, one reads a sentence in five seconds, another reads the same sentence in two seconds, the third takes ten seconds
- style—preferences with regard to ways of proceeding, e.g., one likes to hold his book up when reading, another prefers to leave it resting on the desk, the third doesn't care which position the book is in but likes to have her feet up when she reads
- amount—quantity of work the person does, e.g., during quiet reading time, one of the students stops after reading three or four assigned pages, another stops after the teacher is no longer watching, the third reads as much as he can before the period ends
- quality—care, mastery, and aesthetic features demonstrated in performance, e.g., our three students will be found to differ in how well they understand what they read and in how much the practice period improved their skills

Remember that rate, style, amount, and quality of performance not only reflect levels of developmental competence but also are influenced by levels of motivation to perform. Therefore, efforts to assess a learner's skills in any area of development often are confounded by motivation—especially among individuals whose previous failures make them relatively unmotivated to perform on formal measures.

Specific intervention strategies for matching development are discussed in Chapters 10 and 11.

PERSONALIZATION

By this point, it should be clear to you why it is important to match motivation and development in facilitating the learning of Sally, Bret, Jan, Chris, and others with learning problems. You may, however, still not quite understand what is involved. Therefore, before moving on to a more detailed discussion in Chapters 9 and 10, it may be helpful if we discuss the concept of personalization (Adelman, 1971).

Definition, Key Assumptions, and Major Elements

Personalization can be viewed as a psychological construct. It stresses that whether a learning environment is an effective match depends on whether the *learner* experiences the environment as a good match with what she or he wants to learn and is able to learn.

> Bret and Jerry both are in Mr. Phillips's fifth-period class.
> Jerry may not say so spontaneously, but the class seems to fit him very well. He likes most of what he does in class each day, and he finds it just challenging enough (not too easy and not too hard). All indications suggest he experiences his classroom as a good match motivationally and developmentally.
> Bret finds few things to like about the class. Although the teacher has planned remedial activities that Bret is able to do rather easily, they don't interest him. He is bored and feels unhappy. From his perspective, the learning environment is not a good one.

In general, the emphasis on how the learner perceives the match and on matching *both* development and motivation distinguishes a personalized intervention

from other individually oriented approaches.

Because learning is an ongoing, dynamic,
and interactive process, a learning environment must continuously change to match
changes in the learner. Jerry perceives the
environment as personalized and responds
by learning; the changes in him usually call
for changes in the environment so that it
will continue to be perceived as personalized. What is involved, then, is an ongoing
series of transactions and mutual changes

on the part of the learner and the learning
environment.

Box 8–10 contains a list of some key assumptions and major elements of a personalized intervention program.

Sequential and Hierarchical Framework

The figure in Box 8–11 presents a sequential
and hierarchical framework that can guide
efforts to provide a good match and deter-

Box 8–10

Key Assumptions and Major Elements of a Personalized Program

dividual differences, as well as independent
and cooperative functioning and problem
solving.

Assumptions of a Personalized Program

- Learning is a function of the ongoing transactions between the learner and the learning environment.
- Optimal learning is a function of an optimal
  match between the learner's accumulated capacities and attitudes and current state of being and the program's processes and context.
- Matching a learner's motivation must be a
  prime objective of the program's procedures.
- Matching the learner's pattern of acquired
  capacities must also be a prime procedural
  objective.
- The learner's perception is the critical
  criterion for evaluating whether a good match
  exists between the learner and the learning
  environment.
- The wider the range of options that can be offered and the more the learner is made aware
  of the options and has a choice about which
  to pursue, the greater the likelihood that he
  or she will perceive the match as a good one.
- Besides improved learning, personalized programs enhance intrinsic valuing of learning
  and a sense of personal responsibility for
  learning. Furthermore, such programs increase acceptance and even appreciation of in-

Elements of a Personalized Program

- Regular use of informal and formal conferences for discussing options, making decisions, exploring learner perceptions, and
  mutually evaluating progress
- A broad range of options from which the
  learner can make choices with regard to types
  of learning content, activities, and desired
  outcomes
- A broad range of options from which the
  learner can make choices with regard to facilitation (support, guidance) of decision making
  and learning
- Active decision making by the learner in
  making choices and in evaluating how well
  the chosen options match his or her current
  levels of motivation and capability
- Establishment of program plans and mutual
  agreements about the ongoing relationships
  between the learner and the program personnel
- Regular reevaluations of decisions, reformula-
  tion of plans, and renegotiation of agreements
  based on mutual evaluations of progress,
  problems, and current learner perceptions of
  the "match"

Box 8–11

Sequences and Levels in Providing a Good Match and Determining Least Intervention Needed

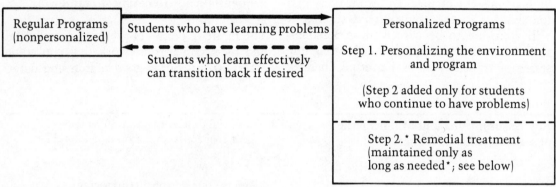

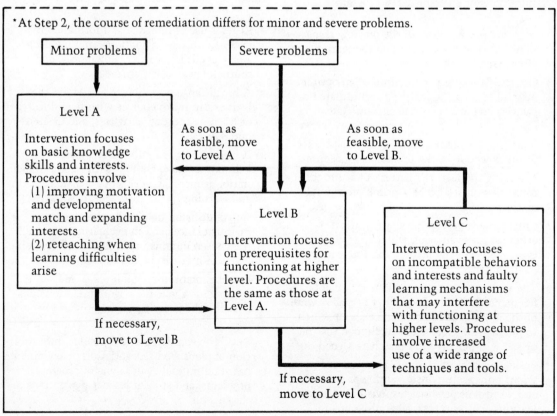

mine the least intervention needed for individuals with learning disabilities and other learning problems. As can be seen, the first step focuses on changing the classroom environment. The changes are meant to make the program more responsive to learner differences in motivation and development. The next step provides remedial treatment as needed.

Specifically, Step 1 involves

(a) establishing a learning environment with a broad array of options;

(b) assisting each student to sample from the range of options and then to make some initial decisions about which ones will be pursued (the primary basis for the choices made is the learner's view of what seems to be a good match); and

(c) monitoring and evaluating effectiveness so that the initial decisions can be modified as needed and so that the effectiveness of the program can be mutually assessed.

Ideally, if the program is effective in enhancing appropriate learning, this first step would be continued until the learner "catches up."

Step 2 is introduced only if the learner continues to have some learning problems or in other ways does not respond well to the first step. This second step involves three hierarchical levels of intervention focus (see Box 8-12).

In pursuing the three levels discussed in Box 8-12, the following strategies are used:

1. For those whose ongoing problems are minor, the range of options is expanded and alternative teaching strategies and techniques are introduced in efforts to improve the match and facilitate learning (Level A). This strategy is used only when and as long as it is needed.

2. If the preceding strategies are not enough or if problems are relatively severe,

the emphasis is on identifying and pursuing missing learning prerequisites (Level B). When this level of activity is no longer needed, the focus shifts back to Level A strategies.

3. If Level A and B strategies do not do the job, treatment takes the form of a one-to-one clinical intervention focused on interfering factors. A broad range of remedial, therapeutic, and behavior change approaches are tried. The specific approach depends on whether the problem is identified (a) as a dysfunction in internal learning mechanisms or (b) as disruptive social and emotional behaviors and interests. As soon as this clinical work is no longer necessary, the intervention focus shifts back to the most appropriate of the levels and strategies listed above. (A graphic representation of the various levels, types, and areas for intervention focus is presented in Box 8-13.)

The sequential and hierarchical framework also provides a sequential strategy for detecting errors in LD diagnoses and for screening different types of learning problems:

• If Step 1 is sufficient in correcting an individual's learning problem, it seems reasonable to suggest that the person does not have a learning disability. Instead, the individual's learning problem may have resulted primarily from the inadequacies of the learning environment.

• If Levels A and B of Step 2 are sufficient, the individual is probably a learner whose natural variations in development or whose minor physical or psychological vulnerabilities require considerably more accommodation than current regular programs provide.

• If Level C of Step 2 is necessary and the problem does not appear to be caused by social or emotional factors, it may well be that the individual has learning disabili-

Box 8–12

Theory and Research
Levels of Intervention

Ideally, the first impact of efforts to personalize learning is to mobilize learners to perform as well as they can. In this way, identifying problems in learning becomes easier and less prone to error.

As the problems become evident, there may be a need to focus on one or more of three levels of intervention:

1. Level A—basic knowledge and skills and interests. Once motivation and development are matched appropriately, individuals diagnosed as learning disabled or as having other learning problems may be found to have no difficulty learning. Such individuals can simply continue to pursue basic skills and other regular activities. Of course, they may have some catching up to do, and they may learn and perform better under procedures that differ from those associated with their previous poor performance.

2. Level B—prerequisites. Some individuals may not have acquired certain prerequisite ("readiness") skills or may not be interested in learning to read, do math, understand science. An individual who has not learned

to order and sequence events, follow directions, and so forth will need to develop such skills before he or she is likely to be successful in learning to read and do math. If the person doesn't see much point in learning the three Rs, development of such interests must be encouraged. This level is adopted only to pursue specific prerequisites as they are identified as missing.

3. Level C—interfering factors. There are two types of interfering factors. If an individual has trouble learning skills in a personalized learning environment even after prerequisites are addressed, it seems reasonable to explore the possibility that internal learning mechanisms are not functioning effectively. The focus of intervention thus shifts to clinical remediation designed to help the individual overcome whatever is interfering with learning.

   The other type of interfering factor appears early in the intervention process. Some individuals do not respond positively for a variety of social and emotional reasons. They display a range of behaviors and interests that are incompatible with pursuing learning in most classrooms, and they usually are not interested in one-to-one instruction. Intervention for these persons may take the form of psychotherapy or behavior change strategies.

ties stemming from a minor CNS disfunction.

SUMMARY

Adopting an interactional perspective makes it clear that learning and learning problems are a function of the match between what the learner brings to the learning environment and what the environment offers and demands. A good match exists when the learner perceives the environment as appropriate in terms of both what she or

he *can* learn and *wants* to learn. Thus, the prime objectives of personalization are to provide enough options with regard to content, activities, and outcomes so that the learner finds those that are most likely to be a good motivational and developmental match. In this context, as a framework for applying the guideline of least intervention needed, a set of sequential and hierarchical strategies has been outlined in this chapter and will be discussed in greater detail in the next two chapters.

Although the concept of the match has been presented here in connection with

Box 8–13

Levels, Types, and Areas of Intervention

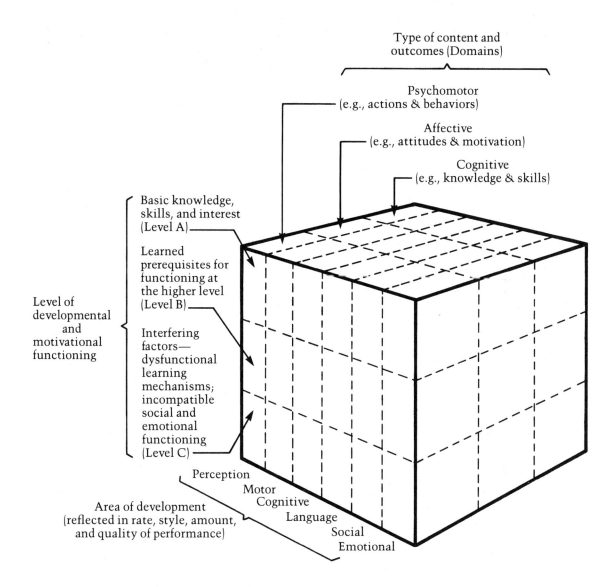

learning problems, it clearly has application in all learning situations. Indeed, if instruction in the early years of schooling were more personalized, a significant number of learning problems probably could be prevented. Moreover, application of sequential and hierarchical strategies in the primary grades could help to identify true learning disabilities at a time and in a way that significantly reduces the negative effects of such handicaps.

AN ENRICHMENT ACTIVITY

Interview a friend about a few of her or his current classes. Get a rating of the degree to which each class is perceived as a good or bad match. Remember to get separate ratings for motivation (valuing, expectations of success) and current patterns of development.

If the match is perceived as not too good, ask for some specific examples of why this is the case.

Also, ask your friend for some specific ideas about what should be changed to make it a good match for him or her.

Finally, ask how many others in the class(s) he thinks might agree that such changes would improve the match for them.

When you are done, you will have conducted a little empirical test of the validity of what you read in this chapter. What are your conclusions?

SPECIAL TOPIC REFERENCES

Should you be interested in further information about *motivation* and *development*, see the following readings.

ADELMAN, H. S., & TAYLOR, L. (1983). *Learning disabilities in perspective.* Glenview, Ill.: Scott, Foresman, Chapter 10.

BRUNER, J. S. (1966). The will to learn. In *Toward a theory of instruction.* Cambridge, Mass.: Belknap Press.

DECI, E. L. (1975). *Intrinsic motivation.* New York: Plenum, Chapter 8.

DECI, E. L. (1980). *The psychology of self-determination.* Lexington, Mass.: Lexington Books.

FURTH, H. G., & WACHS, H. (1975). *Thinking goes to school: Piaget's theory in practice.* New York: Oxford University Press.

MCCOMBS, B. L. (1984). Processes and skills underlying continuing intrinsic motivation to learn: Toward a definition of motivational skills training interventions. *Educational Psychologist, 19,* 199–218.

Should you be interested in further information about interactional models and matching environments to learners, see the following readings.

ADELMAN, H. S., & TAYLOR, L. (1983). *Learning disabilities in perspective.* Glenview, Ill.: Scott, Foresman, Chapters 2 and 13.

CRONBACH, L. J., & SNOW, R. E. (1977). *Aptitudes and instructional methods.* New York: Irvington.

HUNT, D. E., & SULLIVAN, E. V. (1974). *Between psychology and education.* Chicago: Dryden Press.

SMITH, C. R. (1983). *Learning disabilities: The interaction of learner, task, and setting.* Boston: Little, Brown.

Chapter *9*

Teaching Basic Knowledge and Skills: Content

Teaching is a fascinating and somewhat mysterious process. Is it an art, or is it an activity that most people can learn to do?

It is certainly an activity that many people do everyday. Helping someone grow, develop, and learn is one of the most basic forms of human interaction. In some form, we've all taught. And we've all experienced the satisfaction of succeeding in helping others learn and the frustration when they don't "get it."

Frustration is a common feeling when teaching and learning don't go smoothly. The frustration often leads us (teacher, parent, or other helper) to conclude that there's something wrong with people we're trying to help. After all, we explained it right; they should have understood it. And the fact that they didn't is usually seen as indicating a lack of effort ("They would have if they had really been trying") or a lack of ability ("They would have if they were smarter or not handicapped by a brain dysfunction").

Sometimes the frustration isn't just with a particular individual; it is with the poor school performance of large numbers of children and adolescents and with the vast amount of adult illiteracy. Such frustration leads to conclusions that something is wrong with the schools ("We need to get *back to basics!*"), or with certain groups of people ("These youngsters do badly because their parents don't value education"), or with both.

The frustration surrounding learning problems is more than understandable. And where there is frustration, it is not surprising that there are accusations and blaming. But blaming, of course, does not solve the problem. The solution is to be found, in part, in improving the ways in which basic knowledge and skills are taught.

This chapter and the next two chapters explore ways of facilitating the learning of learning disabled individuals with reference to "basics"—and much more. Although the emphasis is on elementary and secondary classroom programs, the strategies have also been used in clinical settings and with learning disabled adults. In this chapter, the focus is on the importance of a broad curriculum. In Chapter 10, the emphasis is on major elements in enhancing motivation and facilitating learning. In Chapter 11, we discuss what's involved when remedial instruction is needed.

Before discussing these ideas, however, it is important to put basic skills and the Back to Basics movement into perspective.

FORWARD TO BASICS: BASICS PLUS

Some people believe there has been a serious decline in the standards of public education. They claim schools have become too soft on students and are offering too many unessential and inappropriate courses. They demand that schools get *back to basics.*

Like so many catch-all phrases, "Back to Basics" means different things to different people. For some, it simply means returning to the way they were taught to read and write; it worked for them, and they don't see why it shouldn't work for everyone. Others mean that the schools should stop wasting time teaching courses in value clarification, sex education, poetry, and the like. In either case, there may also be a demand for stricter discipline and regimentation—"All this motivation talk is a lot of hooey; what some of these kids need is a good swift kick in the pants."

Many who talk about Back to Basics don't strictly mean going back to old methods. They just want a greater amount of time devoted to teaching the three Rs and a few other basics, such as science. They often also want to introduce ways to make teachers more accountable for poor student performance.

There's no question that people need to learn basic skills. What's controversial and at issue are the questions: What is basic?

How are the skills best learned? and What should be offered in the way of other learning opportunities? (See Box 9–1.)

The answers to these questions as reflected in the demand to get Back to Basics do not take into account the experience of those who have been diagnosed as learning disabled. Many individuals with learning problems have been taught by the very procedures advocated by the Back to Basics movement. Thus, rather than a reactive Back to Basics approach, the need is to go *forward* to basics and to develop programs that offer *basics plus.*

Psychology and education have made important advances in recent years in facilitating learning, and it seems naive and wasteful to ignore all that has been learned. A leap back to old-fashioned methods not only ignores important new ideas but also falsely assumes the old methods really worked.

You may believe that you are a good reader because you were taught by a specific approach, say phonics. Some of your friends believe they are good readers because they learned by a whole-word (look-say) method. Whatever method worked for you is probably the one you think should be used for others.

If you did a study, however, you would find that almost every method used has *not* worked for a significant number of people. Experts acknowledge that teaching reading is much more complex than has been implied in teacher education courses on "How to Teach Reading." Experts also disagree about what is the best way to teach reading in public schools.

The terms *forward to basics* and *basics plus* are meant to convey the following points:

- Basic skills involve more than the three Rs and cognitive development. There are many important areas of human development and functioning, and each contains "basics" that individuals may need help in

Box 9–1

Fable
What's Basic?

Once upon a time, the animals decided that their lives and their society would be improved by setting up a school. The basics identified as necessary for survival in the animal world were swimming, running, climbing, jumping, and flying. Instructors were hired to teach these activities, and it was agreed that all the animals would take all the courses. This worked out well for the administrators, but it caused some problems for the students.

The squirrel, for example, was an A student in running, jumping, and climbing but had trouble in flying class, not because of an inability to fly, for she could sail from the top of one tree to another with ease, but because the flying curriculum called for taking off from the ground. The squirrel was drilled in ground-to-air take-offs until she was exhausted and developed charley horses from overexertion. This caused her to perform poorly in her other classes, and her grades dropped to D's.

The duck was outstanding in swimming class—even better than the teacher. But she did so poorly in running that she was transferred to a remedial class. There she practiced running until her webbed feet were so badly damaged that she was only an average swimmer. But since average was acceptable, nobody saw this as a problem—except the duck.

In contrast, the rabbit was excellent in running, but, being terrified of water, he was an extremely poor swimmer. Despite a lot of make-up work in swimming class, he never could stay afloat. He soon became frustrated and uncooperative and was eventually expelled because of behavior problems.

The eagle naturally enough was a brilliant student in flying class and even did well in running and jumping. He had to be severely disciplined in climbing class, however, because he insisted that his way of getting to the top of the tree was faster and easier.

It should be noted that the parents of the groundhog pulled him out of school because the administration would not add classes in digging and burrowing. The groundhogs, along with the gophers and badgers, got a prairie dog to start a private school. They all have become strong opponents of school taxes and proponents of voucher systems.

By graduation time, the student with the best grades in the animal school was a compulsive ostrich who could run superbly and also could swim, fly, and climb a little. She, of course, was made class valedictorian and received scholarship offers from all the best universities.

(Benjamin [1949] credits George H. Reeves with giving this parable to American educators.)

---

acquiring. Moreover, an individual may require special accommodation in any of these areas.

- Motivational considerations play a major role in the acquisition of basic skills. Instruction should stress procedures that provide for a range of meaningful options, personal decision making, and useful feedback. Such processes can underscore intrinsic reasons for learning the skills, eliminate overemphasis on extrinsics, and provide for motivated practice. Individual differences in motivation may also require special accommodation.

- Facilitating learning involves varying three major areas of the learning environment and program: the physical and social setting, program structure and activities, and teacher techniques.

- Remedial procedures must be added to instructional programs for certain individuals, but only after appropriate nonremedial procedures for facilitating learning have been tried.

These points should become clearer as you read on.

A COMPREHENSIVE CURRICULUM

The curriculum for individuals diagnosed as learning disabled tends to be rather limited in scope. Individual Educational Plans (IEPs) often stress goals and objectives bearing only on identified problems. Putting aside the matter of the inaccuracy of many such prescriptions, what is evident is how narrow the focus can become if one is not careful.

How broad should the focus be? By now, we hope it is clear that an adequate approach for the learning disabled must go beyond remediation; it must encompass developmental and enrichment activity as well. And more is at stake than teaching the three Rs and cognitive skills. The focus must be on a variety of areas, types, and levels of instruction and learning (as outlined in Box 8–13).

Let's summarize and build a bit more on what we have already suggested about the nature of a curriculum for individuals who have experienced learning problems.

Remediation in Perspective

Given that teaching is an imperfect process, a particular individual's poor performance may be as much the result of a teaching problem as a learning problem. That is, until one is certain that the program is a good match for the student's current level of motivation and development, the trouble may just as easily be seen with the program as with the student. Thus, the most appropriate time to pursue remediation is after efforts have been made to improve (e.g., personalize) the program as much as feasible.

There has been a tendency in offering remedial instruction to focus primarily on a limited range of factors related to basic skills and to pay relatively little attention to other learning opportunities. Always working on one's problems and trying to catch up can be a grueling experience. One has to be tremendously motivated (and perhaps a bit masochistic) to keep working on fundamentals and problem areas day in and day out. Picture yourself with no other courses but basic requirements and those that you find extremely hard; how would you feel about going to school each day?

Limiting the focus to remediation, then, risks making the whole enterprise rather deadening. Broadening the focus to an increased range of developmental tasks and enrichment activities not only can balance the picture a bit but also may prove to be the key to finding better ways to help an individual overcome his or her problems.

We will have more to say about the specific nature of remediation and strategies for offering remedial help later in this chapter and in Chapter 11.

Developmental Tasks and General Domains of Learning

Most public school curriculum guides and manuals reflect efforts of schools to prepare youngsters to cope with what may be called *developmental* or *life tasks.* Reading, math, biology, chemistry, social studies, history, government, physical education, sex education, and so forth—all are seen as preparing an individual to take an appropriate role in society as a worker, citizen, member of a community, mate, and parent.

Over the years, efforts have been made to discuss developmental tasks related to perceptual-motor activity, cognition, language, and social and emotional functioning. Educators have tried to combine these areas of human functioning into three general categories referred to as the cognitive, affective, and psychomotor domains (Bloom, Englehart, Furst, Hill, & Krathwahl, 1956; Kibler, Barker, & Miles, 1970; Krathwahl, Bloom, &

Masia, 1964). Each domain is seen as encompassing a wide range of instructional content and outcomes (see Box 9–2).

Whatever areas of human functioning are stressed, the "developmental" curriculum is divided into sequential blocks and spread over the years that a youngster is in school. The timing for teaching a specific block depends on data about when most students will need and appear able to learn such materials and on a variety of practical matters.

Of course, not every area is given the same degree of emphasis. Instruction in some areas and for some students is designed to achieve a relatively high level of mastery and in-depth understanding. For example, higher levels of competence are expected for reading than for physical prowess; students planning on going to college are expected to develop higher levels of competence than those who are not. And some topics are presented simply because it is felt that students should be aware of them.

Programs overemphasizing basics risk deemphasizing other important areas of human functioning. They primarily stress basic cognitive skills and knowledge and the level of overall competence that should be expected of an individual, at least minimally. Obviously, however, because of the range of developmental tasks, more is required for successful daily functioning than a minimal level of literacy in the three Rs and in basic academic subjects such as science and history.

Enrichment

Enrichment goes beyond basics and beyond minimal levels of competence. In some people's minds, enrichment is extracurricular activity, something to be taken only if time is left after basics are mastered at an appropriate level. Others see enrichment as elite, special activity to be reserved for the gifted. In either case, the expectation is that what is learned will be something extra and often something hard to identify.

Enrichment in LD programs comprises opportunities for exploration, inquiry, and discovery related to topics and activities that are not part of the expected developmental curriculum. Opportunities are to be offered but need not be taken. If taken, no specific learning objectives are specified. Whatever is learned is fine. The assumptions are that many unpredictable specifics will be learned and, equally as important, an individual may gain a greater sense of the value of instruction and of pursuing knowledge.

Enrichment activities often are more attractive and intriguing than activities offered in the developmental curriculum. In part, this is because they are not required; they generally are not seen as demands, and individuals can seek out those that are a good match for their interests and abilities. Enrichment activities also usually are designed to provide more responsiveness to students; that is, whatever doesn't keep the attention of participants usually is replaced.

Because so many people think of enrichment as a frill, it is not surprising that such activities may not even be considered for individuals having trouble with developmental tasks. After all, these persons are seen as needing all the time that is available for remediation and for catching up. As has been suggested, this view of what is in the best interests of these individuals seems in error. The broader the curriculum, the better the opportunity for creating a good motivational match and for facilitating learning with regard to an important range of developmental tasks and remedial needs.

FOCUSING ON MOTIVATION

"How many psychologists does it take to change a light bulb?"

"Only one. But the bulb has to want to change."

Box 9–2

Theory and Practice
Outline of Goals of Education

The following outline was developed by the Evaluation Technologies Program at UCLA's Center for the Study of Evaluation.* Cognitive, affective, and psychomotor outcomes across all areas of development are reflected in the list. The outline illustrates the broad range of outcomes and content that may be appropriate in any school program, including programs for students identified as learning disabled.

I. Affective and personality traits
    A. Personal temperament
       1. Self-assertion
       2. Emotional stability
       3. Responsibility and self-control
    B. Socialization
       1. Social awareness
       2. Social values and conduct
    C. Attitudes, values, and motivation
       1. School orientation
       2. Self-esteem
       3. Achievement motivation
       4. Interests
II. Arts and crafts
    A. Valuing art
       1. Appreciation of art
       2. Internalization of art
    B. Producing art
       1. Representational skill in art
       2. Expressive skill in art
    C. Understanding art
       1. Art analysis
       2. Developmental understanding of art
III. Career education
    A. Career values and understanding
       1. Knowledge of vocations and careers
       2. Interest in vocations and careers
IV. Cognitive and intellectual skills
    A. Understanding and reasoning
       1. Classification
       2. Comprehension of information
       3. Logical reasoning
       4. Spatial reasoning
    B. Creativity and judgment
       1. Creativity
       2. Evaluative judgment
    C. Memory
       1. Rote memory
       2. Meaningful memory

D. Foreign language skills
   1. Reading comprehension in a foreign language
   2. Knowledge of elements of a foreign language
   3. Conversation in a foreign language
   4. Writing in a foreign language
E. Valuing foreign language and culture
   1. Cultural insight and values
   2. Enjoyment and application of a foreign language
V. Language arts
    A. Writing skills
       1. Spelling
       2. Punctuation and capitalization
       3. Grammatical skills in writing
       4. Penmanship
       5. Purpose and organization in writing
       6. Expression in writing
    B. Reference and study skills
       1. Reference and library skills
       2. Personal study skills and habits
VI. Mathematics
    A. Understanding math
       1. Knowledge of numbers and sets
       2. Knowledge of numeral systems and number principles
       3. Knowledge basic to algebra
    B. Performing arithmetic operations
       1. Whole number computation
       2. Computation with fractions
       3. Decimal and percent computation
    C. Applying and valuing mathematics
       1. Solution of word problems
       2. Personal use and appreciation
    D. Geometry and measurement skills
       1. Knowledge of geometric objects and relations
       2. Measurement knowledge and skills
       3. Use of tables, graphs, and statistical concepts
VII. Music
    A. Valuing music
       1. Appreciation of music
       2. Internalization of music
    B. Performing in music and dance
       1. Singing
       2. Instrument playing
       3. Dancing
    C. Understanding music

1. Music analysis
2. Developing understanding of music

VIII. Perceptual and motor skills
  A. Sensory perception
    1. Visual and tactile perception
    2. Auditory perception
  B. Psychomotor skills
    1. Fine motor skills
    2. Gross motor skills

IX. Physical education and health education
  A. Sports skills
    1. Athletic skills and physical condition
    2. Sports knowledge
  B. Valuing physical education
    1. Sportsmanship
    2. Sports enjoyment and participation
  C. Health habits and understanding
    1. Health and safety behavior and attitudes
    2. Knowledge of health factors
    3. Knowledge of life functions
    4. Knowledge of human sexuality
  D. Understanding hazards and diseases
    1. Knowledge of safety precautions
    2. Knowledge of habit-forming substances
    3. Knowledge of disease and disability

X. Reading
  A. Reading readiness skills
    1. Listening
    2. Speaking
    3. Word attack skills
  B. Familiarity with literature
    1. Recognition of literary devices and qualities
    2. Knowledge of literature
  C. Reading with understanding
    1. Recognition of word meanings
    2. Reading comprehension
  D. Reading interpretation and criticism
    1. Oral reading
    2. Reading interpretation
    3. Critical reading
  E. Valuing literature and language
    1. Response to literature and language
    2. Personal use of reading and language skills

XI. Religion and ethics
  A. Understanding religion
    1. Knowledge of own religion
    2. Knowledge of religions of the world
  B. Personal ethics and religious belief
    1. Ethical code and practice
    2. Religious belief and practice

XII. Science
  A. Investigating the environment
    1. Scientific observation and description
    2. Generalization and hypothesis formulation in science
    3. Experimentation
  B. Understanding science
    1. Knowledge of different life forms
    2. Knowledge of ecology
    3. Knowledge of physical science
    4. Knowledge of the foundations of science
  C. Valuing and applying science
    1. Science interest and appreciation
    2. Application of scientific methods in everyday life

XIII. Social studies
  A. Understanding history and civics
    1. Knowledge of history
    2. Knowledge of government and civics
    3. Knowledge of current events
  B. Understanding geography
    1. Knowledge of physical geography
    2. Knowledge of anthropology and cultural geography
    3. Knowledge of economic processes and geography
  C. Understanding social relationships
    1. Knowledge of family life
    2. Knowledge of social control and conflict
    3. Knowledge of social groups
  D. Valuing and applying social studies
    1. Social studies interest and appreciation
    2. Citizenship
    3. Ethnic and cultural appreciation

NOTE: This material is also presented in CSE Elementary School Test Evaluations, 2nd ed. (Los Angeles: Center for the Study of Evaluation, UCLA, 1976), edited and prepared by R. Hoepfner, M. Bastone, V. Ogilvie, R. Hunter, S. Sparta, C. Grothe, E. Shari, L. Hufano, E. Goldstein, R. Williams, and K. Smith. The original source is out of print but can be retrieved through the ERIC system (ED 143670).

This old joke has the ring of truth about it. Individuals who don't want to change represent a special challenge to professionals, parents, and friends alike.

Good teachers may present lessons that are seen as excellent by most observers. But it is almost inevitable that any particular lesson will not appeal to everyone. For those who aren't interested, the lesson's intended objectives are not likely to be accomplished very well. To meet the objectives in such cases, the teacher must first focus on student motivation.

Despite a teacher's best efforts, students with learning disabilities and other learning problems often are not motivated to work on improving basic skills.

Mr. Johnson is confronted with a "chicken-and-egg" dilemma. He understands, at least intuitively, that if he could improve Sally's skills, he might enhance her motivation for reading. Thus, he proceeds with basic reading skill instruction in ways designed to ensure that she can do the work successfully. However, Sally either refuses or just goes through the motions with regard to each assigned activity. He soon realizes that besides not improving her motivation to read, he is increasing her avoidance.

What is he to do? He can't just ignore her skill deficits; but he doesn't want to increase her avoidance of reading.

Most individuals with learning problems do want to overcome their problems. Sally doesn't like having problems with her reading, and she would love to be a good reader. What she hates and tries to avoid is her remedial reading program.

With regard to motivation, the tasks in helping students like Sally seem to be two. First, the learning environment should be designed to enhance her intrinsic motivation for learning. Then, if she still shows signs of avoidance in overcoming problems,

the program must focus on the reasons for her avoidance.

As long as there have been schools, there has been criticism of schools. In 1632, Comenius noted:

"For more than a hundred years much complaint has been made of the unmethodical way in which schools are conducted, but it is only within the last thirty that any serious attempt has been made to find a remedy for this state of things. And with what result? Schools remain exactly as they were."

We read almost daily of falling achievement test scores, rising illiteracy rates, and lack of respect for school property and personnel. The cry is for competency tests and excellence in education. Remedies proposed include back to basics, increased discipline, longer school days, longer school years, and more homework.

Concerned persons commonly lament that students aren't motivated and don't put enough time and effort into their schoolwork. It is implied that teachers and parents should motivate and, if necessary, demand better learning and performance. Most people agree that motivation is a major problem in schools. They don't agree, however, on what to do about the problem (see Box 9–3).

If it is granted that motivation is of major importance in learning, in general, and learning problems, in particular, then a commitment to correcting learning problems requires instructional reforms that stress motivation (see Reading E). The following discussion explores what might be involved in such a direct focus on motivation.

Enhancing and Expanding Intrinsic Motivation

Let's start with the assumption that a prerequisite for learning at school is the student's perception that the time and effort

Box 9–3

**Should school learning activities
be interesting?**

"A mother said to me not long ago, 'I think you
are making a mistake in trying to make schoolwork so interesting for the children. After all,
they are going to have to spend most of their
lives doing things they don't like, and they
might as well get used to it now.'

"Every so often the curtain of slogans and
platitudes behind which most people live
opens up for a second, and you get a glimpse of
what they really think. . . . Is life nothing but
drudgery, an endless list of dreary duties? Is
education nothing but the process of getting
children ready to do them? . . . One would
expect that people feeling this way about their
own lives would want something better for
their children, would say, in effect, 'I have
somehow missed the chance to put much joy
and meaning into my own life; please educate
my children so that they will do better.'

"Well, that's our business, whether parents
say it or not." (Holt, 1964, pp. 160–61)

Writers such as Holt have suggested that
those who call for increased *pressure* on
students to learn seem to be operating more on
a *training* than on an *educational* model. That
is, they seem to be equating the process of

education with processes that are designed to
teach people selected sets of skills, such as addition and multiplication facts, vocabulary words,
typing, driving, and various other technical activities. Moreover, they fail to recognize that
even such skills as these are learned best when
a person is intrinsically motivated to practice
the skills and to understand underlying concepts—as contrasted, for example, with being
forced to practice and memorize skills by rote.

There can be no doubt about the usefulness
of the training model. If one can exercise control, people and animals can be trained to perform certain behaviors. Such an approach, however, may not be the best way to proceed in
teaching children to read and do math. In fact,
such an approach may be counterproductive if,
besides the skills, the objective also is to establish an attitude of growing interest in the
area—especially interest that continues beyond
the course of instruction.

Think about all the persons who have been
trained to do math fundamentals and who, at
the same time, seem to have learned to hate
math. (Many of these people are now teaching
math; many others have major learning problems related to math.) There is nothing intrinsically to hate about math. It seems likely that
the training approaches widely used in teaching
these skills have negatively affected many people's motivation for learning math and pursuing activities that involve its use.

required to learn effectively and behave
appropriately at school are *worthwhile*.
From our discussion in Chapter 8, remember: what a person values (intrinsic-
ally/extrinsically) interacts with expectations about what will happen, and motivation is one product of the interaction. It is as
if the learner thinks in terms of such questions as, Are the tasks worth doing? (valu-

ing) and Can I do them? (expectations). And
the answers determine whether the tasks
are pursued or avoided and whether a little
or a lot of effort and ability is expended.
Psychologists refer to this view of motivation as expectancy-times-value (E × V)
theory.

In recent years, theorists interested in the
motivational role played by thoughts and

feelings have discussed many factors that influence people's valuing and expectations (see Weiner, 1980). The growing body of theory has many implications for understanding and working with learning problems. One very basic implication is how easy it is to mistake a lack of motivation for a lack of skills. In contrast, it is recognized that individuals with learning problems can display amazing effort and progress under conditions of high intrinsic motivation to learn. If classroom programs ignore these facts, not only may instruction fail to capitalize on motivation, but also motivation may be undermined. Moreover, students may appear to know less than they do, and time will be wasted teaching them what they already know. These are some of the reasons why it is so important to focus first on enhancing and expanding current areas of intrinsic motivation.

All students probably have some areas in which they are highly motivated to learn and other areas in which their motivation is at least positive and will increase if encouraged. It also can be expected that, given the opportunity, they will develop new interests.

Thus, as a first step, learning environments should be designed in ways that maintain currently high motivation, enhance budding motivation, and expand areas of interest. This means establishing learning environments that help students to identify intrinsic reasons for learning and overcoming problems. In doing so, there will be times when it is necessary to reduce external demands to perform and conform.

Overcoming Avoidance Motivation

Sometimes strategies to enhance and expand motivation are sufficient. Students find instructional activities that capture and hold their interest, and they proceed to learn. Where this step is insufficient, the program must expand to include approaches for dealing with avoidance motivation and related problem behavior (see Box 9–4).

Among students with learning problems a significant amount of the problem behavior seen at school may be the result of avoidance motivation. Students who have failed extensively at school are unlikely to expect to succeed with schoolwork or to positively value it. Indeed, they probably have a strong dislike for schoolwork.

When people dislike an activity, but are pushed to do it, they are likely to protest or to try to avoid the activity (see Brehm & Brehm, 1981). If the protest or direct efforts to avoid are unsuccessful, an individual can be expected to react in increasingly negative ways.

> Because of his many experiences of failure at school, Bret tends to perceive learning situations as threatening. Even before he knows much about a situation, he expects to have difficulty coping. Thus, he feels vulnerable, fearful, and sometimes angry at being pushed into such situations.
>
> He would like to avoid the situations, and if he can't do so directly, he tries indirect ways, such as diverting the teacher to a discussion of other matters. When he can't manipulate the situation effectively, he engages in various misbehaviors. This often leads to a power struggle with the teacher, which ends up with his being sent to the principal or home.
>
> After a number of such experiences, he has developed some rather strong negative expectations and attitudes about school and teachers and has learned a rather large range of behaviors to protect himself from what he perceives as bad situations. Unfortunately, the more he displays such behavior, the more those around him tend to think of him as emotionally disturbed.

A great deal of the negative behavior of persons like Bret may reflect reactions to immediate school pressures (see Box 9–5). Those with long or intense histories of problems at school are likely to develop general

Box 9–4

Research and Practice
Motivation Problem Subgroups

In working with learning problems, we have found it useful to identify subgroups of students by patterns of learning, behavior, and motivation problems. We have found it one thing to work with students who have minor avoidance tendencies toward learning literacy skills; it is quite another thing to work with those who have major avoidance tendencies; and it is even harder to work with those who find a variety of interfering behaviors attractive alternatives to school learning and who even view such behaviors as signs of competence.

For instance, truancy, peer interactions including gangs and drug culture, and baiting authority are much more interesting and exciting to some adolescents than any learning activities the school is offering. In these instances, efforts to enhance motivation toward overcoming skill deficiencies generally aren't too successful. What is needed are strategies for correcting the motivation "problems" directly and before efforts to remedy academic and developmental deficits. For example, if a student strongly values and feels committed to behaviors that interfere with classroom learning, procedures are needed to counter this *commitment.* Similarly, procedures are needed to modify the *perceptions* of students who strongly expect to fail or who believe that success is beyond their control.

To understand the range of *motivation* subgroups, consider the following clusters:

Group I—Those who want to attend school and learn some, but not all, of the basic skills demanded.

Group II—Those who want to attend school and to learn all or some of the basic skills but do not greatly value the procedures currently used to teach basics and/or do not expect to succeed with them. This group is further divided into IIa, those who are willing to discuss and explore alternative learning processes, and IIb, those who are not.

Group III—Those who want to attend school but do not want to be taught or to learn what the program currently demands. This group also is divided into IIIa, those who are willing to discuss and explore alternative learning opportunities, and IIIb, those who are not. (This last subgroup includes a large number of adolescents who come to school primarily for peer interactions, and some students who have such major fears of failure that they avoid all discussion of their problem.)

Group IV—Those who do not want to attend school.

What this overview of motivation problems underscores is that for some students motivation is a problem and in some cases may be as much of a problem as a lack of basic skills.

expectations that most classroom experiences will be hurtful. Given such a general expectation, a student may approach all school situations looking for the worst and thus perceiving it. Even when a teacher offers "exciting" new opportunities, they may not be readily seen. (This, of course, can be frustrating to a teacher who has spent a great deal of time developing new procedures to enhance motivation.)

Whatever the reasons, there are clearly times when efforts to enhance motivation do not sufficiently eliminate behaviors interfering with classroom learning. At such times, the next step is to change any environmental factors that seem to be producing the youngster's negative reactions. In particular, this involves making certain that external demands to perform and conform are truly minimized. This strategy is intended

Box 9–5

Theory and Practice
Approach and Avoidance Motivation and Negative Behavior

Sally hates reading and refuses to do her assignments. Chris drops out of school. Bret is seen as a "behavior problem." Jan withdraws into herself.

Youngsters diagnosed as learning disabled frequently display a range of behaviors that are seen as inappropriate and troublesome. Such behavior can reflect approach (as contrasted with avoidance) motivation. That is, noncooperative, disruptive, and aggressive behavior patterns may be rewarding or satisfying to an individual because the behavior itself is exciting or because the behavior leads to desired outcomes (e.g., peer recognition, feelings of autonomy). Intentional negative behavior stemming from

such approach motivation can be viewed as *pursuit of deviance.*

Of course, negative behavior in the classroom also often stems from avoidance motivation. That is, it may be the result of *protective reactions.* Students with learning problems can be seen as motivated to avoid and to protest against being forced into situations in which they cannot cope effectively. For such students, many teaching and therapy situations are perceived in this way. Under such circumstances, individuals can be expected to react by trying to protect themselves from the unpleasant thoughts and feelings that the situations produce. In effect, the negative behavior reflects efforts to cope and defend against aversive experiences. The actions may be direct or indirect and include defiance, physical and psychological withdrawal, and diversionary tactics (see figure following).

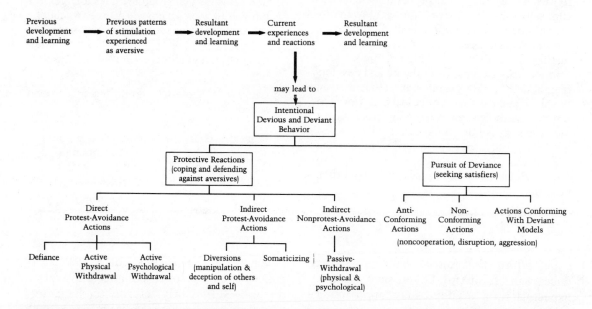

to reduce interfering behavior to a level at which the teacher and student can at least work together. The focus is then on efforts to help the student identify areas in which

vulnerability and distress won't be felt and in which she or he indicates motivation to learn.

General Implications for Instruction

Concern with intrinsic motivation shifts the focus of instruction away from a preoccupation with behavioral objectives (see Box 9–6). Skills and behaviors, however, are not ignored. A motivational focus just stresses the importance of developing *motivational readiness* and *continuing motivation* to learn and to overcome problems. In general, consideration is given to how to enhance and expand an individual's valuing and expectations of success in important areas of learning.

Concern focuses on such matters as: Does Bret perceive the environment as filled with positive opportunities for learning or as something that he is forced to endure? If it is only to be endured, does he perceive himself as being able to do so with minimal discomfort, or does he expect it to be a very painful experience? Does he have a strong attraction to do something else with his time?

Accurate answers to such questions would tell us a lot about why Bret behaves as he does and would give us some hints about what to do to help him overcome his problems. When it is clear that motivation is playing a key role in Bret's problems, formulation of motivation-oriented objectives is indicated.

But how can we know the answers to such questions? To do so, we would have to know what Bret is thinking and feeling.

With motivation as our focus, *assessment* takes on a new direction. What does Bret think and feel about his school program? What is it that Sally sees as worth learning? What other things does she see as worth considering? Why does she say she hates reading? Assessment of motivation relies heavily on a continuing series of dialogues with a student. The focus at first is on finding out what the student wants to learn at school; once the program is underway, progress and problems are discussed.

Given that these matters are assessed, *program planning* must consider each of them. Planning must also consider what

---

Box 9–6

Clinical Example
IEPs and Learning Options

Public Law 94-142 requires specifying an Individual Educational Plan (IEP) for each learning disabled student. The IEP has rapidly become a detailed prescription of content to be taught and of outcomes to be achieved. The prescription is written in the form of behavioral and criterion-referenced objectives. This way of stating objectives tends to shape program content toward overemphasizing certain skills and toward using teaching processes that stress training rather than education.

Two relatively typical examples illustrate these points:

The following is the IEP of a thirteen-year-old LD student who also is a severe behavior problem.

Clearly, these two IEP examples provide no content and outcome *options* for the learner.

Moreover, subsequent work with the youngsters showed just how poorly the objectives matched their current motivation and developmental capabilities. In the case of the first student, the overriding need was that he start to perceive school as a place that had something to offer him. He belonged to a street gang that was trying to convince him that school was a worthless experience; by following the prescription indicated by the IEP, the teacher could not convince him otherwise.

The second student demonstrated tremendous creative talent in his cartooning and his creative stories. He had aspirations for a career in this area, which were not out of line with his talent. His talent and career aspirations were completely ignored by the IEP and, indeed, the prescribed program left him no time for these important interests and strengths.

Box 9–6 continued on p. 138.

The following is the IEP of a thirteen-year-old LD student who also is a severe behavior problem.

Annual Goals	Short-term Objectives	Evaluation
Behavior: develop appropriate modes of behavior	Will employ impulse control. Will submit a paragraph of 4 alternative ways in which inappropriate behavior could have been avoided.	Observation Product assessment
Math: demonstrate basic skills in mathematics	Will multiply a 3-digit no. by a 3-digit no. regrouping as necessary. Will divide a 3-digit no. by a 1-digit no. with and without a remainder.	Observation Product assessment
Reading: increase sight word vocabulary	Will recognize sight words from various content disciplines, e.g., Dolch & Core lists. Will maintain a booklet of synonyms, antonyms, and homonyms	Observation Product assessment
Counseling: improve self-control	Will maintain self-control and comply with adult authority. Will share frustrations and feelings in counseling setting.	Observation

The following is the IEP of a sixteen-year-old LD student.

Annual Goals	Short-term Objectives	Evaluation
Math: develop consumer math skills	Will develop and learn shopping skills and learn to live within a budget. Will tell time to 1 hour with 100% accuracy.	Observation Product assessment
Behavior: develop ability to participate in small groups; develop ability to work on assignments independently	Will attend a small group for 1 class period. Will read aloud in group. Will work on teacher-assigned task independently for 15 mins., asking for help only when necessary.	Observation
Language Arts: improve oral expression; improve sight vocabulary	Will modulate voice for expression. Will use complete sentences in spontaneous speech. Will increase sight vocabulary to 600 words. Will decode unfamiliar consonant-vowel-consonant words with 85% accuracy.	Observation Product assessment
Counseling: increase sense of identity	Will identify feelings and formulate goals. Will express feelings and personal goals appropriately to others.	Observation

else a student might be likely to perceive as worthwhile learning opportunities.

Optimally, all program decisions should be made in ways that don't undermine feelings of competence, self-determination, and effectiveness and that do heighten a sense of personal choice, responsibility, and commitment (Deci, 1980). Also, professionals increasingly recognize the importance of accounting for motivational differences and problems. As a result, the implications for instruction are slowly being spelled out. Besides those mentioned already, we should note the following:

- Optimal performance and learning require motivational readiness. Readiness should not be viewed in the old sense of waiting until an individual is interested. Rather, it should be understood in the contemporary sense of offering stimulating environments that can be perceived as vivid and valued options intended to lead to successful learning and performance.

- Teachers must not only try to increase motivation but must also avoid practices that decrease motivation. For example, they must be careful not to overrely on extrinsics to entice and to reward because to do so may decrease intrinsic motivation.

- Motivation represents both a process and an outcome concern. For example, the program must be designed to maintain, enhance, and expand intrinsic motivation for pursuing both current learning activities *and* learning as a lifelong aim.

- Increasing intrinsic motivation involves affecting a student's thoughts, feelings, and decisions. In general, the intent is to use procedures that have the potential to reduce negative and increase positive feelings, thoughts, and coping strategies with regard to school learning. In particular, this means attempting to identify and minimize experiences that might maintain or increase avoidance motivation.

The point about minimizing experiences that have negative associations deserves special emphasis. Students with extremely negative perceptions of teachers and programs are not likely to be open to personnel and activities that look like "the same old thing." There have to be major changes in approach if the student is even to perceive a difference. Minimally, exceptional efforts must be made to have students (1) view the teacher as supportive (rather than controlling and indifferent) and (2) perceive content, outcome, and activity options as personally valuable and obtainable.

With these implications as background, we are now ready to explore some specific procedures for classroom programs. We begin with the basic operating premise that such programs are to stress intrinsic reasons for pursuing learning activities and overcoming problems. Also, students are to make personal and active choices from among a variety of options and evaluate how well their intrinsic objectives are being met.

Toward these ends, a program must provide for (1) a broad range of content, outcome, and procedural options, including a personalized structure to facilitate learning; (2) student decision making; and (3) ongoing information about progress.

Options. If the only decision Sally can make is between reading book A, which she hates, and reading book B, which she loathes, she is more likely to be motivated to avoid making any decision than to be pleased with the opportunity to decide for herself. Even if she chooses one of the books over the other, the motivational effects the teacher wants are unlikely to occur. Thus:

Choices have to include valued and feasible options.

Sally clearly doesn't like to work on her reading problem at school in any way. In contrast, Bret wants to improve his reading, but he just doesn't like the programmed materials the teacher has planned for him to work on each day. Chris would rather read about science than the adventure stories his teacher has assigned. Jan will try anything if someone will sit and help her with the work. Thus:

Options usually are needed for (a) content and outcomes and (b) processes and structure (see Reading F).

Every teacher knows a classroom program has to have variety. There are important differences among students with regard to the topics and procedures that currently interest and bore them. And in programs for students with learning problems, more variety seems necessary than in classes for those without learning problems.

Moreover, among those with learning problems are a greater proportion of individuals with avoidance or low motivation for learning at school. For these individuals, few currently available options may be appealing. How much greater the range of options needs to be depends primarily on how strong avoidance tendencies are. In general, however, the initial strategies for working with such students involve

- further expansion of the range of options for learning (if necessary, this includes total deemphasis of established curriculum content and processes)
- intially pursuing *only* areas in which the student has made personal and active decisions
- accommodation of a wider range of behavior than usually is tolerated (e.g., a widening of limits on the amount of deviance tolerated)

Learner decision making. From a motivational perspective, one of the most basic instructional concerns is the way in which students are involved in making decisions about options. Critically, the decision-making processes can lead to perceptions of they can affect whether a student's efforts are directed at pursuing planned learning activities and outcomes or at avoiding them (Brehm & Brehm, 1981).

People who have the opportunity to make decisions among valued and feasible options tend to be committed to following through. In contrast, people who are not involved in being coerced and controlled or to perceptions of having a real choice (being in control of one's destiny, being self-determining). Such differences in perception can have contrasting effects on motivation. Specifically, decisions often have little commitment to what is decided. And if individuals disagreed with a decision that affects them, besides not following through, they may react hostilely.

Thus, essential to programs focusing on motivation are decision-making processes that maximize perceptions of having a choice from among personally worthwhile options and that minimize perceptions of having no choice, little value, and probable failure.

Students initially make two basic sets of decisions, each of which must be modified as often as necessary. These are decisions about participation and those about specific program plans (see Reading G).

Continuous information on learning and performance. Because of the potential negative impact of too great an emphasis on extrinsic rewards and punishment, great care must be taken in developing procedures for providing students with information on their progress (see Deci, 1975, 1980). Obviously, information must be provided that highlights success. Feedback, however, also should stress effectiveness in making decisions and the relationship of outcomes to the student's intrinsic reasons for learning.

Handled well, the information should contribute to students' feelings of competence and self-determination.

Feedback can be provided during formal and informal conferences. At such times, products and work samples can be analyzed; the appropriateness of current content, outcomes, processes, and structure can be reviewed; and agreements and schedules can be evaluated and revised if necessary.

Regardless of the form in which feedback is given, the emphasis should be on information clarifying progress and effectiveness; procedures that may be perceived as efforts to entice and control should be avoided. To these ends, self-monitoring techniques and recordkeeping are seen as especially helpful; close supervision and external rewards are seen as procedures to be used sparingly (see Box 9–7).

Dialogues are the easiest and most direct way to know about learners' views of the match between themselves and the program. Many students are ready to evaluate and say what's working well for them and what isn't.

Some students, of course, have yet to develop the ability to self-evaluate to a satisfactory degree; others are motivated to make excuses, to overstate how well they are doing, or to avoid discussing the matter at all. The presence of students who have trouble with self-evaluation is not a reason to return to procedures that stress close supervision and decision making by others. Rather, the problems these students are experiencing become an important focus for intervention.

When students are not motivated to be appropriately self-evaluative and self-directive, they need opportunities to find out how personally valuable these "basic skills" can be to them. Sometimes all they need is to feel that it's safe to say what's on their minds. If they already feel safe and just

---

Box 9–7

Theory and Practice
Evaluative Feedback and Variations in Perception

Why do people arrive at different conclusions about progress and about the reasons for ongoing problems? Sometimes because they perceive events differently.

For example, social psychologists interested in the "attributions" people make about the causes of behavior have stressed that there are some systematic ways that people differ in their perceptions. Research has shown that there is a general tendency for observers to perceive the behavior of others in terms of internal dispositions or traits. "He failed the test because he's lazy (or stupid)." "She's a success because she works very hard (or because she's very smart)." Referring to the same actions, the people carrying out the behavior have a tendency to blame problems they experience on factors in the environment (e.g., poor teaching, hard tasks, bad luck) and to credit their successes to their effort or ability.

Why? Theorists suggest that sometimes it is because people are operating on the basis of different information. This is especially true when one person has information not available to the other, as is often the case for observers as contrasted to those who are actively involved in an event. For instance, when you do poorly on a test because you didn't have time to study, you may be the only one who knows the reason. Others may think it was because you didn't care to put in the time or that you have difficulty understanding the material. In this instance, the observers lack a key bit of information.

However, the different information affecting perceptions may also be due to the perceiver's level of competence and particular philosophical or political interests. That is, people often are selective in what they see because of their motivation or their capacity to understand.

In general, then, differences in evaluation of progress and problems may reflect differences in

Box 9–7 continued on p. 142.

Box 9–7 continued from p. 141.

the information that is actually available to the decision makers or differences in what information they choose to notice and stress. Understanding such factors can be helpful.

Let's take an example.

Jan wants to improve her spelling. From various options, she has chosen to learn five interesting words each day, which she will pick for herself from her experiences at school or at home. She agrees to bring a list of her five chosen words to school each day.

On the first day, Jan shows up without her list. "I lost it," she explains. The next day, still no list. "We had to go visit my grandmother—she's sick."

Naturally, Ms. Evans, her teacher, is suspicious. She knows that many students with learning problems use elaborate excuses and blame everything but themselves for their poor performance. Her first thought is: Jan is telling tales. She really doesn't want to work

on her spelling. She's lazy. Probably I should assign her spelling words.

But then she thinks: Suppose she's telling the truth. And even if she isn't, what will I accomplish by accusing her of lying and by going back to procedures that I know were unsuccessful in working with her before. I must work with what she says and try to help her see that there are other ways to cope besides saying she will do something and then giving excuses for not following through.

Ms. Evans tells Jan: "I want you to think about your program. If you don't want to work on spelling, that's O.K. Or if you want to choose another way to work on it, we can figure out a new way. I won't check up on what you do. When we meet, you can just let me know how you're doing and what help you want."

Jan seemed greatly relieved by this. The next day she told Ms. Evans that she'd decided to find her five words at school each day, and she'd like some help in doing so.

---

haven't acquired the skills, self-monitoring and regular recordkeeping provide a good framework for learning such competence.

Case Example

It was a hard decision, but Bret and his parents decided he should go to a private school to correct his learning problem. Among those they looked into was one that emphasized personalized learning. When they visited the program, they observed a variety of learning options that they were encouraged to explore.

After visiting several programs, Bret was asked which he preferred. His decision was to try the personalized program.

In early September, a meeting was arranged with his prospective teacher, Ms. Hopkins. She used this first meeting to engage Bret in a discussion of his interests, things he was good at, and what he hadn't liked about his previous school experiences. Then, she described, dem-

onstrated, and helped Bret sample as many of the available learning activities as time allowed; she, of course, highlighted those related to his interests.

Before he left that day, Bret indicated to Ms. Hopkins and his parents the specific activities he was interested in pursuing during his first week at school. The program he scheduled consisted of an enrichment class in anatomy dissection, a group focusing on chicken incubation, a guitar class, a soccer class, and participation on the school newspaper. Somewhat tentatively he also indicated a desire to improve his math skills. In all, he had scheduled activities covering 2½ hours a day. Therefore, his school day was initially scheduled to last just that long.

Because the activities did not include a reading program, Bret's parents were concerned. Ms. Hopkins explained that the main focus for now was to let Bret find that learning at school was something worth doing. "We don't want to make the mistake of just recreating the program you left; after all, it was not working for Bret."

Each day of Bret's first week, Ms. Hopkins talked with him several times. Sitting next to him, she informally continued the dialogue begun at their first meeting. Bret indicated that most of the activities were going fine, but the guitar class was not what he had thought it would be, and he was still not sure about the math. The guitar class was dropped, and the time was devoted to helping him explore other options.

As agreed at the first meeting, Bret, his parents, and Ms. Hopkins had another formal meeting at the end of the week. They discussed how the program was shaping up and other concerns. Bret and his parents were pleased with the way things had begun. He really liked the dissection class; he had replaced guitar with a drawing and oil painting class; the school newspaper was his favorite activity. Math was still not quite satisfactory; however, one of the other students who was good at math had agreed to help him. Because they were just getting started, Bret wanted a few more days to see how it would work out. If nothing else, the alliance was a good one since the other student had helped Bret enter a circle of friends quickly. Bret had also agreed to let Ms. Hopkins know anytime he was getting bored and restless so that they could find a good activity rather than letting him fall into old patterns of daydreaming or distracting others.

As the meeting was ending, the parents again expressed concern about Bret's reading. Ms. Hopkins again stressed that the first step was to help Bret experience school as a positive learning environment and that as he became involved in various learning experiences there would be plenty of opportunities to help him improve his basic skills. "For example," she pointed out, "Bret's decision to be on the school newspaper means he spends three hours a week planning what the paper will include and another three hours carrying out reporter assignments and writing up articles."

The program continued to work well over the next few weeks. New activities were added, and his school day was increased to 4½ hours. Then two problems cropped up. Bret started to arrive at school a half hour late several days a week, thereby missing most of his creative writing class. Moreover, toward the end of the day, he would begin to pick on another student, disrupting both their programs.

As soon as she noted the pattern of behavior, Ms. Hopkins arranged a special meeting with Bret. He wasn't too eager to talk about the problems. To engage him, Ms. Hopkins said: "Look, I'm not asking about these things to trap you or blame you or punish you. After all, I didn't send you to the office or call your parents, did I? I just figured something was wrong, and I thought it would be a good time to show you how you can work on solving a problem rather than suffering with it. Let me show you how we do it."

Bret was a bit surprised that the teacher wasn't "coming down on him." And he was intrigued when she went to the blackboard, wrote "Problem Solving Steps," and made three columns, headed "Problem," "Alternatives," and "Pros and Cons." "Let's look at the reasons you get here late," she said. He repeated the excuses he had given over the past few weeks—traffic jams and oversleeping. "Anything else?" she asked. Bret shrugged. Ms. Hopkins smiled: "Sometimes students come late because they don't like what's scheduled."

"Well," said Bret, "Sometimes I don't feel like doing creative writing."

They went on to look at some ways he might handle the problems he had noted—catching an earlier bus, asking his parents to help him not oversleep, spending some time to see if there were ways to make creative writing more enjoyable, and having another activity planned that he could do whenever he didn't feel like doing what was scheduled.

"Each of these ideas has some good points and bad points," Ms. Hopkins noted. "Let's list some of them." She offered a couple; Bret added some more. Then she asked: "Well, now that you've had a chance to think the problem through, do you want to try any of these ways of trying to solve it?" He chose the ideas of looking for ways to make creative writing more enjoyable and having other activities he could do when he didn't feel like doing what was scheduled.

"You did a great job on this Bret. Perhaps you can think about the other problem in the same way, and let me know in a day or two if you come up with some ideas for handling it. If you need help solving it, I'll be glad to work on it in the same way we did this one."

During the next few weeks, Ms. Hopkins used informal daily contacts to follow up with Bret. They found that one of the things that made creative writing a problem for him was the need to come up with new topics each day. They hit upon the idea of his writing a continuing story and using his drawing skills to illustrate it.

With regard to his second problem, Bret reported that he would like to stop the conflict with the other student, but he just didn't know how to do it. Because this had been noted as a long-standing problem for Bret, Ms. Hopkins took the opportunity to suggest that he might like to join a group that was working on how to deal with such problems (see Reading E).

As the year progressed, Bret's program was reviewed and revised regularly. He was given a lot of options to choose from and made a lot of decisions for himself.

By November, he was attending school full time. By midyear, his program consisted of a varied set of activities, including reading instruction. From all reports, he was enjoying school and regaining his self-confidence.

The March conference with Bret and his parents was a happy one. Bret felt he had made good progress and continued to like his program. However, he missed going to school with his neighborhood friends and expressed an eagerness to return to public school the next fall. His parents were pleased with his progress and his attitude and were anxious for him to get back to public school, too. However, they were worried that it might be too soon. Their concerns were explored, and it was agreed that Bret would plan some work that would enable everyone to see whether he was now ready to handle public school.

For the next two months, Bret pursued a regular school program. He had subjects and texts similar to those in public school; he increased his homework time and took weekly quizzes on what he studied. He wrote a special term paper to practice the skills involved in such ac-

tivity. Along with other students preparing to return to public school, he spent an hour a day learning "survival skills." These included study skills and interpersonal problem solving with teachers and other students.

Because Bret was now highly motivated to learn such skills, things that had been "learning problems" and avoided in the past were learned quickly. Moreover, it turned out he already had many skills he had seemed to lack.

SUMMARY

Facilitating the learning of basic knowledge and skills begins with an understanding of which basics are to be taught and what is involved in teaching them. In this chapter, we have emphasized that (1) the basic knowledge and skills needed by most individuals—learning disabled or not—involve more than the three Rs and cognitive development, and (2) in facilitating the learning of such basics, motivational considerations play a major role. This means LD programs must offer a broad curriculum that includes not only remedial instruction in deficit areas but also programs to enhance development and enrich daily learning.

In addition, whatever the initial cause of the learning problem, an individual with long-standing basic skill problems is likely to have negative feelings and thoughts about instruction, teachers, and schools. The feelings include anxiety, fear, frustration, and anger. The thoughts may include strong expectations of failure and vulnerability and low valuing of many learning activities. Such thoughts and feelings can result in avoidance/motivation or low motivation for learning and performing in many areas.

Low motivation leads to half-hearted effort. Avoidance motivation leads to avoidance of activities. Individuals with avoidance and low motivation often also are attracted to socially disapproved activities. Poor effort, avoidance behavior, and active pursuit of disapproved behavior usually interfere with the remediation of learning problems.

Sometimes these interfering behaviors decrease when systematic efforts are made to enhance and expand motivation. When this proves not to be the case, special remedial procedures are necessary. The objectives of such strategies have been introduced in this chapter; the processes for accomplishing these objectives are discussed in some detail in Chapters 10 and 11.

AN ENRICHMENT ACTIVITY

Make a list of what you think are essential things for a person diagnosed as learning disabled to learn.

Then assume that such a person will need to spend time remedying his or her learning problems and therefore will not have enough time to pursue all the things on your list.

Which ones would you propose to cross off?

Why did you list the ones you did, and how did you decide which ones to cross off?

SPECIAL TOPIC REFERENCES

See the references cited at the end of Chapters 10 and 11.

Chapter 10

Teaching Basic Knowledge and Skills: Process

Day after day, Bret's motivation to learn at school increased, and the range of what he wanted to learn expanded. Ms. Hopkins now could focus on facilitating his quest for learning. She always looked forward to the time when "problem" students gained enough motivation that she could really help them experience the sense of competence that comes from valued learning. For Ms. Hopkins, teaching was not simply a job, but a labor of love. She helped her students learn to read and write and to use their skills to explore the wonders of the world. She never stopped being intrigued with what made the process of teaching work—when it did.

FACILITATING THE LEARNING OF BASICS

If the learner is motivated at the start, facilitating learning involves (1) maintaining and possibly enhancing motivation and (2) helping establish ways for the learner to attain his or her goals. In general, the intent is to help the individual learn effectively, efficiently, and with a minimum of negative side effects.

Sometimes all that is needed is for someone to help clear the way of external hurdles to learning. At other times, facilitating learning requires leading, guiding, stimulating, clarifying, and supporting. Although the process involves knowing when, how, and what to teach, it also involves knowing when and how to structure the situation so that people can learn on their own (Joyce & Weil, 1980).

More specifically, the teacher can be viewed as trying to accomplish six comprehensive procedural objectives:

1. to establish and maintain an appropriate working relationship with students (e.g., trust, communication, support, overcoming emotional inhibitors, and fostering motivation),

2. to clarify the purpose of the learning activity, especially specific problems that are to be corrected,

3. to clarify the procedures to be used in facilitating learning and the reasons they can be expected to be effective,

4. to clarify any other procedures, such as evaluative measures, and why they are necessary,

5. to pursue the procedures and produce desired changes, and

6. to terminate the process appropriately.

The focus in facilitating learning is not on one procedure at a time. Teachers usually have some overall theory, model, or concept that guides them to certain procedures and away from others (see Reading H). In general, procedures and content are tightly interwoven, with procedures seen as means to an end. In this connection, it is frequently suggested that learning is best facilitated when procedures are perceived by learners as good ways to reach their goals.

Because there is no proven set of procedures and principles for facilitating learning, our emphasis is on synthesizing current ideas. For example, see Box 10–1, and review the outline in Box 8–4 for key factors relevant to facilitating learning. Also review the discussion of matching the learner's current levels of motivation and development.

With these ideas in mind, let's explore the topics of learning-environment characteristics; structure; activities, techniques, and motivated practice; and the ways in which personalization can be pursued in any classroom.

Environmental Setting

Psychologists studying the effects of settings on behavior have drawn attention to the importance of various physical and social factors in learning contexts (Altman, 1975). Examples of widely discussed factors that can have negative effects include crowding, lack of privacy, and environments that are extremely ill-equipped or poorly arranged.

There are less dramatic factors in classroom settings, however, that if ignored can have a profound negative effect on efforts to facilitate learning. For instance, Jan is rather small in stature and needs a special-sized desk and chair; Chris is left-handed, and at many times during his schooling he lacked appropriate materials to use and patterns to follow (e.g., left-handed scissors to cut with

---

Box 10–1

Theory and Practice
Factors Relevant to Facilitating Learning

Efforts to synthesize ideas for facilitating learning draw upon what is currently known about major facets of human functioning as reflected in such concepts as motivation, attention, information processing, decision making, and interpersonal dynamics. These psychological constructs encompass such topics as the role of realistic goals, choice, commitment, incentives, curiosity, strivings for competence, schedules of reinforcement, negative consequences, feedback, expectation and set, intensity and vividness, cues, stimuli covariation, life circumstances, active participation, massed vs. distributed practice, overlearning, memory and assimilated schemata, group dynamics in informal and formal settings, sense of community, task focus vs. ego-oriented communication, leadership styles, and so forth.

and examples of how to write left-handed); Bret and Sally both need a work space that cuts down on visual distractors when they are doing written tasks at their desks.

In general, key setting and context characteristics can be thought about in terms of three questions:

- What is the composition and organization of the personnel and learners?
- What is the nature and quality of the physical surroundings? (e.g., architecture, materials, furnishings, design, color, lighting, temperature control)
- How is the setting perceived? (e.g., perceptions of physical, social, intellectual, political, and moral atmosphere)

Let's look at a few brief examples of each of these.

The quality of facilitation depends on the presence of a teacher who has both competence and time. Assuming the teacher is reasonably competent, the number of students, their characteristics, and the length of time they spend with the teacher remain major concerns. In general, the greater the number of students, the more critical is the ratio of students to personnel (e.g., teacher, aides, resource specialists). This factor can become even more critical if a large percentage of the students have learning or behavior problems.

For both students with and those without problems, one-to-one instruction is sometimes necessary. And some things are learned best in the context of a group, especially when the group is selected because its characteristics can facilitate what is to be learned. Furthermore, the composition of the class shapes its dynamics and thus can profoundly affect efforts to facilitate learning. Of particular importance is the presence of positive or negative leaders and models. Working with others one likes or admires may change

the learning experience from mediocre to exceptional.

The quality of the physical surroundings also plays an important role. Think about the impact on teachers and students of being in old, run-down buildings in urban ghettos as contrasted to the newer schools found in most suburban areas. And what about the impact of being assigned to a segregated, special program within a larger school setting? Furthermore, think of the difference of having or not having a wide range of appropriate material available.

Of course, whether the environment appears good or bad to others is less important than how it appears to the learner. As we stressed in our discussion of personalization, the learner's *perception* of the setting is one of the most important determinants of whether it is experienced as facilitative.

Structure

Another way to view the setting variables is in terms of the structure they provide to facilitate learning (Adelman & Taylor, 1983; McGrath, 1972). In talking about structure, some people seem to see it as all or nothing. That is, they see a program as structured or unstructured. Moreover, there has been a tendency to equate structure simply with limit setting and control.

When a student misbehaves in a classroom setting, it is common for observers to say that the youngster needs "more structure." Sometimes the phrase used is "clearer limits and consequences," but the idea is the same. The youngster is seen as being out of control, and the need perceived by the observer is for more control.

Most teachers wish it were that easy. There comes a point when efforts to use external means to control behavior can become incompatible with developing the type of working relationship that facilitates learning. Using the term *structure* to describe extreme efforts to control behavior tends to ignore this point.

Structure involves communication, support, direction, and the type of limits or external controls that facilitate learning and performance. The point is to facilitate learning, not just control behavior.

Obviously, it is not possible to facilitate the learning of youngsters who are out of control. Equally obvious, however, is the fact that some procedures used to control behavior also interfere with efforts to facilitate learning. A teacher cannot teach a youngster who is suspended from school, and the youngster may be *less* receptive to the teacher when the suspension is ended. A youngster on medication to control behavior may be less of a behavior problem but may be so sedated that she or he does not learn any better than before the pills were prescribed.

Structure is the type of support and direction available to the learner. Such support and direction is a matter of degree. There can be little or a great amount. Furthermore, how much is offered can vary from task to task. Support and direction include clarifying information and limits (external controls).

Ideally, the type and degree of support and direction used should vary with the learners' needs at the moment. Some activities can be pursued without help and should be if the learner is to attain and maintain independence. Other tasks require considerable help if learning is to occur. Although teachers are not the only source of support and direction in classrooms, they certainly are the single most important source.

In general, figuring out the best way to provide support and direction probably is the most important problem a teacher faces in building a working relationship with a student. The problem is how to make the structure neither too controlling and dependency-producing nor too permissive. The teacher does not want to create an authoritarian atmosphere, and no teacher wants to be pushed around. Although a facilitative working relationship may not have to be positive and warm, the literature tends to support the value of these qualities. Most teachers find that a positive working relationship requires mutual respect; a warm working relationship requires mutual caring and understanding (see Box 10–2).

Activities, Techniques, and Motivated Practice

For providing support and direction to facilitate learning, the structure offered during the pursuit of learning activities is especially important. Not all the structure comes from the teacher. Some degree of structure is inherent in all planned activities.

When more structure is needed, a teacher may introduce activities, employ a variety of techniques, or both. The intent is to increase attractiveness and accessibility and decrease avoidance and distraction.

Although any experience can be a learning activity, not all activities are meant to be vehicles for learning. Some are primarily designed to provide practice to solidify and consolidate what is learned. Practice activities present a special concern because people often find them dull and prefer to avoid them.

Activities. The range of available learning and practice activities is tremendous. For teaching reading, language, and math skills alone, there are a staggering number of packaged and published materials and "programs."

Some activities can be used with a variety of content and techniques. Others (such as programmed materials) prescribe content and outcomes, incorporate a particular set of techniques, and reflect specific ideas about the nature of instruction.

Box 10–2

Theory and Practice
Structure and Working Relationships

Structure is meant to allow for active interactions between the student and the environment, and these interactions are meant to lead to a relatively stable, positive, ongoing working relationship. How positive the relationship is depends on how the learner perceives the communications, support, direction, and limit setting. Obviously, if they are perceived negatively, instead of a positive working relationship, what may evolve is a pattern of avoiding such a relationship.

There appears to be a belief among some teachers that a tight and controlling structure must prevail if students are to learn. This view is caricatured by the teacher's maxim "Don't smile until Christmas!"

Some students, especially those who are very dependent and uninterested or who misbehave, do need a great deal of support and direction initially. However, it is essential to get beyond this point as soon as possible.

As long as a student does not value the classroom, the teacher, and the activities, then the teacher is likely to believe that the student requires a great deal of direction. In general, it is recognized that the less the student is motivated, the more it is necessary to teach and control behavior, and the less successful the whole enterprise of schooling appears to be. Conversely, the more the student is motivated, the less it is necessary to teach and control, and the more likely the student will learn.

To facilitate a positive perception, it seems important to allow students to take as much responsibility as they can for identifying the type and degree of support, direction, and limits they require. In providing communication, it is important not only to keep students informed but also to interact in ways that consistently convey a sense of appropriate and genuine warmth, interest, concern, and respect. The intent is to help students "know their own minds," make their own decisions, and at the same time, feel that others like them and care about them.

To achieve these objectives, procedures must be used that allow students to take as much responsibility as they are ready for in choosing the support and direction they require. That is, there must be a wide range of alternatives available to each student with regard to support and direction. For example, some students request a great amount of direction; others prefer to work autonomously. Some like lots of help on certain tasks but want to be left alone at other times.

When a continuum of structure is made available and students are able to indicate their preferences, the total environment appears less confining. Although we see this as positive, we know that this tends to make many observers think they are seeing an *open classroom* or *open structure,* as these terms are widely understood. This is not necessarily the case. The main point of personalizing structure is to provide a great deal of support and direction for students when they need it and to avoid creating a classroom climate that is experienced by students as tight and controlling. Such an approach is seen as a great aid in establishing positive working relationships.

Because there are so many possible activities, it is necessary to try to group or categorize them (see Box 10-3). Talking of *learning* and *practice* activities suggests the usefulness of distinguishing activities in terms of their purpose. Although this approach would be straightforward and simple, it would not be descriptive enough to convey the many forms of activity and their varied sources.

Thus, thinking in terms of the breadth and type of the content options discussed already (see Reading F), classroom activities for facilitating learning may be categorized, minimally, in terms of

- *purpose* (e.g., communication, learning, practice, creative expression, exploration, recreation, entertainment)

- *form* (e.g., printed material such as texts, workbooks, and library materials; presentations and lectures; writing and performing; one-to-one and group discussions; machines, tools, instruments, and equipment, including audiovisual devices and computers; role playing; games)

- *source* (e.g., publishers, community resources, intervener-made materials)

Box 10–3

Current Practices
Activities

A number of efforts have been made to group specific types of activities into categories. Diedrich (reported in Burton, 1962) lists about one hundred eighty activities organized into eight groupings: visual, oral, listening, writing, drawing, motor, mental, and emotional. The categories seem to reflect an effort to group activities according to their purpose and form.

Darrow and Van Allen (1961) focus on activities people can do independently and offer four groups stressing purpose: searching, organizing, originating, and communicating.

Means (1968) discusses activities and techniques as methodology and organizes them into six groups on the basis of their form: group, dramatic, student-oriented, teacher-initiated, material-focused, and equipment-centered.

With specific regard to learning disabilities, Lerner (1976) groups activities primarily into areas of human development and performance. An outline of her discussion of activities provides the following categories and specific examples:

I. Activities for motor development
   A. Gross motor
      1. Walking activities (e.g., forward, backward, sideways, and variations; animal walks; cross-pattern walking; stepping stones; line and ladder walks)
      2. Floor activities (e.g., angels in the snow, crawling, obstacle crawl)
      3. Balance beam (e.g., forward, backward, sideways, and variations)
      4. Other (e.g., skateboard, stand-up, jumping jacks, hopping, bouncing, galloping steps, skipping, hopscotch, hoop games, rope skills)
   B. Body-image and body-awareness activities
      (e.g., point to body parts, robot man, Simon Says, puzzles, life-sized drawings)
   C. Fine motor
      1. Throwing and catching (e.g., objects, ball games)
      2. Eye-hand coordination (e.g., tracing, cutting, stencils, lacing, paper-and-pencil activities, paper folding)
      3. Chalkboard (e.g., dot-to-dot, geometric shapes, letters and numbers)
      4. Eye movement (e.g., ocular pursuit, visual tracking)

II. Perception
   A. Visual perception
      (e.g., pegboard, block, and bead designs; puzzles; classification; finding, matching, sorting, grouping, tracing, and reproducing shapes, letters, and numbers)
   B. Auditory perception
      1. Auditory sensitivity to sounds (e.g., listening and identifying different sounds of objects and events)
      2. Auditory attending (e.g., responding to rhythmic patterns)
      3. Discrimination of sounds (e.g., near and far, loud and soft, high and low)
      4. Awareness of phonemes or letter sounds (e.g., initial consonants, consonant blends, rhyming words)
   C. Haptic perception: tactile and kinesthetic skills
      (e.g., feeling and touching textures and shapes, perceiving temperature and weight differences)
   D. Cross-modal perception
      (e.g., perceiving and reproducing rhythms, shapes, sounds across modalities such as visual to auditory, tactile to visual, and so forth)

III. Memory
  A. General memory
    (e.g., frequent reviewing, organizing material, mnemonic strategies)
  B. Auditory memory
    (e.g., practice with simple and increasingly complex letter and number retention, following directions)
  C. Visual memory
    (e.g., practice with simple and then increasingly complex recall of objects, designs, letters, numbers, tachistoscopic presentations)
IV. Oral language
  A. Listening
    1. Auditory perception of nonlanguage sounds (see activities listed for perception)
    2. Auditory perception and discrimination of language sounds (e.g., recognition and discrimination of initial consonants, blending of phonemes, identifying rhyming sounds and syllables)
    3. Understanding words (e.g., object naming, verb meanings, object classification)
    4. Understanding sentences and other linguistic units (e.g., following simple directions, learning function words)
    5. Auditory memory (see activities listed for memory)
    6. Listening comprehension (e.g., listening for details, sequencing events, following directions, getting the main idea, making interpretations and drawing conclusions)
    7. Critical listening (e.g., recognizing absurdities, analyzing advertisements and propaganda)
  B. Speaking
    1. Building a speaking vocabulary (e.g., naming objects, supplying missing words)
    2. Producing speech sounds (e.g., exercising speech muscles and organs, feeling vibrations and observing sounds)
    3. Learning linguistic patterns (e.g., morphological generalizations

through auditory and visual presentations)
    4. Formulating sentences (e.g., practice with simple to complex sentences)
    5. Practicing oral language skills (e.g., conversations; discussions; telephoning; reports; role playing; telling jokes and riddles; questions and answers)

V. Reading
  A. "Decoding" approaches to beginning reading
    (e.g., phonics; linguistics; modified alphabet)
  B. Language-experience approach
    (e.g., building on basic language skills and personal experience)
  C. Multisensory approach
    (e.g., using procedures for teaching reading vocabulary that incorporate use of auditory, visual, kinesthetic, and tactile modalities)
  D. Individualized reading
    (e.g., reading materials chosen to match individual needs)
  E. Programmed reading instruction
    (e.g., materials designed to be self-instructional, self-pacing, self-corrective)
  F. Basal reading series
    (e.g., graded sets of readers intended to cover basic reading skills in sequence)
  G. Behavior modification approaches
    (e.g., establishing specified, observable, and measurable objectives and structuring the environment through contingency management)
  H. Technological approaches
    (e.g., computer instruction and various types of audiovisual teaching machines)
  I. "Systems" approaches
    (e.g., packaged multimedia materials including books, games, puzzles, tape cassettes, practice sheets, tests, etc.)
VI. Written language
  A. Handwriting
    (e.g., chalkboard; holding pencil correctly; tracing; dot-to-dot; tracing with cues; unlined paper; template lines)

B. Spelling
(e.g., auditory and visual perception and memory of sounds, multisensory practice, programmed spelling materials, use of dictionary including *Bad Speller's Dictionary*)

C. Written expression
(e.g., composing and dictating to others, copying, taking dictation, rewriting)

VII. Cognitive development
A. Arithmetic
(e.g., practice with basic counting and computational skills; use of materials and apparatus such as counting materials and measuring instruments; practice with matching and sorting; discriminating relationships using concepts of size, length, part-whole, serial order, time, space)

B. Reading comprehension
(e.g., noting facts and details; main idea; following sequence of events; drawing inferences; organizing ideas; applying ideas; critical evaluation)

VIII. Self-concept and emotional attitudes
(e.g., bibliotherapy; classroom group discussion; self-understanding exercises and creative materials; counseling and psychotherapy)

IX. Social perception skills
A. Body image and self-perception
(e.g., body-image motor activities cited before)

B. Sensitivity to other people
(e.g., drawing or gathering pictures of others who are expressing various emotions; analyzing body and voice communications)

C. Social situations
(e.g., use of pictures and stories to focus on understanding social situations and events; differentiating between real and make-believe; practicing comprehension of time, space, and direction)

Techniques. In developing and using activities to facilitate learning, teachers often want to make them more attractive and accessible and to minimize avoidance and distraction. This is accomplished through various techniques (Adelman & Taylor, 1983).

Techniques alter the structure provided for an activity. For example, the same activity can be pursued under different degrees of support and direction by varying the amount of cueing and prompting given to the learner. Some variations are "built in" at the time an activity is developed (such as special formatting in published materials); others are added as the activity is pursued.

From a psychological perspective, techniques are intended to enhance

- *motivation* (attitudes, commitment, approach, follow-through)

- *sensory intake* (perceptual search and detection)

- *processing and decision making* (evaluation and selection)

- *output* (practice, application, demonstration; see box 10–4)

Motivated practice. The idea of motivated learning and practice is not without its critics.

"Your points about motivation sound good. I don't doubt that students enjoy such an approach; it probably even increases attendance. *But*—that's not the way it really is in the world. People need to work even when it isn't fun, and most of the time work isn't fun. Also, if a person wants to be good at something, they need to practice it day in and day out, and that's not fun! In the end, won't all this emphasis on motivation spoil people so that they won't want to work unless it's personally relevant and interesting?"

Learning and practice activities may be enjoyable. But even if they are not, they can

Box 10–4

Theory and Practice
Categorizing Techniques

Techniques are defined as planned variations in the characteristics of a tool or the way it is applied, the immediate intent of which is to increase attraction and accessibility and decrease avoidance and distraction. Ultimately, these variations are meant to enhance one or more of such facets of human functioning as motivation, sensory intake, processing, decision making, and output. Techniques are categorized here in terms of specific objectives they are intended to achieve.

I. Techniques to enhance *motivation*
   A. *Nurturance* (including positive regard, acceptance and validation of feelings, appropriate reassurance, praise, and satisfaction)
   Specific examples:
   - eliciting and listening to problems, goals, and progress
   - statements intended to reassure clients that change is possible
   - increasing the number of interpersonal, but nonauthoritarian and nonsupervisory, interactions
   - increasing the frequency of positive feedback and positive public recognition
   - reducing criticism, especially related to performance
   - avoiding confrontations
   B. *Permission* for exploration and change (including encouragement and opportunity)
   Specific examples:
   - increasing availability of valued opportunities
   - establishing and clarifying appropriate expectations and "set"
   - modeling expression of affect (self disclosing) when relevant
   - encouraging pursuit of choices and preferences

   - reducing demand characteristics such as expanding behavioral and time limits, reducing the amount to be done
   C. *Protection* for exploration and change (including principles and guidelines—rights and rules—to establish "safe" conditions)
   Specific examples:
   - reducing exposures to negative appraisals
   - providing privacy and support for "risk taking"
   - statements intended to reassure clients when risk taking is not successful
   - reducing exposure to negative interactions with significant others through eliminating inappropriate competition and providing privacy
   - establishing nondistracting and safe work areas
   - establishing guidelines, consistency, and fairness in rule application
   - advocating rights through statements and physical action
   D. *Facilitating effectiveness* (See techniques for enhancing sensory intake, processing, decision making, and output)

II. Techniques for *sensory intake, processing, decision making,* and *output*
   A. *Meaning* (including personal valuing and association with previous experiences)
   Specific examples:
   - using stimuli of current interest and meaning
   - introducing stimuli through association with meaningful materials, such as analogies and pictorial representation of verbal concepts, stressing emotional connections
   - presenting novel stimuli
   - participating in decision making

   B. *Structure* (including amount, form, sequencing and pacing, and source of support and guidance)

Specific examples:
- presenting small amounts (discrete units) of material and/or information
- increasing vividness and distinctiveness of stimuli through physical and temporal figure-ground contrasts (patterning and sequencing), such as varying context, texture, shading, outlining, use of color
- varying levels of abstraction and complexity
- multisensory presentation
- providing models to emulate, such as demonstrations, role models
- self-selection of stimuli
- using prompts and cues, such as color coding, directional arrows, step-by-step directions
- verbally mediated "self"-direction ("stop, look, and listen")
- grouping material
- using formal coding and decoding strategies such as mnemonic devices, word analysis and synthesis
- rote use of specified study skill and decision-making sequences
- allowing responses to be idiosyncratic with regard to rate, style, amount, and quality
- reducing criteria for success
- using mechanical devices for display, processing, and production, such as projectors, tape recorders, and other audio visual media, typewriters, calculators, computers
- using person resources such as teachers, aides, parents, peers to aid in displaying, processing, and producing

C. *Active contact and use* (including amount, form, and sequencing and pacing of interaction with relevant stimuli)

Specific examples:
- immediate and frequent review
- allowing for self-pacing
- overlearning
- small increments in level of difficulty, such as in "errorless training"
- use of play, games, and other personally valued opportunities for practice
- role playing and role taking
- use of formal reference aids, such as dictionaries, multiplication charts
- use of mechanical devices and person resources to aid in interactions

D. *Feedback* (including amount, form, sequencing and pacing, and source of information/rewards)
Specific examples:
- feedback in the form of information/rewards
- immediate feedback provided related to all processes and/or outcomes or provided on a contingency basis (reinforcement schedules or need)
- peer and/or self-evaluation
- use of mechanical monitoring and scoring

III. "Technical methods." Sometimes groups of techniques are combined into comprehensive and complex sets of tools (activities/experiences/materials and techniques). Despite the fact they are complex methods, they usually are referred to simply as *techniques* as they are communicated from intervener to intervener.
Specific examples:
- kinesthetic techniques (Fernald, 1943)
- desensitization and relaxation techniques (Wolpe, 1958)
- problem-solving strategies (see Chapter 7)

NOTE: While we have attempted to conceptualize discrete categories, all the examples are not mutually exclusive.

be viewed as worthwhile and experienced as satisfying.

We do recognize that there are many things people have to do in their lives that will not be viewed and experienced in a positive way. How we all learn to put up with such circumstances is an interesting question, but one for which psychologists have yet to find a satisfactory answer. It is doubtful, however, that people have to experience the learning of basic knowledge and skills as drudgery in order to learn to tolerate boring situations.

In response to critics of motivated practice, those professionals who work with learning disabilities stress the reality that many students do not master what they have been learning because they do not pursue the necessary practice activities. Thus, at least for individuals experiencing learning problems, it seems essential to facilitate motivated practice.

One of the most powerful factors keeping a person on a task is the expectation of feeling some sense of satisfaction when the task is completed or from the activity itself. For example, task persistence often is due to the expectation that one will feel smart or competent while performing the task or at least will feel that way after the skill is mastered (Deci, 1980).

Within some limits, the stronger the sense of potential outcome satisfaction, the more likely practice will be pursued even when the practice activities are rather dull. The weaker the sense of potential outcome satisfaction, the more the practice activities themselves need to be positively motivating.

Minimally, facilitating motivated practice requires establishing a variety of task options that are potentially challenging—neither too easy nor too hard (see Box 10–5). However, as we have consistently stressed, the processes by which tasks are chosen must lead to perceptions on the part of the learner that practice activities, task outcomes, or both are worthwhile—especially for their potential as a source of personal satisfaction.

LEAST-INTERVENTION TEACHING

Highly motivated individuals tend to learn a lot more than any teacher can teach. In this sense, the form of teaching that requires the least intervention is self-teaching. Of course, asking students to learn on their own is not the function of schools. Nevertheless, it is useful, in applying the principle of least intervention needed to daily teaching processes, to conceive such processes as a range, with learner-initiated processes anchoring one end and teacher-dominated processes at the other (see figure on p. 158).

As conceived, then, the processes that involve the least intervention are those in which the learner self-selects outcomes and learns on his or her own; the greatest degree of intervention occurs when the teacher selects the outcomes and uses behavioral conditioning techniques to accomplish the desired ends. Obviously, variations in degree of intervention occur when the source and nature differ for outcome selection and instruction. For example, in most classrooms, teachers probably select most outcomes, which then are learned through teacher facilitation.

Learners greatly vary in how much teacher outcome selection and instruction they require and receive. Teachers vary considerably in their attempts to apply the principle of least intervention needed. Thus, it is to be expected that classroom programs and specific facets of such programs vary considerably in the degree to which teaching practices are restrictive, intrusive, and disruptive of natural learning processes.

PERSONALIZING CLASSROOMS

Efforts to apply the least-intervention principle to classroom teaching raise many prob-

Box 10–5

Current Practices
Motivated Learning and Practice

The following examples illustrate ways in which activities can be varied to provide for motivated learning and practice. Because you have experienced a variety of reading and writing activities throughout your schooling, the focus here is on other types of activity.

Learning and practicing by

doing

- using movement and manipulation of objects to explore a topic, e.g., using coins to learn to add and subtract
- dramatization of events, e.g., historical, current
- role playing and simulations, e.g., learning about democratic vs. autocratic government by trying different models in class; learning about contemporary life and finances by living on a budget
- actual interactions, e.g., learning about human psychology through analysis of daily behavior
- applied activities, e.g., school newspapers, film and video productions, band, sports
- actual work experience, e.g., on-the-job learning

listening

- reading to students, e.g., to enhance their valuing of literature
- audio media, e.g., tapes, records, and radio presentations of music, stories, events
- listening games and activities, e.g., Simon Says; imitating rhymes, rhythms, and animal sounds
- analyzing actual oral material, e.g., learning to detect details and ideas in advertisements

or propaganda presented on radio or television; learning to identify feelings and motives underlying statements of others

looking

- directly observing experts, role models, and demonstrations
- visual media
- visual games and activities, e.g., puzzles, reproducing designs, map activities
- analyzing actual visual material, e.g., learning to find and identify ideas observed in daily events

asking

- information gathering, e.g., investigative reporting, interviewing, and opinion sampling at school and in the community
- brainstorming answers to current problems and puzzling questions
- inquiry learning, e.g., learning social studies and science by identifying puzzling questions, formulating hypotheses, gathering and interpreting information, generalizing answers, and raising new questions
- question-and-answer games and activities, e.g., twenty questions, provocative and confrontational questions
- questioning everyday events, e.g., learning psychology by asking about what people value and why

These activities can be pursued in one-to-one or group interactions. From a motivational perspective, friends often work particularly well together on projects. Friends with common interests can provide positive models and support that can enhance productivity and even creativity.

lems. This is especially the case when classes contain large numbers of students, when many of the students have learning and behavior problems, and when resources are inadequate. It would be foolish to suggest that such circumstances do not make the task of the teacher seem impossible at times.

In recent years, the term *burn out* has

NATURE AND SOURCE OF INTERVENTION

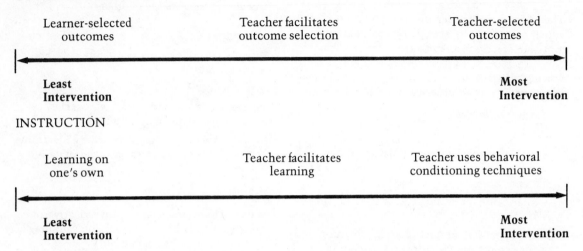

OUTCOME SELECTION

| Learner-selected outcomes | Teacher facilitates outcome selection | Teacher-selected outcomes |

Least Intervention ← → **Most Intervention**

INSTRUCTION

| Learning on one's own | Teacher facilitates learning | Teacher uses behavioral conditioning techniques |

Least Intervention ← → **Most Intervention**

been used to describe the exhaustion and discouragement teachers often experience when confronted with students who do not seem to want to learn. Obviously, the situation could be improved by reducing teacher-student ratios and increasing availability of appropriate resources. Unfortunately, progress in this regard is likely to be somewhat slow and limited.

The concept of personalization provides a key to ways to facilitate learning with increased effectiveness under less than optimal conditions. Such increased effectiveness can reduce burn out. Personalizing a classroom program is not easy, and it is not without its problems. But personalization is no harder than many other current approaches and has the potential to be a lot more satisfying for teachers and students at both the elementary and the secondary level (Adelman & Taylor, 1983).

What does it take to personalize a classroom? First of all, the teacher must expect and value individual differences in students' motivation and development. The teacher also must be willing to offer available resources as options and help students make decisions among these learning alternatives.

The emphasis in such decision making must be on encouraging students to pursue what they perceive as a good match in terms of learning activities and structure. And as new information about what is and isn't a good match becomes available, there must be a willingness to revise decisions.

When a teacher is highly motivated to personalize a classroom program, both the students and the teacher have to become accustomed to the special elements of the approach. Thus, it is usually necessary to move toward personalization through a series of transition steps (see Box 10–6). In general, this means developing an appropriate variety of learning options to offer as a starting point, facilitating student understanding of what the new approach involves, and establishing procedures so that most students can work independently while the teacher pursues one-to-one and small-group interactions.

All of this, of course, assumes that schools and teachers are ready to change. Some are; some aren't. The transition toward personalization may have to begin with major policy and organizational changes (see Box 10–7).

Box 10–6

For Example
**Transition Steps Toward
Personalizing Classrooms**

I. Preparing the class
   A. An enthusiastic explanation to the class of the why, what, when, and how of the intended changes (e.g., with the emphasis on the special personal opportunity of the new approach for them)
   B. Identifying available options and increasing the variety to reflect the range of interests and capabilities usually present in the class
   C. Teaching students to be relatively self-sufficient at times and to ask others for help when necessary (e.g., a range of independent activities are introduced and students are shown how to use them, how to transition to other tasks on their own, and how to use aides, peers, and volunteers for support and direction when the teacher is working with others)
   D. Recruitment of aides, peers, and volunteers and teaching them how to provide help that may be needed by class members when the teacher is occupied with others
   E. Making trial runs to evaluate if students, aides, etc., can function effectively while the teacher holds individual conferences; continuation of development of self-sufficiency and trial runs until class is minimally effective in this regard
   F. Giving demonstrations and opportunities to sample learning options
   G. First conferences focusing on discussion of each student's interests and strengths, available options, other options each would like to have available, and amount of structure the individual views as needed; first conferences should be oriented particularly to building a sense of valuing the opportunity to interact with the teacher in making program decisions
   H. Over the first weeks, focusing also on working with students, aides, and volunteers to develop additional learning options in keeping with students' specific requests
II. Additional conditions to facilitate individual conferences and small-group and one-to-one facilitation of learning
   A. Establishment of a quiet area where others will not interfere or be distracted
   B. Scheduling of such sessions when other students are involved in independent activities or there is sufficient help available
   C. Establishment of recordkeeping and information procedures for use by both student and teacher (e.g., objective checklists, records from last conference, products, work samples, tests materials, etc.)
III. Ending the transition phase
   A. Establishment of working agreements with each student regarding learning plans (e.g., intended outcomes, procedures, and products, needed support and direction)
   B. Establishment of procedures for regular individual conferences with students to improve, evolve, and expand the quality of the learning activities
   C. Establishment of procedures for implementing remediation if necessary

SUMMARY

Regardless of which basics are stressed, the process of facilitating learning can be understood by analyzing key elements in learning situations. Of particular relevance are the ways in which learning environments, structure in learning situations, and instructional methods can be varied to provide an appropriate match with the learner's current level of motivation and development. The concept of personalization provides one model

Box 10–7

Theory and Practice
Organizational Change

The major prerequisite to correcting many learning problems in public schools is to change the way schools are run.

As unhappy as people in and out of schools seem to be with the organization of school programs, major changes aren't very frequent. Change, of course, always is easier to advocate than accomplish. For a variety of reasons, systems tend to resist change. Therefore, it is helpful to know a bit about the factors that seem to overcome such resistance.

According to the organizational literature, creation of an appropriate climate for policy and organizational change appears to require at least the following:

• appropriate incentives for change (e.g., intrinsically valued outcomes, expectations of success, recognitions, rewards)

• procedural options so that those who are ex-

pected to implement the changes can select one that they see as workable

• establishment of mechanisms to facilitate the efforts of those who have responsibility for installing changes (e.g., participatory decision making, special training, resources, rewards, procedures designed to improve organizational health)

• agents of change who are perceived as pragmatic rather than as idealistic

• not trying to accomplish too much, too fast (e.g., facilitating readiness, planned transition or phasing in of changes)

• appropriate feedback regarding progress of change activity

• ongoing support mechanisms to maintain changes as long as they remain appropriate

Some of these points may seem familiar. At least, they should. They are similar to points we have stressed in connection with the concepts of facilitating learning and personalization.

for facilitating learning in any classroom and provides an important foundation for the type of remedial activity that we are now ready to explore in some detail.

AN ENRICHMENT ACTIVITY

Interview some friends about music lessons.

Find out how many were forced to take instrumental music lessons as children.

How many learned to play well?

How many came to dislike the lessons and the practicing and dropped out as soon as they could?

How many professional musicians do you think had to be regularly forced to practice?

SPECIAL TOPIC REFERENCES

Should you be interested in further information about procedures that might be useful with students with low or *avoidance motivation*, see the following readings.

BIXBY, L. W. (1977). *The excitement of learning, the boredom of education.* Roslyn Heights, N.Y.: Libra Publishers.

BORTON, T. (1970). *Reach, touch, and teach.* New York: McGraw-Hill.

DE CHARMS, R. (1976). *Enhancing motivation.* New York: Irvington Publishers.

DREW, W. F., OLDS, A. R., & OLDS, H. F. (1974). *Motivating today's students.* Palo Alto, Calif.: Learning Handbooks.

FADER, D. (1975). *The new hooked on books.* Berkley, Calif.: Berkley Publishing Co.

GREER, J. G., SCHWARTZBERG, I. M., & LAYCOCK, V. K. (1977). *Motivating learners with instructional games.* Dubuque, Iowa: Kendall/Hunt Publishers.

MARTIN, R. J. (1980). *Teaching through encouragement.* Englewood Cliffs, N.J.: Prentice-Hall.

WLODKOWSKI, R. J. (1978). *Motivation and teaching: A practical guide.* Washington, D.C.: National Educational Association.

Should you be interested in further information about *facilitating learning*, see the following readings.

ASHTON-WARNER, S. (1963). *Teacher.* New York: Simon and Schuster.

BEECHHOLD, H. F. (1971). *The creative classroom.* New York: Scribner's Sons.

DREIKERS, R., GRUNWALD, B. B., & PEPPER, F. C. (1982). *Maintaining sanity in the classroom,* 2nd ed. New York: Harper & Row.

FISK, L., & LINDGREN, H. C. (1974). *Learning centers.* Ridge, N.J.: Exceptional Press.

FOSTER, J. (1972). *Discovery learning in the primary school.* London and Boston: Routledge & Kegan Paul.

JOHNSTON, H., HALEY-JAMES, S., BARNES, B., & COLTON, T. (1978). *The learning center handbook: Activities for the elementary and middle grades.* Boston: Allyn & Bacon.

MAMCHAK, P. S., & MAMCHAK, S. R. (1977). *Handbook of discovery techniques in elementary school teaching.* West Nyack, N.Y.: Parker Publishing.

MOFFIT, J., & WAGNER, B. J. (1976). *Student-centered language arts and reading, k–13: A handbook for teachers,* 2nd ed. Boston: Houghton-Mifflin.

MUESER, A. M., RUSSELL, D. H., & KARP, E. E. (1981). *Reading aids through the grades: A guide to materials and 501 activities for individualized reading instruction,* 4th ed. New York: Teachers College Press.

VOIGHT, R. C. (1971). *Invitation to learning: The learning center handbook.* Washington, D.C.: Acropolis Books.

YOUNG, R. M., & SAVAGE, H. H. (1982). *Better learning.* Englewood Cliffs, N.J.: Prentice-Hall.

And then there is the *microcomputer.*

The use of microcomputers to facilitate the learning of persons with learning disabilities has been increasing at an amazing rate. Interested readers should see the following works.

BENNETT, R. E. (1982). Applications of microcomputer technology to special education. *Exceptional Children, 49,* 106–113.

BUDOFF, M., THORMAN, J., & GRAS, A. (1984). *Microcomputers in special education.* Cambridge, Mass.: Brookline Books.

GREENFIELD, P. M. (1984). *Mind and media: The effects of television, videogames, and computers.* Cambridge, Mass.: Harvard University Press.

HUMMEL, J. W., & FARR, S. D. (1985). Options for creating and modifying CAI software for the handicapped. *Journal of Learning Disabilities, 18,* 166–188.

LEPPER, M. R., & MALONE, T. W. (in press). Intrinsic motivation and instructional effectiveness in computer-based education. In R. E. Snow & M. J. Farr (Eds.), *Aptitude, learning, and instruction: III. Conative and affective process analyses.* Hillsdale, N.J.: Erlbaum Associates.

SALEND, S. J., & SALEND, S. M. (1985). Implications of using microcomputers in classroom testing. *Journal of Learning Disabilities, 18,* 51–53.

In addition:

The *Journal of Learning Disabilities* carries a "Computers in the Schools" section in each issue which usually consists of one to two discursive articles and several reviews of available software (referred to as "courseware" in this journal).

The *Learning Disability Quarterly* also offers a comprehensive review of a major software package in each issue.

Chapter *11*

Remediation

Remediation is an extension of normative efforts to facilitate learning. Thus, before a remedial focus is introduced, the best available nonremedial instruction should have been tried. Optimally, this means trying procedures to improve the match between the program and a learner's current motivation and development. A significant number of learning problems may be corrected and others prevented by introducing optimal nonremedial instruction before remediation is considered.

There does come a time, however, when remediation is necessary for some individuals. In this chapter, we outline the criteria for deciding who needs it, the general features of remediation, and the focus and form of remedial methods.

WHEN IS IT NEEDED?

Stated simply, an individual needs remediation when the best nonremedial procedures are found to be ineffective. As we have suggested, remediation is used for motivation problems and for those who have difficulty learning or retaining what they have learned (see Box 11–1).

Because remediation in all areas usually is unnecessary, as much learning as possible will probably continue to be facilitated with nonremedial approaches. Besides facilitating learning, such procedures provide an essential foundation and context for any remedial strategy, especially if they are valued by the learner.

WHAT MAKES REMEDIATION DIFFERENT FROM REGULAR TEACHING?

Techniques and materials designated as remedial often appear to be very different from regular teaching practices. However, the differences often are not as great as appearance

Box 11–1

Research and Practice
Criteria for Implementing Remediation

To determine who needs remediation, a variety of sequential criteria and assessment procedures have been evolved.

In one type of experimental approach, efforts are made, first, to be certain that a sound personalized program has been developed. This is viewed as essential for differentiating between motivational problems and learning disabilities. For up to several months, an individual's program may be designed around areas of expressed interest. For example, if a student is not motivationally ready to risk pursuing basic skill areas such as reading or math, consideration is given to accommodating this motivational preference initially. The rationale for doing so is to minimize poor performance due to low or avoidance motivation.

For children and adolescents, the first criterion indicating the need for remediation is the student's decision not to select and actively pursue *any* area of learning at school. Students who do not make an immediate choice are encouraged to explore options and to experience the personalized program for one to two weeks before the criterion is applied. When the student opts not to get involved in any learning activity after two weeks, the preliminary assumption is that a severe and pervasive motivation problem is present. (The remedial steps for this group are discussed in Chapter 9.)

Students who don't meet this criterion are assumed to be functioning under reasonably optimal conditions, motivationally and developmentally, with regard to the areas of learning they have chosen. Thus, assessment is made of the amount of learning pursued and of retention. In this connection, criterion-referenced and rating procedures are used to identify learning problems in each area where the student has made an effort to learn.

More specifically, records are kept of skills and content learned, and periodically, at least weekly, the student is asked to demonstrate retention. In addition, both the student and teacher are asked to rate whether the amount learned was adequate with reference to agreed-upon objectives.

It is, of course, difficult to know what standard should be applied in judging when the amount learned and retained is adequate. With the standards currently used in this approach, learning or retention that falls below 75 percent in an area where the student is motivated to learn represents a remedial problem. To allow for common fluctuations, however, remediation is not implemented unless the student's performance falls below this standard for at least two weeks. As a further precaution against misidentification, daily performances (e.g., work samples) are analyzed to determine whether a retention problem occurs in situations other than test and formal review sessions.

Of course, a student may learn and perform well only in a few self-selected areas and show little interest in major areas of a school's curriculum. Thus, after the youngster is functioning appropriately (with or without remedial help) in areas of interest, an assessment must be made of whether the breadth of interest is expanding adequately. The appropriate standard for judgment here is even harder to agree on than for amount and retention of learning. In this regard, public schools obviously want students following the regular curriculum, especially for the basic skills. However, individuals overcoming learning and motivational problems may have renewed difficulty if they are expected to return to such a curriculum too rapidly.

suggests. Some remedial practices are simply adaptations of regular procedures. This is even the case with some packaged programs and materials specially developed for problem populations. In general, regular and remedial procedures are based on the same instructional principles.

Because all teaching procedures are based

on the same principles, the question is frequently asked: "What's so special about special education?" The answer to this question involves understanding (1) the factors that do differentiate remedial from regular teaching and (2) the special task of special education.

What *do* differentiate remedial from regular teaching are the following six factors:

Sequence of application. Remedial practices are pursued after the best available nonremedial practices have been found inadequate.

Teacher competence and time. Probably the most important feature differentiating remedial from regular practices is the need for a competent teacher who has time to provide one-to-one instruction. While special training does not necessarily guarantee such competence, remediation usually is done by teachers who have special training. Establishing an appropriate match for learners with problems is difficult. Indeed, a great deal of this process remains essentially a matter of trial and appraisal. Thus, there must be additional time to develop an understanding of the learner (e.g., strengths, weaknesses, limitations, likes, dislikes). There also must be access to and control over a wide range of learning options.

Outcomes and content. Along with basic skills and knowledge, other content and outcome objectives usually are added. These are aimed at overcoming missing prerequisites, faulty learning mechanisms, or interfering behaviors and attitudes.

Processes. Although instructional principles underlying remedial and nonremedial procedures do not differ, remediation usually stresses an extreme application of the principles. Such applications may include reductions in levels of abstraction, intensification of the way stimuli are presented and acted

upon, and increases in the amount and consistency of direction and support—including added reliance on other resources. Although such processes do not have to be carried out in special settings (e.g., outside regular classrooms), they often are.

Resource costs. Because of the type of factors already cited, remediation is more costly than regular practices with regard to time, personnel, materiel, and space.

Psychological impact. The features of remediation already mentioned are highly visible to students, teachers, and others. Chances are they are perceived, at least in part, as stigmatizing. That is, they are seen as "different" in a negative sense. As a result, the psychological impact of remediation is likely to have a negative component. The psychologically sensitive nature of remediation is another reason it should be implemented only when necessary. This feature also underscores the need for ways that can result in the learner perceiving remediation as a special and *positive* opportunity (see Reading I).

In addition to the factors that differentiate remedial from regular teaching, special educators have a special task to perform in education and schooling. That is, while all educators share the same basic concerns about educating the populace, special educators are asked to take on an additional concern. Their responsibility is to clarify whether general answers to educational matters are adequate for everyone and, if not, how the answers should be modified to account for specific subgroups of learners (Adelman, 1972). Moreover, special educators often find themselves working in areas of concern where no answers have been offered. Until much more is known about how to meet the needs of those who are not well served by regular classroom programs, there will certainly remain a role for remedial teaching and special education.

CONTENT FOCUS OF REMEDIATION

Because the focus of the LD field is on problematic conditions of persons, the outcomes sought are usually identified as problems in specific areas of functioning. The following problem (or content) areas are major remedial concerns. Some prominent names associated with each of these areas were highlighted in Chapter 2. Over the years, there have been major controversies about strategies proposed for dealing with the various problems listed here. Readings discussing remedial programs for problems in each area are presented at the end of the chapter.

Perceptual-Motor Problems

Some of the most prominent programs in the field during the 1940s and 1950s focused on perceptual-motor problems. Indeed, as noted in Parts 1 and 2, until recently, the evolution of the field has been dominated by such interventions and by those persons associated with them. The general content focus has been on

- motor skills and patterns
- perception, i.e., ability to recognize and interpret sensory stimuli
- perceptual-motor integration, i.e., organization and coordination of sensory stimuli with motor activity and use of motor activity to monitor and correct perceptions
- relationship of motor and perceptual development to more complex cognitive development

Note:
Perceptual problems differ from sensory acuity problems, e.g., a person may have 20/20 vision and thus be able to receive visual stimuli well but still have trouble interpreting what is seen.

In response to concerns about perceptual-motor functioning, remedial activity has been directed at improving

- laterality and directionality
- body image and differentiation
- balance and posture
- locomotion
- gross and fine motor coordination
- ocular control
- figure-ground perception
- constancy of shape
- position in space
- spatial relationships
- perceptual-motor coordination
- auditory and visual integration
- tactile and kinesthetic integration
- multisensory integration
- rhythm
- agility
- strength, endurance, flexibility
- catching and throwing

In addition to the psychoeducational focus on perceptual-motor problems, there has been a focus on such matters as eye movement and physiological functioning, e.g., ocular training and prescription of stimulant drugs, on the part of other professional groups involved in offering treatments in this area.

Language and Psycholinguistic Problems

The 1940s and 1950s also saw a group of prominent programs and pioneers in the field stressing language remediation. The general content focus since then has been on

- listening skills
- speaking skills
- reading skills
- writing skills

- spelling skills
- grammar
- usage (written expression)
- processing abilities underlying language

In response to concerns about language and psycholinguistic functioning, remedial activity has been directed at improving

- basic skills in each of the content focus areas; e.g., for reading, the focus might be on sound-symbol associations, word recognition, phonics and structural analysis, and comprehension
- underlying abilities in each of the content focus areas; e.g., for psycholinguistics, the focus has been on such factors as auditory and visual reception, association, closure, and sequential memory

As linguists and psycholinguists improve our understanding of language and communication, the areas of focus for remediation are expanding.

Math Problems

Only recently have comprehensive efforts been made to relate remedial math, although long a concern, to the LD field. Prominent examples are the work of Jack Cawley and his colleagues and Englemann and Carnine (see special topic references at the end of the chapter). The general content focus has been on

- computational skills
- conceptual processes associated with quantitative relationships

In response to concerns about math performance, remedial activity has been directed at improving functioning related to

- shape and size discrimination

- sets and numbers
- one-to-one correspondence
- counting
- place value
- computational aids
- graphs, charts, maps
- measurement
- money and time concepts
- word problems
- algorithms
- algebraic addition
- geometric relationships
- descriptive statistics

Remediation to improve math skills also often focuses on prerequisite skills, underlying abilities, and compensatory tools related to perceptual-motor development, language, cognition, and motivation.

Cognitive Prerequisite Problems

Concern about cognitive prerequisites has expanded greatly in recent years with the re-emergence of cognitive psychology. The work of Piaget, Bruner, and many others has contributed greatly to efforts to understand what factors may be worthy of remedial concern. The general content focus has been on

- attentional skills, i.e., short-term and sustained voluntary attention
- memory, i.e., organization (coding), storage (retention), and retrieval of information
- conceptual skills, i.e., cognitive structuring of perceived stimuli and operations to order, sequence, classify, etc.

In response to concerns about deficiencies in cognitive prerequisites, remedial activity has been directed at improving

- attention to tasks
- following directions
- rote memory
- short-term or immediate memory
- serial or sequential memory
- long-term memory
- spatial or temporal sequential ordering
- classification to understand relationships

In addition, prerequisites for cognitive development, such as motivation and perceptual, motor, and language development are relevant.

Maria Montessori was an early advocate of focusing specifically on facilitating development of cognitive prerequisites. Her ideas are reflected in many remedial programs for all the basic skills. One example is her emphasis in teaching arithmetic and science on the use of concrete materials that represent abstract principles.

With the increasing interest in attentional and memory problems, these areas are becoming a major focus of remediation. Efforts to improve attention and memory usually stress ways to improve efficiency in using basic abilities. The objectives are learning specific skills and strategies and learning to compensate for any impairment in basic ability.

Learning Strategies and Reasoning Problems

Along with the trend toward viewing learning disabilities as the result of inefficient learning has been an increasing emphasis on the notion that poor learners have deficiencies in general learning strategies and reasoning skills. These students are seen as needing to learn to (1) think about how to learn and (2) use what they have learned. The general content focus is on

- pacing and timing skills

- thinking and questioning skills
- organizing and structuring skills
- problem-solving skills

In response to concerns about deficiencies in learning strategies and reasoning skills, remedial activity has been directed at improving

- study strategies
- strategies for describing and judging phenomena
- strategies for grouping and classifying phenomena
- hypothesis testing
- problem analysis
- self-monitoring and evaluating
- strategies for generating alternatives
- strategies for evaluating options
- strategics for differentiating and generalizing
- use of visual and verbal imagery

Alley and Deshler and their colleagues (see references at end of chapter) have done a great deal to bring the attention of the LD field to this area. They stress that the objective is to teach any strategy that can help the individual acquire, organize, store, retrieve, and use information. Their work suggests that such remediation is most appropriate for those who are of at least average intelligence, who are reading at a third-grade level or better, and who can deal with abstract as well as concrete tasks.

Social and Emotional Problems

Social and emotional problems were an early concern to those dealing with learning problems. As the LD field focused more intently on perceptual-motor and language problems, social and emotional problems were pushed into the background. Currently, there is a reemergence of interest in the relationship of such problems to learning disabilities and in their remediation. The general content focus has been on

- interpersonal functioning, e.g., social perception
- intrapersonal functioning, e.g., self-concept

In response to concerns about social and emotional functioning, remedial activity has been directed at improving

- awareness of self
- awareness of others
- mastery of interpersonal skills
- empathy
- choice and decision making
- coping
- assertion
- intrapersonal and interpersonal problem solving

Remedial ideas dealing with social and emotional problems draw on the literature that deals with psychological phenomena such as self-concept, anxiety, dependency, aggression and withdrawal, social perception, interpersonal relationships, and moral development. Particularly influential has been the vast literature on psychotherapy and behavior change.

Motivational Problems

Although motivation has always been a concern to those who work with learning disabilities, the stress usually has been on how to use extrinsics to mobilize the learner and maintain interest. A recent emphasis has been on the relationship of learning problems to deficiencies in intrinsic motivation. The general content focus has been on

- increasing feelings of self-determination
- increasing feelings of competence and expectations of success
- increasing the range of interests and satisfactions related to learning

In response to concerns about deficiencies in intrinsic motivation, remedial activity has been directed at improving

- awareness of personal motives and true capabilities
- learning to set valued and appropriate goals
- learning to value and to make appropriate and satisfying choices
- learning to value and accept responsibility for choice

Current work in psychology has brought renewed attention to motivation as a central concept in understanding learning and learning problems. This work is just beginning to find its way into applied fields and programs for those with learning and related problems.

Interfering Behaviors

Throughout the 1950s and 1960s, it became evident that remediation, especially in classroom contexts, often was delayed because so many individuals with learning problems also manifested behavior problems. Such individuals were frequently described not only as learning disabled but also as hyperactive, distractable, impulsive, behavior disordered, and so forth. Their behavior patterns were seen as interfering with efforts to remedy their learning problems, and thus, it was concluded that such interfering behaviors would have to be eliminated or minimized in order to pursue remediation. The general content focus in this connection has been on any actions of an individual that compete with the intended focus of remediation.

Besides trying to reduce the frequency of deviant and disruptive actions directly, programs have been designed to alter such behavior by improving

- impulse control
- selective attention
- sustained attention and follow-through
- perseverance
- frustration tolerance
- social awareness and skills

Variations in focus have been the result of how interfering behaviors have been viewed. Some professionals have seen the problem as a skill deficiency and have tried to improve the situation through instruction. Others see the problem as a matter of control and have addressed it through the use of control techniques. For those children diagnosed as hyperactive or as having attentional deficit disorders with hyperactivity, a number of controversial nonpsychoeducational interventions also have been advocated, e.g., use of stimulant drugs and special diets to avoid chemical additives in food.

REMEDIAL METHODS

Discussions of remedial procedures often begin with concerns about remedial classroom settings. "Isn't it harmful to segregate a student in a special classroom?" "Shouldn't everyone be kept in the mainstream of education?"

Whether remedial approaches should be administered in special or in regular classrooms is a secondary consideration and one that, for now, is best decided in practical terms. The primary consideration is to provide students with a teacher who has the competence, time, and resources to facilitate learning appropriately. If such conditions are available in regular classrooms, it is always preferable not to segregate students just because they need remedial help.

Some special remedial methods are based on specific theoretical formulations about the nature of an individual's learning problem. For example, procedures emphasizing stimulus bombardment, stimulus simplification, modality isolation, or multisensory integration have been designed for particular types of problems. What is usually referred to as "theories" of remediation in the LD field are the rationales, orientations, and models used in developing remedial strategies. In general, such theories reflect views about faulty learning mechanisms and stress ways to improve sensory intake, processing and decision making, and output (review Box 10–4).

Advocates of most remedial procedures argue that their approach is needed to deal with some factor within the learner that is interfering with learning. The factor may be seen as an underlying processing deficit, a motivational or emotional problem, a developmental delay in selective attention, inefficient use of learning strategies causing poor retention, and so forth.

Furthermore, advocates of all remedial methods argue that their approach cannot be expected to be effective unless it is applied appropriately, e.g., with regularity and consistency.

When a procedure is applied and an individual improves, advocates of the approach, of course, believe that the progress validates the procedure. They also tend to believe the approach has corrected the underlying problem and see this as supporting their assumption about what caused the learning problem.

In contrast, when a procedure is applied and the individual doesn't improve very much, advocates of the approach tend to suggest that either it wasn't applied properly or that a different underlying factor must have been causing the problem. Those who favor competing ideas and methods, of course, see the procedure's lack of effectiveness as evidence that it and its underlying rationale are both invalid.

Generally ignored in the skirmishes is the fact that when an approach appears to be effective in any particular instance, there is no way to be very confident about why. For one thing, adequate research usually will not have been conducted, and therefore, events other than the approach may well have been responsible for the outcomes. Even when satisfactory evaluative research has been carried out, there inevitably are other competing explanations for the procedure's effectiveness that will not have been adequately explored.

For instance, analysis of most remedial methods suggests that they not only have the potential to influence the factor they were designed to affect (e.g., processing deficits, selective attention) but also have the potential to enhance motivation and to facilitate performance. Thus, before the approach can be credited with correcting any assumed underlying factor, these other factors must be ruled out.

As a specific example, in Box 11–2 and in Reading J, we describe and analyze an approach that we use regularly with some youngsters and that has a long-standing and well-deserved positive reputation. The approach is often referred to as the Fernald Method or Technique, the multisensory approach, the VAKT (visual-auditory-kinesthetic-tactile) technique, or simply the kinesthetic or tracing method (Fernald, 1943).

The example illustrates that techniques and materials designated as remedial often have much in common with regular teaching practices. In fact, all special remedial procedures can be reanalyzed in terms of how they affect motivation, attention, and performance. Thus, regardless of the problem for which a remedial practice has been developed, it may prove to be a useful aid for a variety of problems. For instance, a procedure developed for use in perceptual-motor training can be a novel and effective procedure for improving skills in listening and in following directions.

By reanalyzing procedures in terms of general instructional principles, the variety of alternatives available for remediation can be greatly increased. There are, of course, a great range of remedial procedures available on the market and discussed in the literature. Most can be readily adapted and many more procedures can be created by anyone who understands what is involved in facilitating learning. A great deal of remedial instruction can be accomplished using only paper and pencil and commonly available objects.

Essentially, all remedial activity is intended to correct a problem, compensate for a problem, or both. There is considerable debate as to what is correctable, what needs to be compensated for, and what compensatory strategies are appropriate and effective. At this point, the pragmatic position suggests that if direct approaches do not appear to remedy the problem, compensatory approaches should be tried. There are two ways to help a learner compensate for a deficit. The teacher can change the demands to accommodate the learner's handicap, or the learner can be taught a strategy to be self-initiated whenever it is needed, or both approaches can be employed.

LEVELS OF REMEDIATION

Specialized psychoeducational procedures to facilitate learning in developmental areas can be applied at any of three levels (as outlined in Chapter 8):

1. Level A—basic knowledge, skills, and interests involved in current life tasks
2. Level B—learned prerequisites needed to function at Level A
3. Level C—factors interfering with learning

Box 11–2

Concern in the Field
Remedial Methods

Grace Fernald viewed many reading and language problems as due to the fact that the methods used in public schools were not adapted to the needs of certain individuals (Fernald, 1943; also see Reading J). In particular, she saw some individuals as "thinking" in auditory or kinesthetic terms. In some cases, she assumed this may have been due to brain dysfunctioning. However, unless the ability to learn was completely disrupted, she believed that the only thing interfering with the individual's progress was the failure of instructional methods to account for the way the individual learned best. She also recognized that learning problems almost inevitably produced emotional problems.

Because the prevailing procedures used in schools stressed auditory and visual modalities, Fernald argued that an approach that also emphasized kinesthetic and tactile modalities would benefit those who learned best through such senses. She developed a series of technical steps and stages, incorporating multisensory learning, to help individuals learn and practice skills related to basic school subjects.

At the same time, Fernald stressed that all techniques (including the kinesthetic approach) should be applied within the context of intrinsically valued learning activities. She was concerned that the activities be ones that could be done successfully and would not add to emotional upset. The major emphasis she placed on such matters unfortunately has been widely ignored by those who have adopted the kinesthetic technique. What Fernald was advocating was an overall methodological stance toward teaching and learning as well as some specific techniques to help when individuals had special difficulty. She underscored the importance of changing the fixed and emotionally disruptive way in which children tend to be taught in schools.

Take for example, what she said about written language problems:

". . . many children fail to learn to spell because the methods used by the schools actually prevent them from doing so. These children are forced to write over and over again words they do not know, until bad habits are fixed. The child knows he is not writing [the] words correctly and is emotionally upset on this account. When he gets back . . . written work with misspelled words marked in red and with disparaging remarks concerning [the] attempts to write, the negative attitude becomes established as part of the total problem. As a matter of fact, it is much more important that a child should love to write than that he should write in perfect form. To teach spelling in such a way that the development of form takes the joy and life out of writing is a futile process." (p. 13)

Over the years, the kinesthetic techniques described by Fernald for remedying reading problems have been tried by many teachers around the world. Not surprisingly, specific research findings have been inconclusive. But for the most part, those who use the steps say they are very effective for many students.

Ironically, at the clinic school that Fernald founded, kinesthetic techniques are used more sparingly than in other settings where Fernald Techniques are advocated. Moreover, sometimes we use such techniques, as indeed Fernald did, for their value in enhancing motivation, attention, and performance rather than with any thought that the youngster is a "kinesthetic thinker." That is, the novelty and the high degree of support and direction provided by the specific steps that a learner follows are seen as useful for individuals with a variety of learning problems.

More important, however, is the fact that whenever we use techniques advocated by Fernald or anyone else, we do so in the context of activities that emphasize intrinsically worthwhile learning. This has always been an essential ingredient of the "Fernald Method," and it may be one of the most important features of any remedial method. Unfortunately, research on the effectiveness of remedial methods has tended to ignore this point.

Basic knowledge, skills, and interests.   Current life tasks involve a variety of basic knowledge, skills, and interests as part of day-by-day living at school, home, and on the job. These include reading, writing, interpersonal and intrapersonal problem solving, and so forth. At this level, remediation essentially involves reteaching—but not using the same approach that has just failed. Alternative ways must be used to present the material that the student has had difficulty learning. This is accomplished by further modifying activities in ways likely to improve the match with the learner's cur-

rent levels of motivation and development. Throughout Part 3, we have discussed how this is done.

You may recall we pointed out that teachers have access to a range of environmental factors that influence the match (e.g., review Box 8–4). Also emphasized has been the point that a wide range of techniques can be used to vary such factors in order to enhance (1) motivation, (2) sensory intake, (3) processing and decision making, and (4) output (review Box 10–4 and see Box 11–3).

Box 11–3

Theory and Practice
Remedial Strategies Used to Teach Reading

Because reading problems are so prevalent, remedial procedures in this area are among the most highly developed strategies. *Regular* approaches for teaching reading tend to emphasize one or a combination of six approaches:

- phonics
- look-say (or visual)
- linguistics
- language experience
- individualized (including programmed) instruction
- personalized

Any one or more of these may be used as a foundation for remedial reading instruction for individuals with learning disabilities.

From a theoretical perspective, the choice would be based on one's theoretical position about (1) how reading skills are learned and (2) what has caused and what must be done to correct a particular individual's learning disability.

The theoretical debate over the first matter has centered on whether approaches should stress (a) the meaning of language (e.g., language

experience strategies) or (b) "breaking the code" (e.g., strategies that emphasize phonetic analysis). With regard to the practical implications of theories of the cause and correction of LD, the debate has been whether to stress procedures that build on strengths and avoid any weaknesses an individual may have in a particular modality for learning to read (e.g., how much stress should be placed on phonetic analysis for a person with weak ability to make auditory perceptual discriminations). There can, of course, be a dilemma if the theory of reading instruction one has adopted favors a phonics approach but the individual to be taught appears to have severe problems in making auditory discriminations and little or no difficulty discriminating among visual symbols.

For those with severe learning disabilities, all of the basic approaches to reading instruction have to be modified in some way (review Box 10–4). Major examples of strategies for modifying reading instruction involve (a) special alphabets, such as the Initial Teaching Alphabet (ITA) and color-coded alphabets; (b) multisensory approaches, such as the Fernald Techniques and the Gillingham-Stillman method; and (c) audio-visual and interactive devices, such as audiotapes with accompanying printed material, teaching machines that can say words and direct active responding and give feedback on accuracy, and computers with a growing variety of special programs.

Prerequisites. At this level, the focus is essentially on identifying missing prerequisites and teaching them. The types of prerequisites that may not have been learned are outlined in Box 11-4. The procedures used are the same as those already described for facilitating learning related to current life tasks.

Interfering factors. At this level, the possibility of faulty learning mechanisms must be faced. As discussed in Part 1, a variety of underlying processing deficits, language disabilities, and poorly developed learning strategies have been suggested as interfering with learning. Remedial approaches have been designed to overcome such deficiencies by directly correcting the problems or indirectly compensating for them. (The prevailing underlying-abilities or therapy-oriented approaches to remedying interfering factors are discussed in Chapter 6, e.g., see Box 6-1; and commonly used remedial activities are

---

Box 11-4

Theory and Practice

Prerequisites

In general, individuals should have the following important prerequisites if they are to benefit appropriately from instruction in the three Rs.

Language

1. Expressive—working vocabulary and ability to speak clearly and plainly enough to be understood
2. Receptive—ability to understand what is said
3. Use—ability to use at least simple sentences and to express ideas, thoughts, and feelings; understanding of the relationship between spoken and written language

Perception

1. Visual discrimination—ability to discriminate differences and similarities in letters, words, numbers, and colors and to see the relationship of a part to a whole
2. Auditory discrimination—ability to discriminate differences and similarities in sounds of letters

Cognition and Motivation (including attentional, memory, and conceptual skills)

1. Interest in what is being taught

2. Ability and desire to follow simple directions
3. Ability and desire to stay at one's desk for sufficient periods of time to complete a simple classroom task
4. Ability and desire to remember simple facts
5. Ability and desire to answer questions about a simple story
6. Ability and desire to tell a story from a picture (i.e., associate symbols with pictures, objects, and facts)
7. Ability and desire to stay focused on material (pictures, letters, words) presented to the class by the teacher
8. Ability and desire to solve simple task-oriented problems
9. Ability and desire to tolerate failure sufficiently to persist on a task
10. Ability and desire to make transitions from one activity to another
11. Ability and desire to carry on with a task over several days
12. Ability and desire to accept adult direction without objection or resentment
13. Ability and desire to work without constant supervision or reminders
14. Ability and desire to respond to normal classroom routines
15. Ability and desire to suppress tendencies to interrupt others

highlighted in Box 10-3. Also see the references at the end of this chapter.)

SEQUENCING REMEDIATION

When a youngster has a learning problem at school, the teacher and student must decide whether instruction in that area should be delayed until learning might be easier. For instance, the need for such decisions is common with young children (five- to eight-year-olds) whose perceptual development may be slower than the mean for their age group. This strategy also may have to be considered with adolescents and adults who are so anxious or so unmotivated that they are not ready to pursue learning vigorously in a particular area. Remediation is most productive with students who express a desire for help.

When remediation is indicated, the teacher may focus on any of the three levels described. However, the sequence and level differ depending on whether the student has minor and occasional problems or is found to have severe and pervasive problems. The process involves the following sequence:

For learners with minor or occasional problems, the initial focus is on facilitating learning related to current tasks and interests and on expanding the range of interests. The procedures involve (1) continued adaptation of methods to match and enhance current levels of motivation and development and (2) reteaching specific skills and knowledge when the student has difficulty. (This level of focus is Level A in Boxes 8–11 and 8–12; a portion of the figure in Box 8–11 is reproduced in Box 11–5).

If the problem continues and is assessed as severe, the focus shifts to assessment and development of missing prerequisites (Level B) needed for functioning at the higher level. Again, procedures are adapted to improve the match, and reteaching is used when the learner has difficulty. If missing prere-

quisites are successfully developed, the focus returns to Level A.

The intent in proceeding in this sequential and hierarchical way is to use the simplest and most direct approaches first whenever problems appear minor. However, if available data indicate the presence of severe and pervasive motivation or developmental problems, instruction at Level B is begun immediately.

And if help at Level B is not effective, the focus shifts to Level C. Only at this level is the emphasis on factors that may interfere with functioning, that is, incompatible behaviors and interests and/or dysfunctional learning mechanisms.

At Level C, there is increased and intensified use of a wide range of psychoeducational techniques (see Box 10–4). As soon as feasible, the focus shifts back to prerequisites (Level B) and then on to current tasks and interests (Level A). These remedial strategies are used whenever and as long as necessary.

Even among those with pervasive and severe problems, there are likely to be some areas in which the problem is not severely handicapping. These are areas in which learning can proceed without remediation or, at least, in which remediation can be focused more directly on Level B or A. In such cases, an individual would be pursuing learning at several levels at once.

A couple of examples may help further clarify this sequential and hierarchical approach to remediation.

Larry had a minor reading problem. Joan's was somewhat more severe.

Mr. Johnston's first efforts to help Larry improve his reading skills involved a variety of reteaching strategies. The activity focused on current reading tasks in which Larry had indicated an interest. The reteaching strategies were not simply a matter of trying more of the same—more drill, for example. He tried alternative procedures ranging from commonly

Box 11–5

Program Example
Sequencing of Hierarchical Strategies

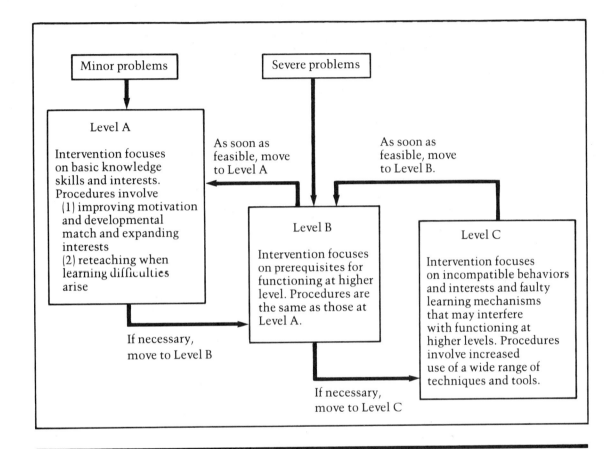

used explanations, techniques, and materials (such as another example or analogy, a concrete demonstration, a memorization strategy) to less common, specialized, *remedial* techniques (such as a multisensory method).

After working on this level for a week, Mr. Johnston found that over the preceding years, Larry had not learned a number of prerequisites widely viewed as reading-readiness skills. For example, Larry had difficulty following directions involving more than one point at a time, and he had problems ordering and sequencing events described to him. He also seemed to have little awareness of the relationship between the spoken and the printed word. As he assessed these problems in his daily work with Larry, Mr. Johnston pointed them out, and they agreed to include them as a major focus of instruction.

In other cases, Mr. Johnston had found that once the missing prerequisites were learned, students had little problem learning basic reading skills. This turned out to be the case with Larry.

Joan's situation, however, proved to be more difficult. Because her problem was more severe, Mr. Johnston had focused from the start on absent reading prerequisites. As he worked with her over a period of several weeks, he found that she had trouble learning most of the prerequisites he taught her and retained only a small amount of what she learned. Thus, he moved on to try to detect any dysfunctional learning mechanisms that might be interfering with her learning.

Over a period of weeks, it became clear that Joan was having widespread difficulty discriminating sounds and was continuing to have severe trouble recalling what she had learned the day before. Rather than have her continue to experience failure, Mr. Johnston shifted the focus of instruction. The time usually spent on reading instruction was devoted to helping overcome her learning handicaps. Activities she wanted to do were identified; as she had trouble, he worked with her using techniques that stressed multisensory involvement. To improve her retention, he encouraged her to take smaller amounts, and together they identified a variety of interesting activities with which she could immediately apply and practice what she was learning.

At first, Joan was hesitant to try things that she had failed at previously. Mr. Johnston did not push. He followed her lead and, at the same time, increasingly encouraged her to risk exploring new things. It should be noted that one of Mr. Johnston's goals with Joan was to help her increase her feelings of competence. When he first began working with her, however, she perceived the special help as another sign of her lack of competence, and this made her feel worse. Such a reaction is common. In the end, as was usually the case with such students, Mr. Johnston found Joan's progress to be slow but steady.

SUMMARY

In Chapter 9, we stressed that remedial programs often tend to reduce the focus of instruction by narrowing the curriculum. As important as the three Rs and cognitive development are, other basic areas of human development and functioning must not be ignored. Thus, even though a student may need a great deal of remediation, it is important to maintain a balanced program—including a broad range of developmental and enrichment options. That is, remediation is not intended to replace effective and interesting opportunities that can facilitate development and provide enrichment; special help is to be added to such activity as needed.

In general, the task of regular and remedial teachers is the same—facilitating learning. For motivated learners (with and without learning problems), this involves (1) maintaining and possibly enhancing motivation and (2) helping establish ways for learners to attain their goals.

In this chapter, remediation has been presented as an extension of nonremedial processes for facilitating learning. We have focused on the criteria for deciding when such a special focus is needed, reviewed the major features that differentiate remediation from regular teaching, outlined the problems remedial strategies are designed to address, and explored the nature of remedial methods and applications.

Remedial strategies involve no new principles of instruction. What makes such approaches appear different is the rationale given for their use, the extreme degree and consistency with which they must be applied, and their application on levels of functioning other than current life tasks. How well remediation works and why it does—when it does—remain unclear. What may make any remedial procedure work is the fact that it is different from those a student has already tried and found ineffective. Special procedures have the benefit of being new and novel and, therefore, have motivation- and attention-inducing value.

As a general stance regarding remedial activity, we concur that "learning disabilities cannot be corrected or 'cured' by a specific teaching method or training technique. It is imperative that teachers have a wide range of instructional materials and techniques at their disposal and that they are imaginative and flexible enough to adapt these to the specific needs of their pupils." (Koppitz, 1973, p. 137)

We would add, however, that effective flexibility and imaginativeness in facilitating learning stem from a sound understanding of what is involved in personalizing regular and remedial instruction.

AN ENRICHMENT ACTIVITY

Now that you've read Chapters 8 through 11, what do you think:

Is teaching an art, or is it an activity that most people can learn to do?

Why do you think so?

SPECIAL TOPIC REFERENCES

Should you be interested in further information about *remedial methods*, see the general overviews provided in the following readings.

ALLEY, G., & DESHLER, D. D. (1979). *Teaching the learning disabled adolescent: Strategies and methods.* Denver: Love Publishing Co.

HAMMILL, D. D., & BARTEL, N. R. (1982). *Teaching children with learning and behavior problems,* 3rd ed. Boston: Allyn & Bacon.

KIRK, S. A., & CHALFANT, J. C. (1984). *Academic and developmental learning disabilities.* Denver: Love Publishing Co.

LERNER, J. W. (1985). *Learning disabilities: Theories, diagnosis, and teaching strategies,* 4th ed. Boston: Houghton-Mifflin.

MERCER, C. D., & MERCER, A. R. (1981). *Teaching students with learning problems.* Columbus, Ohio: Charles E. Merrill.

MYERS, P. I., & HAMMILL, D. D. (1982). *Learning disabilities: Basic concepts, assessment practices, and instructional strategies.* Austin, Texas: Pro-Ed.

SMITH, D. D. (1981). *Teaching the learning disabled.* Englewood Cliffs, N.J.: Prentice-Hall.

STEPHENS, T. M. (1977). *Teaching skills to children with learning and behavior disorders.* Columbus, Ohio: Charles E. Merrill.

WALLACE, G., & KAUFFMAN, J. M. (1978). *Teaching children with learning problems.* Columbus, Ohio: Charles E. Merrill.

For more on specific areas, see the following readings.

Perceptual-motor

AYRES, A. J. (1972). *Sensory integration and learning disorders.* Los Angeles: Western Psychological Services.

BARSCH, R. H. (1968). *Enriching perception and cognition,* Vol. 2. Seattle: Special Child Publications.

CRATTY, B. (1971). *Active learning: Games to enhance academic abilities.* Englewood Cliffs, N.J.: Prentice-Hall.

FROSTIG, M., & HORNE, D. (1964). *The Frostig program for the development of visual perception.* Chicago: Follett.

GETMAN, G. N., KANE, E. R., & McKEE, G. W. (1968). *Developing learning readiness: A visual-motor tactile skills program.* Manchester, Mo.: Webster Division, McGraw-Hill.

KEPHART, N. C. (1971). *The slow learner in the classroom.* Columbus, Ohio: Charles E. Merrill.

Language and psycholinguistics

BANGS, T. E. (1982). *Language and learning disorders of the preacademic child with curriculum guide,* 2nd ed. Englewood Cliffs, N.J.: Prentice-Hall.

BERRY, M. (1980). *Teaching linguistically handicapped children.* Englewood Cliffs, N.J.: Prentice-Hall.

BURNS, P. C. (1980) *Assessment and correction of language arts difficulties.* Columbus, Ohio: Charles E. Merrill.

BUSH, W. J., & GILES, M. T. (1977). *Aids to psycholinguistic teaching*, 2nd ed. Columbus, Ohio: Charles E. Merrill.

ENGLEMANN, S., & BRUNER, E. (1974). *DISTAR Reading: An instructional system.* Chicago: Science Research Associates.

FERNALD, G. M. (1943). *Remedial techniques in basic school subjects.* New York: McGraw-Hill.

GILLINGHAM, A., & STILLMAN, B. (1966). *Remedial teaching for children with specific disability in reading, spelling, and penmanship*, 7th ed. Cambridge, Mass.: Educators Publishing Service.

HARRIS, A. J., & SIPAY, E. R. (1980). *How to increase reading ability: A guide to developmental and remedial methods*, 7th ed. New York: Longman.

HEGGE, T. G., KIRK, S. A., & KIRK, W. D. (1970). *Remedial reading drills.* Ann Arbor, Mich.: George Wahr.

JOHNSON, D., & MYKLEBUST, H. (1967). *Learning disabilities.* New York: Grune & Stratton.

LEE, L., KOENIGSKNECHT, R. A., & MULHERN, S. T. (1975). *Interactive language development teaching.* Evanston, Ill.: Northwestern University Press.

McLEAN, J. E., & SNYDER-McLEAN, L. K. (1978). *A transactional approach to early language training.* Columbus, Ohio: Charles E. Merrill.

MINSKOFF, E., WISEMAN, D. E., & MINSKOFF, J. G. (1972). *The MWM program for developing language abilities.* Ridgefield, N.J.: Educational Performance Associates.

WIIG, E. H., & SEMEL, E. M. (1980). *Language assessment and intervention for the learning disabled.* Columbus, Ohio: Charles E. Merrill.

Math

ADAMS, S. and colleagues (1979). *Adston mathematics skill series.* Baton Rouge, La.: Adston Education Enterprises.

BLEY, N. S., & THORNTON, C. A. (1981). *Teaching mathematics to the learning disabled.* Rockville, Md.: Aspen Systems.

CAWLEY, J. F., FITZMAURICE, A. M., GOODSTEIN, H. A., LEPORE, A.V., SEDLAK, R., & ALTHAUS, V. (1976). *Project MATH.* Tulsa, Okla.: Educational Development Corporation.

CONNOLLY, A. J. (1982). *Key math early steps program.* Circle Pines, Minn.: American Guidance Service.

COPELAND, R. W. (1979). *Math activities for children: A diagnostic and developmental approach.* Columbus, Ohio: Charles E. Merrill.

DUNCAN, E. R., COPPS, L. R., DOLCIANI, M. P., QUAST, W. G., & ZWENG, M. J. (1970). *Modern school mathematics: Structure and use K–6.* Boston: Houghton-Mifflin.

ENGELMANN, S., & CARNINE, D. (1982). *Corrective mathematics.* Chicago: Science Research Associates.

REISMAN, F. K. (1977). *Diagnostic teaching of elementary school mathematics: Methods and content.* Chicago: Rand McNally.

SULLIVAN, M. R. (1973). *The Sullivan Basal Mathematics Program.* Palo Alto, Calif.: Behavioral Research Laboratories.

Cognitive prerequisites and learning strategies

The preceding readings cover many cognitive prerequisites and learning strategies. A few additional readings follow.

ALLEY, G., & DESHLER, D. D. (1979). *Teaching the learning disabled adolescent: Strategies and methods.* Denver: Love Publishing Co.

DESHLER, D. D., ALLEY, G. R., WARNER, M. M., & SCHUMAKER, J. B. (1982). Instructional practices for promoting skill acquisition and generalization in severely learning disabled adolescents. *Learning Disability Quarterly, 4*, 415–21.

DESHLER, D. D., SCHUMAKER, J. B., LENZ, B. K., & ELLIS, E. (1984). Academic and cognitive interventions for LD adolescents: Part II. *Journal of Learning Disabilities, 17*, 170–79.

GELZHEISER, L. M., SOLAR, R. A., SHEPHERD, M. J., & WOZNIAK, R. H. (1983). Teaching learning disabled children to memorize: A rationale for plans and practice. *Journal of Learning Disabilities, 16*, 421–25.

KAIL, R. V., Jr., & HAGEN, J. W. (1977). *Perspectives on the development of memory and cognition.* Hillsdale, N.J.: Lawrence Erlbaum Associates.

KOPS, C., & BELMONT, I. (1985). Planning and organizing skills of poor school achievers. *Journal of Learning Disabilities, 18*, 8–14.

MASTROPIERI, M. A., SCRUGGS, T. E., & LEVIN, J. R. (1985). Mnemonic strategy instruction with learning disabled adolescents. *Journal of Learning Disabilities, 18,* 94–100.

MEICHENBAUM, D. (1977). *Cognitive-behavior modification: An integrative approach.* New York: Plenum.

MONTESSORI, M. (1964). *The Montessori method.* New York: Schocken Books.

PARRILL-BURNSTEIN, M. (1981). *Problem solving and learning disabilities: An information processing approach.* New York: Grune & Stratton.

REESE, H. W. (1976). *Basic learning processes in childhood.* New York: Holt, Rinehart & Winston.

Social and emotional problems and interfering behaviors

See references in Reading E.

Motivational Problems

ADELMAN, H. S. (1978). The concept of intrinsic motivation: Implications for practice and research related to learning disabilities. *Learning Disability Quarterly, 1,* 43–54.

ADELMAN, H. S., & TAYLOR, L. (1983). Enhancing motivation for overcoming learning and behavior problems. *Journal of Learning Disabilities, 16,* 384–92.

DE CHARMS, R. (1976). *Enhancing motivation.* New York: Irvington Publishers.

DECI, E. L. (1975). *Intrinsic motivation.* New York: Plenum.

McCOMBS, B. L. (1984). Processes and skills underlying continuing intrinsic motivation to learn: Toward a definition of motivational skills training interventions. *Educational Psychologist, 19,* 194–218.

RUBLE, D. N., & BOGGIANO, A. K. (1980). Optimizing motivation in an achievement context. In B. Keogh (Ed.), *Advances in special education.* Greenwich, Conn.: JAI Press.

Chapter 12

Evaluating Effectiveness

Accountability! It's becoming an increasingly familiar topic. More than that, it's becoming an increasingly common demand.

Everybody agrees that professionals should be accountable. There are, however, major disagreements about just what that means (see Box 12–1). Unfortunately, in fields such as education, psychology, and medicine, evaluation is not a simple matter.

Box 12–1

TEACHER: "Yes, Butch, what is it?"

BUTCH: "I don't want to scare you, but my dad says if I don't get better grades someone is due for a spanking."

Accountability means that professionals working with learning disabilities must show that their work is effective. But effective in what way? To what degree? At what cost?

It is not uncommon to hear professionals say, "If it works, use it!" This statement suggests that, in choosing their practices, they are selecting those that are effective. Unfortunately, there rarely is adequate *evidence* about what really works.

It is one thing to want and need accountability; it is quite another to work out a satisfactory way to find out whether a program is any good. It is as easy to demand accountability as it is difficult and costly to carry out appropriate evaluation.

As we explore the approaches to evaluation and concerns about it, some will be familiar to you because we have already discussed them in relation to other assessment practices. Many evaluation concerns are basic to any assessment effort. Remember: evaluation is one of the major functions or purposes for which assessment is used (review Box 6–8).

WHAT IS THE PROGRAM TRYING TO ACCOMPLISH?

A program may be evaluated simply in terms of whether it accomplishes its intended outcomes. People, however, also tend to evaluate a program in terms of whether they agree with what it is trying to do.

What a program intends to do is reflected in its rationale. Programs with different rationales may look alike in some ways, but they will certainly differ in important ways. Thus, evaluations of whether a program is any good usually reflect judgments about the appropriateness of its rationale—with specific reference to the major ways the rationale results in the program differing from other programs.

All programs for individuals with learning disabilities are designed with the hope that the individuals served will be able to cope effectively with day-to-day demands. All such programs intend to do something positive and to minimize negative side effects.

Some LD programs, however, focus on a narrow range of basic academic skills; others stress a broad range of goals related to motivation and development. When one doesn't agree with a program's rationale, one will not likely approve of the program—even if evaluation data indicate it is effective.

Whose Rationale? Whose Judgment?

Everyone may agree that

- people should learn to read, write, and do basic mathematical computations
- remedial procedures should be used to help individuals overcome learning and behavior problems
- a remedial program should improve a person's skills so that the individual can

again function as effectively as those without learning problems

As program details are worked out, however, it often becomes clear that different individuals and groups have *very* different ideas about what they want accomplished and how they want it done.

Reading programs, for instance, obviously teach reading. However, daily objectives and procedures can differ tremendously.

One program may be designed by the program staff primarily to teach a set of basic reading skills; little time may be spent on activities for increasing enjoyment and valuing of reading. Thus, specific skills are taught, and evaluation focuses on whether they are learned. Little attention is paid to whether students' enjoyment and pursuit of reading outside of school increases or decreases.

Another program may be concerned both with skills and with enjoyment of reading. And both skills and attitudes are evaluated.

In general, there are a variety of persons and agencies with different vested interests who make decisions about programs (see Box 12–2). Whether they are sophisticated, directly involved, or have any control over the situation, each interested party is likely to have beliefs and values about what a program should be doing and how to evaluate and judge its worth. The more diverse the perspectives of the interested parties, the more the likelihood of conflict (Strupp & Hadley, 1977).

Conflict among interested parties always highlights issues of the appropriateness of what the program is trying to do and of the criteria and standards used in judging its effectiveness. Moreover, conflict always underscores the concern over whose perspective should prevail and the need for processes to decide the matter. When there are no established procedures for determining whose perspective should prevail, program planning is usually shaped by the beliefs and

Box 12–2

Parties Who Directly or Indirectly Shape a Program's Rationale and Evaluation

I. Directly involved interested parties
   A. *Subscribers* — including private individuals and representatives of organized bodies who are seeking intervention for themselves, others, or both
   B. *Objects to be changed* — including individuals and those in settings who seek change or are referred by others
   C. *Interveners* — those who, in addition to whatever self interests are involved, may base their activity on the stated desires

or interpreted needs of subscribers, the objects of change, or both

II. Indirectly involved interested parties, i.e., those whose influence has the potential to produce a major impact on the intervention
   A. *Immediate or primary environmental influences* — e.g., family, friends, employers, teachers, co-workers, local representatives of funding sources
   B. *Secondary and tertiary environmental influences* — governmental agents related to health, education, welfare, and law enforcement; professional and lay organizations; theorists, researchers, and instructors; i.e., those who lobby for, underwrite, study, evaluate, and teach about intervention.

---

values of those with greatest authority in the situation.

Program Purposes and Evaluation

One basic conflict that often arises concerns the question of whether a program's rationale and evaluation should primarily reflect the interests of the individual enrolled in the program or the interests of the society. For example, a very important difference in

programs for problem populations is the degree to which a program is intended to *help* individuals or to *socialize* them. When the intent is socialization, programs are designed to accomplish society's aims and are evaluated from the perspective of society's standards. Helping programs are designed to meet the individual client's needs and are evaluated in terms of the standards of the client or the client's advocates (see Box 12–3).

Box 12–3

Theory and Practice
Helping Relationships vs. Socialization

Programs for individuals with problems are established to meet varying and, at times, conflicting needs and ends. Differences particularly arise when programs are designed with reference to the interests of the society rather than the interests of the "client." This, of course, is a

frequent occurrence in school programs that enroll students with learning and behavior problems.

School systems are established by society as socializing agencies, with helping services added when feasible. Parents of students experiencing problems generally want a greater emphasis on helping but usually also value the school's socializing functions — especially when their youngster's problems include bad behavior. In contrast, students do not often like the socializing facets of schooling and usually don't see school programs as designed to be all that helpful.

Ironically, many students diagnosed as learning disabled are individuals who have not responded to the socialization efforts of public schools in the past and have been singled out for remediation because of this fact. Moreover, many students' learning problems go uncorrected because so much teacher effort is devoted to procedures designed only to establish social control.

All of this should not be surprising. Students with learning problems often are found to be hard to control. And, even though individuals with learning problems need help, schools are not established to create helping relationships.

Nevertheless, the need of such individuals for help leads many parents and students to believe that their school program should become more help oriented. This view often

brings them into conflict with those whose responsibility it is to maintain the school's socialization agenda. When there is conflict, a great deal of valuable time and energy usually is wasted as parents, students, teachers, and administrators engage in a struggle over whose rationale, interests, and criteria are to prevail.

Factors differentiating helping relationships from socialization are highlighted in the following diagram.

The key to differentiating helping and socialization rests in the matter of whose interests are being served. Helping relationships are defined as serving the individual's interests; socialization serves the interests of the society. Sometimes there is no conflict of interests; often there is. When there is, the conflicting parties hold very different views about such matters as the appropriate aims of a program and the criteria and standards that should be used in identifying problems, prescribing what should be done, and judging effectiveness.

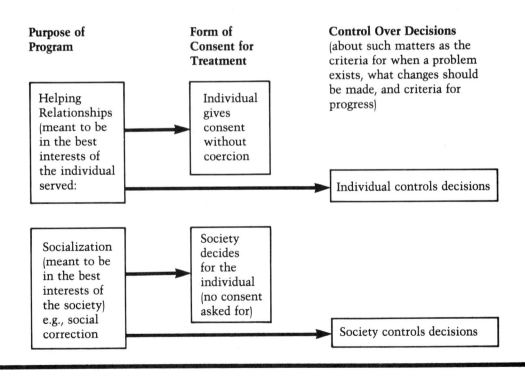

Another basic conflict arises between proponents of the underlying-abilities and those of the observable-skills orientations, the prevailing orientations toward learning disabilities. You will recall that, although each orientation intends to remedy an individual's learning problems, the approaches set about doing so in very different ways and with very different initial objectives and timetables (review Chapter 6).

From a motivational perspective, conflicts also arise when programs stress only developmental problems and ignore motivation and attitudes. Similarly, from an interactional perspective, conflicts arise when programs ignore the need for environmental changes and focus only on changing individuals, especially when major problems in the school and home environments have been identified.

Obviously, the program's purposes may be judged as inappropriate prior to any measure or judgment of program effectiveness. Moreover, data on effectiveness may be gathered in terms of the program's intentions or in terms of anything else the evaluator thinks is important.

Breadth of Program Focus and Evaluation

As the discussion to this point indicates, evaluation should be used to determine (1) if one agrees with what the program is trying to accomplish and (2) how well the program is achieving the full range of what is desired. The less a program is trying to achieve, the easier it is to determine these matters. It is hard to evaluate most school programs because they are trying to accomplish many different things (see Worthorn & Sanders, 1973).

Not coincidentally, however, the longer that a program is the focus of formal evaluation, the less it may try to accomplish. At least this appears to be one of the negative effects of the big push toward behavioral and criterion-referenced objectives as ways to improve accountability (review discussion in Chapter 6).

Behaviorist-oriented instructional objectives and other naive accountability trends often seem to be putting the cart before the horse. That is, the emphasis on evaluation is so strong that the primary focus of instruction shifts from the program's rationale (e.g., long-range aims) to a limited set of objectives that can be measured immediately. As greater attention is paid to what can be measured, the breadth of instructional focus often is reduced (see Box 12–4).

Thus, if one is not careful, the desire for data on effectiveness can result in a program being redesigned to pursue only that which can be measured currently. This is a negative form of teaching to the test because, in the process, many important things are ignored simply because they will not be on the test.

Comprehensive evaluation should stress the full scope of desired aims. That is, even if certain processes and outcomes are not easily measured, they still need to be evaluated as well as is possible, and they need to be kept in the forefront in discussions about a program's worth. (For example, is the program leading to greater interest, desire, and participation in learning on the part of students?)

In general, then, evaluations of whether a program is any good must first address the question: Is what the program is trying to accomplish appropriate? The frame of reference for such evaluations may be the program's rationale or what others think the program should be doing. Generally, this means clarifying such matters as: Who or what is to be the focal point of intervention—a person, the environment, or both? and What changes are desired?

Box 12–4

Viewpoint
**Specifying Remedial Outcomes
for Evaluation**

Because of increasing demands for accountability, the primary focus in preparing IEPs for students with learning problems tends to be on remedial outcomes. Furthermore, the prevailing emphasis is on specifying them in terms of behavioral and criterion-referenced objectives.

These trends no doubt are a major aid in efforts to evaluate whether remedial outcomes are accomplished. However, the tendency to limit the focus to remediation ignores the school's responsibility to facilitate ongoing development and to provide enrichment opportunities. An overemphasis on remediation also can be counterproductive to overcoming problems if the program involves little more than a set of laborious and deadening experiences.

In general, the danger is that important intervention aims and goals will be lost in the emphasis on specifying *all* program plans in terms of highly concrete and easily measurable objectives. Not all of the complex long-range aims a program must pursue can be stated as short-term or immediate behavioral objectives. Nor should they all be specified in this way.

Attitudes, motivation, and creative functioning in the arts and sciences, for example, do not lend themselves to being stated in terms of simple behaviors.

For the most part, only a relatively limited set of skills can be specified in highly concrete, behavioral terms—and even in these instances, it may not be desirable to do so for instructional purposes. Besides the fact that specifying everything in this way would result in far too many objectives to teach, the trend also contributes to an overemphasis on *teaching* at the expense of *learning*.

A teacher's job is to facilitate a student's efforts to learn—not to establish a program in which everything to be learned must be taught. The point of evaluation is to sample the broad range of what has been learned—not to measure a limited range of skills that have been taught. Although it is worth making the job of evaluation as easy as possible, this should not be done in ways that limit the learning opportunities of the individuals who are evaluated.

Finally, specifying and evaluating remedial outcomes keeps the focus on individuals and the changes they are to make. This contributes to the tendency to ignore environmental and program changes. Obviously, at times, the environment or specific interactions between individuals and the environment are the appropriate objects of change. It seems unfortunate that current approaches to evaluation in the LD field have become another force colluding with narrow models of the causes and correction of learning and behavior problems.

After the appropriateness of what is wanted or expected is judged, the program's intended breadth of focus should guide efforts to evaluate effectiveness. However, not everything can be measured in a technically sophisticated way at this time. This means that some things will be poorly measured or simply reviewed informally. Obviously, this is less than satisfactory. Nevertheless, as long as the inadequacies of the evaluation are recognized, it is better to keep attending to the full range of what is intended than to adopt evaluation approaches that inappropriately reduce the focus of instruction and evaluation.

With this as background, we now turn to the topic of measuring what's happening.

MEASURING WHAT'S HAPPENING

One of the reasons that conflicting orientations exist in the LD field is the difficulty of validly measuring what works and what doesn't. A considerable amount of research has been reported. However, measurement and other research methodology problems have made it impossible to *prove* the worth of the programs studied (e.g., see Tindal, 1985).

In recent years, the increasing demand for accountability, especially from funding agencies, has led to mandated evaluation. It is easy to mandate such accountability. Unfortunately, such mandates ignore the fact that current evaluation practices are terribly inadequate. Thus, while mandated evaluation goes on continually, comprehensive and valid evaluation is rare.

What's Done Currently to Evaluate Effectiveness?

Most commonly, programs are evaluated using paper-and-pencil tests of ability and performance, self-reports and interviews, and systematic observations of behavior. (Examples are cited in Reading A.) Besides test scores, grades and ratings are relied on heavily. Unfortunately, many of the measurement instruments used are not highly reliable and valid.

As stated already, accountability pressures have led to an overemphasis on measuring immediate, behavioral outcomes. Moreover, many important facets of a program are not easily measured (e.g., self-concept, attitudes toward learning, problem-solving capabilities, creativity).

Usually, decisions as to what and how to evaluate are made by those administering or funding the program. Currently, there is little student or parent involvement in such decisions, and not surprisingly, there is little emphasis on consumer judgments of whether a program is a good one.

Because evaluations have been narrowly focused, many educators and psychologists argue that current interventions are judged unfairly (e.g., Horn, O'Donnell, & Vitulano, 1983). These professionals tend to reject negative findings and are critical of current evaluation purposes and practices (see Box 12–5).

What Is Evaluation?

Essentially, evaluation involves determining the worth or value of something (Stake, 1967; 1976). For purposes of this discussion, evaluation is defined as a systematic process designed to describe and judge the overall impact and value of an intervention for purposes of making decisions and advancing knowledge.

More specifically, the goals and objectives of evaluation include the following:

- to *describe* and *judge* an intervention's (1) rationale, including assumptions and intentions, and (2) standards for making judgments
- to *describe* and *judge* an intervention's (1) actual activity, including intended and unintended procedures and outcomes, and (2) costs (financial, negative effects)
- to *make decisions* about continuing, modifying, or stopping an intervention for an individual or for all those enrolled in a program
- to *advance knowledge* about interventions to improve (1) practices, (2) training, and (3) theory

The information needed to meet these purposes comes from comprehensive evaluations that include both immediate and long-term program data. The full range of data that may be gathered is suggested by the particular evaluation framework adopted (see Box 12–6).

Box 12–5

Research
How Effective Is Remediation?
How Effective Is Evaluation?

After reviewing a set of relevant long-term studies, Spreen (1982) concluded that

> "most children who are referred to a clinic for a learning or reading disability do not catch up. In fact, their disability is likely to become worse with time. In addition, remedial instruction has not been shown to improve the prognosis for these children." (p. 483)

In the November 1983 issue of the *Journal of Learning Disabilities*, Horn, O'Donnell, and Vitulano take another look at twenty four of the long-term outcome studies in learning disabilities. They discuss reports going back to 1960 with an eye not only to outcomes but to methodological problems in evaluation research.

They stress that neither outcome data nor procedures used to gather the data has been particularly good. Therefore, they caution against interpreting the body of findings as indicating that remediation is not effective. They conclude that until better evaluations are conducted, such a pessimistic conclusion would be unfortunate and premature.

To support their conclusions about the poor quality of evaluation practices, they cite finding major methodological problems with the sample reported and with the lack of appropriate control and comparison groups. They also note that decisions to measure different outcomes often lead to very different conclusions about effectiveness.

In connection with samples, for instance, they note a lack of clear and precise descriptions of the populations studied and the procedures used to select the samples. In addition, they found that comparisons commonly were made between samples apparently quite dissimilar with reference to severity of problem and a variety of demographic factors, such as age and socioeconomic status. Moreover, they stress that emphasis on total group functioning tended to mask possible gains by subgroups.

The reviewers also point out that one of the most important decisions in conducting evaluative research involves choosing which outcomes to measure. They identify three major classes of outcomes used as measures of effectiveness in the studies they reviewed: (1) measures of educational/vocational attainment, such as grades, years of schooling, occupation; (2) tests of basic skill areas, such as achievement or perceptual functioning; and (3) indices of behavior/emotional functioning, such as parent reports of problems or symptoms. From their analyses of the data reported, they conclude that these three classes of outcome measures produce different findings and thus result in different conclusions about program effectiveness.

Horn and his colleagues' overall conclusion about the effectiveness of remediation is that

> "While it does appear that LD persons have enduring deficits in basic skills areas, their relatively good educational/vocational outcome indicates that many persons are able to compensate for their continued deficits . . . . The challenge for future research is to identify the kinds of compensatory strategies that contribute the most to helping which particular subgroups of LD persons achieve satisfactory educational and vocational goals while minimizing emotional and behavioral difficulties." (p. 554)

Steps in Evaluation Planning

Awareness of steps involved in planning an evaluation provides another way to understand the process. Such steps reflect the necessity in evaluation planning of making decisions about the focus of the evaluation, its specific objectives, and appropriate methodology and measures.

Box 12–6

Theory and Practice
A Framework for Evaluation

A framework formulated by Robert Stake (1967) provides a useful specific example of the type of models used by evaluators. Stake's framework offers a graphic and comprehensive picture of various facets of evaluation and how they relate to each other (see figure here).

In brief, Stake emphasizes that "the two basic acts of evaluation" are description and judgment. Descriptions take the form of data gathered by formal or informal means. Judgments take the form of interpretive conclusions about the meaning of the data, such as whether a procedure is good or bad, a student is above or below norm, a behavior is pathological or not. In practice, judgments are used for purposes of decision making. When it comes to deciding specifically what to describe and judge, evaluators often are guided by their understanding of the decisions to be made at the conclusion of the evaluation.

Stake stresses that proper program evaluation requires data and criteria for analyzing the degree to which

- conditions anticipated prior to the program (antecedents), planned procedures (transactions), and intended outcomes are consistent with the program rationale and are logical in relation to each other

- intended antecedents, transactions, and outcomes actually occur

An example may help further clarify Stake's framework for evaluation. Let's use Sally's reading program to illustrate each cell of the matrix shown in this box.

Rationale

Sally's teacher has decided that because Sally's auditory functioning seems stronger than her visual abilities, he will teach her phonics as a way to improve her reading.

Intents

Antecedents: The teacher knows that Sally has the ability to learn phonics and that he taught her vowel sounds on Monday.
Transactions: He plans to teach her initial consonant sounds on Wednesday.
Outcomes: He decides she should be able to reproduce vowel and initial consonant sounds during a review test on Friday.

Observations

Antecedents: The teacher notes Sally did not put much effort into learning the vowel sounds on Monday.
Transactions: Because of a field trip on Thursday, there was not enough time for her to practice the sounds she had learned on Monday and Wednesday.
Outcomes: On Friday's review, Sally was unable to reproduce half of the sounds she had been taught.

Standards

Antecedents: The teacher expects Sally to be motivated enough to put in the effort to learn whatever he teaches as long as the material is not too difficult.
Transactions: He considers the procedures used to teach the material to be extremely good ones, and he has found them effective for about 90 percent of the other students in the class.
Outcomes: On Friday's review, other students in the class reproduce 95 percent of the sounds correctly.

Judgments

Antecedents: Looking back to Monday, the teacher judges his work with Sally as having been unrealistic. He now thinks that if she was not motivated to work, she was not really learning what he was teaching.
Transactions: Besides not particularly wanting to do the lesson on Monday, Sally tells him

that she did not understand the lessons on both days.

Outcomes: Sally's inability to reproduce half the sounds was judged unsatisfactory and was seen as the result of unrealistic teaching practices.

In general, the types of data Stake's framework indicates should be gathered can provide a wealth of information for use in describing and judging programs and making decisions about ways to improve them.

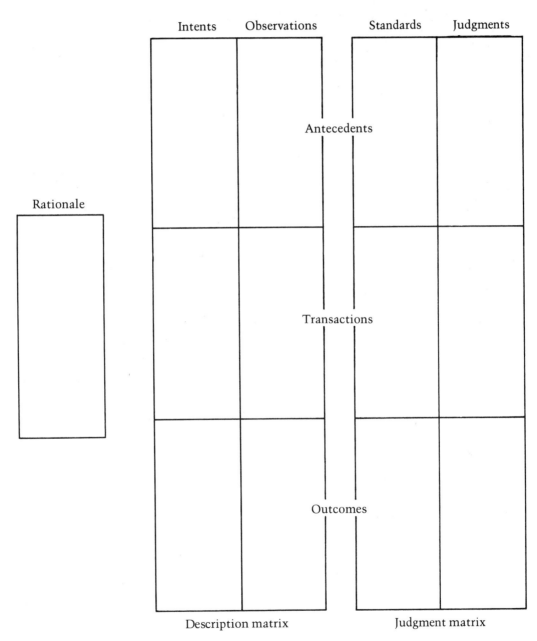

A layout of statements and data to be collected by the evaluator of an educational program.

One formulation of key steps follows:

1. *Clarification of the intended use to be made of the information.* Most important at this step is awareness of who wants the data and why they need it, e.g., what types of decisions they need to make. Also, it is important to anticipate the reactive impact—politically and motivationally—of evaluation processes and findings.

2. *Understanding of the program's rationale.* Often, the program's rationale is clarified as part of Step 1 because evaluation data generally are used to make judgments related to the program's rationale. This may not be the case, however, when the evaluation is designed to judge the program with reference to some standard set of basic objectives. This occurs, for example, when the same standardized test of reading is administered in all schools. Of course, even in such cases, it may be desirable to evaluate whether a program is accomplishing the other things that it has set out to do.

3. *Formulation of evaluation questions.* The matters to be evaluated are translated into a set of *major* questions. For example: How effective are Procedures A v. B for students with severe learning problems? Are LD students more motivated to learn in special or in regular classes? Because all programs are likely to have some negative effects, one standard question always is: What negative impact does the program produce? (See Box 12–7).

4. *Specification of data to be gathered.* For each major question, it is necessary to specify relevant descriptive data that should be gathered (e.g., on intended and unintended antecedents, transactions, and outcomes). At this point, specific instructional objectives are noted—along with the other matters about which data are to be gathered. The more things one is interested in evaluating, the more one has to settle for samples of information. That is, it often is not feasible (e.g., because of time, money, personnel) to gather all the data that are desired.

5. *Specification of procedures.* Further problems in gathering desired data arise as one attempts to specify procedures. Sometimes there is a good test or other measuring instrument; sometimes only weak procedures are available; sometimes there is no currently feasible way to get the information. Thus, decisions about the data to be gathered are shaped first by what one wants to know and then by practical considerations.

6. *Specification of a design.* An evaluation design is used so that data can be gath-

---

Box 12–7

Viewpoint
On Looking for Negative Consequences

Few, if any, major interventions can claim to have no negative features. A contemporary example is the increasing recognition of the potential negative consequences, both physical and psychological, of treating "hyperactivity" with stimulant drugs. Another example is the increasing levels of dependency on teachers that is a by-product of many remedial approaches.

Even when negative consequences are known, often little attention is paid to them. And, of course, many are undoubtedly unknown because so little effort has been made to detect them. Obviously, there is little justification for ignoring negative effects and, indeed, to do so is unethical. Consequently, evaluation efforts must include a direct focus on all major negative consequences that can be *anticipated*; evaluative research must also be directed at finding *unexpected* negative outcomes.

ered and interpreted appropriately. When someone asks how good a program is, the judgment made is based on the available data and is relative to some standard of comparison. A sound design ensures that appropriate data are gathered on the program under evaluation and that there also is a set of data for use as standards in judging the evaluation findings.

7. *Designation of time and place for data collection.* These matters are determined, in part, by the design and, in part, by practical factors such as resource availability.

One major evaluation concern not reflected in these steps involves decisions about what role various interested parties should play. For example, as suggested in Step 2, there may be different rationales about what should be evaluated. When this is the case, whose rationale should prevail? Almost at each step, evaluators will be influenced by the decision made about this matter.

Another evaluation concern not specifically addressed in the steps involves decisions about ethical matters associated with evaluation activities. Many of the ethical concerns are similar to those that arise in connection with assessment and treatment. Thus, at each step, evaluators must be concerned with how to minimize possible bias, conflicts of interest, and negative consequences that can arise from evaluation itself (see Box 12–8).

Box 12–8

Viewpoint
The Power of Evaluation to Inappropriately Shape Schooling

"Elementary school students almost invariably regard mathematics as the most important subject in the curriculum—not because of its elegance, but because math has the most homework, because the homework is corrected the most promptly, and because tests are given more frequently than in any other subject. The youngsters regard spelling as the next most important subject, because of the frequency of spelling tests. 'To a pupil,' Professor White explains, 'the workload and evaluation demands obviously must reflect what the teacher thinks is important to learn.'" (Silberman, 1970, p. 147)

Similarly, with the increasing demands for accountability, teachers quickly learn what is to be tested and what will not be evaluated, and slowly but surely greater emphasis is placed on teaching what will be on the tests. Over time what is on the tests comes to be viewed as what is most important. Because only so much time is available to the teacher, other things not only are deemphasized, they also are dropped from the curriculum. If allowed to do so, accountability procedures have the power to reshape the entire curriculum.

What's wrong with that? Nothing—if what is being evaluated reflects everything we want students to learn in school. Unfortunately, this is not the case.

Current accountability pressures reflect values and biases that have led to evaluating a small range of basic skills and doing so in a narrow way. For students diagnosed as LD, this is seen in the fact that their school programs increasingly have been restricted to improving skills they lack. As a result, they are cut off from participating in learning activities that might increase their interest in overcoming their problems and that might open up opportunities and enrich their future lives.

TEACHER: "I can hardly read your handwriting. You *must* learn to write more clearly."

STUDENT: "Aw, what's the use! If I write any clearer, you'll complain about my spelling."

SUMMARY

Evaluation is a key to the future of the LD field. Evaluation is a difficult process, which many would prefer to avoid; but it is a process that can improve programs, protect consumers, and advance knowledge.

In point of fact, everyone evaluates the programs with which they come in contact. Teachers judge whether their own and others' programs are going well. Students are quick to formulate likes or dislikes of teachers and school programs. And administrators will tell you which programs they think are working and which aren't.

Whenever anyone decides that a program is or isn't a good one, an evaluation is being made. Many times such evaluations simply reflect an individual's or group's informal observations. At other times, however, the judgments reflect careful data gathering and analyses and the use of an appropriate set of standards. Sometimes the judgments reflect differences in opinion about what a program should be doing; sometimes the judgments are about the degree to which the program is being effective.

Systematic efforts to evaluate programs involve decisions about

- the focus of evaluation (e.g., person or environment, immediate objectives vs. long-range aims)
- whose perspective is to determine the evaluation focus, methods, and standards to be used (e.g., the views of teachers, parents, students, or funding agencies)
- the best way to proceed in gathering and interpreting data (e.g., specific measures, design)

In making such decisions, concerns arise because

- what can be evaluated currently is far less than what a program may intend to accomplish

- inappropriate bias and vested interests can shape what is evaluated, thereby influencing whether a program is seen as good or bad

- evaluation processes can produce a variety of negative effects (e.g., over time what is evaluated can reduce and reshape a program's intended aims; evaluation can lead to invasion of privacy, an undermining of the ability of students and professionals to self-evaluate, and so forth)

Unfortunately, many professionals caught up in the day-by-day pressure of providing programs for individuals with problems feel that evaluation is just one more unnecessary chore. It just takes time away from carrying out the program.

Indeed, programs often get into trouble because everyone is so busy "doing" that there is no time to evaluate whether there might be a better way. One is reminded of Winnie-the-Pooh:

> "Here is Edward Bear, coming downstairs now, bump, bump, bump, on the back of his head behind Christopher Robin. It is, as far as he knows, the only way of coming downstairs, but sometimes he feels that there really is another way, if only he could stop bumping for a moment and think of it." (A. A. Milne, 1926, p. 1)

There is an obvious need for LD professionals to improve their practices and to be accountable. There is an equally obvious need to improve current evaluation practices. Because evaluations can as easily reshape programs in negative as in positive directions, it is essential that such practices be improved and that accountability pressures not be allowed to inappropriately narrow a program's focus. This is especially important for special education programs in which the tendency already is to limit evaluation to specific remedial objectives.

Finding out if an LD program is any good is a necessity. But in doing so, it is wise to recognize that evaluation is not simply a technical process.

Evaluation involves decisions about what and how to measure, and these decisions are based in great part on values and beliefs. As a result, limited knowledge, bias, vested interests, and ethical issues are constantly influencing the descriptive and judgmental processes and shape the decisions made at the end of the evaluation.

Ultimately, the decisions made affect not only individuals with learning disabilities but also the entire society.

AN ENRICHMENT ACTIVITY

1. Write down what you think are the most important things that should be taking place to facilitate learning in a classroom. (In a sense, you will be stating your rationale for what makes a program good.)

2. Observe a classroom for an hour.

3. Write down your observations as follows:

   a. Divide your paper into two columns—label the left-hand column "Descriptions" and the right-hand column "Judgments."

   b. Write down your descriptions in the left-hand column before making any judgments. (This may be a bit harder than you imagine at first. As you write out the descriptions of what you saw, you should keep asking yourself: Have I excluded all judgments?)

   c. Then write your judgments in the right-hand column. (Essentially, you will be making good-bad statements; be certain you think in terms of degree, e.g., how good or bad.)

4. Look over your judgments and think about *why* you decided something was good or bad. This will help you get in touch with both the standards you are using to make such judgments and the factors that have led you to adopt these particular standards. You might give particular thought to the following:

- Are the standards you are using appropriate to every classroom situation?

- Are they more appropriate for classrooms serving students who don't have learning problems than they are for students who do have problems?

- Do your standards reflect what you found was effective in your own schooling?

- Do you think you tend to assume that what worked for you—or what you now believe would have been a better approach for you—should be used with everybody else?

- If so, how might such an assumption be a problem?

SPECIAL TOPIC REFERENCES

If you want to read more about trends in *program evaluation*, see the following readings.

BRYK, A. S. (1983). *Stakeholder-based evaluation.* San Francisco: Jossey-Bass.

CAMMANN, C. (1982). Feedback systems for teachers. In J. Bess (Ed.), *New directions for teaching and learning: Motivating professors to teach effectively.* San Francisco: Jossey-Bass.

COOLEY, W. W. (1983). Improving the performance of an educational system. *Educational Researcher, 12,* 4–12.

CRONBACH, L. J., & Associates (1980). *Toward reform of program evaluation.* San Francisco: Jossey-Bass.

Part IV

LEARNING DISABILITIES: WHERE DO WE GO FROM HERE?

If you don't care much about where you get to, it doesn't matter which way you go.

Although relatively young, the field of learning disabilities rapidly has become an important force in efforts to combat learning problems. As we look to the future, we anticipate the field will continue to make significant contributions and will overcome many of the concerns that confront it. Among those that are particularly pressing are the ongoing problem of defining learning disabilities and the many issues related to how to provide for the increasing numbers diagnosed as learning disabled from preschool on into adulthood. In addition, there are service dilemmas, research issues, and the ongoing debate over what LD professionals-in-training should be taught. And there is the ever-present and overriding problem of where funds are to be found to finance the needed services and training as well as to underwrite the research that must be pursued if the field is to improve its knowledge base.

Our objectives in Part 4 are to encourage you to (1) think about what you have learned so far, (2) reflect on the evolving nature of the field, and (3) anticipate the field's personal relevance for you in the future. Chapter 13 explores major ongoing concerns and new concerns that are emerging about accountability, ethics, and the social impact of practices used with individuals manifesting learning and behavior problems. Chapter 14 is designed to give you an opportunity to think through and assimilate some of the major facts, ideas, and concerns you have read so far in this text. Finally, in Chapter 15, we focus on ways you may find yourself involved with the LD field in the future.

Our intent in Part 4 is not to predict the future. Our answer to the question Where do we go from here? stresses concerns that must be attended to by professionals and nonprofessionals alike. A few thoughts about ways in which some of these concerns may be addressed are offered—but only as examples. We take this approach because we believe the future of the field depends less on specific prescriptions for progress than on people strongly caring about improving educational systems and establishing ways to work together toward dealing with shared concerns.

Chapter *13*

Continuing and Emerging Concerns

The LD field continues to grow. As it does, responsible professionals struggle with the ongoing problems and issues of finding the learning disabled and improving daily practice and research. They are also confronted with emerging concerns over accountability, ethics, and the degree to which current practices are compatible in serving the needs of individuals and society.

Let's take a brief look at these areas of continuing and emerging concern.

CONTINUING CONCERNS

Throughout this book, we have referred to the *field* of learning disabilities. Some people question whether there is such a thing as the LD field (see Box 13–1).

Those of us who argue that there is a field do so because we believe a group of individuals exist whose problems should be differentiated from other individuals who have learning problems. For us, the former are individuals who have faulty learning mechanisms.

If for no other reason, these individuals deserve to be differentiated because it's likely they need different forms of remedial help. This has many implications. One of the most basic is that efforts of researchers to demonstrate the effectiveness of remedial approaches have been hampered because of the failure to distinguish the truly learning disabled from those with other learning problems.

Finding the Learning Disabled

Ongoing concern about who is or isn't learning disabled is reflected in efforts to improve the definition (as discussed in Chapter 1) and in efforts to improve diagnostic procedures (as discussed in Chapters 4 and 5). Ironically, for many years, some researchers have skirted right past this concern to the

Box 13–1

Concern in the Field
Noncategorical Special Education

Past and present classification schemes for categorizing individuals with special educational needs such as learning disabilities have been criticized widely as inadequate and often harmful (e.g., Blatt, 1972; Fisher, 1967; Goldstein, Arkell, Ashcroft, Hurley, & Lilly, 1975; Hobbs, 1975; Reger, Schroeder, & Uschold, 1968). Concerns raised by educators suggest that current categories deemphasize common characteristics relevant to learning and instruction; imply more of a need for specialization among teachers than is necessary; are inequitable; and produce negative consequences for many.

One controversial solution advocated has been to replace current categories and labels with a noncategorical or cross-categorical approach (e.g., Dunn, 1968; Hallahan & Kauffman, 1977; Meyen, 1971; Sabatino, 1981; Schwartz, Osteroff, Brucker, & Schwartz, 1972; Quay, 1968). Most prominent advocates of a noncategorical or cross-categorical approach have not argued against the importance of some form of classification (e.g., Mann, Davis, Boyer, Metz, & Wolford, 1983). Their interest is in replacing current categories used in schools with a system by which the special needs of each individual are identified (1) only as they become

relevant in providing an appropriate education and (2) in terms that have direct relevance to intervention.

The implications of a noncategorical/cross-categorical approach are profound—encompassing theoretical, practical, legal, and ethical matters. For example, such an approach affects the way in which exceptional individuals are described and studied, alters assessment and teaching practices, and requires extensive revision of teacher training and certification (see Adelman, 1973).

Given the scope of the implications of a noncategorical system, it is not surprising that the debate about such an approach has been vociferous (e.g., Phipps, 1982; Sparks & Richardson, 1981). Opponents, for instance, warn that a noncategorical approach will lead to inequities and that all who need special help will not be appropriately served by such a strategy. More specifically, they argue that the special needs of some individuals will be ignored because teachers will lack the competence and time required to deal with the diversity of educational needs in their classrooms. In addition, they worry that support for special education will be jeopardized because the general public, elected officials, policymakers, judges, administrators, and so forth will not understand or appreciate the special needs of the individuals involved should current or comparable labels denoting handicapping conditions no longer be stressed.

problem of identifying subgroups of disabled individuals. Although recent attempts to identify learning disability subgroups are conceptually more sophisticated than earlier efforts, in practice they have not proved to be much more useful. The reason for this is that the assessment data that a researcher in this area must rely on to diagnose a person as disabled are not as precise as are needed (e.g., see Morrison, MacMillan, & Kavale, 1985). Before there can be meaningful research on subgroups of learning *disabilities*, one must be able to distinguish *validly* the

disabled from persons with other types of learning problems. The warning of computer analysts is relevant: they constantly caution researchers that the quality of what comes out of the computer is only as good as the data fed into the computer. Or, as they are more likely to say, "GIGO—garbage in, garbage out."

New approaches are needed (see Box 13–2).

One direction pursued focuses on improved neuropsychological test batteries. We discussed this activity in Chapters 4 and

Box 13–2

Research
Identifying Children with Learning Disabilities: Needed a New Approach

In reporting on a study of diagnostic procedures used to identify LD children (grades K–6) in fourteen school districts, Perlmutter and Parus (1983) state:

"Results of our survey revealed similarities in diagnostic procedures in that all districts used standardized achievement tests and teacher referrals, and communicated at some point with the referral child's parents. However, except for certain tests which enjoyed popularity, districts did not agree on how to identify specific disabilities. Thus, differences were found in (a) number of tests given, (b) use of tests and subtests, (c) use of intelligence tests, (d) choice of testing instruments, (e) cutoff points for determining learning disabilities, (f) composition of multidisciplinary teams, and (g) the point at which parents were consulted during the diagnostic process. In addition, while some districts established specific guidelines for determining which students should be classified as LD, others relied almost entirely on clinical judgment.

"The teacher played a major role in the identification process. Thus, teacher referrals constituted the majority of initial contacts and teacher assessments made up the primary diagnostic screening device used by most districts." (p. 326)

Citing others, the investigators note:

"The identification problem influences research on LD populations as well as school classification systems. In a review of 229 articles, Harber (1981) found that 'in more than two-fifths of the studies involving LD subjects, the criteria for such classification were not provided,' and that 'studies which did not operationally define learning disabilities utilized a wide range of criteria' (p. 372). In a further condemnation of classification systems used in research on learning disabilities, Kavale and Nye (1981), after having reviewed 307 studies, concluded that 'the learning disabilities research literature presents a divergent picture of the nature and characteristics of learning disabilities and reflects a lack of consensus regarding standard identification criteria'" (p. 383).

The researchers conclude:

"The problem of improper or unreliable identification procedures is of concern to both frontline school personnel and researchers in the field."

"If there is disagreement and uncertainty among researchers in the field, it should come as no surprise that individual districts do not agree on how to diagnose and deal with potential LD students. One recurring complaint heard while conducting this study was that the ambiguity of the definition made it difficult to be confident in any given diagnosis." (pp. 327–28)

---

5. The approaches appear useful for studying brain-behavior relationships in individuals with undisputed signs of brain damage. It will be many years, however, before neuropsychological testing is able to provide valid, *direct* evidence for use in diagnosing the type of *minor* central nervous system (CNS) trouble often associated with learning disabilities.

It will also be many years before adequate data are gathered and evaluated to determine the usefulness of neuropsychological test batteries in providing valid, *indirect* evidence of learning disabilities. Thus, efforts to detect learning disabilities through neuropsychological testing must be viewed as being in the early stages of experimentation.

Another proposed approach to differential diagnosis of learning disabilities tries to avoid the limitations of current test batteries and to account for the fact that environmental factors cause some learning problems. The strategy involves a sequence of activity, the first step of which is program improvement. This step is designed to prevent and screen out those learning problems not appropriately labeled as learning disabilities. Learning disabilities among the remaining pool of learning problems then are identified by using diagnostic teaching procedures.

For example, preschool, kindergarten, and primary school programs could be upgraded to improve their capability for serving a wider range of individual differences. This would reduce the proportion of learning problems. That is, some would be prevented; others would be corrected soon after onset.

The relatively small group of individuals whose learning problems remained uncorrected—despite program improvements—would become candidates for diagnostic consideration as learning disabled. The diagnosis would be made over a period of weeks as part of a program of one-to-one diagnostic teaching. Such teaching would be carried out in connection with an area of instruction each individual had identified as interesting. Certain levels of difficulty in acquiring or retaining material that the individual is trying to learn would be used as criteria for a diagnosis of learning disability. That is, poor performance under *optimal* learning circumstances would be used as minimal criteria.

A great deal of research is needed before the usefulness of any new strategy can be demonstrated. However, unlike the test approaches, the program improvement strategy is seen as consistent with the principle of the least intervention needed and as having obvious immediate positive side effects.

In highlighting these strategies, our intent is not to overemphasize any particular approach. The point is to stress the importance of exploring new directions. There is little doubt that current approaches for finding the learning disabled can be improved. Unfortunately, not all developers of new strategies take cognizance of the limitations of prevailing models and procedures, and many research efforts are hampered by measurement problems.

Improving Programs

Whether or not programs are improved as a strategy for differential diagnosis of learning disabilities, current instructional approaches definitely must be upgraded. A number of ongoing concerns are worth noting here.

A central concern is that many general and special education teachers have become convinced that every procedure developed for learning problems is *special*. As stressed throughout Part 3, a variety of seemingly different practices can and probably should be understood in terms of some very general underlying concepts. Helping those who are inattentive or who learn slowly may only require providing more support and guidance and improving the teaching-learning match (see Box 13–3).

Another continuing concern stems from the fact that so many individuals placed in programs for the learning disabled are likely to have been *misdiagnosed*. This fact makes it essential that such programs be redesigned to deal systematically with the full range of learning problems of those enrolled. In particular, those who have no disability should not be viewed or treated as if there is something wrong with their learning capability.

Ongoing efforts also are being made in programs for those with learning problems to avoid limiting them to remediation. One of the important helping strategies is to include activities they like, even if the indi-

Box 13–3

Research and Practice
Improving Schools

It would be nice if all that was required to improve programs for LD students was to buy new equipment and materials or teach teachers a few new remedial techniques. Such steps can help. So can new ideas from clinical and laboratory research specifically focused on remediation. But in the long run, what are needed are findings about how schools can be improved in general.

Reporting on a seven-year study of more than one thousand schools across the United States, John Goodlad (1984) concludes that focusing on any one part of the system of formal schooling is to arrive at simplistic analyses and solutions. Indeed, he sees the continuing failure to make major improvements in schooling as the result of piecemeal and poorly conceived reforms. He stresses the need for reforms in almost every facet of the educational system—from the way program rationales are formulated to who should make decisions, from the way time and teachers are used to the content of the curriculum and the way students are grouped, from how schools are organized to the way teachers are trained.

In general, schools are seen as too often forcing students into a passive role in their education. Teachers and principals are seen as having too little to say about how their school programs can be improved. Parents are seen as too rarely consulted or informed. Students, teachers, principals, and parents—all are seen as having the ability to play a much greater role in making schools a place where people work together actively and cooperatively toward agreed-upon educational goals.

---

viduals can do them without difficulty. Similarly, programs are supposed to avoid aggravating vulnerability. Few people want to spend most of their time in situations in which they are required to rely primarily on their weaknesses.

In the same vein, while evident that those with learning problems have areas of weakness, such problems do not affect the competence of most people to communicate and make choices. Thus, it has been suggested that greater emphasis be devoted to direct dialogue with individuals to arrive at decisions about what is to be done to help them overcome their problems. As one writer has noted:

"To help another . . . you have to know what the other needs, and the only way to find out what the other needs is for him to tell you. And he won't tell you unless he thinks you will listen . . . carefully. And the way to convince him you will listen carefully is to listen carefully." (Nyberg, 1971, p. 181)

Finally, not all concerns about program improvements are associated with academic programs for children and adolescents. For some time, it has been recognized that there is a chronic need to develop and evolve vocational and postsecondary level programs for the learning disabled. Surveys show, for example, that many learning disabled students want to attend college and that too many who try are forced to drop out because of lack of appropriate programs to accommodate their special needs (see Box 13–4 and Reading K).

Other program concerns could be highlighted. But listing all the issues and problems is less important than noting that there is some dissatisfaction with current intervention approaches and that directions for improvement have been identified.

Box 13–4

Concern in the Field
**Postsecondary Education and
Vocational Training**

Postsecondary and vocational programs for LD students have only recently appeared on the scene, and they are developing rather slowly. One reason for this is that such programs are somewhat controversial.

For some time, it was widely assumed that so few LD students were interested in going to college that special programs for them were not needed. Figures were generated in the 1970s and early 1980s to counteract this assumption.

After the assumption of lack of interest was undermined, the debate shifted to the matter of whether such students would be able to survive in college even with special help. This assumption was bolstered by figures that showed how few LD students who began college actually graduated. To rebut this argument, it has been emphasized that even when special programs are offered, the tendency is to promise more than is delivered; thus, students are not getting the support necessary for success.

The fact that special programs at the college level are costly and difficult to set up also is a factor that tends to cause resistance. The issue raised here is that of priorities. Given that only so much money is available, should it be used to bolster existing, regular programs that are undersupported or should it be used to create additional services for those who need special help to survive in college?

Anyone interested in the topic of college programs for LD students (issues, components, and available programs) can start with the November 1982 issue of the *Journal of Learning Disabilities,* which featured a series of articles on the subject. Also relevant is a two-part article entitled "College Possibilities for the Learning Disabled," by Mangrum and Strichart, published in May and June 1983 in *Learning*

Disabilities (a one-article-a-month journal published by Grune & Stratton, Inc.). Further discussion and guides to colleges for learning disabled students are included in Liscio (1985) and Mangrum and Strichart (1985).

More controversial than postsecondary programs has been the topic of vocational training for those with learning disabilities. The roots of the issue are found in the type of menial jobs that many vocational programs for the handicapped have emphasized. Critics say such programs often demean and underutilize the potential of those enrolled and certainly limit their options for the future.

To deal with the criticism, the trend seems to be toward increasing the range of vocational options for which training is made available. Lack of money and resources, of course, are stumbling blocks. Therefore, critics still worry that vocational programs are likely to remain low-level programs.

As long as there are any vocational programs, there also is controversy over who should be enrolled in such programs and how enrollment decisions are made.

If you are interested in reading more about vocational training, career planning, and services for the LD adult, you can consult works discussing the topics, including *Career-Vocational Education for Handicapped Youth* by Miller and Schloss (1982); *Handbook for Career Planning for Special Needs Students* by Harrington (1982); the summer, 1983, issue of *Teaching Exceptional Children;* an article in the *Journal of Learning Disabilities* (April, 1982), "Problems and Issues in Delivering Vocational Instruction and Support Services to Students with Learning Disabilities," by J. P. Greenan; and two articles in the fall, 1981, issue of *Learning Disability Quarterly,* "Services for the LD Adult: A Working Paper," by R. A. Gray, and "Learning Disabilities and Eligibility for Vocational Rehabilitation Services: A Chronology of Events," by P. J. Gerber.

Upgrading Research

A sad-funny fact about most research reports is that the final paragraphs usually contain some form of the statement "More research is needed." More research is always needed. But an even greater truism is that better research is needed.

One key to improving research in learning disabilities obviously lies with improved identification of who is learning disabled. Toward this end, there has been an increasing effort to convince researchers that some common set of descriptors or "marker variables" should be reported for every study of persons designated as learning disabled (see Box 13–5).

Another direction long advocated for improving research in LD identification is doing more comprehensive studies of the causes and correction of learning problems. In this connection, there is interest in countering premature acceptance of correlates as causes, widening the range of possible causes investigated, and using data on apparently effective corrective strategies as clues about certain causes. A particular concern in this area has been the relative failure to gather data on daily teacher-student transactions,

---

Box 13–5

Research
Describing Participants in LD Research

In 1983, a committee of the Council for Learning Disabilities formulated a set of recommendations regarding the description of LD research participants. The recommendations are made in a draft of a paper entitled "Minimum Standards for the Description of Subjects Used in Learning Disabilities Research Reports" (CLD Research Committee, Sept., 1983). The recommendations draw heavily on the "marker variable" research project conducted by Barbara Keogh and her colleagues (1982).

As guidelines, the committee suggests that both quantitative and qualitative data on participants be reported, presented in one of two tables and in a narrative section. The table proposed for "applied behavioral" research would include:

**Sample Table for Description of Subjects for
Analysis of Behavior Research**

Numbers:	Specific achievement:	SES:	Educational
male _____	area _____	high _____	placement:
female _____	mean _____	middle _____	type of
total _____	range _____	low _____	placement _____
Age:	test(s) used _____	IQ:	number _____
mean _____	Ability:	mean _____	type of
range _____	area _____	range _____	placement _____
Race:	mean _____	test(s) used _____	number _____
Anglo _____	range _____	Overall achievement:	Years receiving special
Hispanic _____	test(s) used _____	mean _____	services:
Black _____		range _____	mean _____
other _____		test(s) used _____	range _____

For group research, the following table is proposed:

Sample Table for Description of Subjects for Group Research

Experimental Group	*Control Group*	*Experimental Group*	*Control Group*
Numbers:	Numbers:	IQ:	IQ:
male _____	male _____	mean _____	mean _____
female _____	female _____	range _____	range _____
total _____	total _____	test(s) used _____	test(s) used _____
Age:	Age:	Overall	Overall
mean _____	mean _____	achievement:	achievement:
range _____	range _____	mean _____	mean _____
Race:	Race:	range _____	range _____
Anglo _____	Anglo _____	test(s) used _____	test(s) used _____
Hispanic _____	Hispanic _____	Specific	Specific
Black _____	Black _____	achievement:	achievement:
Other _____	other _____	area _____	area _____
		mean _____	mean _____
		range _____	range _____
		test(s) used _____	test(s) used _____
(SES) Socioeconomic	SES:	Ability:	Ability:
status)	high _____	area _____	area _____
high _____	middle _____	mean _____	mean _____
middle _____	low _____	range _____	range _____
low _____	Educational	test(s) used _____	test(s) used _____
Educational	placement:	Years receiving	
placement:	type of	special services:	
type of	placement _____	mean _____	
placement _____	number _____	range _____	
number _____	type of		
type of	placement _____		
placement _____	number _____		
number _____			

In preparing either table, it is stressed that (1) when data on a particular item are unavailable, (UN) should be entered, (2) any other available test information should be added in an appropriate place, and (3) whenever other specific test data are relevant to the particular type of study, they should be included.

With regard to the narrative section, the committee states:

"By using a table to describe the demographic subject information, the narrative section could be rather brief. In cases, however, where the researcher cannot obtain the demographic information requested in the table, information about the school districts' criteria for placement needs to be detailed. In particular, the IQ and achievement criteria must be provided.

"In addition, information should be included on the following topics: (1) motivation of the student(s), (2) students' educational background, (3) background and description of the experimenters or teachers."

especially for purposes of detecting misdiagnosed students.

A basic ongoing concern in all efforts to study assessment and corrective strategies is how to control or account for motivational effects. Although aware of the problem, LD researchers generally have not paid great attention to the matter. Analyses of research reports show that the implications of the widespread impact of motivational factors have yet to be addressed adequately. Of course, the bottom line in improving LD research is money. And the availability of research money is a matter of political policy and priority. What now appears evident is that priority is given to meeting short-term service needs—and to programs of research that claim they can quickly demonstrate how to meet these needs. Unfortunate, but true, this type of activity has not led to much new knowledge about how to significantly improve interventions.

We may conclude, therefore, that the type of research that can best provide major advances in the LD field is not easily, cheaply, or rapidly carried out. Clearly, policymakers have accepted the idea that immediate services and resources are needed to help persons experiencing learning disabilities. Apparently, it remains hard for them to accept the idea that well-designed, long-term, and usually costly research studies are indispensable if new and fundamental knowledge is to be made available to practitioners.

EMERGING CONCERNS

Learning disabilities exist in a societal context. Therefore as the field matures, new concerns are emerging about the role society plays in shaping what goes on in LD programs and about the responsibilities the field has to the society at large (see Box 13–6).

As with most problem populations, the public seems concerned but not sure how much to help those diagnosed as learning disabled. In recent years, legislation and litigation in the United States have reflected both the concern of society and its fluctuating support.

There have been demands for increased and better student services and greater protection of student rights. There has been a call for accountability related to such outcomes as improved basic skills and reduced behavior problems. Yet, along with the mandates to provide more help, protection, skill building, behavior control, and evaluation, there has been a major reduction in financial support for LD services, training, and research.

Not surprisingly, then, society's approach to dealing with the learning disabled has raised a variety of issues and problems. Currently, three topics are emerging as of particular concern: (1) social control, (2) ethics, and (3) accountability.

Social Control

Society's role related to problem populations has been widely discussed. As one writer nicely summarizes the matter:

> "Society defines what is exceptional or deviant, and appropriate treatments are designed quite as much to protect society as they are to help the child."
>
> "'To take care of them' can and should be read with two meanings: to give children help and to exclude them from the community." (Hobbs, 1975, pp. 20–21)

The topic of social control encompasses three concerns that increasingly appear to need the field's attention. These can be discussed in terms of tendencies on the part of practitioners toward *excessive* use of (1) power, (2) limits, and (3) expert role-playing in relating to clients.

Box 13–6

Viewpoint
Schooling and Helping

Over the years, we have seen the number of students with learning problems increase well beyond the resources available to help them. At first, our primary interest was in that subgroup who had learning disabilities. We wanted to understand their problems and *help* them and, in doing so, demonstrate respect for rights, liberties, dignity, and worth. We also saw our work as a way to serve society and perhaps improve the quality of education and of psycho-educational practices in general. Such straightforward motives were soon confounded.

We discovered that learning problems were often *schooling* and *societal* problems and that it was impossible to identify and thus limit our focus to any one subgroup of learning problems. We also found that schooling and helping are very complex phenomena, which sometimes are compatible but very often come into conflict.

These realities led us to reflect on the role of school environments and professional helpers in contributing to the cause of certain learning problems. It did not take long, however, to realize that blaming professionals was to miss the point; that is, there are circumstances that often make schooling and helping incompatible, especially for students who do not fit in.

Professionals working in schools struggle against horrendous odds in efforts to make programs work for most students. Many beat the odds and are remarkably successful. Even the most successful teacher, however, has a few problem students. And in some school districts, there are large numbers of students for whom no one seems to know what to do.

One can debate who is at fault and what labels and definitions seem appropriate. What is beyond debate, however, is that students in trouble at school need help.

Many school professionals who could provide such help, and who want to, indicate that conflicting societal priorities and pressures on school systems prevent them from doing so. They are asked increasingly to assume functions other than helping or educating, including a wide variety of activities related to caretaking, housekeeping, classroom management, record-keeping to meet naive accountability demands, and babysitting and police work.

At times, teachers and other school personnel seem to be asked to solve some of society's most difficult problems—illiteracy, delinquency, racial prejudice, and poverty. And as the years go by without any solution for these complex problems, school professionals seem to be the target of society's frustration.

Power. As if dealing with the complexities of learning and learning problems were not enough, LD practitioners often find their work confounded by students' behavior problems. Students behind in their reading also may have trouble with peers, their family, and even with legal authorities. Older students, in particular, often are involved with drug or alcohol abuse and truancy.

When confronted with behavior problems, practitioners experience the dilemma of trying to help and socialize at the same time. In order to help, they need the individual's cooperation. To gain cooperation, interfering behaviors must be brought under control. Because those who misbehave usually are not viewed as likely to control their own behavior, practitioners tend to see their only recourse as to use external pressure to gain control. Whether they are successful in doing so depends, in part, on the degree to which they have exercised and can exercise real power in the situation.

Power stems from the political nature of

the relationships between society and its citizens; among members of organizations, groups, families; and between professionals and their clients. In any specific situation, the source of power can be identified by clarifying who makes the decisions that have the greatest influence over the most important processes and outcomes.

Ironically, most of us can easily identify situations in which decisions are made for us, and we feel coerced. It is, however, more difficult to recognize situations in which we are coercive (see Box 13–7).

In general, then, the use of power in efforts to control negative behavior raises concern about coercion and the loss of freedoms and rights. Behavior modification, medica-

tion, screening, referral, placement, suspension, expulsion—all may be beneficial; but such procedures also may be used simply to *force* individuals to behave as others think they should. All may be misused in ways that deprive individuals of their rights.

Limits. In recent years, it has become clearer that the limits imposed in order to teach in schools and to control problem behavior often conflict with helping. As one writer has noted, one would not be surprised to hear any student say to a teacher "If you are here to help me . . . why must I do everything your way?" (Weinberg, 1974, p. 15).

Box 13–7

Viewpoints
Social Control in the Classroom

"I do not wish to refer to the traditional school in ways which set up a caricature in lieu of a picture. But I think it is fair to say that one reason the personal commands of the teacher so often played an undue role and a reason why the order which existed was so much a matter of sheer obedience to the will of an adult was because the situation almost forced it upon the teacher. The school was not a group or community held together by participation in common activities. Consequently, the normal, proper conditions of control were lacking. Their absence was made up for, and to a considerable extent had to be made up for, by the direct intervention of the teacher, who, as the saying went, 'kept order.' He kept it because order was in the teacher's keeping, instead of residing in the shared work being done."

"I am not romantic enough about the young to suppose that every pupil will respond or that any child of normally strong impulses will respond on every occasion. There are likely to be some who . . . because of previous experience, are bumptious, and unruly and per-

haps downright rebellious. But it is certain that the general principle of social control cannot be predicated upon such cases. It is also true that no general rule can be laid down for dealing with such cases. The teacher has to deal with them individually. He or she cannot, if the educational process is to go on, make it a question of pitting one will against another in order to see which is the strongest, nor yet allow the unruly and non-participating pupils to stand permanently in the way of the educative activities of others. Exclusion perhaps is the only available measure at a given juncture, but it is no solution. For it may strengthen the very causes which have brought about the undesirable antisocial attitude. . . ." (Dewey, 1938, pp. 55–57)

"We like children who are a little afraid of us, docile, deferential children, though not, of course, if they are so obviously afraid that they threaten our image of ourselves as kind lovable people whom there is no reason to fear. We find ideal the kind of 'good' children who are just enough afraid of us to do everything we want, without making us feel that fear is what is making them do it." (Holt, 1964, pp. 167–168)

One of Chris's remedial teachers exercised control by insisting that students complete assignments exactly in the manner prescribed, ask for permission before doing anything other than what they were directed to do, and not talk with each other or move around the class. Chris and most of the other students in the class hated the teacher and the program. Some rebelled and were punished—even to the point of expulsion; others simply did the minimum necessary to avoid severe punishments.

In contrast, the teacher who was most successful in helping Bret worked with each student to evolve a setting where they could talk quietly while working, move about as needed, and add personal experiences and interests to assignments as they desired. Bret and the others responded well to such an approach, and there was very little misbehavior.

Many writers have suggested that the overreliance on power and tight limits in many classrooms probably is short-sighted and counterproductive (see Deci, 1980; Dewey, 1938). Such tactics may have an immediate impact on some negative behaviors, but they may interfere with learning and even with the intended long-term socialization. A concern for the future is how to teach practitioners and parents to avoid an *overemphasis* on using power and tight limits to establish control and to evolve helping procedures that can lead to cooperation and appropriate social functioning (see Box 13–8).

Neither license nor naive permissiveness is an answer to concerns about excessive use of power and limits to control student behavior. What emerging approaches suggest is (1) to increase the range of valued options and realistic choices in classroom programs and (2) to get rid of limitations that disrupt students' feelings of self-determination and appear to interfere with the establishment of helping relationships. The alternative to taking such steps seems to be a continuation of a large number of student and teacher dropouts, psychologically if not physically.

Expert Role-Playing.   Tremendous pressures are exerted on professionals in the LD field to provide immediate answers and services to the public. In meeting this pressure, cautious optimism, self-criticism, and professional standards often seem to give way to expert role-playing.

Overselling expertise by practitioners and researchers alike is a major concern in all fields. One facet of overselling expertise has been a trend toward large-scale use of procedures before their appropriate validation.

In general, the tendency to overstate expertise appears to be highly related to the fostering of fads, panaceas, and mystical thinking (see Frank, 1961; Illich, 1976). Such fads and panaceas reflect an uncritical acceptance of what are often very poor services. As the public is "burned" by many unfulfilled hopes and promises, they become disappointed, frustrated, and angry. The result often is a backlash in the form of malpractice suits, demands for greater accountability, and increasingly detailed government regulation.

Suggestions for dealing with the tendency to overstate expertise center on increased activity to demystify the general public. Key professionals in such activity are those who teach and write about learning disabilities, those who help shape policy, and those who provide services. The message they need to deliver is simple: Not only don't we know all the answers, we may not be asking some of the most important questions (see Box 13–9).

Ethics

As a field matures, it often finds that during the period of rapid growth there has been relatively little time devoted to ensuring that high ethical standards have been established and maintained. The LD field has not been an exception. Increasingly, leaders in the field are recognizing the need to identify

Box 13–8

Theory and Practice
On Limits

Limits may be defined as the degrees of freedom or range of choices allowed an individual in any given situation. Stated differently, limits are the restraints placed on an individual's freedom of choice and action.

The concept of limits provides a basis for understanding the difference between permissiveness and license. The tendency is to use the term *license* when someone goes well beyond or is encouraged to go well beyond commonly accepted boundaries for behaving. If Chris completely ignores the limits that have been set for him and others like him, we see him as taking, or believing he has been given, license to behave very inappropriately.

When the term *permissiveness* is used, the tendency is to apply it to observed efforts to expand commonly accepted limits. If one agrees with such efforts, one may see them as a move toward establishing greater freedom and liberty; if one doesn't like the direction, it probably is seen as a step toward license and anarchy.

The following diagram graphically suggests that varying criteria may be used in establishing limits.

Everyday you experience differences in the limits you are expected to stay within. As you go from one setting to another, you will observe that different criteria are used regarding what is acceptable behavior. What is appropriate at home is not appropriate at school. What friends expect is not usually the same as what parents expect.

In which situation do you experience the strictest limits?

For students with problems, schools and particularly special classrooms often are the places where the greatest sense of being controlled and losing freedom are experienced. Often the narrow limits imposed by their school program are much more restrictive than the students are likely to experience anywhere else currently or later in life. It has been suggested that this excessive control adds to their dislike of school and teachers (Koestner, Ryan, Bernieri, & Holt, 1984). What seems surprising is not that many rebel and misbehave under such circumstances but that so many accept as much control as they do.

---

unethical practices and to reduce their frequency by establishing clear ethical guidelines and standards (see Box 13–10).

Currently, in deciding whether a procedure is ethical, LD practitioners often make judgments based primarily on their need to use the procedure. For instance, those who need diagnostic labels (e.g., administrators)

Box 13–9

Viewpoint
On Easy Answers

"There's always an easy solution to every human problem—neat, plausible and wrong." H. L. Mencken

focus on the usefulness of existing labels and diagnostic procedures. Those who don't need to make differential diagnoses often brand current labels and identification procedures as unnecessary, harmful, and unethical.

Although the tendency to make ethical judgments in terms of personal usefulness is understandable, ethical concepts and principles provide a better basis for arriving at ethical conclusions (see Reading L). Thus, leaders in the LD field want evolving guidelines to be based on such considerations.

With regard to specific ethical dilemmas, three topics are emerging as critical. These involve the degree to which current practices ensure that (1) intervention benefits outweigh costs, especially physical and psy-

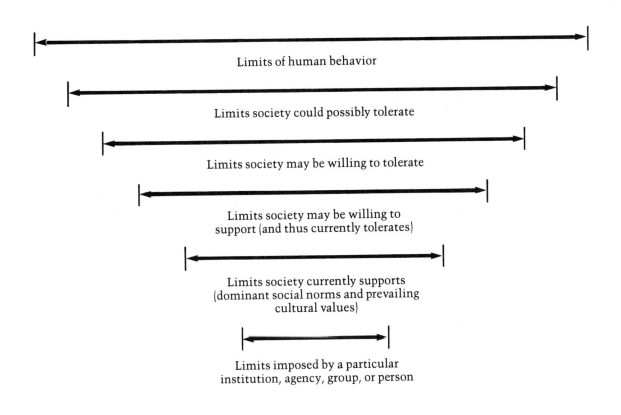

Limits of human behavior

Limits society could possibly tolerate

Limits society may be willing to tolerate

Limits society may be willing to
support (and thus currently tolerates)

Limits society currently supports
(dominant social norms and prevailing
cultural values)

Limits imposed by a particular
institution, agency, group, or person

chological harm, (2) informed consent is given, and (3) the general public is not deceived or mystified.

Cost-Benefit. Ethically, all individuals are entitled to help with problems, such as learning disabilities, for which they are not responsible. There is, of course, no way to provide the needed help without cost. Indeed, if the society finds the help costs too much money, it may not at all be feasible to meet this ethical responsibility.

Even when the financial costs do not outweigh the potential benefits, some negative consequences (side effects) usually are inevitable. Thus, the decision as to whether a practice is ethical also depends, in part, on whether it is seen as having the potential to

do more good than harm (see Beauchamp & Childress, 1979). The current problem, in this regard, is that too little data are available for estimating either the positive or negative long-term effects of most practices in the LD field. (The need for such data makes improvement of evaluative research a high priority ethically—as well as practically.)

Informed Consent. As discussed in Chapter 5, informed consent and other due process concepts increasingly are becoming major issues in the LD field (Biklen, 1978). This is not surprising in any society that values justice and personal liberty.

In the United States, federal legislation has been enacted, e.g., Public Laws 93-380 (1974)

Box 13–10

Current Practices
**Welfare of the Individual Served—
Standards Stated in the Council for
Learning Disabilities Code of Ethics (1978)**

"Because the members of DCLD are both *consumers* and *producers* of service programs and technology that may affect an individual's life significantly, members must engage in a process whereby each individual identified as possessing learning disabilities is guaranteed that his/her welfare is of primary importance.

"a. All members engaged in the identification, evaluation, and treatment of individuals designated learning disabled should adhere to practices that are in keeping with legal standards. Members must guarantee each individual served his/her constitutional rights. No practice that violates a person's legal rights should be condoned.

"b. Any discrimination on the basis of race, sex, religion, or national origin in the identification, evaluation, and treatment of learning disabled individuals should not be condoned by members of DCLD.

"c. Members of DCLD should assume responsibility for their roles as helping members of our society and should realize the significance [of] the trust given to them because of their position to offer services to those in need. They should also present to the public a realistic picture of the limitations of the knowledge base and should not make the claim that they or members of their profession are able to solve all the intricate problems individuals with learning disabilities may manifest. Furthermore, no attempts should be made to promote personal gains by capitalizing in any way upon the educational and social needs of those with learning problems.

"d. In keeping with the legal standards, members of DCLD should safeguard the confidentiality of information obtained during the process of identifying, evaluating, and/or delivering services to learning disabled individuals. The individual or their representatives should be consulted before information is released to other interested professionals."

NOTE: At the time the Code was developed, the Council for Learning Disabilities (CLD) was called the Division for Children with Learning Disabilities (DCLD).

and 94-142 (1975), designed to establish procedures to curtail identification of children as handicapped and their placement in special school programs without due process. As safeguards, the law specifies that parents have the right to be notified in their native language about proposed changes in their child's school program, to examine records, to have the child evaluated in a culturally normative manner, to have an independent evaluation, to register complaints, and to have appeals and impartial hearings. In place of parents, a suitable surrogate (e.g., child advocate) is to be appointed, if needed, to protect the child's rights.

Determining competence is a pivotal concern in ethical considerations associated with seeking consent. Recent research on children's competence to give informed consent has explored the influence of cognitive capabilities, demographic factors such as socioeconomic status, personality variables such as locus of control, and tendencies of youngsters to be deferent. In addition, research has focused on the risks and benefits of involving children in consent procedures. As yet, there are no conclusive findings. Some workers in the area suggest that providing children with information about their problems and alternatives for treatment can facilitate positive child-welfare goals and enhance shared decision making by children, parents, and teachers. Other professionals suggest that children may not be mature enough to make important decisions and that they still need adult protection (see Box 13–11).

Demystification. One of the most basic ethical obligations in any field is to be open and honest and to avoid conflicts of interest (American Psychological Association, 1981). Besides providing relevant information as part of informed consent procedures, this also means making a major attempt to avoid deceiving and mystifying others. Comprehensive activity designed to inform and clarify and to correct misinformation is called *demystification.*

At this time, the general public has difficulty knowing the limitations of current LD practices. Even many professionals are uncertain about just how valid some procedures are.

Widespread use of jargon and failure to clarify the limits, uncertainties, and controversial nature of many practices used in the field not only fails to inform but tends to deceive and mystify. The failure to demystify the public probably accounts, in part, for the many fads and panaceas that have plagued the LD field.

Arguments against efforts to take the time to explain matters to clients and the general public often stress that nonprofessionals don't have the ability to understand the complexities of professional practices or that they are not really interested (see Box

---

Box 13–11

Theory and Practice
Informed Consent

Levine (1975) enumerates eleven elements of information that should be communicated and understood.

1. statement of overall purpose
2. defining the role of the subject
3. informing the prospective subject why he or she has been selected
4. a fair explanation of the procedures, including the setting, the time involved, with whom the subject will interact
5. description of discomforts and risks
6. description of benefits
7. disclosure of alternatives
8. offer to answer questions
9. offer of consultation
10. noncoercive disclaimer
11. consent to incomplete disclosure

To facilitate communication and understanding, such information may need to be presented in a variety of ways. Repeated verbal or written communications, translations, media presentations, question-and-answer follow-ups to evaluate whether information was understood, feedback from other consumers—all may be relevant at various times.

The emphasis on information elements and the very term, *informed* consent, probably somewhat misrepresents the nature of what is involved. As Biklen (1978) says of the term:

"It suggests that the key element of consent is the provision of information to people who are giving consent. Consent is a legal concept that has been referred to and implicitly defined in court cases and in legislation. It has three major aspects: capacity, information, and voluntariness. All three elements are equally relevant to any consent procedure or decision. Simply stated, one must have the ability to give consent in order to do so; one must have adequate information to do so in a knowledgeable way; and one must be free from coercion or any other threat to one's voluntariness." (p. 99)

13–12). To counter this argument, it has been pointed out that one of the most frequent formal complaints from clients and consumers is about practitioners who fail to explain the limitations and uncertainties of the procedures they use.

Besides the straightforward ethical matter of honesty is the matter of practices that mystify (such as the overselling of expertise), thereby tending to undermine people's ability to protect and take care of themselves. Such practices make people believe that if they go to professionals their problems will be solved. And it makes them believe that the *only way* to solve such problems is to go to professionals. Increasingly, a major negative consequence of the failure of practitioners to demystify their activity is that people in modern societies are evolving an unhealthy overreliance on professionals. A large majority of our society believe that they are incompetent to deal with problems in certain basic areas of personal and interpersonal functioning without the services of a professional (Illich, 1976). This, of course, is good for business. But it raises serious ethical concerns about self-serving tendencies on the part of professionals.

The range of ethical considerations we have outlined hardly scrapes the surface. In coming years, professionals in the LD field will be grappling with these and many others (e.g., see Stephens, 1985). Minimally, they must deal more systematically with the following ethical responsibilities:

1. the obligation to be aware of potential negative consequences, such as immediate and long-term harm to individuals, groups, and society,

2. the obligation (ethically and often legally) to inform prospective clients of potential positive and negative consequences,

3. the dual obligation to *minimize* potential negative effects and *maximize* potential benefits during intervention,

4. the obligation to anticipate subsequent negative consequences and to take steps to counter them—especially by preparing clients to protect themselves, and

5. the obligation to acknowledge when in-

Box 13–12

Viewpoint
Mystifying Clients

"If there is, in fact, an area in which one does know things that the client doesn't know, it is extremely easy to believe that one knows generally what is best for the client. . . . In addition there is the fact . . . the client has a serious problem or concern which has rendered the client weak and vulnerable. This, too, surely increases the disposition to respond toward the client in a patronizing, paternalistic fashion. The client of necessity confers substantial power over his or her well-being. . . . Invested with all of this power both by the individual and the society, the . . . profes-

sional responds to the client as though the client were an individual who needed to be looked after and controlled, and to have decisions made for him or her . . . with as little interference from the client as possible." (Wasserstrom, 1975, pp. 21–22)

"The parents of a child who has been labeled and is physically, psychologically, or academically deficient are usually avid consumers of ideas that promise help. These parents are struggling to understand what may be incomprehensible. But answers come easy, and all too often they are given by individuals with well-lubricated ethics in a forceful, professional, quasi-scientific and logical manner." (Pihl, 1975, p. 23)

tervention outcomes (including assessment findings) are inconclusive and to avoid rationalizing and dismissing uncertainties and incongruities.

Understanding ethical concerns, of course, is no guarantee that persons will behave ethically. Indeed, ethical considerations often appear to be honored more in discussion than in practice. Although professional LD organizations have committees to deal with ethical concerns, no one claims that such committees create ethical practitioners. Ultimately, ethical practice is a matter of individual understanding, conscience, and action.

Accountability

In the LD field's early years, the matter of evaluating programs in any systematic and comprehensive way was relatively ignored. Currently, it is one of the most discussed, and least understood, concerns in the field.

Although some practitioners would prefer to ignore the topic, two facts make this impossible. One, evaluative research is essential to the improvement of interventions. Two, this is an age of accountability, and therefore evaluation increasingly is mandated by legislation and government regulations (e.g., see Scheffelin, Ragsdale, & Martinez, 1985).

There can be no doubt that professionals must be accountable. The concern remains how to do it.

Unfortunately, the great need for program evaluation has outstripped the field's present ability to meet this need. As discussed in Chapter 12, comprehensive and valid procedures for use on a wide scale are yet to be evolved.

Comprehensive evaluation requires a considerable set of valid procedures, and development of such procedures requires a considerable financial commitment. Some legislators seem to think that all that is required is for them to demand accountability. For the most part, they have not shown readiness to underwrite the costs of comprehensive evaluation. Indeed, because of the costs, accountability usually remains a token item in most program budgets.

Although evaluation is costly, a number of writers have tried to encourage professionals to see ways to proceed that are not too expensive. They emphasize that there are many ways to reduce costs, such as sampling if a large population is involved, using existing data-gathering procedures whenever possible, systematically developing (over a period of years) new procedures to supplement existing valid instruments, and cutting costs of analyses through the use of microcomputers.

Of course, accountability goes beyond program evaluation. Professionals must be accountable for the degree to which the field as a whole oversells itself. As already discussed, when data are insufficient to support widespread use of a procedure or when data suggest potential problems, professionals always must proceed cautiously. The concern is that unvalidated procedures should be used much more conservatively than they often are and in a controlled, experimental fashion (see Box 13–13).

In general, accountability is a matter of judgments about how close the field comes to being a "good profession." What makes a profession a good one? According to a proposal made in 1965 by the American Psychological Association, members of a good profession:

"1. Guide their practices and policies by a sense of social responsibility;

"2. Devote more of their energies to serving the public interest than to 'guild' functions and to building ingroup strength;

"3. Represent accurately to the public their demonstrable competence;

"4. Develop and enforce a code of ethics primarily to protect the client and only secondarily to protect themselves;

"5. Identify their unique pattern of competencies and focus their efforts to carrying out those functions for which they are best equipped;

"6. Engage in cooperative relations with other professions having related or overlapping competencies and common purposes;

"7. Seek an adaptive balance among efforts devoted to research, teaching, and application;

"8. Maintain open channels of communication among 'discoverers,' teachers, and appliers of knowledge;

"9. Avoid nonfunctional entrance requirements into the profession, such as those based on race, nationality, creed, or arbitrary personality considerations;

"10. Insure that their training is meaningfully related to the subsequent functions of the members of the profession;

"11. Guard against premature espousal of any technique or theory as a final solution to substantive problems;

"12. Strive to make their services accessible to

Box 13–13

Viewpoint
Accountability in a Broad Sense

"The field is at a critical stage in its development. In the last few years, we have had a great deal of the public's 'good will.' This has helped us in many ways. If we don't take steps to avoid the expert trap, we are quite likely not only to lose that good will, but to experience a very painful backlash. I believe the most appropriate way to demonstrate our expertise is to take responsibility for not overstating it. This is not only an ethical stance, although the ethics of the situation should be a compelling enough reason for taking such responsibility. In the long run, it may be a most practical consideration in preventing the loss of much needed support and avoiding the enactment of overly restrictive, mandated guidelines on services and research activity which can adversely affect our efforts to advance the state of the art." (Adelman, 1978, p. 466)

" 'Accountable' is a good word. *Webster's Third* defines it as both 'capable of being accounted for' and 'subject to giving an account.' In the second sense, state legislators and policymakers, including those at the district level, have been diligent in seeking to make

others educationally accountable but have been restrained with respect to their own responsibility for articulating priorities based on careful studies of need and sound educational concepts.

"If it is a message that educators and others are looking for, let that message be couched in the most compelling terms and have the highest professional appeal. The time has come, past come, for the 50 states to articulate as basic policy a commitment to a broad array of educational goals in the four areas that have emerged in this country over more than three hundred years.

"These goals should be revised as needed and endorsed by each successive governor and legislature. Each local district should then reiterate the state's commitment and assume responsibility for assuring every child and youth a sequential, balanced program of academic, civic and social, vocational, and personal studies.

"We have been told frequently in recent years that people want to go back to an earlier, simpler time in our history when the 3 Rs were the sole expectation for schools. If the preceding review of our educational history is reasonably correct, there never was such a time. I doubt that this time has come now." (Goodlad, 1984, pp. 49–50)

all persons seeking such services, regardless of social and financial considerations." (APA, 1968, p. 10)

A SURVEY LOOKING TO THE FUTURE

In 1984, we undertook the task of surveying prominent LD professionals to clarify what they viewed as the most fundamental concerns facing the field. Our intent in doing the survey was to begin a process that would stimulate more systematic thought and planning for the future.

We mailed the brief survey to persons listed as (1) editorial consultants to the *Journal of Learning Disabilities* and the *Learning Disability Quarterly*, (2) officers of the Council for Learning Disabilities (CLD), the Division of Learning Disabilities (DLD), and the Association for Children and Adults with Learning Disabilities (ACLD), (3) fellows and members of the International Academy for Research in Learning Disabilities (IARLD), and (4) authors of learning disability textbooks.

Although a few respondents expressed concern that perhaps there wasn't such a thing as an LD field or that there would be no LD field in the not-too-distant future, most accepted its existence and were concerned with improving the field. The range of problems and issues they wanted to see resolved reflects that concern.

Respondents cited the need for general improvements in theory, research, practice, and training. Improvement in the quality of theoretical analyses was seen as essential to upgrading research; better theory and research were seen as providing the foundation for improving practice, training, and policy and as the key to maintaining the integrity of the field.

For the majority, concern about defining LD (e.g., arriving at a conceptual and operational consensus of just what constitutes a learning disability) was seen as basic to ef-

forts to advance the field. At the same time, the conflicting views that make it so difficult to deal with the matter of defining LD were seen in the responses of those who want the definition broadened vs. those who want it narrowed.

There were also expressions about the need for more and better programs to enhance public awareness, improved legislation, and less politicization of the field. With regard to who might provide guidance in resolving current problems and issues, it was implied that much of the field's future is in the hands of those working for government agencies, major research groups, the leaders of professional and lay organizations, and journal editors and editorial boards.

A sample of some of the specific concerns raised by respondents is provided here. For a more detailed presentation, see the original report (Adelman & Taylor, 1985).

Theory and Research

The most fundamental theoretical concern expressed was that the field does not draw adequately on the theoretical advances of those disciplines relevant to understanding learning, learning problems, and their correction. Specifically cited was the need for systematic effort to

- clarify differences in paradigms and their implications for theory, research, and practice
- base LD theories on psychological and neurophysiological theories of normal human development and functioning
- incorporate transactional, cognitive, and motivational theories into discussions of LD
- develop and clarify, in developmental terms, psycholinguistic analyses of reading and writing
- clarify theoretical bases for intervention practices (assessment, instruction, treat-

ment, service delivery systems, public education)

Deficiencies in theory and lack of agreement about what constitutes LD were seen as seriously handicapping research. Research needs cited ranged from further clarifying who we are talking about to development and validation of effective and efficient identification procedures and corrective interventions (including preventive strategies) for all age levels. In this connection, major issues were raised about whether and when to broaden or narrow the theoretical focus that determines which correlates, hypotheses, and programming considerations are explored.

On a less applied level, the primary concern was for continued investigation of brain-behavior relationships associated with LD, e.g., of neurophysiological/neuroanatomical bases for LD and its manifestations. Other basic research concerns stressed the need for more study of information processing related to memory and attention problems and of language and psycholinguistic development related to learning to read and write.

Also proposed was investigation of a variety of correlates seen as likely to have major implications for intervention. Social competence, problem-solving deficiencies, child abuse, juvenile sexual trauma, familial patterns, sex and cultural (including immigrant group) differences were noted specifically. The importance of developmental comparisons between the nondisabled and those with learning disabilities was frequently stressed.

Many concerns about applied research could not be readily separated from those pointing to immediate needs for improving daily practices. Therefore, these are covered in the following discussion of concerns related to practice.

Practice

Four major areas of concern to practitioners were identified: subtyping, differential pro-

gramming, expanding intervention focus and improving efficacy, and prevention and early intervention.

Subtyping. Most frequently mentioned (by over half the respondents) was the necessity of developing valid procedures for differential diagnosis and subtyping, e.g., for defining, identifying, and classifying the subgroups to be served.

This concern included expression of the need for

1. theory-based activity directed at clarifying the relevant differences between LD and other handicapped individuals at all ages and within the group identified as LD (e.g., differentiating dyslexia from other forms of LD, gifted LD from those with average intelligence)
2. developing valid assessment procedures and criteria for differential diagnoses

In this context, several issues were raised. One was whether to continue seeking agreement on what constitutes a severe discrepancy between aptitude and achievement or whether to develop other criteria for operationally defining LD. Another focused on the advisability of broadening the field by defining as LD any learning problem that is not readily understood.

Differential programming. The next most frequently cited practitioner concern focused on differential instruction and treatment. Included were recognition of the need to accommodate persons whose differences and disabilities interfere with their ability to meet conventional standards.

This concern encompassed expression of the need to develop and validate corrective intervention strategies and related assessment procedures for appropriately identified subgroups and to implement them in ways that remove or minimize stigma.

In the context of differential programming for major subgroups, the issue raised was whether the same ends could be accomplished by programming more effectively for individual differences. Paralleling this concern was the view that too many students are being labeled as LD and provided with special education resources who do not really need such specialized assistance, i.e., those able to learn satisfactorily if motivated and in programs that can accommodate a wide range of individual differences.

Expanding Intervention Focus and Improving Efficacy. The third most frequently cited set of applied concerns stressed the need to expand the nature of intervention activity and improve efficacy through evaluation research. The major focus was on traditional and recently introduced practices, e.g., with particular reference to investigating factors that facilitate and interfere with efficacy. There was, however, also considerable emphasis on creating new approaches.

Specifically cited were the need for

- expansion and improvement of academic, vocational, career, and self-help programs, especially for adolescents and young adults, i.e., a more comprehensive approach to providing services and programs to meet the range of problems and needs that arise at each stage of life for those with LD

- emphasizing more than deficits, e.g., increasing the focus on interests, talents, and strengths of those with LD

- expansion and improvement of services for LD in public school settings

- development and validation of a greater variety of instructional procedures that minimize the drudgery of learning basic skills (e.g., use of microcomputers, increased range of program and personal options)

- development and validation of specific roles that family members can play in helping the LD individual

- development and validation of procedures that improve the degree of generalization and maintenance of what LD students are taught

- long-term follow-up studies to clarify LD treatment efficacy and postschool status with reference to subtypes (or at least contrasting mild with severe/profound problems)

- exploration of psychophysiological/neuropsychological interventions

- clarification of system variables that interfere with and those that best facilitate the learning of individuals with LD

Prevention and early intervention. The fourth most frequently cited major area expressed the desire to prevent or at least identify and correct LD at an early age. Specified as needs were (1) further research on genetic factors and on the relationship between at-risk individuals (infants, young children) and the onset of learning disabilities, (2) intervention and applied research focused on prereferral populations and on detection and intervention at preschool age and in primary grades, and (3) programs to better accommodate individual delays in development.

Training

In addition to higher standards in preparing LD practitioners and researchers, training concerns stressed the need to educate all professionals who have contact with the LD population and to broaden the range of functional consultation to health professionals and families and expand public education programs. The major training issue mentioned was the matter of categorical vs. generic training and certification. In this connection, the validity of separate competency lists for training and certifying LD professionals was questioned. The issue of categorical vs. generic training, of course, is basic to the continuation of the LD field as a separate entity.

Particular emphasis on the following points about training programs was advocated:

- more clarity about what is actually known regarding the constitutional bases for LD and the range of specific disabilities among individuals labeled as LD
- more attention to behavioral facets of LD
- clarification of the implications of developmental and motivational differences for understanding learning, learning problems, and the correction of such problems
- how to adapt and create corrective strategies rather than overrelying on conventionally accepted but unproven approaches

Taken as a whole, the survey responses can be interpreted as prescribing the following future agenda for the LD field. Now that the initial period of exploration and debate in the field is over, the time has come to strengthen conceptual formulations related to (1) identifying the causes of LD, (2) differentiating LD from other learning problems and differentiating among relevant subgroups of learning disabilities, and (3) intervening to ameliorate and prevent. With improved conceptualization, more sophisticated research and practical applications can be pursued.

To accomplish such ends, there must be changes in training, including recruitment from among the best and the brightest. Professionals must be prepared to use and advance the latest in theoretical analyses and related basic and applied research approaches. Besides recruitment and training of new professionals, there remains a need to attract highly able professionals from a variety of disciplines who can help resolve the fundamental concerns.

Finally, a field's survival probably depends as much as anything on the strength of organization and activity manifested by the groups who represent the field. Formal organizations are a major source of advocacy of ideas and actions and a major source of lobbying for recognition and support. As a field matures, its organizations must mature. The focus must move beyond the concern for immediate survival to an analysis of the fundamental obstacles to advancing the field's knowledge base and practices. And the analysis must be followed by coordinated action dedicated to overcoming the obstacles (see Box 13–14).

SUMMARY

The LD field has grown rapidly. In many ways, prevailing orientations and practices have been useful frames of reference for research and practice. They are, however, not sufficient. The status quo must be understood, and that understanding must be used as a springboard for change. Not change for the sake of change or simply to produce more growth. What is needed now is a major transformation. It is time to consider new concepts, develop new frameworks, and explore new approaches.

Most practitioners would like the opportunity to improve their practices and evolve the field. Instead, they usually have to settle for getting through their next activity. To those in this position, it often seems unrealistic to talk about anything but how best to cope with current daily pressures. A common response to proposals for long-term reform is "I'm in favor of anything that will improve the field—but what do I do tomorrow?"

From the perspective of immediate survival, such a response is very understandable. In terms of changing things for the bet-

Viewpoint
On Working Together

Collaboration, networks, partnerships—these terms all reflect a recognition that solutions to the complex concerns confronting fields such as education, psychology, and medicine require the joint effort of all who may be affected or hope to benefit. John Dewey stressed the point in discussing education just before the turn of the twentieth century. Provocative thinkers, such as Seymour Sarason and John Goodlad, continue to emphasize similar ideas today.

As Sarason (1982) states:

"In almost all of the research and evaluation literature on educational change there has been surprisingly little discussion about the parochial conception of constituency that the proponents of change have had. That teachers have to be part of the change process has gained some acceptance, but it still amazes me in 1981 how frequently that acceptance is rhetorical and not actual. . . ."

"The rationale that justifies involving teachers in the change process, beginning with planning, is precisely the rationale that justifies involvement of parents and other community groups. This is not, I must emphasize, a matter of courtesy or the recognition of legal rights. It is a matter that derives from the principle that those who are or may be affected by the change should have some part in the change process because only through such involvement can they become committed to the change. They, like the teachers, come to see the change as *theirs*." (p. 294)

And, with a growing appreciation that parents and other community groups should be a part of collaborative efforts, we hope that there will be an increased awareness of the importance of including youngsters as well.

If you want to read more about this topic, see the following:

GOODLAD, J. I. (1984). *A place called school.* New York: McGraw-Hill.
SARASON, S. B. (1982). *The culture of the school and the problem of change,* 2nd ed. Boston: Allyn & Bacon.

ter, however, the narrow focus on survival probably tends to perpetuate many problems—including the need to settle for daily survival rather than improving the quality of our world.

Too often, changes seem to result primarily in reaction to demands for accountability and other indications of a backlash in public opinion. Reactions of this type seldom produce carefully formulated reforms. Indeed, they usually are harmful to a field.

To prevent further negative reactions to the LD field, professionals have been urged to move quickly to establish higher standards of practice and mechanisms for change. Of particular importance are the following concerns, which have been discussed throughout this chapter:

- Differentiating learning problems: developing procedures that can validly differentiate those who are learning disabled from those with other types of learning problems
- Improving current programs: dealing systematically with the full range of learning problems, recognizing the commonalities among supposedly specialized procedures, not limiting programs to remediation, understanding what help is wanted, and evolving postsecondary and vocational/career programs

- Upgrading research: specifying some common set of descriptions of individuals studied, increasing efforts to control and account for motivational effects, and pursuing new approaches for validly identifying and correcting learning disabilities
- Addressing emerging concerns of social control, ethics, and accountability

Obviously, major changes take time. There is no lack of ideas for improving and eventually transforming the field. Such ideas represent a starting point for those who are concerned with the future.

" . . . creating the future begins with transforming the present.

"If each of us begins with his or her part of the envisioned ecosystem—the piece we understand best and can control most easily—we may be able to shape the necessary evolution." (Goodlad, 1984, p. 357)

Chapter 14

Learning Disabilities: What Do You Think?

I hear, and I forget;
I see, and I remember;
I do, and I understand

(Old Chinese proverb)

In discussing anatomy, one seventh grader wrote: "Anatomy is the human body made up of three parts, the head, the chest, and stummick. The head holds the skull and the brains, if there is any. The chest holds the liver, and the stummick holds the vowels, which are *a, e, i, o, u,* and sometimes *w* and *y.*"

Obviously, it can take a while for any learner to effectively assimilate the many basic things that she or he has been studying.

The preceding chapters have offered a great deal of information and ideas. Either you will soon forget most of what you have read, or you will assimilate the material, and it will become part of the way you view things in the immediate future. Probably what will determine which of these two possibilities takes place is the degree to which you have reason to use what you have learned in the days to come.

One reason that may arise for using the material would be if someone asked you what you thought about some of the issues and problems confronting the field. If so, what might they ask?

What follows are eight questions that reflect basic concerns about learning disabilities that people currently ask about or that we think they should ask about. We encourage you to take this opportunity to see what you think about these matters now. The activity will provide you with a good basis for thinking about the discussion in Chapter 15, which focuses on your possible future involvement with the LD field.

Use a blank sheet of paper to answer each question. In case you should want to review material for a particular question, we have noted some sections of the book in which matters relevant to the topic are discussed. References to other sections can be found in the index.

Remember, there are no simple answers. There are, however, some fascinating practices and ideas and some very interesting controversies that you can share with others to help them understand the current status of the LD field.

1. "I've heard that *learning disabilities* is a special term that should not be used as a catchall label for everyone who has a learning problem.

   "Who should be called learning disabled?"

   See sections in Chapter 1, "Learning Disabilities Defined" and "Learning Disabilities in Perspective."

2. "What causes a learning disability?"

   See Chapter 3.

3. "My youngster's school says that they're going to start a program to identify learning disabilities in kindergarten. I've heard that some professionals are concerned about such screening programs.

   "Should I encourage my child's school to screen kindergartners to find learning disabilities?" (Why or why not?)

   See section in Chapter 4, "Assessing Cause," and review Chapter 5. You may also want to look at Reading B.

4. "What are some limitations of the approaches that are widely used to diagnose and treat learning disabilities?"

   See Chapters 6 and 7.

5. "What are some concepts and steps that can be applied to follow the principle of using the least intervention needed in helping those diagnosed as LD?"

   See Chapter 8.

6. "In working with motivational problems, what are some alternatives to commonly used behavior modification strategies?"

   See section in Chapter 8, "Matching Motivation," and review Chapter 9.

7. "I've heard that not everyone with learning problems needs remediation and that those who do should not be placed in special classes.

   "Who does need remediation and what is the best way to provide for their special learning needs?"

   See Chapters 9 through 11.

8. "There was an editorial in the newspaper calling for greater accountability on the part of educators.

   "How effective are practitioners who work with the learning disabled and should they be made to be more accountable for the outcomes of their work?"

   See Chapter 12 and a section in Chapter 13, "Accountability."

AN ENRICHMENT ACTIVITY

If you tried the study skill activity outlined in the enrichment exercise at the end of Chapter 7 (the SQ3R method), how did it work out for you?

How do you understand this outcome?

Many people who are taught such study skills or skills for memorizing material or who go through other skills training approaches do not follow through. That is, they learn them, may use them briefly, and then give up using them.

Why do you think this happens? (Think in terms of the relationships between motivation and learning and performance discussed in Part 3.)

Chapter *15*

Your Future Relationship with the LD Field

AS A CONSUMER—CLIENT, PARENT, OR REFERRER

AS A CAREER PROFESSIONAL

AS A CONCERNED CITIZEN

By now, you know quite a bit more about learning disabilities than most people do. Because of your new awareness, you probably are starting to notice how many times during the course of daily living the topic of learning disabilities or other learning and schooling problems comes to your attention. Television, newspapers, magazines, friends, and family members—all may bring up concerns related to such topics.

With your new knowledge, you are in a good position to evaluate thoughtfully media and professional presentations and to help clarify a variety of matters for family, friends, and acquaintances. Moreover, you may be among that group of readers who have become (or already were) so intrigued with the matters discussed throughout the text that you are thinking about some type of related professional career. At the very least, as a concerned citizen, you have a role to play in shaping the future direction of efforts to deal with learning disabilities.

This final chapter is devoted to highlighting a few additional points that may help you in your future roles related to the LD field. The focus is on the three major ways most people find themselves involved—as a consumer, as a career professional, or as a concerned citizen.

AS A CONSUMER—CLIENT, PARENT, OR REFERRER

Bret, Chris, Sally, Jan, Johnny, Mary, Jenny, you, your friends and family, us—much of the population of the world can be divided into those who are either directly involved or have significant indirect contact with learning and related problems. For our purposes here, anyone who has any degree of involvement is seen as a consumer.

What are they consuming? Information and services about learning and related problems.

For example, whether directly involved or not, you may find yourself confronted with the question, What should a person who may have a learning disability do about it or what should those responsible for that person do?

Any answer to this question should convey the type of information that clarifies rather than mystifies. The need is for appropriately cautious information to aid in (1) putting the matter into proper perspective, (2) looking at general options for dealing with the problem, and (3) making decisions and following through. Unfortunately, the hardest time for people to get information and sort things out for themselves seems to be when there is a pressing concern. Thus, they may need help from others.

Help can come from various sources. Here, we group such sources as (1) self-help resources (including help from acquaintances and friends) and (2) professional contact.

Self-help. If so inclined, you can use nonprofessional resources to find the information you need. The advantages in doing so are many, not the least of which is the money that may be saved. Three major types of nonprofessional resources are consumers' groups, parents' and self-help organizations, and media presentations such as popularized books and magazine articles.

Consumer information groups gather together and reproduce available information. A major resource for consumer information products is the Consumer Information Center (Department DD, Pueblo, Colo. 81009), an agency of the U.S. General Services Administration. It publishes a catalogue listing booklets from almost thirty agencies of the federal government. The majority of the booklets are free. The titles of four relevant available works are

- "Learning Disability: Not Just a Problem Children Outgrow"
- "Plain Talk About Children with Learning Disabilities"
- "Your Child and Testing"
- "Plain Talk About When Your Child Starts School"

The Foundation for Children with Learning Disabilities (FCLD) is a privately funded organization established in 1977 with one of its primary goals to promote public awareness of learning disabilities. In 1984, the group published a 249-page resource entitled "The FCLD Guide for Parents of Children with Learning Disabilities." The guide provides basic information about learning disabilities (warning signs, guidelines for seeking help, children's rights, alternatives beyond high school), lists sources of information and help, and includes an annotated list of relevant books, periodicals, directories, and audiovisual materials. For a free copy, write

> FCLD
> 99 Park Ave.
> New York, N.Y. 10016

The National Association of College Admissions Counselors publishes the "Guide for Learning Disabled Students," which lists twenty-one schools that provide comprehensive programs for such students. Write

> 9933 Lawler Ave.
> Suite 500
> Skokie, Ill. 60077

More generally, Higher Education and the Handicapped (HEATH) acts as a clearinghouse, providing information about secondary education for the learning disabled. It offers fact sheets, lists of directories, and information about testing, types of programs, and organizations. Also available are bibliographies of recently published pamphlets and books about learning disabilities. Write

> 1 Dupont Circle NW
> Washington, D.C. 20036

Although the information in the materials cited here is presented clearly, not enough effort is made in these materials to clarify issues and consumer concerns.

Consumer advocate groups are more likely to provide the general public with *critical* as well as informative overviews of what to do and what not to do when one has an educational, psychological, or medical problem. For example, an organization called Public Citizen (Health Research Group, 2000 P St., NW, Washington, D.C. 20036) has produced a number of booklets stressing consumer guidelines for careful selection of professional health services. Their approach provides information and instructs consumers in how to ask about and evaluate services to protect themselves when shopping for and using professional help. Although their work has not focused specifically on learning disabilities, it is still relevant because learning disabilities practitioners often model themselves after the medical and mental health professions. Three examples of the Health Research Group's products are

- "A Consumer's Guide to Obtaining Your Medical Records"
- "Through the Mental Health Maze: A Consumer's Guide to Finding a Psychotherapist, Including a Sample Consumer/Therapist Contract"
- "Consumer's Guide to Psychoactive Drugs"

With the rapid changes in laws, regulations, policies, and administrative mechanisms, legal resource networks have developed to provide information to parents and others concerned with individuals with special needs. Three major resources are the Parent Information Centers, Closer Look Information Project, and the Protection and Advocacy Network (see Box 15–1).

Parents played a major role in establishing the LD field, and the organizations parents established continue to play a major role. The obvious example is the Association for Children and Adults with Learning Disabilities (ACLD, 4156 Library Road, Pittsburgh, Pa. 15234 or Kildare House, 323 Chapel, Ottawa, Ontario KIN 7Z2, Canada), with fifty state affiliates and more than 775 local chapters in the United States and abroad. Among its various functions, the organization serves as a referral center, publishes a newsletter, operates an LD literary depository, and provides general information about the field. It also sponsors an annual international conference. ACLD prides itself in its breadth of concern for parent and self-help needs.

Adults diagnosed as LD are beginning to band together to help each other. In the United States, there is the National Network of Learning Disabled Adults (P.O. Box Z, East Texas Station, Commerce, Tex. 75428). Besides general information of use to interested parties, this organization has compiled a list of local self-help groups.

There are books and books and books— some useful, some questionable. There are many texts, journals, and works primarily for professionals. Books for the general public are fewer and have mostly focused on simple explanations and advice. They tend to stress descriptions of the problem and offer suggestions about what parents might do to help their child. Three examples follow.

- Brutten, M., Richardson, S. O., & Mangel, C. (1973). *Something's wrong with my child: A parents' book about children with learning disabilities.* New York: Harcourt Brace Jovanovich.
- Miller, J. (1973). *Helping your child at home.* San Rafael, Calif.: Academic Therapy Publications.
- Osman, B. (1979). *Learning disabilities: A family affair.* New York: Random House.

While professional works have raised many issues and problems, popular books presenting a systematic *critical* look at the

Box 15–1

Current Practice
Legal Resource Networks

As described by Massenzio (1983):

"The Parent Information Centers and the Closer Look Information Project were funded in the 1970s by the U.S. Office of Education. . . . From 1969 to 1972, a major focus of the Closer Look Project . . . was on the location and identification of existing special education facilities and resources. But between 1972 and 1975 . . . , the emphasis shifted to dissemination of the basic issues surrounding the right to education . . . judicial decisions, statutes, and regulations. . . . In 1978–79, the Closer Look Project added intensive training of potential parent-advocates to its activities. . . .

"Parent Information Centers dialogue with state and local officials often centered around issues of policy interpretations, provisions regarding IEP's, notice and due process, and the coordination of state plans and interpretations with federal requirements. Most importantly, information provided by Parent Information Centers has been of that finely tuned variety which could respond to more precise questions about timeliness, participants in meetings, due process, and the like. . . .

". . . a growing number of the activities of state Protection and Advocacy Offices for developmentally disabled persons throughout the nation are concerned with special education issues. . . . In many localities, they represent an important source of information for all aspects of educational law . . . [and] policy matters. . . . The issues presented have recently required a broader knowledge of all aspects of special education implementation and a greater sophistication of analysis . . . The offices tend not only to answer questions, but to define them as well." (pp. 274–75)

LD field are nonexistent. The closest any popularized account has come is a work by P. Schrag and D. Divoky entitled *The Myth of the Hyperactive Child and Other Means of Child Control.* This 1975 book contains an all-out attack on the concepts of hyperactivity and learning disabilities and on some treatments used with those given such diagnostic labels.

Professional Contact.   Even if not done for self-help purposes, one would do well to gain a little consumer sophistication before contacting a professional resource. Not because professionals are out to rip people off (although there are a few shady practitioners in any profession) but because the majority of professional services by their very nature have built-in pathological biases and usually reflect prevailing treatment fads. Thus, a specific practitioner may promote her or his view of the problem and the treatment need-

ed, and the interventions may be extremely disruptive and restrictive. They may also use jargon and perhaps overly complex and unproved theories and practices.

With the need for caution in mind, let's quickly review a range of possibilities people may consider in contacting professionals for help. Also keep in mind that in looking for help, the consumer's problem is twofold—to identify feasible resources and then to evaluate their appropriateness.

As a first professional contact, telephone "helplines" appear to be increasingly popular (see Box 15–2 and Reading M). Well designed and highly visible helplines can provide a means to both inform and protect the public by providing ready access to information. Such services, however, can be abused. For example, besides the general problems of bias noted already, practitioners seeking clients may use the guise of a helpline primarily to solicit new customers for other services.

For many parents, public schools and related public agencies provide the most natural and ongoing contact point for discussing a youngster's learning problems. Indeed, in the United States, federal guidelines stress the obligation of schools to identify learning disabilities and inform parents of their rights related to special programs (see Box 15–3). Thus, a very common and reasonable first referral involves directing people to a public school counselor or psychologist for information.

As an alternative, local universities and colleges often have training or research programs focusing on learning and related problems. They may offer direct services or at least can be a good source of information about reputable local resources (see Reading M). Similarly, mental health agencies and government departments for vocational rehabilitation may provide relevant services or referrals. Some public libraries also have established referral reference lists.

If public resources are not available or are not seen as appropriate, private practitioners are considered. Private resources vary widely in terms of professional affiliation, available services, and competence. They range from referral, testing, and consultation services to training and remedial services in the form of tutoring and special schools; also very much part of the picture are the array of medical or medically related and psychological treatments discussed in earlier chapters.

Identification of public and private programs and practitioners can be done through the type of referral resources already described or by reference to any of a variety of referral directories. One free directory focused specifically on learning disabilities is the *1985–86 Directory of Facilities and Services for the Learning Disabled—Tenth Edition* ($1.50 postage/handling) by Academic Therapy Publications (20 Commercial Blvd., Novato, Calif. 94947–6191).

Evaluating the appropriateness of a potential resource is not an easy task. In the introduction to the 1983–84 edition of the directory by Academic Therapy Publications, it is noted that

---

Box 15–2

Current Practices
Helpline and Consumer Information

In October 1983, the Closer Look Information Project/The Parents' Campaign for Handicapped Children and Youth established the LD TEEN-LINE (toll free 800-522-3458, Monday–Friday, 10 A.M.–4 P.M.). This service is for parents of LD teens, LD teens themselves, and educators who work with adolescents.

The volunteer staff offers information and referrals related to educational advocacy, vocational and postsecondary education and training, vocational rehabilitation, community resources, and publications. A special TEEN Packet is offered that contains information and advice for parents and educators preparing adolescents for the future.

"We are frequently asked: How does one evaluate a facility or service to be sure it meets the needs of an individual? Clearly, the best way is to visit the facility and meet with its director and staff. A second avenue is to talk candidly with someone who has had a family member enrolled. If neither of the above strongly recommended practices is possible, then a letter of inquiry should be directed at the facility requesting a copy of its brochure and full information on the program, staff (credentials), fees, et cetera. At the same time, a descriptive statement on the child should be included so that the director of the facility can determine whether or not the program offered is appropriate." (p. iv)

Some referral services are designed to aid in the task of evaluating potential programs (see Reading M). However, the final judgment is always the consumer's. Thus, for

Box 15–3

Current Practice
Parent Rights and Appeal Procedures

The following is a document prepared for parents by the Los Angeles Unified School District.

"I. General Rights
  • All handicapped children have the right to a free and appropriate public education.
  • Individuals have the right to privacy and confidentiality of all educational records including the right to see, review, and if necessary, challenge the records in accordance with the Family, Educational Rights and Privacy Act of 1974.
  • Individuals have the right to request a copy of the education records prior to meetings.
  • All handicapped children have the right to placement in the least restrictive learning environment, to the program with least restrictive alternatives, and the right to enjoy the same variety of programs as are available to the nonhandicapped.
  • All individuals have the right to receive a full explanation of all procedural safeguards and rights of appeal.

"II. Rights Related to Assessment
  • The right to initiate a request for educational assessment.
  • The right to give or withhold written consent for any proposed activities.
  • The right to have 10 days in which to give or withhold consent.
  • The right to obtain an independent outside assessment. Procedures for obtaining such assessment shall be provided upon request.
  • The right to an assessment that is designed to be free of racial or cultural discrimination.
  • The right to have a description of the procedures and tests to be used and to be fully informed of the assessment results.

"III. Rights Related to Individualized Education Program
  • The right to be notified prior to, and to participate and/or be represented at, meeting(s).
  • The child's right to participate in the meeting(s) as appropriate.
  • The right to have the meeting within 35 school days from date of receipt of signed consent.
  • The right to have the meeting conducted

---

visiting and evaluating a facility or service, the specific consumer's perspective is the most important frame of reference (see Box 15–4).

If any single consumer-oriented guideline is to be emphasized, it is the importance of obtaining as clear a picture as possible about the *competence* of the individual(s) who will actually be working with the person to be helped. Brochures, written program descriptions, the charm of the person representing the program, fancy offices and material displays, and other such professional trappings are not completely irrelevant. They are sim-

ply much less important than the quality of the practitioners who are to spend the greatest amount of time with the person to be helped. Do these practitioners seem to know what they are doing? Are they willing to take the time to explain what it is they do and why? At the first meeting, how well do they do in trying to relate to the person to be helped?

Somewhere in between self-help and turning the problem over to a professional is the expanding movement toward workshops and manuals designed to train parents and other nonprofessionals to work more effec-

in your primary language/communication mode.

- The right to at least an annual review of the Individualized Education Program.
- The right to appeal any decision of the Committee.

"IV. Rights Related to Appeals
"A. Informal Conference
- The right to have the informal conference within 10 days of receipt of written request for hearing.
- The right to be accompanied by a representative.
- The right to examine and have copies of any related educational documents.
- The right to referral to the fair hearing panel where the informal conference fails to resolve concerns.
- The right to be informed of available free or low cost legal or other relevant services.
- The right of the individual to remain in his/her present placement pending all appeals.
"B. Fair Hearing
- The right to a hearing held at a time and place of mutual convenience and

within 45 days following receipt of written requests.
- The right to 10 days notice prior to hearing date, the notice to include date, time and place of hearing.
- The right to select one of the 3 panel members.
- The right to a decision within 10 days after appeal is heard.
- The right to request an administrative review of the decision of the fair hearing panel.
"C. Administrative Review by the Superintendent of Public Instruction
- The right to file a request within 20 days following the fair hearing panel decision.
- The right to be heard within 30 days following receipt of written request.
- The right to knowledge of all rights related to the administrative review.
- The right to be informed within 10 days of the date, time and place of administrative review.
- The right to a written decision within 15 days following the administrative review.
- The right to appeal the decision to a court of competent jurisdiction."

SOURCE: Procedural Safeguards and Appeal Procedures for Individuals with Exceptional Needs, from Bulletin 23, Division of Special Education. Reprinted by permission of Los Angeles Unified School District.

tively with youngsters. Currently, most of these programs are designed to improve parenting in general or to train parents of youngsters whose behavior is hard to handle and parents of very slow learners.

AS A CAREER PROFESSIONAL

When people think about careers related to the LD field, the tendency is to think primarily of teaching. That's not bad. The field needs as many good teachers as it can

recruit (see Box 15–5). However, there are, in fact, a variety of professional and paraprofessional roles open to anyone who wants to focus on learning disabilities and related problems.

Relevant careers are available through training in education, psychology, medicine, social welfare, and numerous other areas. Jobs may involve direct services to clients, college teaching, research, administration, and policymaking. That is, one may be a practitioner; or one may pursue activities designed to improve current practices by training professionals, advancing knowledge, planning and guiding programs, or affecting policy. Specific functions include instruction and training, screening and diagnostic assessment, remediation and therapy, counseling and consultation, program planning and evaluation, experimentation and program development, advocacy and lobbying (see Reading N).

Box 15–4

Program Example
Consumer Guidelines for Evaluating Potential School Placements

The emphasis in the following guidelines is on the student's evaluation. Obviously, parents are involved in the decision making in many if not most cases in which students are to be enrolled in special programs. The reason the guidelines stress the youngster's perspective is because it is so often ignored.

Guidelines

Before visiting the program, ask yourself the following five questions:

1. What kind of teacher do I work best with?
2. What things do I like to do in school?
3. What do I want to learn about?
4. What type of help do I like and need from the teacher?
5. What do I expect to get from my schooling? (What are my goals?)

You will want to keep your answers to these questions in mind as you try to find out what kind of teacher(s), activities, and support are available to you in the program you visit.

The following are things to ask and look for during a program visit:

Classroom observation

1. Do the students seem interested in what they are doing?
2. Are there things you would like to do?
3. Do the activities and tasks seem like you can do them?

Interview the teacher or someone else such as a counselor

1. Tell what type of program you would like, especially the things you want and need from a program.
2. Ask how the program is run, e.g., rules, schedules, homework, grading, opportunity to pursue personal interests.
3. Ask about what you would be expected to do, e.g., behavior limits, skill level expectations.
4. Ask how hard it will be to make changes if parts of the program do not work out as you want them to.

Interview one or more students in the program

1. Ask how they like it and why.
2. Ask if they can ask for and get help when they need it.
3. Ask what they would suggest you do to prepare for making this program a good one for you should you enroll.
4. Ask what they think is the most important thing you would need in order to do well in the program.

Find out what other types of help the program would have available for you, e.g., tutoring, counseling.

Box 15–5

Research
Who Aspires to Teach?

Roberson, Keith, and Page (1983) report a study designed to look at factors involved in who decides to prepare for a career in teaching. By way of introduction, they note that

"Having come full circle from the shortage of the '60s, through the surplus of the '70s, to yet another shortage predicted for the '80s, we still know too little about the influences on and motivations of those who decide to teach, despite the ups and downs of the profession. Here, path analysis was used to study the relative importance of various background variables, attitudes, and perceived motivations on the occupational aspirations of high school seniors who aspire to teach compared to those who do not. . . ." (p. 14)

Their data and analyses lead them to the following conclusions about who aspires to teach in the 1980s:

"1. Now, as in the past, it is primarily white females who aspire to teach. Seventy-five percent of those aspiring to teach (in the present sample) were white females.

"2. Those aspiring to teach are much less concerned with earning a good income than are those choosing other professions. This effect seems especially true for males.

"3. Job security, once reported as an important motivation for entering teaching, does not appear to be an important consideration today, except for blacks. Today's teacher aspirants are influenced by a desire to work with friendly people, and (for blacks and males) are not especially concerned with 'success.'

"4. Consistent with previous research, it appears that teacher aspirants today are somewhat less able intellectually than their classmates. Lower ability is a notable influence for females and blacks who aspire to teach, but not for white males. It seems possible that affirmative action, while creating opportunities for women and minorities, may drain off some teaching talent to professions with higher rewards. . . ."

"Currently, those who desire a good income do not enter the teaching profession. Those who do enter teaching, while less concerned with income, are also often less able than others. Clearly, if we desire excellence in teaching, we need to reward it. . . ."

"Those teachers who choose to enter the profession despite low wages seem motivated to do work that they enjoy, with other people whom they also enjoy. These are the intrinsic rewards associated with teaching. However, if we permit teaching to remain as extrinsically unsatisfying as it presently is by not budgeting to the profession wages comparable to those of other professions, then we can expect to no longer see studies that address the issue, 'Who Aspires to Teach?' This title will have been replaced with 'Does *Anyone* Aspire to Teach?'" (p. 20) (From "Now Who Aspires to Teach?" by Sandra D. Roberson, Timothy Z. Keith, and Ellis B. Page, EDUCATIONAL RESEARCHER, Volume 12, Number 6, June–July 1983. Copyright © 1983 American Educational Research Association. Reprinted by permission.)

What do you think about these conclusions? How do they fit with your own experiences? Those of friends you know who teach or are preparing to teach? Those who decided against teaching as a career?

Some specific examples of relevant service positions found in the public and private sectors are as follow:

Teaching	Classroom aides
	Regular classroom teacher
	Reading specialist
	Special education teacher
	Adaptive physical education specialist
	Vocation career education specialist
	Resource room teacher
	Resource specialist or consultant
	Tutor or educational therapist
Psychological Services	School psychologist
	Educational psychologist
	Clinical psychologist
	Developmental psychologist
	Neuropsychologist
	Medical psychologist
Medical Services	Pediatrician
	Neurologist
	Psychiatrist
	Ophthalmologist
Social Services	Social welfare worker
	Community advocate
Support Services	Speech therapist
	Recreational-movement-dance therapist
	Occupational therapist
	Optometrist

In addition, more and more lawyers and lobbyists are working for public agencies and for professional and parent organizations concerned with individuals with special needs. And, with rapidly expanding computer applications, there are increasing opportunities for those with interest and training in the use of computers in the classroom and as an aid in assessment, program planning and evaluation, and so forth.

As important as daily service is, a critical need in advancing a field is acquisition of new knowledge. Research careers in almost any of the biological and social sciences can be directed toward problems of concern to the LD field. Basic researchers concentrating on language development, psycholinguistics, neurology, pharmacology, sociology, anthropology, and so forth may make contributions in ways yet to be imagined.

Obviously, many careers are open to those who find the topic of learning disabilities fascinating (see Box 15–6).

Box 15–6

JILL: "What do you want to be when you grow up?"

JACK: "A psychologist."

JILL: "Oh, you want to help people who have problems."

JACK: "No, I'm just nosey!"

AS A CONCERNED CITIZEN

"The present is not pregnant with one future, but with many possible futures. That fact alone requires us to avoid despair and nihilism and to pursue the goals of change." (Sarason, 1982, p. 298)

We all have a role to play in shaping tomorrow.

Whether or not you ever have specific consumer or career interests in the LD field, you will have plenty of opportunity to play a role as an informed and concerned citizen. You will also experience positive and negative effects as a result of the field's activities. Your tax money pays for much of what the field does. The culture of which you are a part shapes how individuals with problems such as learning disabilities are viewed. In turn, practices by LD professionals influence how those around you view their competence to deal with such problems.

If you have a child, you will be concerned about schools and education (see Box 15–7 and Reading O). If your youngster does not have a problem, you will not want his or her education to be negatively affected by those who do have problems. You probably will want to see greater effort expended to pre-

vent such problems in order to minimize the likelihood of your child or friends experiencing difficulty.

If you feel that those with special needs deserve special help, you will want to see such programs funded. And if resources are tight, you may have to help decide about priorities.

Many questions are being raised about the future of education in general that will affect the LD field. In just what way, however, often is not clear. Moreover, because schools are critical to the current functioning and future of society, you have a stake in any decisions that affect schools.

If there is a widespread move toward allowing the use of public funds for private schooling (e.g., voucher systems), will this

---

Box 15–7

Viewpoint
Learning Disabilities: Everyone's Concern

"The learning-disabled child presents all of us concerned with the education of children with a monumental dilemma: How can we provide all of our children an equal educational opportunity? The plight of the learning-disabled child is, I believe, symptomatic of some of the most central problems that presently plague our educational system. Dissatisfaction with our schools is widespread. Children are said not to be learning the basic skills of reading, writing, and arithmetic. Seemingly more and more children are said to create discipline problems. According to some experts, as many as 15 to 30% are said to be learning disabled. So-called cultural disadvantagement creates enormous problems for educators and, in turn, for the poverty and minority groups whose disadvantagement creates problems for themselves and for the schools. Never have the schools been so attacked through the courts. Suits alleging improper administration of funds, utilization of special class placement as

a tool of racial segregation, failure to provide handicapped children with services necessary for their education, and inability to educate normal pupils in the basic skills are not uncommon. Teachers are equally dissatisfied, and strike for better working conditions and higher pay. Parents are also demanding to be heard and frequently find themselves at loggerheads with the school administration. While trying to keep the lid on, and also to hold the line on the quality of instructional programs for the children, administrators seek extra funds to meet teacher demands. Legislatures are reluctant to appropriate more money because they do not obtain mandates from the people to provide the (failing?) schools more funds. Half of the school bond issues are now being defeated.

"The picture I am painting is bleak indeed, but I am not so much concerned here about arguing the severity of the present problems as much as recognizing that the problems appear to permeate the system rather than being something that will either pass in time or be solved by a council of experts." (Senf, 1981, p. 85)

have a positive or negative effect on the LD field? What about activities related to civil rights and equal opportunities for minorities? How do you feel about merit pay for teachers? Hazard pay for working with difficult populations? Differentiated staffing patterns and salaries?

You can play a role in the ongoing discussion about such matters—in your neighborhood, at work, and even in public meetings that are a part of efforts to spell out the implications of potential shifts in public policy. You will also play a role when you vote. You may have a direct opportunity to support certain programs by voting for school bond issues or specific school board members. Even if you don't have a chance to vote directly, your elected representatives do, and you may want to let them know what you think.

Moreover, everyone has a role to play in efforts to encourage high-quality people to seek careers in education.

This brings us to the bottom line—more money for education. While we all believe current funds could be reallocated and put to better use, it is a fallacy to believe that the reforms so many people are calling for can be done without a greater investment of money and the resources money buys. Professions compete for the talents of the best people in a society. If education is to get a fair share of the best and the brightest, the salaries simply must be higher. Over twenty years ago, Sterling M. McMurrin (1963), former U.S. Commissioner of Education, made the point in straightforward and strong language:

> "Our average citizen has taken it for granted that teaching, especially in the secondary and elementary schools, is a profession entirely appropriate for persons of second- or third-rate ability. We have all too commonly, therefore, proceeded to pay them third- or fourth-rate salaries." (p. x)

As several of the major reports on education have noted about the public's expectations of schools, "We want it all." We want the schools to accomplish a comprehensive set of aims; we want such aims met for all youngsters; we want such aims set in ways that reflect the highest possible standards. The question must be asked: Are we willing to pay for all this?

If we really want it all, the only possible answer is *yes.*

READINGS AND RESOURCES

The following set of readings and resources has been compiled to provide (1) material that can expand your understanding of the topics covered and (2) additional resources that may be of use to you now or in the future.

If you haven't done so already, you may want to take some time to browse through the material at this time. The titles and a brief description of each of the readings are presented here for your convenience.

- Reading A—"Procedures and Instruments for Assessment in the LD Field" designates resources for identifying and evaluating assessment procedures and instruments and provides a categorized list of major assessment tools and source references.

- Reading B—"Technical Concerns About Assessment" discusses why so many of the procedures listed in Reading A must be used with great care and discretion.

- Reading C—"Controversial Medically-Related Services" highlights vision training, stimulant medication, diets, vitamins, and CNS training.

- Reading D—"Fads and Claims" stresses major reasons why the LD field has been so vulnerable to treatment fads.

- Reading E—"Enhancing Motivation and Skills in Social Functioning" expands the text's focus on the topic of the relationship between motivation and skill development with special reference to interpersonal functioning.

- Reading F—"Options to Enhance Motivation and Learning" further outlines the nature and range of content and process options that can help enhance motivation for learning among individuals diagnosed as learning disabled.

- Reading G—"Learner Decision Making to Enhance Motivation and Development" stresses specific ways that the learner can be involved in decision making to further increase motivation for learning.

- Reading H—"Theories of Instruction and Models of Teaching" contains brief abstracts from C. H. Patterson's review of the work of Maria Montessori, Jean Piaget, Jerome Bruner, B. F. Skinner, and Carl Rogers, all of which have relevance to efforts to develop theories of instruction; also outlined is a categorization of models of teaching by B. Joyce and M. Weil.

- Reading I—"To the Rescue" describes the negative dynamics that can arise when helping is approached in the wrong way.

- Reading J—"Fernald's Techniques in Their Motivational Context" reviews Grace Fernald's well-known set of remedial techniques, the VAKT or tracing approach to reading and written language remediation, and clarifies the motivational features that have not been widely stressed.

- Reading K—"Guidelines for Serving the LD Adult" summarizes twenty-five guidelines proposed by R. Gray.

- Reading L—"Ethical Concerns About Negative Effects" expands on the general text discussion of negative consequences that may arise from intervention activity and the ethical considerations raised by such unfortunate outcomes.

- Reading M—"Toward Services with an Informed Consumer Orientation" presents three service models designed to provide information and guidance to consumers and assessment and consultation for persons with learning problems in ways that encourage self-direction and personal problem solving.

- Reading N—"Areas of Professional Competence" highlights the movement toward detailed listing of the types of competence professionals are supposed to have and presents the list of LD professional competencies formulated by the Council for Learning Disabilities.

- Reading O—"Perspectives" offers a smattering of thought-provoking commentary from a variety of writers regarding many of the topics discussed throughout the text.

Reading *A*

Procedures and Instruments for Assessment in the LD Field

Assessment procedures are essential ingredients in most facets of practice and research in the LD field. The demand for better procedures is so great that new procedures are appearing at a faster rate than most of us can keep up with.

An estimated 250 million standardized tests are given each year in school settings. While most of these are routine achievement tests, a considerable amount of this and related assessment is directed at diagnosing and planning for special populations.

An estimated thirteen to fifteen hours of professional time per person may be involved in assessment and decision making for individuals with psychoeducational problems (Ysseldyke & Algozzine, 1982). One observer has suggested the cost of such activity in school settings may be as much as eighteen hundred dollars for each targeted individual (Mirkin, 1980).

To document the nature of some of this activity, Thurlow and Ysseldyke (1979) surveyed forty-four federally funded model LD programs. They found a great deal of variability in the tests used; they also found frequent instances in which tests developed for one purpose were being used for other purposes.

Generally speaking, the specific type of assessment procedures used in the LD field tend to reflect the orientation of the practitioner. As discussed in Part 2, those who focus on central nervous system (CNS) causes use assessment procedures that attempt to measure and prescribe treatment of underlying processing problems. In contrast, those who deemphasize looking for initial causes tend to rely on assessment devices designed to identify and aid in planning corrective interventions for missing skills and learning strategies and for factors that may be currently interfering with correction.

In looking for assessment tools, practitioners find many worthwhile devices on the market. They also find more than a few that are not very good. The caution made by Buros (1974) is one we can all take to heart.

"At present, no matter how poor a test may be, if it is nicely packaged and it promises to do all sorts of things which no test can do, the test will find many gullible buyers. When we initiated critical test reviewing in the *1938 Yearbook*, we had no idea how difficult it would be to discourage the use of poorly constructed tests of unknown validity. Even the better informed test users who finally become convinced that a widely used test has no validity after all are likely to rush to use a new instrument which promises far more than any good test can possibly deliver. Counselors, personnel directors, psychologists, and school administrators seem to have an unshakable will to believe the exaggerated claims of test authors and publishers. If these users were better informed regarding the merits and limitations of their testing instruments, they would probably be less happy and less successful in their work. The test user who has faith—however unjustified—can speak with confidence in interpreting test results and making recommendations. The well-informed test user cannot do this; [this person] knows that the best of our tests are still highly fallible instruments which are extremely difficult to interpret with assurance in individual cases. Consequently, [the user] must interpret test results cautiously with so many reservations that others wonder whether [the person] really knows what he is talking about." (p. xxxvii)

In identifying what is available and as an aid in evaluating how good a procedure is, one can turn to a variety of sources. For example, a major resource is the *Mental Measurements Yearbook* (Buros, 1978). This is a series of critical reviews and bibliographies of published psychometric tests. A companion work, *Tests in Print II* (Buros, 1974), provides a comprehensive bibliography, by category, of tests used in psychology, education, and industry. Tests specifically used with individuals manifesting learning and behavior problems are discussed in various texts (e.g., Salvia & Ysseldyke, 1981). In addition, *the journal Remedial and Special Education*

regularly compares categories of tests used with special education populations. They employ a rating system developed by Hammill, Brown, and Bryant (in press; see Brown & Bryant, 1984).

Since so many procedures are unpublished, efforts have been made to compile surveys. See, e.g., Chun, Cobb, & French, 1975; Comrey, Backer, & Glaser, 1973; Johnson & Bommorito, 1971; Johnson, 1976; and Orvaschel, Sholomskas, & Weissman, 1980.

In Box A–1, we list, by category, a range of procedures and instruments that are used for assessment in the LD field.

Box A–1

Types of Procedures and Instruments Used for Assessment in the LD Field

I. Observations or rating of current behavior (by parents, students, or professionals)
    A. In natural settings such as classrooms, home, or free play situations
        1. For prevention and identification
            a. Child Behavior Rating Scale (Cassel, 1962)
            b. Individual Learning Disabilities Classroom Screening Instrument (Giles, Meier, & Cazier, 1973)
            c. Student Rating Scale (Adelman & Feshbach, 1971; Feshbach, Adelman, & Fuller, 1977)
            d. The Pupil Rating Scale Revised (Myklebust, 1981)
            e. Devereux Child Behavior Rating Scale (Spivack & Spotts, 1966) and Devereux Adolescent Behavior Rating Scale (Spivack, Spotts, & Haimes, 1967)
        2. For diagnosis, treatment planning, or evaluation
            a. Burks' Behavior Rating Scale (Burks, 1969)
            b. Peterson-Quay Problem Behavior Checklist (Quay & Peterson, 1967)

            c. Target Behavior analysis procedures (O'Leary, 1972)
            d. Conners Rating Scale (Conners, 1979)
    B. In special assessment situations
        1. For prevention and identification
            a. Early Detection Inventory (McGahan & McGahan, 1967)
            b. Gesell Developmental Tests (Ilg & Ames, 1964)
            c. Developmental Indicators for the Assessment of Learning—Revised (Mardell & Goldenberg, 1975; 1983)
        2. For diagnosis, treatment planning, evaluation
            a. Checklist for Student's Behavior (Smith, Neisworth, & Greer, 1978)
            b. While standardized measures are almost nonexistent, observations of behaviors during psychological and medical examinations tend to be the most heavily relied on data in confirming presenting problems (Adelman, 1978; Wade & Baker, 1977)
II. Interviews and written personal reports by parent, students, or professionals (responses to oral and/or written questions, or inven-

tories of items, related to medical, psychological, educational, and socioeconomic background and status with emphasis on traumatic incidents and developmental problems)

Note: While some of the data elicited may be factual, there is undoubtedly an important bias toward subjective reinterpretation (Yarrow, Campbell, & Burton, 1970).

A. Histories
   1. Medical information related to pregnancies and birth, illnesses, and injuries (Seidel & Ziai, 1975)
   2. Developmental information related to social, emotional, motor, language, and cognitive areas, e.g., Gesell's Illustrative Behavior Interview (Gesell & Amatruda, 1947)
   3. School history focusing on important events or patterns regarding school experiences (Wallace & Larsen, 1978)
   4. Family information including socioeconomic data, relevant medical, developmental or school history of family members (Mercer & Lewis, 1977)

B. Current status (present concerns and perceived causes of problems)
   1. Medical status—current health status, recent illnesses, injury, or physical complaints (Schain, 1972)
   2. Developmental status—current social, emotional, motor, language, and cognitive status, e.g., Vineland Adaptive Behavior Scale (Sparrow, Balla, & Cicchetti, 1984)
   3. School status—current school problems and perspectives by all participants as to the causes and possible corrections
   4. Family status—current family events, living arrangements, impending changes

III. Verbal and performance measures
   A. For prevention and identification
      1. de Hirsch Predictive Index (de Hirsch, Jansky, & Langford, 1966)
      2. The Satz Battery (Satz, Friel, & Rudegeair, 1976)
      3. Denver Developmental Screening Test (Frankenburg, Dodds, Fandall, Kazuk, & Cohrs, 1975)

   B. For diagnosis, treatment planning, evaluation
      1. Cognitive area and aptitudes
         a. Wechsler Intelligence Scales; WPPSI, WISC-R, WAIS-R (Wechsler, 1955, 1967, 1974)*
         b. Stanford Binet Intelligence Test (Terman & Merrill, 1973)
         c. Boehm Test of Basic Concepts (Boehm, 1970)
         d. Slosson Intelligence Test (Slosson, 1971)
         e. McCarthy Scales of Children's Abilities (McCarthy, 1972)
         f. Peabody Picture Vocabulary Test—Revised (Dunn & Dunn, 1981)
         g. Ravens Progressive Matrices (Ravens, 1956)
         h. System of Multicultural Pluralistic Assessment (Mercer & Lewis, 1979)
         i. Achievement tests such as the California Achievement Test (Tiegs & Clark, 1963)
         j. Psychoeducational tests such as the Woodcock-Johnson Psychoeducational Battery (Woodcock & Johnson, 1977)
         k. Learning Potential Assessment Device (Feuerstein, 1979)
         l. Kaufman Assessment Battery for Children—K-ABC (Kaufman & Kaufman, 1983)
      2. Language area
         a. Illinois Test of Psycholinguistic Abilities (Kirk, McCarthy, & Kirk, 1968)*
         b. Wepman Auditory Discrimination Test (Wepman, 1973)*
         c. Slingerland Screening Test (Slingerland, 1974)
         d. Test of Written Language (Hammill & Larsen, 1978)
         e. Achievement tests such as Metropolitan Achievement Tests: Language Instructional Battery (Balow, Hogan, Farr, & Prescott, 1978)
         f. Reading readiness tests such as

Metropolitan Readiness Tests
(Nurss & McGauvran, 1976)

3. Perceptual motor area
   a. Bender Visual-Motor Gestalt Test (Bender, 1938; Koppitz, 1963, 1975)*
   b. Developmental Test of Visual Perception (Frostig, Maslow, Lefever, & Whittlesey, 1964)*
   c. Lincoln-Oseretsky Motor Development Scale (Sloan, 1955)*
   d. Graham-Kendall Memory for Designs (Graham & Kendall, 1960)*
   e. Purdue Perceptual Motor Survey (Roach & Kephart, 1966)*
   f. Developmental Test of Visual Motor Integration (Beery & Buktenica, 1967)
   g. Southern California Sensory Integration Tests (Ayres, 1972)

4. Social and emotional areas
   a. Vineland Adaptive Behavior Scales (Sparrow, Balla, & Cicchetti, 1984)
   b. California Test of Personality (Thorpe, Clark, & Tiegs, 1953)
   c. Kuder Personal Preference Record (Kuder, 1954)
   d. Goodenough-Harris Drawing Test (Harris, 1963)
   e. Children's Apperception Test (Bellak & Bellak, 1965)
   f. Early School Personality Questionnaire (Coan & Cattell, 1970)
   g. Piers-Harris Children's Self-Concept Scale (Piers & Harris, 1969)

5. School performance
   a. California Achievement Test (Tiegs & Clark, 1978)
   b. Stanford Achievement Test (Madden, Gardner, Rudman, Karlsen, & Merwin, 1973)
   c. Metropolitan Achievement Tests (Prescott, Balow, Hogan, & Farr, 1978; Farr, Prescott, Balow, & Hogan, 1978; Hogan, Farr, Prescott, & Balow, 1978; Balow, Hogan, Farr & Prescott, 1978)
   d. Iowa Tests of Basic Skills (Hieronymus, Lindquist, &

Hoover, 1978); Tests of Achievement and Proficiency (Scannell, 1978)
   e. Gates-MacGinite Reading Tests (MacGinite, 1978)
   f. Wide Range Achievement Test (Jastak & Jastak, 1965; 1978)
   g. Peabody Individual Achievement Test (Dunn & Markwardt, 1970)
   h. Psychoeducational tests such as Woodcock-Johnson Psychoeducational Battery (Woodcock & Johnson, 1977)
   i. Kaufman Test of Educational Achievement—K-TEA (Kaufman & Kaufman, 1985)
   j. Skill diagnostic inventories such as Criterion Reading (Hackett, 1971), Brigance Diagnostic Inventories (Brigance, 1977, 1978, 1980) and Diagnostic Mathematics Inventory (Gessell, 1977)

IV. Physiological tests and neuropsychological exams
   A. Physical examination—a nonspecialized exam including measurement of height, weight, head circumference, blood pressure, and exams of various physiological systems including visual acuity using Snellen wall or E charts
   B. Sensory acuity—specialized tests
      1. Vision tests to assess refractive errors, nystagmus, faulty eye movement
         a. Keystone Telebinocular (e.g., Walton & Schubert, 1969)
         b. Massachusetts Vision Test (e.g., Foote & Crane, 1954)
         c. Bausch and Lomb Orthorater (e.g., Salvia & Ysseldyke, 1981)
      2. Hearing
         a. Sweep audiometry (e.g., Schain, 1972)
         b. Pure tone audiometry (e.g., Northern & Downs, 1974)
   C. Neurological exam
      1. Evaluation of mental status, speech, muscle tone, fine and gross motor control—"hard" neurological signs such as bilaterally exaggerated ten-

don reflexes, and various "soft"
neurological signs such as confused
dominance, asymmetrical reflexes,
overflow or crossover movements.
(e.g., Schain, 1972)*
2. Electroencephalogram—amplifica-
tion, recording, and analysis of electrical activity of the brain (e.g., Ellingson, 1966)*
D. Neuropsychological tests
1. Luria-Nebraska Neuropsychological
Battery—Children's Revision
(Golden, 1981)
2. Holstad-Reitan Neuropsychological
Battery (Reitan & Davison, 1974)
Note: As distinct from neurological
exams, neuropsychological exams
involve a battery of tests measuring
intelligence, sensory and motor
functioning and achievement, with
the aim of relating performance to
brain dysfunction (Reitan &
Davison, 1974).
E. Special procedures to test hormonal,
chemical, or structural defects (e.g.,
Schain, 1972)
1. X-ray studies of the skull for intracranial calcification or tumor
2. Metabolic tests, e.g., brain metabolism, ferric chloride test for PKU
3. Chromosomal studies

V. Available records and data
A. Past
1. Medical reports from pediatricians,
neurologists, other medical
specialists
2. Psychological—test data, results,
and reports from school
psychologists or other professionals
3. Educational
a. Review of past school products
(e.g., written papers, tests, projects)
b. Reports from teachers and tutors
c. Cumulative school records
(grades, teacher comments, test
scores, attendance, school health
records)
B. Current (within the past three months)
1. Medical—report from the most recent physical and/or neurological
exam
2. Psychological—test data, results,
and reports from school
psychologists or other professionals
who have been consulted recently
3. Educational
a. Review of current school products (e.g., written papers, tests,
projects)
b. Reports from current teachers
and tutors

Note: Examples and specific references are cited when relevant and available.

This has been one of the ten most frequently recom-mended tests and evaluations for a learning disabilities battery as noted by authoritative publications from 1968 to 1978 (Coles, 1978).

SPECIAL REFERENCE RESOURCE

The following list of references cited in Box A–1 and elsewhere in Reading A is provided as an aid in finding and evaluating *assessment procedures.*

ADELMAN, H. S. (1978). Diagnostic classification of learning problems: Some data. *American Journal of Orthopsychiatry, 48,* 717–26.

ADELMAN, H. S., & FESHBACH, S. (1971). Predicting reading failure: Beyond the readiness model. *Exceptional Children, 37,* 349–54.

AYRES, A. J. (1972). *Southern California sensory integration tests.* Los Angeles: Western Psychological Services.

BALOW, I. H., HOGAN, T. P., FARR, R. C., & PRESCOTT, G. A. (1978). *Metropolitan achievement tests: Language instructional battery.* New York: Psychological Corporation.

BEERY, K. E., & BUKTENICA, N. (1967). *Developmental test of visual-motor integration.* Chicago: Follett.

BELLAK, C., & BELLAK, S. (1965). *Children's apperception test.* Larchmont, N.Y.: CPS.

BENDER, L. (1938). A visual-motor gestalt test and its

clinical use. *American Orthopsychiatric Association Research Monograph, 3.*

BOEHM, A. E. (1970). *Boehm test of basic concepts.* New York: Psychological Corporation.

BRIGANCE, A. (1977). *Brigance diagnostic inventory of basic skills.* North Billerica, Mass.: Curriculum Associates.

BRIGANCE, A. (1978). *Brigance diagnostic inventory of early development.* North Billerica, Mass.: Curriculum Associates.

BRIGANCE, A. (1980). *Brigance diagnostic inventory of essential skills.* North Billerica, Mass.: Curriculum Associates.

BROWN, L., & BRYANT, B. R. (1984). A consumer's guide to tests in print: The rating system. *Remedial and Special Education, 5,* 55–61.

BURKS, H. (1969). *Burks' behavior rating scales.* El Monte, Calif.: Arden Press.

BUROS, O. K. (Ed.) (1974). *Tests in print II.* Highland Park, N.J.: Gryphon Press.

BUROS, O. K. (Ed.) (1978). *The eighth mental measurements yearbook.* New York: Gryphon Press.

CASSEL, R. N. (1962). *The child behavior rating scale.* Los Angeles: Western Psychological Services.

CHUN, K., COBB, S., & FRENCH, J. R. P., Jr. (1975). *Measures for psychological assessment.* Ann Arbor, Mich.: Institute for Social Research, The University of Michigan.

COAN, R., & CATTELL, R. (1970). *Early school personality questionnaire.* Champaign, Ill.: Institute for Personality and Ability Testing.

COLES, G. S. (1978). The learning disabilities test battery: Empirical and social issues. *Harvard Educational Review, 48,* 313–40.

COMREY, A. L., BACKER, T. E., & GLASER, E. M. (1973). *A sourcebook for mental health measures.* Los Angeles: Human Interaction Research Institute.

CONNERS, C. K. (1979). A teacher rating scale for use in drug studies with children. *American Journal of Psychiatry, 126,* 884–88.

DE HIRSCH, K., JANSKY, J., & LANGFORD, W. S. (1966). *Predicting reading failure.* New York: Harper & Row.

DUNN, L., & DUNN, L. (1981). *Peabody picture vocabulary test—revised.* Circle Pines, Minn.: American Guidance Service.

DUNN, L., & MARKWARDT, F. (1970). *Peabody individual achievement test.* Circle Pines, Minn.: American Guidance Service.

ELLINGSON, R. J. (1966). Relationships between EEG and test intelligence: A commentary. *Psychological Bulletin, 65,* 91–98.

FARR, R. C., PRESCOTT, G. A., BALOW, I. H., & HOGAN, T. P. (1978). *Metropolitan achievement tests: Reading instructional battery.* New York: Psychological Corporation.

FESHBACH, S., ADELMAN, H. S., & FULLER, W. (1977). Prediction of reading and related academic problems. *Journal of Educational Psychology, 69,* 229–308.

FEUERSTEIN, R. (1979). *Dynamics assessment of retarded performers: The learning potential assessment device.* Baltimore: University Park Press.

FOOTE, F. M., & CRANE, M. M. (1954). An evaluation of vision screening. *Exceptional Children, 20,* 153–61.

FRANKENBURG, W., DODDS, J., FANDALL, A., KAZUK, E., & COHRS, M. (1975). *Denver developmental screening test, reference manual, revised.* Denver: LA-DOCA Project and Publishing Foundation.

FROSTIG, M., LEFEVER, W., & WHITTLESEY, J. (1964). *Developmental test of visual perception.* Palo Alto, Calif.: Consulting Psychological Press.

GESELL, A., & AMATRUDA, C. S. (1947). *Developmental diagnosis: Normal and abnormal child development,* 2nd ed. New York: Harper & Row.

GESSELL, J. K. (1977). *Diagnostic mathematics inventory.* Monterey, Calif.: CTB/McGraw-Hill.

GILES, M. T., MEIER, J. H., & CAZIER, V. O. (1973). *Individual learning disabilities classroom screening instrument.* Evergreen, Colo.: Learning Pathways.

GOLDEN, C. J. (1981). The Luria-Nebraska children's battery: Theory and formulation. In G. W. Hynd & J. E. Obrzut (Eds.) *Neuropsychological assessment and the school-age child: Issues and procedures.* New York: Grune & Stratton.

GRAHAM, F. K., & KENDALL, B. S. (1960). *Memory for designs test.* Missoula, Mont.: Psychological Test Specialist.

HACKETT, M. G. (1971). *Criterion reading: Individualized learning management system.* Westminister, Md.: Random House.

HAMMILL, D. D., BROWN, L., & BRYANT, B. R. (in press). *A consumer's guide to tests in print.* Austin, Tex.: PRO-ED.

HAMMILL, D. D., & LARSEN, S. (1978). *Tests of written language.* Austin, Tex.: PRO-ED.

HARRIS, D. B. (1963). *Children's drawings as measures of intellectual maturity: A revision and extension of the Goodenough draw-a-man test.* New York: Harcourt, Brace & World.

HIERONYMUS, A. N., LINDQUIST, E. F., & HOOVER, H. D. (1978). *Iowa tests of basic skills.* Lombard, Ill.: Riverside Publishing Co.

HOGAN, T. P., FARR, R. C., PRESCOTT, G. A., & BALOW, I. H. (1978). *Metropolitan achievement tests: Mathematics instructional battery.* New York: Psychological Corporation.

ILG, F. L., & AMES, L. B. (1964). *School readiness: Behavior tests used at the Gesell Institute.* New York: Harper & Row.

JASTAK, J. F., & JASTAK, S. R. (1965). *The wide range achievement test* (rev. ed.). Wilmington, Del.: Guidance Association of Delaware.

JOHNSON, O. G. (1976). *Tests and measures in child development: Handbook II.* San Francisco: Jossey-Bass.

JOHNSON, O. G., & BOMMORITO, J. W. (1971). *Tests and measurements in child development: A handbook.* San Francisco: Jossey-Bass.

KAUFMAN, A. S., & KAUFMAN, N. L. (1983). *Kaufman assessment battery for children (K–ABC).* Circle Pines, Minn.: American Guidance Service.

KAUFMAN, A. S., & KAUFMAN, N. L. (1985). *Kaufman Test of Educational Achievement (CK-TEA).* Circle Pines, Minn.: American Guidance Service.

KIRK, S. A., McCARTHY, J. J., & KIRK, W. D. (1968). *Illinois test of psycholinguistic abilities.* Urbana: University of Illinois Press.

KOPPITZ, E. M. (1963). *The Bender-Gestalt test for young children.* New York: Grune & Stratton.

KOPPITZ, E. M. (1975). *The Bender-Gestalt test for young children: Vol. II: Research and application, 1965–1973.* New York: Grune & Stratton.

KUDER, R. (1954). *Kuder personal preference record.* Chicago: Science Research Associates.

McCARTHY, D. (1972). *Manual for the McCarthy scales of children's abilities.* New York: Psychological Corporation.

McGAHAN, F. F., & McGAHAN, C. (1967). *Early detection inventory.* Chicago: Follett.

MacGINITE, W. (1978). *Gates-MacGinite reading tests.* Boston: Houghton-Mifflin.

MADDEN, R., GARDNER, E. R., RUDMAN, H. C., KARLSEN, B., & MERWIN, J. C. (1973). *Stanford achievement test.* New York: Harcourt Brace Jovanovich.

MARDELL, C. D., & GOLDENBERG, D. S. (1975). *Developmental indicators of learning: Manual* (renormed 1983). Edison, N.J.: Childcraft Educating Corp.

MERCER, J. R., & LEWIS, J. F. (1977). *System of multicultural pluralistic assessment.* New York: Psychological Corporation.

MIRKIN, P. K. (1980). Conclusions. In J. Ysseldyke & M. Thurlow (Eds.), *The special education assessment and decision making process: Seven case studies.* Minneapolis: University of Minnesota Institute for Research on Learning Disabilities.

MYKLEBUST, H. R. (1981). *The pupil rating scale revised.* New York: Grune & Stratton.

NORTHERN, J. L., & DOWNS, M. P. (1974). *Hearing in children.* Baltimore: Williams & Wilkins.

NURSS, J. R., & McGAUVRAN, M. E. (1976). *Metropolitan readiness tests, teacher's manual, Part II: Interpretation and use of test results (Level I & II).* New York: Harcourt Brace Jovanovich.

O'LEARY, K. D. (1972). *The assessment of psychopathology in children.* In H. C. Quay & J. S. Werry (Eds.), *Psychopathological disorders of childhood.* New York: Wiley.

ORVASCHEL, H., SHOLOMSKAS, D., & WEISSMAN, M. M. (1980). *The assessment of psychopathology and behavioral problems in children: A review of scales suitable for epidemiological and clinical research (1967–1979).* DHHS Publication No. (ADM)80-1037. Washington, D.C.: U.S. GPO.

PIERS, E., & HARRIS, D. (1969). *The Piers-Harris children's self-concept scale.* Nashville: Counselor Recordings and Tests.

PRESCOTT, G. A., BALOW, I. H., HOGAN, T. P., & FARR, R. C. (1978). *Metropolitan achievement tests: Survey battery.* New York: Psychological Corporation.

QUAY, H. C., & PETERSON, D. R. (1967). *Manual for the behavior problem checklist.* Unpublished manuscript, University of Illinois.

RAVENS, J. C. (1956). *Progressive matrices.* London: H. K. Lewis.

REITAN, R. M., & DAVISON, L. A. (1974). *Clinical neuropsychology: Current status and applications.* New York: Winston Wiley.

ROACH, E. G., & KEPHART, N. C. (1966). *The Purdue perceptual motor survey.* Columbus, Ohio: Merrill.

SALVIA, J., & YSSELDYKE, J. E. (1981). *Assessment in special and remedial education,* 2nd ed. Boston: Houghton-Mifflin.

SATZ, P., FRIEL, J., & RUDEGEAIR, F. (1976). In J. Guthrie (Ed.), *Aspects of reading acquisition.* Baltimore: Johns Hopkins.

SCANNELL, D. P. (1978). *Tests of achievement and proficiency.* Lombard, Ill.: Riverside Publishing Co.

SCHAIN, R. J. (1972). *Neurology of childhood learning disorders.* Baltimore: Williams & Wilkins.

SEIDEL, H. M., & ZIAI, M. (1975). Pediatric history and physical examination. In M. Ziai (Ed.), *Pediatrics.* Boston: Little, Brown.

SLINGERLAND, B. H. (1974). *Slingerland screening tests.* Cambridge, Mass.: Educators Publishing Service.

SLOAN, W. (1955). Lincoln-Oseretsky test of motor development. Chicago: Stoelting.

SLOSSON, R. L. (1971). *Slosson intelligence test.* East Aurora, N.Y.: Slosson Educational Publications.

SMITH, R. M., NEISWORTH, J. T., & GREER, J. G. (1978). *Evaluating educational environments.* Columbus, Ohio: Merrill.

SPARROW, S. S., BALLA, D. A., & CICCHETTI, D. V. (1984). *Vineland adaptive behavior scales.* Circle Pines, Minn.: American Guidance Service. This is a revision of E. A. Doll's *Vineland social maturity scale.*

SPIVAK, G., & SPOTTS, J. (1966). *Devereux Child behavior rating scale.* Devon, Pa.: Devereux Foundation Press.

SPIVAK, G., SPOTTS, J., & HAIMES, P. (1967). *Devereux adolescent behavior rating scale.* Devon, Pa.: Devereux Foundation Press.

TERMAN, L. M., & MERRILL, M. A. (1973). *Stanford-Binet intelligence scale.* Boston: Houghton-Mifflin.

THORPE, L., CLARK, W., & TIEGS, E. (1953). *California test of personality.* Monterery, Calif.: California Test Bureau.

THURLOW, M., & YSSELDYKE, J. (1979). Current assessment and decision making practices in model programs for learning disabled students. *Learning Disability Quarterly, 2,* 15–24.

TIEGS, E., & CLARK, W. (1963). *California achievement test.* Los Angeles: California Test Bureau.

WADE, T., & BAKER, T. (1977). Opinions and use of psychological tests: A survey of clinical psychologists. *American Psychologist, 32,* 874–82.

WALLACE, G., & LARSEN, S. C. (1978). *Educational assessment of learning problems: Testing for teaching.* Boston: Allyn & Bacon.

WALTON, H. N., & SCHUBERT, D. G. (1969). Vision-perception testing and training program: Clerical operations. *American Journal of Optometry, 46,* 840–47.

WECHSLER, D. (1955). *Wechsler adult intelligence scale—manual.* New York: Psychological Corporation.

WECHSLER, D. (1967). *Manual for the Wechsler preschool and primary scale of intelligence.* New York: Psychological Corporation.

WECHSLER, D. (1974). *Wechsler intelligence scale for children—revised.* New York: Psychological Corporation.

WEPMAN, J. (1958). *Wepman auditory discrimination test.* Chicago: Chicago Language Research Associates.

WOODCOCK, R. W., & JOHNSON, M. B. (1977). *Woodcock-Johnson psycho-educational battery.* Boston: Teaching Resources Corporation.

YARROW, M. R., CAMPBELL, J. D., & BURTON, R. V. (1970). Recollections of childhood: A study of the retrospective method. *Monographs of the Society of Research in Child Development, 35,* No. 5.

YSSELDYKE, J. E., & ALGOZZINE, B. (1982). *Critical issues in special and remedial education.* Boston: Houghton-Mifflin.

Reading B

Technical Concerns About Assessment

How good are the assessment procedures listed in the outline of procedures and instruments, Box A–1? Some are terrible. Some are useful. Even the best are not good enough.

Many widely used assessment devices, even those that are commercially marketed, have technical deficiencies. To understand why this is so requires knowledge of what is meant by the concepts of *reliability, validity, norms,* and *standards.*

Assessment procedures (e.g., tests, rating scales, interview and observation schedules) produce descriptive data that vary in their degree of reliability and validity. In judging and interpreting the meaning of the data, assessors use norms and standards that also vary in their reliability and validity.

What does it mean for an assessment procedure to be reliable and valid? What are norms and standards? Let's look at each of these matters.

RELIABILITY

In common usage the term *reliability* refers to dependability, accuracy, and precision. As related to assessment, the concept is used to indicate how consistent and reproducible assessment data are.

Just as assessment is not limited to tests, the concept of reliability is relevant to all assessment activity. Furthermore, it is used to determine whether findings are consistent and reproducible over time, in different settings, and with regard to differences in assessors. The concept also often is used to describe the consistency among procedures that claim to measure the same thing, such as several measures of intelligence.

Reliability, however, says nothing about what the procedure is measuring. The concept of validity deals with the matter of what the findings mean.

In technical terms, reliability refers to the degree a procedure is free of random error. Mathematically, reliability is presented as a number that varies from zero to one. This number is called a correlation or reliability coefficient. The coefficient for a totally unreliable procedure would be .00; perfect reliability is indicated by a figure of 1.0.

A common way to arrive at a reliability coefficient is to analyze the findings from several comparable administrations of an assessment procedure. Assuming what is being measured has not changed, the findings should be similar.

When the findings are not similar, it may be because of deficiencies in the procedure or because what is being measured has changed. On the other hand, highly reliable findings do not always mean that a procedure is technically sound; highly reliable findings can also be produced by biased administration or interpretation (nonrandom error).

No psychological assessment procedure is completely dependable or free from random error. With regard to tests, it has been pointed out that

"Unless the test is perfectly reliable, and such instruments do not exist to the authors' knowledge, there is likely to be some margin of error in every test score. Indeed test theorists conceive that, were a hypothetical individual given the same test a great many times (assuming that learning and practice effects did not systematically change scores), there would be a range of score values observed, with the range being narrow for reliable tests and broad for unreliable tests. The examinee's 'true' score would be the average of all the observed scores. This conception is an elaboration of the idea of reliability, and is presented in an easily comprehended manner in materials developed by test publishers such as the Educational Testing Service. Users of many of the tests published by this organization are advised to make decisions about individual students not in terms of the precise score obtained, but rather in terms of a band or interval extending on each side of the score. This 'confidence band' is calculated on the basis of the reliability coefficient for the test and is to be interpreted as having a sufficiently high probability of including the student's true score." (Skager & Weinberg, 1971, pp. 121–22)

VALIDITY

Valid data and decisions are the main concerns of assessors.

The concept of validity applies both to assessment processes *and* to decisions based on assessment findings. If data are not highly valid, we cannot be very certain about what they mean. This leads to controversy and a great many errors in interpreting the findings and making decisions.

Discussions of the validity of assessment procedures can be confusing. The concept can be understood in general terms with reference to concerns over whether assessment and decision making procedures are leading to meaningful

- descriptions of a phenomenon, e.g., Does the procedure measure what it says it does? Only what it says it does? All of what it says it does?
- interpretations and judgments of a phenomenon, e.g., Are the inferences justi-

fied? How appropriate are the norms and standards?

- decisions, e.g., How relevant are the data for the decisions that must be made?

To understand the concept in more specific terms requires looking at several of the related types of validity discussed in the assessment literature. Furthermore, while reliability is established in a relatively technical and objective way, validity usually is determined through a great deal of rational and subjective activity.

Three basic types of validity are

- content, e.g., How well does the procedure assess the knowledge, skills, and behavior it claims to measure?
- criterion-related (including predictive, concurrent, and diagnostic validity), e.g., How well does the procedure assess the relationship between currently measured phenomena and future, concurrent, or past phenomena?
- construct, e.g., How well does the procedure assess some theoretical concept, such as intelligence or anxiety?

Content Validity

Content validity refers to how well the items on such procedures as standardized achievement tests and course exams actually sample learned skills, knowledge, and behavior. For example, several items that require adding two single-digit numbers (e.g., 4 + 7) may be used to test whether a youngster has learned this skill.

How do we know if a procedure has high content validity? We know because we or someone else makes a judgment that it does.

In the example given, the content validity of the items seems so evident that they are seen by most people as appropriate on their "face value"—thus the term *face validity*.

However, when a great many possible items can be included on a test, judgments about the content validity of many of them may be challenged. (Think about the items on any recent test you have taken; chances are you thought some were not a valid assessment of your knowledge and abilities.)

When more than face validity is necessary, expert judgments are used to establish content validity. However, the more comprehensive the content area to be assessed, the harder it is to sample and the more likely experts are to disagree.

Take any standardized achievement test as an example. The content validity of such tests almost always is judged to be high. That is, some expert or group of experts has designed and judged the items to be a good, representative sample of skills in a particular area such as reading. At the same time, inspection of the popular reading tests on the market shows they vary markedly in their content. All claim high content validity, yet all are different in many important ways. The experts clearly have different opinions about what the content of this type of test should be, and one suspects that each would disagree with the judgments of others. And since reading is an area in which content has been relatively well defined, the problems can only be greater in areas where knowledge and skills have not been clarified very well.

Even when there is expert consensus about the high content validity of a test, it may be a poor measure for some individuals and groups. For instance, a math test that requires reading directions or has a short time limit is a poor measure of what a person knows about arithmetic for any individual with a reading problem or anyone who works slowly.

In sum, statements about content validity reflect someone's subjective judgment. For most consumers, this means they must choose from among expert opinions. In doing so, it is helpful to have clearly in mind what one wants to assess and why as one basis for discriminating among conflicting expert views.

Predictive, Concurrent, and Diagnostic Validity

Criterion-related (including predictive, concurrent, and diagnostic) validity refers to how well current assessment data can be used to help understand some future, present, or past concerns.

An example is assessment designed to predict future school failure. To establish predictive validity in such a case, research must show a strong *relationship* between the data used to predict and some *criterion* representing subsequent school failure, such as poor grades or low achievement scores. As with reliability, correlation coefficients are used to indicate the strength of the relationship.

Criterion-related validity coefficients for comprehensive psychoeducational assessment procedures generally are not high. Coefficients as high as .60 are rare. Some assessment experts recommend that procedures with coefficients as low as .30 can still be useful (Garrett, 1954; Guilford, 1956).

Decisions as to whether a procedure is valid enough depend on how much new and unique information the data represent. If a procedure has the potential to add a piece of important information that will otherwise not be available, it may be worth using even if it has a low coefficient. On the other hand, it makes little sense to use a procedure that adds no new information even if it has a relatively high coefficient.

Ultimately, the point is to make good decisions. Every criterion-related procedure results in some errors. In screening for future reading problems, for instance, some individuals will be identified as future problems but turn out not to be; this type of error is called a false-positive error. Some individ-

uals will not be identified as future problems but turn out to have difficulty learning
to read; these are called false-negative errors.

The number of errors can be used as another way to look at the validity of the assessment and decision-making procedures.
That is, computation of the number of correct predictions and the number of errors expressed as proportions provides another index of validity.

One major complication for efforts to establish criterion-related validity is the selection of appropriate criteria with which to
correlate assessment data. For instance,
what is the most appropriate criterion of
school success or failure? Grades? Amount
learned? Ability to apply what has been
learned? Positive attitudes toward learning?
Obviously, each is debatable. In choosing a
criterion, four major qualities have been
stressed: (1) relevance, (2) freedom from bias,
(3) reliability, and (4) availability (Thorndike
& Hagen, 1977).

Another complication is that the validation process requires a criterion measure
that is highly reliable and valid. For the
measurement of complex psychoeducational
criteria, such measures simply do not exist.
At best, what is available has moderate validity. Thus, the irony often is that researchers must use criterion data gathered by measures that have rather limited reliability and
validity; this includes most of the procedures listed in Box A–1.

A variety of other factors can confound
the validation process related to criterion-
referenced assessment. They need not be reviewed here. The point is that all these complications and confounding factors make it
evident why so many of the available predictive and diagnostic assessment procedures
should be used with great care and discretion.

In choosing such procedures, the question
is not which will avoid making errors. They
all make errors. The question is which will
produce the smallest number of errors. And

although the procedure that produces the
smallest number of errors is the best that is
available, it may not be good enough. Certainly, it will not be good enough for individuals for whom the findings are in error.

Finally, we note that there is a tendency
to infer causation from criterion-related
measures. For example, a test may predict
failure, but this is not sufficient evidence
that what the test measures is the cause of
the failure. This type of jumping at conclusions reflects the common mistake of observing correlates and believing one is seeing cause and effect. The establishment of
cause-effect connections requires construct
validation.

Construct Validity

Construct validity refers to how well an
assessment procedure measures something
that is not directly observable, such as theoretical concepts or abstractions, e.g., intelligence, anxiety, perception, motivation.
It also is used in theorizing about relationships among concepts and things that are observable (Nunnally, 1978).

The term *construct* is used to clarify that
what we are trying to measure is a theoretical or hypothetical idea *constructed* by scientists to help organize thinking about
something that can't be seen directly. In effect, a construct is a myth that is found to be
a useful and convenient way to understand
and communicate about a theoretical notion. Of course, it is rarely discussed as a
myth as long as enough scientists find it
useful.

Because constructs are not directly observable, they are not directly measurable.
What then is measured?

Let's take intelligence as an example. Intelligence is an idea that has been constructed to reflect an attribute of people that
many of us find interesting and important.
Theories have been formulated to suggest

the nature of this attribute and the behaviors that should be directly and indirectly associated with it. For instance, it has been suggested that one of the abilities that reflects intelligence is the ability to reason using verbal, graphic, and mathematical symbols. It also is argued that some groups of persons, such as the majority of university students, are likely to be more intelligent than others, for example, the majority of those who drop out of high school. Efforts to develop a test of intelligence will include—among other items—some that measure verbal reasoning. Efforts to determine the construct validity of the measure of intelligence, then, might involve comparing groups of university students and high school dropouts with regard to their performance on tests of verbal reasoning ability. If the majority of university students are found to score higher, the findings will be seen as providing some evidence for the construct validity of the measure.

Obviously, no one set of findings is enough. Construct validation requires consistent findings from many different studies.

"Construct validity is established through a long-continued interplay between observation, reasoning, and imagination. . . . The process of construct validation is the same as that by which scientific theories are developed." (Cronbach, 1970, p. 142)

As with content and criterion-related validity, then, reasoning and judgment play an important role in construct validation. Also, as with content validity, there is no one correlation coefficient that describes how valid a construct measure is. However, unlike content validation, expert judgment alone cannot be used to validate a construct measure. Conclusions must be justified by an extensive body of research.

A major complication in the validation process is that constructs, such as intelligence, motivation, and learning disabilities,

often are defined differently by those who develop the procedures used to measure the phenomena. Thus, procedures that claim to be measuring the same construct may be very different from each other. This means the findings from validation studies using different measures often are not comparable. Therefore, even though many studies may have been done, it may not be appropriate to combine them as evidence for construct validity.

There is wide recognition of the difficulty of validating measures of constructs such as visual perception, psycholinguistic ability, and minimal cerebral dysfunctioning. Thus, it is obvious that many assessment and decision-making procedures used in diagnosing such factors require a substantial amount of additional validation.

NORMS AND STANDARDS

One of the most basic aspects of human behavior is that people try to make sense out of what they see. Complex things are observed and conclusions are made: the new neighbor appears to be wholesome and friendly; the person walking behind you in an unlit parking lot at night looks like a mugger or worse; students are judged by their teachers to be smart or not too smart; teachers are judged by students to be good or terrible.

What is the basis for such conclusions? Obviously, people are influenced by the information available to them in a given situation. They also draw on past experiences. In addition, they may be influenced by some general ideas, theories, attitudes, values, and beliefs they have developed.

Because of differences in the information available and factors influencing how the information is processed, people often arrive at different conclusions about what seems to others to be the same phenomenon. In interpreting the same assessment data on an individual, one assessor may arrive at a diagnosis of learning disabled, and another assessor may conclude the person is not disabled; among a group of students experiencing the same program, some may adore it, others may hate it, and the rest may think it's merely OK.

Given that people are seeing the same things, the differences in their conclusions probably reflect the use of different norms and standards in making judgments. For our purposes, the term *standard* refers to the use of values or a theoretical idea to make judgments about what has been assessed. The judgments often are about whether what is assessed is a problem or not, good or bad, or consistent with some theory.

Norms are not standards. They are not value statements or theoretical statements. Norms are empirical. That is, they are based on what has been found out from research and systematic observation. For example, a set of previous findings can be used as a set of norms in judging assessment data. Are the current findings higher, lower, or the same as the previous findings? How much higher or lower?

Assessment norms reflect data gathered on various research samples. The score for someone subsequently assessed then is compared to the scores for the previous samples. The individual's score will be described in terms of how it compares to the average (mean or median) score for the research samples. That is, it may be found to be above or below average or typical or atypical.

After norms are used, it is commonplace to apply some set of standards to make judgments about *good* and *bad*. This can happen so quickly that it often is not apparent that judgments have been made. For example, a score above or below average may be quickly translated into a judgment that the performance was acceptable or unacceptable, passing or failing. This is understandable, especially with tests of achievement. However, it is important to understand that a value

judgment—a standard—has been used. The use of norms by themselves do not lead to a judgment of good or bad.

Why the distinction between norms and standards is important can be seen by taking a closer look at judgments based on commonplace assessments of behavior and performance. For example, we may have norms that show that an individual's activity level is well above the average found in research samples. On the basis of this information, should we conclude that the individual is highly active, or *hyper*active, a judgment that carries with it the implication of a problem and pathology? Such a judgment may not be necessary based on the norms—especially if many of those studied previously who scored at the same level were not found to have problems. Thus, the judgment of hyperactivity would reflect someone's *standards*, e.g., the assessor's standards based on theory. Somebody else might use the same findings and norms, but a different set of standards, and decide the individual is not hyperactive.

In general, then, the decisions that follow assessment activity usually are influenced by the norms and standards that have been used in making judgments about the meaning and significance of the assessment findings. Unfortunately, adequate norms are frequently unavailable, and the standards used in making judgments often are extremely controversial.

To illustrate the problem, we can look at the matter of norms for intelligence tests. The individual intelligence test for children developed by Wechsler is among the best assessment devices available to LD professionals. With regard to available norms, there is more data on this instrument than on almost any other major procedure. But as we have suggested already, the statement "best available" should not be too readily interpreted as meaning that the instrument is unquestionably a "good" procedure. As published in 1949, the sample used to standardize and establish norms for the test included only white children. In the years prior to the test's 1974 revision, countless individuals were tested and decisions were made based on norms from this extremely narrow sample. The inadequacy of the norms (and apparent bias in the test's content) with regard to the types of youngsters included in the original samples led to enormous criticism, including judicial action. In an attempt to correct the situation, the 1974 revision used samples that reflected proportions of population subgroups in the 1970 U.S. Census. However, considerable criticism is still directed both at the content and at the fact that the construct validity for many subgroups in the population remains to be established. Furthermore, there is controversy over the widespread tendency to use IQ levels as standards for judging people as good or bad in a variety of contexts.

Understanding the concepts of reliability, validity, norms, and standards allows one to appreciate the current state of the art and the hurdles that must be overcome if psychoeducational assessment and decision-making practices are to be improved. Such hurdles are not insurmountable. To do so, however, will be costly and require the talents of many.

Reading *C*

Controversial Medically-Related Services

If an individual is frequently sick or cannot see or hear well, there is an obvious need for medical or medically related help. These problems may or may not be affecting learning, but standard treatments for such problems are well accepted and are hardly controversial.

There are, however, medically related treatments advocated for individuals diagnosed as learning disabled that are quite controversial. A few prominent examples are reviewed here.

Vision training. One ongoing controversy surrounds "visual training" with those who have learning problems (Keogh & Pelland, 1985). Many optometrists offer such treatment; most ophthalmologists say such training is not worth the time, money, or effort.

Optometrists are trained to examine eye functioning and to prescribe corrective lenses but cannot treat eye diseases or prescribe medication. Some also offer activities that they claim can improve how the eyes move and function and how the individual organizes visual information. Some claim such vision training will help those with learning problems.

Ophthalmologists are medical doctors who specialize in treating eye diseases and injuries. They can also prescribe corrective lenses and could offer vision training if they wanted to.

Essentially, vision training for those with learning problems is based on two related beliefs. One is that many learning problems are caused by faulty eye movements and poor organization of what is seen. Two is that these visual deficiencies can be overcome by training.

Critics argue that faulty eye movements and poor visual organization are not causes of learning problems. Rather, they suggest that such visual deficiencies often are simply side effects of learning problems. Moreover, the view of a growing consensus in the field of learning disabilities is that the visual training procedures do little to help anyone overcome learning problems.

Medication. A variety of drugs have been explored in connection with learning problems. The most common and controversial have been the stimlant medications used to treat those whose learning problems are associated with hyperactivity. Studies of treatment prevalence suggest that approximately 1 to 2 percent of elementary age children in the United States (300,000 to 600,000 youngsters) receive psychotropic drugs—usually stimulants—for hyperactivity (Gadow, 1981).

Part of the intrigue that surrounds the use of such drugs with this group is how a stimulant makes highly active individuals less active. Although the impression has been created that such medication can be a major part of efforts to *cure* learning disabilities, the usual argument for its use claims much less. Advocates suggest primarily that those who are given the medication will attend better and therefore learn better. Why this may happen has been widely debated. Both neurological and psychological explanations have been offered (Barkley, 1977; Whalen & Henker, 1976).

Research on the use of medication has been extremely difficult to do (Adelman & Compas, 1977; Gadow, 1983). For this reason, conclusions favoring its widespread use are not based on satisfactory evidence. There seems to be some immediate impact on children who are given relatively high doses. Some seem more controllable and often will do more of the simple tasks they tend not to do when off medication. However, well-designed studies have not shown any consistent evidence that this immediate impact leads to a cure of learning disabilities or to major improvements in reading and other academic learning (or even to getting along better with others over the long run).

Thus, youngsters may *appear* to be attending better to school work; however, if they are, the increased attention has not yet been shown to have the desired long-term effects. That is, stimulant medication has not been shown to help children make major advances in overcoming their learning problems. Moreoever, although not adequately researched, there is great concern over possible harmful side effects, such as loss of sleep and weight loss.

As with so many treatments of this type, in the absence of adequate research the dominant view expressed in the literature shapes practice. The dominant view regarding medication is that it may help in some cases. Although critics argue that this view is misleading, it prevails. Thus, stimulant medication treatment remains very widely relied upon.

Special diets and megavitamin therapy. Most people recognize that good nutrition is an important part of everyday living. It is also clear that some individuals are allergic to certain foods. Thus, it is not controversial to suggest that poor nutrition or eating food

that causes allergic reactions can cause other problems. Conflicts arise, however, with the suggestion that not eating certain things or taking large doses of vitamins can help people overcome hyperactive behavior and learning problems.

As with research on medication, there is little evidence to support currently advocated special diets and megavitamin therapy. Unlike the situation with stimulant medication, the dominant view in the field remains one of skepticism about such treatments. As with medication, cautions are frequently raised about possible harmful effects (see Chapter 6). Because of the poor quality of studies done to date, proponents argue that no conclusions should be made until appropriate research has been done.

Central nervous system training. In Chapter 3, we discussed efforts to retrain the brain when a person has lost certain functions because of brain damage. We also explored some of the efforts to retrain dominance and laterality.

Although the consensus seems to be that the functions of damaged and dysfunctioning areas of the brain can be taken over by other areas, it is not clear what conditions allow this to occur. The success of individuals who have regained lost functions has reinforced the idea that the functioning of the central nervous system (CNS) can be improved through training and "reprogramming." As a result, many treatment approaches are advocated. Two that have been rather controversial in the field of learning disabilities are the "patterning" approach (Delacato, 1966) and "sensory-integration therapy" (Ayres, 1969, 1978).

Patterning, for example, is based on the theory that poor neurological organization is the result of failure to pass through established developmental stages. To correct the problem, the treatment proposes to flood the sensory system with an intense program of stimulation designed to elicit a response from the motor system. Beginning at the earliest stage of motor development, exercises are designed to take the individual through successive stages of growth. This is supposed to correct damage by inducing proper neural connections.

What makes most of such approaches controversial is the tremendous disagreement among experts about assumptions made regarding how the CNS develops and functions, how current learning problems are connected to the way the individual's CNS has developed and is functioning, and how specific treatment steps improve neurological functioning. Furthermore, particularly in the case of patterning, there has been considerable concern over the potential harm that can arise from treatments that require so much time commitment, physical effort, and financial investment from families.

Reading D

Fads and Claims

The field of learning disabilities has been particularly vulnerable to treatment fads and irresponsible claims of effectiveness. Four prominent reasons why this has been the case are discussed here.

First, the field is relatively young. When a field is new, there are not enough established, effective treatments available. Everyone is looking for *the* answer. Professionals look for every small clue that might suggest a useful treatment. They are not particularly looking for why a practice may have an effect or whether effects are temporary and superficial. And they don't particularly look for limitations and side effects. Often, premature statements are made about the promise of some training activity, test, material, drug, diet, and so forth. And, of course, the media and individuals primarily interested in making money are always ready to exploit a proposed treatment as long as there are eager consumers (see Box D–1).

A second reason for the field's vulnerability to fads and irresponsible claims is that learning disabilities are poorly defined. As long as so many types of learning problems can be identified as learning disabilities, it is easy to claim that any treatment that is effective with any learning *problem* may be effective with a learning *disability*.

Third, evaluating treatment effectiveness is extremely difficult. There are severe limitations related to all efforts to evaluate a specific treatment. This is true with regard to both positive and negative outcomes. As a result, it is not possible yet to base claims of treatment effects on comprehensive research. This is why placement and treatment choices reflect decision makers' beliefs more than they do adequate research evidence. Without comprehensive evaluations of treatments, it is relatively easy for anyone to make positive claims as long as the approach they are pushing has an intuitive appeal. At the same time, the absence of adequate research findings makes it difficult to present conclusive arguments against such claims.

Finally, misinterpretations of reasons for positive outcomes are easy to make. Because a specific treatment takes place in the context of a variety of events and usually occurs over a period of time, many other factors besides the treatment may actually cause a positive change in a specific individual. For example, medical practitioners know that positive changes sometimes are the result of psychological factors rather than a specific treatment. In fact, sometimes placebos (e.g., sugar pills) are given in place of drugs when a doctor finds that a certain patient stops having symptoms simply by taking what he or she thinks is medication. Getting older and maturing is another factor that can produce positive changes regardless of treatment. When these factors operate, as they usually do for some individuals involved in any treatment, the tendency is to assume the specific treatment worked in these cases. Apparent success leads to recommendation of the treatment to others. The more enthusiastic and influential the recommenders, the more likely the word will spread about the promise of the treatment.

When there is a considerable amount of money that can be made if a treatment comes into vogue, it can be expected that special interests will help to publicize the promise of their product. In such cases, it really becomes a matter of "buyer beware!" (see Box D–2).

Box D–1

Examples
Media Promotion of a Fad

The following item appeared in *Newsweek*, October 8, 1973.

"How Coffee Calms Kids"

"About five in every 100 U.S. gradeschool children suffer from hyperkinesis, a disorder marked by restlessness, disruptive classroom behavior, and inability to concentrate. In many cases, the condition can be controlled by the administration of stimulant drugs such as amphetamines that have a paradoxical calming effect on hyperkinetic youngsters and improve concentration. But the use of potent stimulants in children is controversial, mainly because they often produce side effects, which include a loss of appetite, insomnia, and abdominal pain. However, a South Carolina psychiatrist seems to have found a simple way out of this therapeutic dilemma: two cups of coffee a day may be as effective as drugs to calm the hyperactive child. Dr. Robert C. Schnackenberg happened upon the solution while taking the histories of hyperkinetic children at the William S. Hill Psychiatric Institution in Columbia, S.C. He was surprised to learn that an unusually high percentage of the youngsters regularly drank coffee. When he asked why, many of the children said the beverage had a calming effect and helped them in school. . . . Coffee drinking, Schnackenberg thinks, may

account for the paucity of reports on hyperkinetic children in South America where many youngsters drink the beverage. The disorder undoubtedly exists there, Schnackenberg says, but children may be 'inadvertently treating their own symptoms.'"

Can you criticize the conclusions made in this article?
Sieben (1977) warns that

"We must resist the temptation to follow each treatment fad willy-nilly. We must realize that newspapers and news broadcasts are poor sources of medical information. Simplistic new theories offer hope and have news value, but their refutation is a tedious and thankless task which holds little interest for such media. The burden of proof is on the promoter of a new theory. . . . To promote a hypothesis as fact without first submitting it to rigorous testing is a tremendous disservice to the patient and to the public . . . [and] an abuse of the very children we presume to be helping. . . . We should be alert for signs that a proposed treatment may be poorly substantiated. . . . We should be particularly careful in drawing conclusions from anecdotal case reports. . . . They afford fresh insights into familiar problems. Yet they are by their very nature biased, subjective, and impressionistic. . . . Such cases are provocative, but they do not establish the validity of new treatments. We have been misled too many times. . . ."

Box D–2

Viewpoint
Selling Treatments

Treatments for learning disabilities are highly marketable commodities. To meet the growing demand for treatments to correct learning disabilities and related behavior problems, an increasing number of persons, agencies, and companies are selling tests and programmed materials, training exercises, medication, and anything else that people can be convinced to buy.

If the sales pitch is good enough, people tend to ignore the limitations and potential harm of many practices. Ironically, some procedures come to be accepted as valid simply because they are so widely used. People seem to think that a practice must be good or else why would so many textbooks discuss it, professionals offer it, companies sell it, legislative bodies endorse it, and consumers buy it. This type of validation has been jokingly called "market" or "cash validity."

Reading *E*

Enhancing Motivation and Skills in Social Functioning

Persons with learning disabilities and other learning problems often do not behave in ways others think they should. Recently, there has been a trend to view these behavior "problems" as an indication of immature social development, especially a lack of skills for interpersonal functioning and problem solving. This trend has led to a variety of "social skills training" programs.

How promising are programs for training social skills? Recent reviewers have been cautiously optimistic about the potential value of several proposed approaches. At the same time, however, concerns have been expressed that such skill training seems limited to what is specifically learned and to the situations in which the skills are learned. Moreover, the behaviors learned seem to be maintained only for a short period after the training. These concerns have been raised in connection with (1) training specific behaviors, such as teaching a person what to think and say in a given situation, and (2) strategies that emphasize development of specific cognitive or affective skills, such as teaching a person how to generate a wider range of options for solving interpersonal problems.

As with other skills training approaches, the limitations of current approaches seem to result from a failure to understand the im-

plications of recent theory and research on human motivation. It is evident that many social skills training programs lack a systematic emphasis on enhancing participants' motivation to avoid and overcome interpersonal problems and to learn and continue to apply interpersonal skills to solve such problems.

In keeping with the ideas presented in Part 3, we have been exploring ways to initially engage a student in a variety of activities intended to overcome or minimize avoidance and enhance positive motivation for improving social functioning, especially the solving of interpersonal problems. The general assumptions underlying this work are discussed in Chapters 8 through 11. In addition, with regard to social functioning, we assume that

1. not all problems with social functioning are indications that a person lacks social skills;

2. assessment of social skills deficiencies is best accomplished after efforts are made (a) to minimize environmental factors causing interpersonal problems and (b) to maximize a student's motivation for coping effectively with such problems; and

3. regular teaching and remedial strategies to improve skills for social functioning are best accomplished in interaction with systematic strategies to enhance motivation (a) for avoiding and overcoming interpersonal problems and (b) for continuing to apply social skills.

The specific steps we have developed so far to address major motivational considerations in overcoming interpersonal problems are outlined in Box E–1. Steps in enhancing skills are outlined in Box E–2.

Because we have not addressed the topic of social skills in any depth in the text, a few words about the steps outlined in Box E–1 seem in order. The interest in training social

Box E-1

Initial Steps for Enhancing and Maintaining Motivation to Solve Interpersonal Problems

Such activities as direct discussions, responses to direct questions, sentence completion, Q-sort items, role playing, audiovisual presentations,* etc., are used as vehicles for presenting/eliciting and clarifying the following:

1. Specific times when the individual experiences interpersonal problems (without assigning blame).

2. The form of the problems (again, no judgments are made).

3. The individual's perceptions of the causes of the problems.†

4. A broader analysis of possible causes (e.g., the individual's thoughts about other possible reasons and about how other people might interpret the situation; intervener examples of other perceptions and beliefs).

5. Any reasons the individual might have for wanting the interpersonal problems not to occur and for why they might continue.

6. A list of other possible reasons for people not wanting to be involved in such problems.

7. The reasons that appear to be personally important to the individual and why they are significant, underscoring those that are the individual's most important reasons for wanting not to be involved in such problems.

8. General ways in which the individual can deal appropriately and effectively with such problems (i.e., avoid them, use available skills, and develop new skills).

9. The individual's (a) general desire not to continue to experience interpersonal problems, (b) specific reasons for wanting this, and (c) desire to take some action.

10. The available alternatives for avoiding problems, using acquired skills, and developing new skills.

11. The available options related to activities and objectives associated with learning new skills (e.g., the specific activities and materials, mutual expectations, etc.).

12. Specific choices in the form of a mutually agreeable plan of action for pursuing alternatives of steps 10 and 11.

Any step can be repeated as necessary, e.g., because of new information. Also, once the skill development activities are initiated, some of the above steps must be repeated in order to maintain an individual's motivation over time.

---

*Videotapes are particularly useful to make points vividly; e.g., to portray others in comparable situations, to present others as models, etc.

†Each step does not require a separate session; e.g., steps 1 through 3 can be accomplished in one session.

---

skills has resulted in a rapidly growing body of literature specifying skills and procedures (see references at the end of this Reading). Although most social skills curricula await further evaluation, we have drawn upon available work to arrive at what appears to be a promising synthesis of "skills" and practices. Furthermore, our approach to teaching the skills uses a general problem-solving sequence. In essence, individuals are taught to (1) analyze interpersonal problem situations,

(2) generate and evaluate a range of options and specific steps for resolving problems, and (3) implement and evaluate the chosen option, and then (4) if necessary, select another alternative.

These abilities can be practiced as lessons or when natural interpersonal problems arise in the classroom. For those who are interested and capable, the problem-solving framework itself can be taught.

When formal lessons are used, small-

Box E–2

Steps to Enhance Skills for Solving Interpersonal Problems

1. Presentation of examples of interpersonal problem solving (read by the instructor using visual aids or a videotape presentation).*

2. Group discussions of examples stressing (a) why the person in the example wanted to solve the problem, (b) the way the problem was analyzed, (c) possible solutions which were generated, and (d) the way in which pros and cons of solutions were considered, and choices made, implemented, and evaluated.

3. Presentation of an interpersonal problem and group discussion of why the person involved wants to resolve the problem and of how to analyze it.

4. Presentation of an appropriate analysis of a problem and group discussion and categorization of options.

5. Presentation of a range of options and specific steps for solving a problem; group discussion of pros and cons for evaluating which one should be pursued.

6. Presentation of a chosen alternative for solving a problem; group discussion of how to evaluate its effectiveness and to choose another option if necessary.

7. Presentation of a new problem with the above steps repeated as needed.

It is proposed that at least four problems be pursued in this fashion. By the fourth, the individual is to be able to do each facet of the problem-solving sequence during a given session. If not, up to three additional problems should be presented.

---

*As appropriate, during any step the discussion may include role playing, use of puppets with younger children, etc. Initially, the intervener provides categories of ideas which may have been missed. All ideas generated during discussion are to be charted by category for subsequent reference.

Evaluative feedback should be used to underscore progress and satisfaction associated with accomplishment of program objectives and solving interpersonal problems at school. Consequences which the individual experiences when such problems are not solved appropriately also should be highlighted.

---

group instruction is favored because it provides a social context for learning about social matters; however, individuals should be given private lessons when necessary. We propose that groups meet each day for thirty to forty-five minutes over a period of about eight weeks.

For each step, three guidelines shape the choice of specific instructional objectives. Recognizing that both motivational and developmental readiness must be accommodated, the guildelines stress the following:

- Not teaching previously learned skills or those that the individual does not want to pursue currently. (In such instances, scheduled lessons are replaced by enrichment activities. Needed skills instruction is

postponed until sufficient interest can be established.)

- Teaching the skills most needed in pursuing current relationships. (Lessons are not necessarily presented in the order listed in Box E–2. Optimally, objectives are keyed to match the individual's current needs. Such needs are identified by the individual involved or by school personnel who have assessed the deficiencies by closely observing well-motivated attempts at solving interpersonal problems.)

- Developing missing prerequisites for learning and performing needed skills. (When necessary, individuals are involved in additional exercises to improve (1) communication, (2) divergent thinking, (3) recognition and understanding of individual differences, and/or (4) understanding the value of respect and concern for others.)

Obviously, the ideas discussed here represent only a beginning. Given the growing interest in the areas of systematic enhancement of motivation and the training of social skills, we anticipate that programs for individuals with learning and behavior problems will increasingly incorporate procedures that reflect strategies for simultaneously enhancing motivation and skills.

SPECIAL TOPIC REFERENCES

Should you be interested in further information about current approaches to improving *social functioning*, see the following.

BRYAN, J. H. (1981). Social behavior of learning disabled children. In J. Gottlieb & S. S. Strichart (Eds.), *Developmental theory and research in learning disabilities*. Baltimore: University Park Press.

CARTLEDGE, G., & MILBURN, J. F. (Eds.) (1980). *Teaching social skills to children: Innovative approaches*. New York: Pergamon Press.

GRESHAM, F. M. (1981). Social skills training with handicapped children: A review. *Review of Educational Research, 51*, 139–76.

Learning Disability Quarterly, 5, entire issue, Fall 1982.

PHILLIPS, E. (1978). *The social skills basis of psychopathology: Alternatives to abnormal psychology.* New York: Grune & Stratton.

SPIVAK, G., PLATT, J., & SHURE, M. (1976). *The problem solving approach to adjustment.* San Francisco: Jossey-Bass.

STEPHENS, T. M. (1978). *Social skills in the classroom.* Columbus, Ohio: Cedars Press.

TROWER, P., BRYANT, B., & ARGYLE, M. (1978). *Social skills and mental health.* Pittsburgh: University of Pittsburgh.

Reading F

Options to Enhance Motivation and Learning

If Sally dreams of being a musician and wants to spend time learning more about music, is this an option? If Bret's great passion is collecting baseball cards and memorizing facts and statistics about the game, can his program include a project focusing on baseball? Chris is curious about electronics, but he doesn't want to take a standard electric shop course because making buzzers and one-tube radios seems pretty far removed from television and computers. Can he have time to explore the topic in ways that uniquely interest him?

And if Sally, Bret, and Chris are allowed to pursue such content, what outcomes (skills, knowledge, and attitudes) and what level of competence (budding awareness, moderate levels of mastery) should be expected from their activity?

Content and Outcome Options

From a motivational perspective, the answers to such questions are reasonably clear. Learners should be able to explore content that has personal value. In the process, they should be helped to pursue outcomes and levels of competence that reflect their continuing interest and effort (Deci, 1980; Perlmuter & Monty, 1979).

Most individuals will find personal reasons for acquiring basic skills and informa-

tion while exploring intrinsically valued content. For example, the more that Chris pursues his interest in electronics, the more he will discover that he needs to improve his reading and math skills. Thus, his ongoing exploration of electronics can indirectly lead to a personal desire to improve math and reading skills as he comes to view these skills as a means to his ends — rather than as something everyone else wants him to do.

There are three ways in which classroom content and outcomes can be readily expanded to provide a broad range of interesting options. The first involves expanding options to include a wide sampling of topics that are currently popular with the majority of the students (see Box F–1). The second way involves asking students, especially those who still think there are too few positive options, to identify additional topics they would like to have included. Third, there are options the teacher identifies as important and worthwhile, which hopefully can be introduced in ways that expand student interests.

The more severe the student's learning problem, the more that variations from established content and outcomes can be argued worth offering to mobilize and maintain the student's motivation. Indeed, with a severe motivation problem, it may be necessary to include options not usually offered to such students (e.g., auto mechanics, video production, photography, work experiences).

Even more controversial may be the necessity to allow such students to "opt out" of certain content (e.g., reading, math) for a while. This occurs most frequently with students whose failures have led them to strongly avoid particular subjects.

Along with strong dislikes, students with motivation problems often have an area of strong interest that can be made the focus of their program. The intent in doing so is to allow a youngster to explore some intriguing area in depth and in ways that uniquely interest him or her.

Actually, such a comprehensive discovery-oriented project can be a useful option when any student wants to learn a great deal more about a topic. Projects give an intrinsic sense of form, direction, and immediacy to learning. (Any of the examples in Box F–1 may be undertaken as a project.)

Moreover, in pursuing comprehensive projects, students not only can discover more about a specific content area, they can also rediscover the personal value of improving reading, language, and a variety of other basic skills. After all, what makes certain skills "basic" is that they are necessary for pursuing many interests and tasks in daily living. When students come to understand this, they often develop a renewed interest in learning such basic skills.

In general, the many options illustrated here suggest that rather than going "back to basics" it may be better to go "forward to basics" by enabling students to rediscover intrinsic reasons for learning such skills. While we're discussing the matter, we also should reemphasize that there has been a broadening of current views about what is and isn't a basic skill. There is more to coping with everyday situations than having competence to use the three Rs. Another prominent set of basic skills students need, for instance, is the ability to interact positively in social situations. (Reading E outlines a motivation-oriented program in this area.)

The "back to basics" movement underscores the fact that there is always a conflict between required curriculum content and topics that have contemporary interest and are popular. From a motivational perspective, it would be nice if a way were found to achieve some sort of satisfactory balance. This might result in a decrease in time devoted to the established curriculum but, hopefully, also would increase positive attitudes toward learning and school. Even if such a balance seems unnecessary for most students, it does appear justified in cases of

learning problems, since the established curriculum has proved not to be effective.

Process and Structure Options

Content, of course, interacts with processes. An exciting presentation can make a topic really come to life. As with content and outcomes, there are three ways in which process options can be readily expanded—by adding procedures that are widely popular, by adding those of special interest to specific students, or by adding those newly identified by the teacher.

Again, we stress that students who have learning problems will have had negative experiences with a variety of instructional processes. Therefore, it is necessary to show them there are good alternatives to the procedures that led to their failures. For example, in pursuing projects, students with reading problems cannot be expected initially to rely heavily on reading. Visual- or audiovisual-oriented material, such as picture books and magazines, films and filmstrips, records, videotapes and audiotapes, field trips, teacher and other student presentations—all can be used. Products can include some written and some dictated material, along with artwork (drawings, graphs, model constructions, photographs, collages) and oral presentations.

Chris, for example, failed a seventh-grade social studies class and was scheduled to repeat it. The curriculum content for the course consists of specific historical, political, and cultural events and some basic geography.

At the end of the course, students are expected at least to be able to identify the events and geographical features covered and to use source materials (atlas, almanac, encyclopedia, card catalogue) for finding additional historical and geographical material. More ambitiously, the intent is to equip students with the knowledge to ana-

Box F-1

Program Example
Popular Content Options

The following topics have been extremely popular with the majority of students with whom we work. Although the topic may be one that is regularly taught in schools, the reference here is not to a set curriculum. Our students usually are interested in how a topic relates to the world as they know it, or they are intrigued with some exotic subtopic. They do not want to pursue a set curriculum.

- Animals—care, training, and breeding; incubating chickens; learning about prehistoric and exotic animals and about those who live in special climates
- Arts and crafts—expressive drawing and painting, constructing and building, exploring the work of others
- Career and vocation—adolescents, in particular, often want presentations and opportunities to observe to find out about jobs that may be worth pursuing
- Computers—basic uses, graphics, language and logic
- Consumer activity—comparing prices, learning about false advertising and advertising gimmicks, learning how to find a particular product
- Cooking to eat and sell—food planning, purchasing, and preparation keyed to specific interests of the students involved
- Creative writing—fiction and poetry
- Cultures of other peoples—comparing the way one lives with how others live (e.g., rituals, beliefs, music, food, dress, art, education)
- Design—graphics, drafting, architecture, construction
- Drama—writing plays; acting; staging performances; observing and criticizing TV, film, and stage productions; learning more about favorite people and current trends in theater, film, and TV
- Driving—at age 15½ and older, of course, most have a strong interest in preparing for driving
- Health and safety—first aid, CPR, personal care, sex education
- History—specific events such as the invention of the automobile, space exploration, World War II; the background to a current event, such as the turmoil in the Mideast
- Math puzzles and measurement—number and graph puzzlers; how to handle one's money;

lyze and discuss significant past events and relate them to life today.

The class Chris failed used primarily the following procedures:

- Each week the teacher assigned a chapter to be read and questions to be answered and turned in; then, there was a multiple-choice, true-false test on the material at the end of the week.
- In class each day, the teacher spoke about the material covered in the text and had the students take turns sharing their answers to the assigned questions. Once a week they practiced looking up assigned material in atlases, almanacs, etc. Once a month they went to the library to learn how to use its resources.
- During the year, each student was to present four current events to the class on topics relevant to the material being discussed.
- Three times during the school year, films were shown.
- Students who wanted extra credit could do a special term paper chosen from a list of topics the teacher had prepared or could choose three books from a prepared list and do reports on them.

how to keep records on material related to one's hobby; how to measure in pursuing a particular interest, such as model building, wood construction, cooking, sewing, computers, video; how to compare sizes and weights; creative activities using math

- Motor trends—almost everything related to cars and motorcycles has proved to be of interest to one student or another
- Music—learning to play an instrument or sing, reading music, composing, learning more about favorite people and trends, reviewing and critiquing
- Newspaper and yearbook publication—all facets of planning, preparing, and distributing publications
- Photography—camera operations, picture composition, darkroom skills, creating interesting effects, display
- Private enterprise/running a business—establishing and running a small business for profit at school, such as a small food service or offering for sale products that are made on the premises
- Psychology—learning more about the views of others in one's immediate environment, understanding why specific individuals and groups behave as they do

- Science—underwater creatures and plants, especially those that can be seen by scuba diving; electricity, especially as used in everyday life; chemical reactions; personal anatomy and biology; current events in science and medicine
- Space—other planets, space travel, constructing and flying rockets
- Sports—learning more about the present and past of favorite personalities, events, and equipment; learning to coach or referee
- Travel—learning what's interesting to visit locally and what's worth seeing in other countries, planning and taking trips, learning to use public transportation; learning about travel aids and skills such as map reading
- Video—writing, producing, acting, directing, camerawork, editing
- Work experience—some students want to include work experience as part of their school program in order to earn needed money or to feel a sense of competence

A major concern in expanding options is that additional materials usually are needed. This concern can be minimized by asking those interested in the option to help gather the desired materials. (When topics are popular, several class members usually can be mobilized.)

- Grades were based primarily on test scores and extra credit work. However, grades were lowered when current event presentations or answers to the assigned reading questions were poor.
- When students, such as Chris, were found to be having difficulty, the teacher recommended that the parents spend more time helping with homework or find a tutor.

Because Chris failed the class, it seems reasonable to consider the procedures as not a good match for him. Indeed, if in repeating the course he was confronted with the same

processes, it would not be surprising if his behavior reflected a good deal of avoidance motivation.

What would a set of alternative procedures look like? Box F–2 provides an example (also see Box F–3).

Besides specific processes, there is the matter of *structure*. Sally, Bret, Chris, and Jan need and want different amounts of support, direction, and external control (or limit setting) to help them learn. They have each identified some things they can readily do on their own, but they know there are tasks and situations they will handle better with

Box F–2

Program Example
**Offering Alternative Processes
for the Same Content**

A teacher using a topic exploration approach might proceed as follows:

- Rather than assign material, the teacher prepares ten varied topics covering the course content. He also identifies a long list of activities for pursuing such topics, each of which includes use of the desired basic research skills.

- At the beginning of the course, the teacher uses the first few classes to explain the ten varied topics and to help the students explore and choose from them.

He explains that each student can choose one or more topics and can choose from among a wide range of activities in learning about a topic. He also notes that each student can choose to work on a topic alone or in a small group. To help students get a good idea of the choices, he uses pictorial aids, an overhead projector, and filmstrips. The bulletin boards contain a variety of materials, such as pictures of other places and other times, historic newspaper clippings, and brief descriptions relevant to understanding the topics and activities being explored. There also are examples of what students have done in the past. A variety of pertinent reading material at different reading levels (magazines, pamphlets, fiction, and different texts) have been placed on the shelves and some opened for display. The teacher encourages the students to get up and look through the materials and to talk about the various alternatives. He answers questions as they arise. Finally, the teacher asks if any of the students have any relevant and feasible topics and activities they would like to have added. The one guideline he invokes is that groups have no more than four members.

- After aiding the students in choosing their topics and related activities, the teacher meets during classtimes with groups and individuals to assist and provide support and resources as they pursue their topics.

- Throughout the year, students share what they have learned about their topics with each other. For example:

One group studying how the effects of slavery are still felt in current race relations performs a play they have written.

Another group studying the western movement in the United States forms a wagon train to experience the process and problems involved in undertaking such a trek (budgeting, buying supplies, dealing with changes in the weather, surviving harsh terrains); they report their progress and adventures periodically to the rest of the class.

One student chose to study the development and forms of money used from ancient times to the present and, as soon as the information is gathered, reports on each historical stage.

Another student decided to learn research skills by tracing her "roots"; she not only shares her family history with the class but also is able to tell the others about a wide range of available historical resource material.

- To link the material together and cover anything that might be missed, the teacher prepares a series of periodic presentations (lectures, films, video) and related supplementary reading and discussions.

- Each student turned in a written progress report summarizing what he or she had learned about the topic at the end of each month. Multiple-choice, true-false, and essay exams were given at midyear and at the end of the year. The reports and exams were used to evaluate how well the students had learned what the course was intended to teach. Students who had trouble reading or writing were given the exams orally. Grades were based on a combination of effort and performance.

Box F–3

Viewpoint
Different Processes, Different Outcomes

In recent years, there has been a major push for greater accountability in education. Everyone agrees that school programs should be more effective. But not everyone agrees with the extreme emphasis on highly specific objectives as advocated by some evaluators, especially when it ignores the processes used to reach desired objectives.

Some evaluators have even gone so far as to say they don't care what means are used as long as the ends are achieved. This extremist view ignores a simple fact: although two procedures may accomplish the same set of narrow objectives, they also may produce a variety of other different outcomes.

Take the approach used with Chris and the one described in Box F–2, for example. A motivational perspective suggests the two courses may lead to very different attitudes about the material learned.

Lecture/text/test approaches tend to produce a distaste for social studies, history, geography, and similar subjects and for those who teach them. Moreover, teachers who teach in this way find little satisfaction in the process other than the sense of having pulled another group of students through.

In contrast, exploratory approaches lend themselves much better to personalization of learning and thus to the fostering and enhancement of intrinsic motivation along with the learning of specific content and skills. Moreover, students and teachers seem to find many personal satisfactions, i.e., valued learning and special friendships.

---

help. To have their changing needs matched, they must have the option of working alone or seeking support and guidance as often as is appropriate.

It is to be expected, of course, that those with the lowest motivation are likely to need the most support and guidance. At the same time, they are likely not to seek help readily. Moreover, those with avoidance motivation tend to react negatively to structure they perceive as used to control them.

In general, a greater range of options with regard to content, outcome, process, and structure are required for those with motivation problems. We will return to this topic after stressing the importance of options designed to enrich the experience of schooling and living.

Enrichment, Discovery, Inquiry, and Serendipity

As important as specific planning is, it is a mistake for school programs to overprescribe

the specifics of what and how to learn. There must be time for sampling and exploring unscheduled topics and activities. This, of course, assumes there are interesting things available to investigate. The time for exploring can be viewed as an enrichment opportunity.

Some remedial programs are much too preoccupied with a student's problems and the tasks that must be pursued in remedying them. When this happens, enrichment experiences tend to be ignored and the learning environment takes on an air of pathology, drudgery, and boredom—all of which are contrary to enhancing motivation.

The model provided by programs for the gifted is a good example of the type of environment that may have a positive motivational impact on any learner. Such programs offer a rich set of learning centers that focus on topics such as those listed in Box F–1 and on many more. Enrichment activities are useful for enhancing motivation and reducing negative behavior and, of course, can lead to important learning.

Although enrichment activity may be seen as a frill for many students, it is seen as important, motivationally, for students with learning problems. The richer the learning environment, the more likely students will discover a surprising variety of new interests, information, and skills.

From a motivational perspective, enrichment options are not designed to teach specific information and skills. There are, of course, specific, and often predictable, outcomes that come from contact with any topic. However, almost by definition, an enrichment option produces many incidental and unpredictable (serendipitous) outcomes.

Furthermore, enrichment activities are not designed to operate as if everything a student learns is taught by the teacher. The "hands-on" nature of enrichment centers encourages independent exploration, experimentation, and learning. As questions arise, students can choose to use whatever information or help is available.

In the end, what students learn depends a great deal on their interest and effort. Some may decide to go into a topic in great depth and to acquire a good deal of mastery over it; others may simply dabble and gain a surface awareness, which they may or may not follow up on later.

As a general strategy, enrichment opportunities can be established by offering an attractive set of discovery and inquiry centers and helping the students explore the materials and ideas.

Let's look at Sally's experience with an enriched program.

Sally's teacher explains that there are a variety of centers in the room which will change as the school year progresses. At the moment, there are centers dealing with electricity, tropical fish, computers, chemical reactions, African cultures, creative math, and many more. In order to offer a variety of centers each week, some are offered twice and some three times a week.

Sally is given a chance to sample the centers. She then is given the opportunity to choose one or two that really interest her. It is made clear that these are "electives" and that she can drop out at any time.

Sally is attracted to the tropical fish. She wants to know if it is hard to take care of them. She thinks she'd like to have some at home. Where do you buy them? Are they expensive? How long do they live?

The teacher answers a few of her questions and then points out that there is a group meeting on Monday, Wednesday, and Friday. They are learning all about where the fish come from, which can live with each other, how to breed them, and whatever else the group wants to explore about aquariums and fish.

Sally is intrigued but a little suspicious. She wants to know if the activity includes reading or other assignments and tests. The answer is an unequivocal no. She can come and learn whatever she wants, in the way that she wants, and no one will ask her to prove anything. It is her questions that are important—not the teacher's.

It is all so inviting that Sally decides to give it a try. And she finds it's as good as it looks and sounds. As she attends regularly, it becomes evident to all who observe her that she is a bright, interested, and attentive learner whenever she is motivated by the topic. She remembers what she has learned and works well with others.

Not long after joining the group, her teacher notices Sally has gone to the library and checked out picture books on tropical fish. A few days later, Sally approached her to ask for a little help in reading some of the captions.

Options for Those with Motivation Problems

The first work with such students involves exploration to find what the individual's interests are: Sports? Rock music? Movies? Computer games? Such personal interests are used as a starting point. The interest is explored until the student identifies a related topic, no matter how unusual, that he or she would like to learn more about (see Box F–4).

After identification of a topic, learning activity options are reviewed to find those that are a good match with the student's needs, interests, and styles. For example, talkative students may prefer to work in small discussion groups. Other students will want a work area that is private and quiet. Students

---

Box F–4

Program Example
Options for Students with Motivation Problems

Harry comes to school with no intention of working on what his teachers have planned. He will spend as much time as he can get away with talking with his friends and looking for some excitement to make the time pass faster. He is frequently in the middle of whatever trouble is occurring. Everyone is waiting for him to do something bad enough that he can be removed from his present class.

There is an alternative to letting this tragedy run its course. Time can be spent helping Harry identify one area of personal interest that he would like to learn more about, e.g., pop culture, rock music, current teenage fashions. Then, a personalized program can be developed with his identifying a topic he would like to explore and some ways he would like to explore it.

Approached in this way, most students like Harry will identify a topic and activities that interest them. However, one topic and a few activities won't fill up much time—perhaps an hour, maybe less. What then?

Well, Harry could be asked to pursue a regular program for the rest of the school day; but the odds are that he would simply resume his previous pattern of negative behavior. In the long run, this would probably defeat what the alternative program is trying to accomplish.

Our solution to the problem is as simple as it is controversial. We have students such as Harry attend school only for that period of time during which they have planned a program they intend to pursue.

Our reasoning is twofold: (1) we know that students tend to work best when they are working on what they have identified as desirable, and (2) for students like Harry, it seems likely the rest of the time is wasted, including getting into trouble. Obviously, if they are not at school a full day, they are less likely to get into as much trouble. But, more important, the less we are in the position of coercing them, the less we are likely to cause the variety of reactive misbehaviors that characterize such students. Moreover, we find that once we no longer have to do battle with them, many youngsters evolve an increasing range of academic interests, including renewed interest in becoming competent in the areas of reading and writing. The energy they had been devoting to fighting teachers and school may now be redirected to exploring what it is they are interested in doing for themselves. As Harry's range of interests increase, he will want a longer school day and is likely to make better use of it.

We recognize the many practical, economic, and legal problems involved in cutting back on the length of a student's school day. However, we think these problems must be contrasted with the costs to society and individuals of ignoring the fact that for certain students a lengthy school day interferes with correcting their problems. Indeed, in some cases, it only makes the problems worse.

For older students, of course, a shortened day paired with a parttime job or apprenticeship may be a most productive experience. Among the results of work experiences can be an increased feeling of self-worth and competence and enhanced intrinsic motivation toward overcoming learning problems. A job also can provide a student with a source of income, which may be needed, and can even help to establish career directions.

with high activity levels may choose to work with manipulable materials. Most will prefer to work on time-limited activities.

In accommodating a wider range of behavior, classroom rules and standards are redefined to accept behaviors such as nondisruptive talking and movement about the classroom. For some individuals, certain "bad manners" (e.g., some rudeness, some swear words) and eccentric mannerisms (e.g., strange clothing and grooming) may have to be tolerated initially.

The most basic process option, of course, is that of not participating at times or at all.

There are times when Bret simply doesn't feel like working. He wants the option of drawing, playing a game, or resting for about an hour. There are days when Sally doesn't want to go to school. And there came a day when Chris concluded he was ready to drop out of school.

Which, if any, of these should be offered as options? For whom?

At this point, you may think that such options are too inappropriate even to consider. However, if you have time to read about student decision making in Reading G, you will see that such options may play an important role in efforts to reduce avoidance motivation.

SPECIAL TOPIC REFERENCES

See references at the end of Chapters 10 and 11.

Learner Decision Making to Enhance Motivation and Development

Decisions about *participation* are the primary foundation upon which all other decisions rest (Adelman, et al., 1984; Taylor, et al., 1985). If the individual initially does not want to participate or subsequently comes to that point of view, all other decisions become highly problematic.

For students diagnosed as learning disabled, the decision process related to participation begins with the discussions about placement. Whether a student with problems is placed in a special program or maintained in regular classes, the immediate motivational concern always is whether the individual has decided that the program is right for him or her. And, of course, even if the initial answer is yes, the student's perception of the situation may change. Thus, decisions about placement must be continuously reevaluated.

The next most basic decisions are those related to *specific program options*. The objective is to help the student pinpoint alternatives that match personal interests and capabilities. Again, initial decisions have to be modified in keeping with changes in the student's perceptions of what is a good match.

As the following discussion illustrates, the best decision-making processes include opportunities to physically explore and sample options. Thus, all initial decisions can be seen simply as extended opportunities to investigate options.

In overcoming severe motivational problems, it appears important not to insist that a student continue to work in areas she or he wants to avoid. This strategy is intended to reduce the type of psychological and behavioral reactions that occur when individuals think they are being forced to do something they don't want to do. In particular, we don't want to increase avoidance, either in the form of withdrawal (including passive performance) or of active resistance (e.g., disruptive behavior).

Thus, if a student initially indicates not wanting instruction in a specific area, it seems wise to hold off instruction temporarily—even if the area is a basic skill, such as reading or math. The time is better spent on activities that may eventually lead to renewed interest in the avoided area.

Not providing instruction as a step in renewing positive interest in an area seems to go against common sense. We recognize that this is a controversial and, for some, an alarming strategy. It is not one to be adopted lightly or naively, and remember, it is a strategy to deal with motivation problems. From a motivational perspective, it is clearly rational to pursue areas of positive interest. And the case can be made that to focus solely on positive interests may be the best way to eventually overcome motivation *and* skill problems related to reading and other basics.

Let's look at Sally in this context.

Sally doesn't want reading instruction. The teacher agrees to set her reading program aside for now. If reading were completely ignored, the best outcome the teacher should expect is that Sally's avoidance motivation would not be significantly increased. For many persons, this might be an acceptable outcome with regard to art and music and other areas not seen as basic

271

skills. It would not be acceptable to most people when it comes to the three Rs.

Fortunately, what makes basic literacy skills *basic* is that most facets of daily living involve their application. Moreover, the fact that they are designated as basic makes them a major point of focus by almost everyone in the society.

Thus, it is likely that most of what Sally chooses to learn about at school and much of her other experiences will lead to frequent natural encounters that cause her to realize that she has a personal need for such skills. And, of course, these daily encounters inevitably bring her into contact with people who convey to her their assumption that she already has or is in the process of acquiring such skills. These experiences affect her feelings and attitudes about acquiring basics.

As Sally's intrinsic awareness of the value of basic skills increases, she can be helped to learn any specific skills she identifies as needed in coping with natural encounters. Eventually, Sally should arrive at a level of motivational readiness at which she will accept the teacher's offer to pick up with formal reading instruction. Equally important, if her intrinsic motivation has increased enough, the time she spends reading may be considerably greater than the time spent in formal instruction.

Appropriate decision processes, then, can increase personal valuing and expectations of success, thereby enhancing motivation for learning and overcoming problems. By "appropriate" processes, we mean those that enable a student to self-select from desirable and feasible options. Besides improving motivation, such processes also provide opportunities for strengthening a student's ability to make sound choices.

Students, of course, may differ greatly in their motivation and ability to make decisions (see Box G–1). That is why we believe learning to make decisions should be a basic focus of instruction and why it is so important to be ready to help youngsters with decision making.

Steps in Helping Students Make Decisions

In helping with student decision making, it is useful to view the process as a series of steps.

First, a student must understand the value of making his or her own decisions. Minimally, this means the student's knowing that the process provides opportunities for taking greater control over one's life and overcoming one's problems.

"We want to work with you in ways you think are good. Therefore, we've put together as many helpful and exciting learning opportunities as we could. While we think there are many good choices, we know that you are the best judge of what you like. So the first thing you might want to do is to look over and sample some of these options and see if any appeal to you. You may also want to suggest some other topics and activities. We only want to work with those that you choose as worth doing. We want you to have more control over your activities and program schedule than may have been the case in the past. Would you like to take some time and see what's available?"

Second, the process must include ways for students to actively sample and select from available options and to propose others whenever feasible.

"You can spend some time looking over the various options, including watching other students who have chosen them. As you do this, I will be glad to answer any questions you may have. We can also talk about other things you would like to do and learn about that may not be here yet. Let's try to find a topic that personally interests you. The important thing is that you get a chance to decide which things you want to spend your time at school learning about."

Third, working out program details should be done as soon as choices are made. This is necessary so that the student is clear about the implications of following through on decisions. With such information, a stu-

Box G–1

Research and Practice
Are Students with Learning Problems Competent to Make Good Decisions?

Making a sound decision involves having the necessary information about alternatives and about positive and negative outcomes. It also involves having the competence to evaluate available information. Not surprisingly, when someone is perceived as not competent to decide, they often are not given the information or opportunity to prove the perception is incorrect.

Who is competent to decide? This is one of the more difficult and controversial questions confronting professionals, parents, and society in general.

Is it a matter of age? Education? Intelligence? If someone has a learning problem, are they less competent to make certain decisions than individuals without learning problems?

As yet, there are no satisfactory answers. There is, however, a rapidly growing body of research on the competence of youngsters with and without learning problems to participate in decision making (e.g., Baumrind, 1978; Melton, 1983; Weithorn, 1983).

Findings to date suggest that many youngsters and their parents believe that children as young as ten should participate in making decisions about everyday matters such as what clothes to buy and wear, what food to eat, what time to go to bed, and what friends to make. Parents and youngsters also generally agree that minors (thirteen and older) should participate in decisions regarding school programs and placements and physical and mental health treatment. Studies comparing youngsters' and adults' decisions as to treatment and research participation indicate that the decisions of children as young as nine are similar to those made by adults; and by the time they're fourteen, minors seem able to think as competently as adults in weighing certain decision risks and benefits.

In contrast to this research, studies of practitioners' views of minors' competence tend to be less optimistic about youngsters' competence to decide. Unfortunately, research on practitioners' views of minors' competence to participate in decision making is sparse. In a survey of mental health professionals, we found that slightly less than half of those who were willing to respond indicated they asked clients under eighteen to participate in the treatment decision. However, those who did ask, asked children as young as twelve. Moreover, this group of professionals judge that 72 percent of those they asked did turn out to have the necessary level of competence for making the decisions. Of particular relevance to the ideas presented here, the reason most cited for why they asked children to participate in such decision making was to enhance their motivation for treatment (Taylor, et al., 1985).

Despite the inadequacy of the available literature, findings to date support the importance of avoiding presumptions about students' lack of competence. Furthermore, classroom programs ought to be designed to facilitate and not delay development of increased levels of decision-making competence. And, finally, we suggest that motivation often can be enhanced by encouraging students' participation in making decisions.

None of what has been said here is meant to imply that students will always make good decisions; nor will they always stick to a decision — nor should they. All we are proposing is that students (with and without learning problems) should be offered a wide range of learning options and should be helped to sample the options so that they have reasonable information upon which to base decisions. Moreover, after they have experienced an activity for a brief while, they may well decide that they made a mistake, and so all such decisions should be renegotiable. As we understand motivation and learning, such options and renegotiations are major factors in determining whether students want to follow through on decisions and whether they become good at making decisions.

dent can either back off from a choice because it involves too much work or can publicly commit to follow through.

> "Let's talk about your decision to learn how to use a computer. That group meets each day, over ten weeks, for an hour a day. Before you will get to do graphics, you will have to spend the first week learning basic computer operation. There is some reading material available; if you need help, several advanced students will be ready to explain the basics to you. If that sounds O.K. to you, let's have you write it on your posted schedule, and you can begin tomorrow."

Fourth, from the moment the student begins an activity, it is important to monitor motivation. If interest drops, the activity should be altered to better match the student; and if it can't be modified, the student should have the option of changing activities. Such monitoring is discussed in Chapter 9.

Teacher frustration is a frequent problem in helping students to make decisions and to improve their ability to do so. Many of a student's initial decisions don't hold up well. For a variety of reasons, a student may quickly lose interest in a topic or activity. This may happen, for example, if a youngster has a disability or does not work hard enough. However, early in the efforts to help youngsters make effective decisions, such "blaming" conclusions about why a particular choice didn't work can be premature and harmful. In general, when early decisions must be altered, it is important both to avoid blaming the student and to help the student avoid blaming himself or herself.

On the other hand, if the student manifests the common tendency to externalize blame (i.e., the activity is described as too hard or too boring), it may be useful at first simply to accept the reasons at face value. By working on changes that reflect the individual's stated "alibis," in time, it will become evident whether the student is merely making excuses.

Again, the point is that the ability to make good decisions is learned. Making decisions and evaluating their outcomes can be a good process for developing this basic skill. However, if the process is contaminated by accusations and blame, motivation for decision making can be undermined. As with all areas of learning, interactions over time will clarify whether students who continue to make poor decisions do so because of developmental or motivational problems.

Dialogues with Students

As suggested already, decision processes that lead to positive student perceptions involve ongoing dialogue between student and teacher. One result is a series of mutual agreements about what is to be done and how to proceed.

The mechanism for carrying on the dialogue often is called a conference, and the agreement often is referred to as a contract. However, terms like *conference* and *contract* do not convey the full sense of what is involved and at times have been interpreted in ways that are contrary to the meaning used here.

From a motivational perspective:

- Decisions must not be made for the student.

- Decisions must be modifiable whenever necessary.

- Dialogues should be designed to give, share, and clarify information seen as potentially useful to a student who is making a decision.

- Dialogues should involve not only conversational exchanges but also actual exploration and sampling of options.

The importance of the dialogue as a two-way process cannot be overemphasized. A conference should be a time for persons to say what they need, want, and are hoping for from each other. When problems exist, time should be devoted to problem solving. One conference often is insufficient for arriving at a major decision. Therefore, the dialogue is an ongoing formal and informal process.

Although the stress here is on student decisions, good agreements are not one-sided. In general, the processes are meant to establish, maintain, and enhance a positive commitment on the part of both the student and the teacher toward working in a collaborative relationship.

Conflicts Over Decisions

Suppose Sally, Jan, Bret, or Chris makes a decision that others don't like. This will inevitably happen because a number of other "interested parties" are affected by the decisions that are made. Critically, there are at least three interested parties besides the student: parents, teachers, and policymakers, such as principals, school boards, and funding agencies.

What if a student's choices are not acceptable to one or more of these other interested parties? Obviously, the dilemma can be resolved in one of three ways: the student's choice can be allowed to prevail, the decisions of others can prevail, or compromises can be sought.

Let's look at an example. When Chris was fifteen, he felt strongly that he no longer wanted to stay in a special class. The special class made him feel stigmatized, and he didn't see that he was making any progress. He wanted to try regular classes and have a tutor help him. His parents and teacher, however, both thought that he wouldn't be able to handle the work. Furthermore, they believed that rather than making him feel better about himself, the experience would only make him feel worse. An additional concern was that the school had no established way of providing appropriate tutoring.

Because both the parents and the teacher were in agreement, it was decided they "knew best"—so Chris spent another year in the special class program. It was a disastrous

year in which he did no real work and got into a lot of trouble. As soon as he was sixteen, he was so frustrated that he insisted on dropping out of school; his parents and the school were so frustrated, they simply went along with this decision. In looking back, they all wondered if some compromise should have been worked out when he wanted to leave the special class program.

What compromise? Several might have been considered:

- Chris could have spent some time each day in regular classes and some in the special program where tutoring could have been provided.

- He could have been offered a one semester trial period in carefully selected regular classes with some volunteer tutoring (from community resources or advanced students).

- The transfer could have been approved, with the provision that, first, Chris work with his teacher to (1) identify any missing prerequisite skills essential for survival in the regular program and then (2) work on acquiring these skills for a specific time period (no more than an additional semester).

Other compromises probably have occurred to you. Whether any would have worked is uncertain. What is obvious is that the decision to ignore Chris's proposal did not lead to positive outcomes and seemed to have a negative effect on his motivation to overcome his problems. From a motivational perspective, a compromise that he perceived at least as an effort to help him pursue what he saw as in his best interests might have mobilized him toward positive activity.

As the example illustrates, differences in perception lead people to different decisions. Sometimes the perceptions differ because the same information is not available to all interested parties; sometimes the perceptions are shaped by the fact that the parties have different interests (see Box G–2).

Box G–2

Viewpoint
In Whose Best Interest?

Chris almost always makes decisions in terms of what he sees as his best interests. However, his parents and teacher think that many of his decisions reflect mostly current interests rather than what may be in his long-range best interests. (It is common for adults to see children and adolescents as being unable to delay immediate gratification.) Because of this, they often find Chris's decisions unacceptable.

Are adults' decisions always in a youngster's long-range best interests? Obviously not.

But because notions about what is best in the long-run are based on judgment, it is not surprising that adults feel their additional years of experience have equipped them to make better judgments than youngsters. And they have the legal power to control decision-making processes. Thus, they often let a minor make a decision only when they agree with it or see it as not very important. "After all," they say, "we are responsible for looking out for the youngster's best interests."

As noted in Box G–1, whether the adult actu-

ally is competent to make better decisions is a question researchers are investigating. There are, however, philosophical and political issues tied up in all this that should not be ignored.

Whose interests are really being served?

Because there are several interested parties in decisions made about a youngster's schooling and treatment, each party may be operating in the interests of the youngster or in their own interests. When Chris's parents and teacher decided he should stay in the special program rather than return to regular classes, they obviously felt their decision was in Chris's best interests. But were other interests involved as well? For example, were the parents concerned that they would have the added cost of paying for a special tutor if Chris were in a regular class? Was the teacher concerned about keeping enough students enrolled in special programs? Did the adults believe that the special program would do a better job than regular classes in shaping Chris to fit into society?

While youngsters' views of what is in their best interests may be the same as that of the adults who are responsible for their care, there often is a conflict of interests. One way to understand this is in terms of the difference between adults' *socializing* role (in a social philosophical and political sense) and the role they have in *helping* the young in a society.

The responsibilities for socializing the young include making decisions that ensure youngsters learn the skills and behaviors needed to become contributing members of society. Politically, as may be expected, when individual interests conflict with the essential needs of the society, individual interests will be suppressed.

Society establishes schools to socialize the young. Teachers are hired to carry out this agenda. Such an agenda may or may not be in the best interests of the student. Thus, to ensure that the right decisions are made (i.e., those in society's best interests), school personnel control decision-making processes.

When a student has a learning problem, teachers often are caught in a dilemma. They want to help the student overcome the problem. They tend to think in terms of *helping relationships*. But because schools are designed to socialize, procedures that teachers are supposed to use reflect a socialization rather than a helping agenda. The socialization agenda is seen clearly in the compulsory nature of schooling,

in the way in which grades are used, and in the one-sided nature of decision-making processes. The result often is that rather than helping, the procedures increase the student's avoidance motivation and negative reactions.

A helping relationship requires putting the individual's interests over those of the society when there is a conflict of interests. It often means trying procedures not associated with socialization and which maximize the likelihood that the student's best interests are being served.

For making certain that the student's interests are being served, we suggest that an important step can be that of enabling students to make their own decisions. Furthermore, we hypothesize that a philosophical commitment to helping and a political commitment to children's rights may be important factors distinguishing professionals and parents who do encourage youngsters to make their own decisions. Such views may also be guiding those whose practices are effective in overcoming the avoidance motivation of individuals with learning problems.

Theories of Instruction and Models of Teaching

Despite how long formal schooling has been with us, there is, as yet, no such thing as a theory of instruction. In 1966, Jerome Bruner published a work entitled *Toward a Theory of Instruction*, and since then, there has been an increasing interest in the development of such theory.

The discussion here provides a glimpse of efforts to synthesize ideas about instruction and teaching. First, we focus on a work by Patterson (1977), entitled *Foundations for a Theory of Instruction and Educational Psychology*; then we highlight Joyce and Weil's (1980) effort to categorize models of teaching.

THEORIES OF INSTRUCTION

In exploring theories of instruction and educational psychology, Patterson cites the work started by five individuals, which he sees as providing a foundation for the development of such theories. Specifically, he focuses on (1) the Montessori Method, (2) Piaget's ideas on how intellect develops, (3) Bruner's ideas on the processes of education and instruction, (4) Skinner's technological ap-

proach, and (5) Rogers's humanistic approach. Patterson's summary of each approach is abstracted here.

Montessori Method. Maria Montessori's Method offers a set of practices and principles based on the view that learning is a natural developmental process with sensitive periods to which teaching must accommodate. Patterson interprets Montessori as follows:

> "Since learning depends upon the natural development of the child, then the child should be allowed the greatest liberty or freedom within the limits of the freedom of others who are in association with her or him. The appropriate materials and resources must, of course, be made available to the child in a 'prepared environment.' Respect for children, trust in their ability to grow and develop through use of and interaction with their environment, and patience in allowing them to progress at their own time and rate, are fundamental to the Montessori method. . . ." (p. 45)

> "Montessori was concerned with the whole child . . . physical, social, emotional, and cognitive development. The attitudes of the teacher toward the child, and the relationship between the teacher and the child were recognized as important." (p. 61)

Piaget. Jean Piaget's ideas on the origins of intellect have major implications for teaching. Piaget recognizes that the individual interacts with, rather than reacts to, the environment. Piaget discusses processes and structures in terms of such interactions. He sees development as an orderly, continuous process, progressing through stages, with qualitative individual differences appearing at each stage. Learning begins with the concrete and moves to the abstract; it is an active process that is facilitated by first allowing children to manipulate objects ("do") to experience ("see") a principle operating in their own actions. Then, the perceptual and motor supports can be reduced.

Many of Piaget's implications for education are neither new nor unique. The work does provide support for the ideas of innovators such as Dewey and Montessori and is consistent with concepts such as discovery learning.

On the implications of Piaget's ideas for teaching, Patterson notes:

"The contention, or perhaps better, the recognition, that thinking precedes the acquisition of language constitutes a challenge to education, which almost universally places emphasis upon language as the foundation for all education. Piaget emphasizes that thinking begins with, and is built upon, and grows out of sensorimotor activities. Thinking must begin with concrete objects and experiences before abstract or representational thinking can develop. The concept of cognition-as-action would radically change much of the instruction in school. . . .

"One of the most important of Piaget's ideas for education is his conception that the purpose of education is to facilitate the development of the thinking process. This is perhaps not original with Piaget; but heretofore there has been little basis for implementing it. Piaget provides a basis. With the information and knowledge explosion, it is becoming apparent that education cannot cram children with all they need to know; even if it could, much would be obsolete and useless by the time formal education was completed. The development of ability to think, not only in cognitive areas but in areas such as social and interpersonal relations, values, and morality and ethics, is certainly a priority in our current world.

"With all its difficulties and deficiencies, the work of Piaget, in quantity and in quality, provides one of the best existing foundations for a theory of instruction." (pp. 129–30)

Bruner. Jerome Bruner has written cogently on the processes of education and instruc-

tion. Bruner sees formal education as a necessity in complex societies because the young cannot learn all they need to know as adults by observing and imitating others.

To facilitate instruction, Bruner stresses that we must know something about the predispositions in the learner that influence learning, about how to structure knowledge and present material, and about the role of rewards and punishments. He views people as natural learners—active, curious, seeking mastery and competence, with a "will to learn"; natural learning is seen as self-rewarding.

Problems are seen as arising in the artificial setting of schools because teaching emphasizes telling rather than doing and because natural "knowledge of results" is replaced with grades and other unnatural forms of feedback. Under such conditions, content often seems irrelevant and motivational problems arise.

Schools also seem to discourage intuitive (as contrasted with analytic) thinking. Intuitive thinking is seen in sudden insights and problem solutions. Bruner views such thinking as deriving from poetry, art, myth, and the humanities and as providing fruitful hypotheses and creative ideas that can be tested later by application of analytic thinking or scientific methodology. He sees the emphasis on giving correct answers as restricting intuitive thinking, while encouragement of risking a guess is seen as fostering it.

As Patterson notes, in summarizing the implications of Bruner's work for teaching:

"Subject matter can be made interesting and still be presented accurately. The personalization of knowledge—making it meaningful and useful in relation to the child's thinking, attitudes, and feelings—creates interest. Learning is an active process, and the child should participate actively in the learning process. Activity promotes interest. The discovery method also engages the interest of the learner. The solving of real problems arouses interest. Curiosity, interest, and the urge toward competence and mastery lead to exploration, which is necessary for real learning and problem solving.

"Bruner's dictum that any subject can be presented to a learner of any age in a form that is interesting and honest rests on the idea that any subject matter can be converted to a form appropriate for any level of cognitive development. This involves the structuring of subject matter in terms of basic themes, fundamental ideas, principles, issues, and relationships. These can be represented as a set of actions (enactive representation), by a set of images (ikonic representation), or by symbols (symbolic representation). Subjects can be presented sequentially in these modes, with the addition of detail and content, as students progress in school, thus constituting what Bruner calls the spiral curriculum. Later learning is easier when built upon earlier learning. Such structuring of subject matter or knowledge maintains the interest of the student. It also makes for economy in teaching and learning, and fosters retention and transfer, or generalization.

" . . . Learning situations which are self-correcting are ideal; here the effects of actions become immediately apparent, as in experiments using apparatus such as balances. Extrinsic, external reinforcement does not foster continuation or persistence of learning. It may actually interfere with learning, by arousing too high a level of anxiety or by restricting attention and learning to the specific activities which are rewarded, thus discouraging transfer or generalization; and by weakening the satisfactions of intrinsic rewards through focusing the learner's attention on the 'pay-off' or on satisfying the teacher." (pp. 180–81)

Skinner. B. F. Skinner's technology of teaching is based on a behavioral analysis of human functioning that stresses that all behavior is shaped by environmental factors.

Skinner sees teaching as a matter of establishing conditions by which desired behavior will be emitted and responses are then reinforced and shaped using appropriate types and schedules of reinforcement. He sees rewards as more powerful reinforcers than punishment.

For Skinner, inner states, such as thoughts and feelings, are simply covert behaviors that are learned in the same way overt actions evolve. They are not seen as causing behavior and thus don't have to be accounted for when environmental conditions are established to facilitate learning. Motivation simply is seen in terms of states of deprivation and use of related reinforcement contingencies.

Skinner criticizes education as currently being too artificial and irrelevant and as promoting conformity rather than diversity. He sees these problems as easily corrected through the *appropriate* technical use of behavioral principles.

Patterson summarizes Skinner's technological approach as having had three major applications:

"1. In classroom management, the principles of behaviorism can be used to assure that children attend class, engage in those behaviors necessary for learning to take place, and do not manifest behaviors which are disruptive to learning. Discipline is achieved through the application of contingencies of reinforcement, emphasizing positive reinforcement. . . .

"2. Programmed instruction utilizes principles of behavioral analysis in selecting and defining objective terminal behaviors which are desired as the outcome of learning, and then constructing a graded sequence of steps toward the objective, each of which is reinforced until it is established, at which time the next step is presented. Behaviors are elicited . . . [and] reinforced when they occur. . . .

"3. Teaching machines are an efficient method of presenting programmed instruction. Programs can be constructed in advance. . . . Short steps which are necessary for some learners can be gone through rapidly by better students. Programs can be constructed at different levels. Delivery of reinforcements can be more systematic and immediate. . . . Students are active in the learning process, constructing rather than selecting answers, and can progress at their own rate, and review if they wish. The teacher is freed for those activities which cannot be done by a machine. . . .

"[In general, the approach] focuses on the specification of desired terminal behaviors and the process of achieving them through the application of the principles of programming. Technology increases the teacher's productivity and thus leads to a sense of accomplishment." (pp. 271–72)

Recognizing that many behaviorists who advocate some of the approaches proposed by Skinner have added some other ideas, Patterson notes that for them

"Behavior is not completely or automatically determined by its actual consequences. Consequences provide information which guides action. Consequences motivate behavior by representing possible outcomes which can be dealt with cognitively, so that the individual can decide to act or not in order to obtain or avert certain outcomes. Anticipated rather than actual consequences thus influence behavior. Behavior can also be influenced without direct experiencing of consequences by vicarious experience (observation of others), by reading about something, and by listening, activities which involve no objective stimulus, no overt response, and no contingencies or actual reinforcement.

"Behavior is also influenced by social experiences. But in a social context, personal elements or standards also are involved: A person may eschew an external reinforcement because it is inconsistent with consequences for the self-concept.

"Thus, it is increasingly being recognized that, while the principle of reinforcement is valid, it does not operate simply, automatically, or without the influence of internal affective and cognitive factors in much of human behavior." (p. 274)

Rogers. Carl Rogers's ideas reflect a humanistic approach. From his theories of personality and therapy, Rogers has attempted to evolve an approach to education and teaching. He begins with the view that people are basically good and rational. They are motivated toward actualizing their positive potentialities and only act badly as a defensive reaction to threats to their psychological well-being. That is, Rogers suggests that people, given the right opportunities, will develop into self-actualized or fully functioning persons.

In this approach, the goal of education is seen as the development of fully functioning or self-actualized persons. In defining what facilitates such development, Rogers stresses three key conditions that should be created in the teacher's interaction with others. These conditions involve conveying empathic understanding, respect (trust, positive regard), and genuineness. In general, the process of teaching is seen as requiring consistent commitment to providing opportunities for self-initiated, self-directed learning, for being genuine, and for conveying regard and empathic understanding in interacting with learners.

In summarizing Rogers's views on education, Patterson states:

"To educate toward a fully functioning person requires that education cease focusing on imparting facts, information, and knowledge, that it go beyond the objectives of development of the intellect or of thinking persons, to concern for the development of the affective, emotional, and interpersonal relationship qualities of individuals. The whole person must be educated.

"Learning related to development of the whole person is significant learning, learning which is personal and experiential and which makes a difference in the person. The individual doesn't have to be motivated toward significant learning—the motivation is inherent in the drive toward self-actualization. Significant learning occurs when the learner perceives the subject matter as relevant for his or her own purposes. . . . learning is facilitated when external threats to the self are at a minimum. Freedom from threat enables the learner to explore, to differentiate, to try new ideas, to change. Significant learning is facilitated by experiential involvement with real problems. Initiation of the process and participation in it by the learner fosters significant learning. Self-evaluation rather than external criticism and evaluation fosters independence, creativity, and self-reliance. Significant learning, involving all these elements, is learning how to learn. . . .

"Learning also depends, of course, upon the learner. Motivation is a normal, natural characteristic of human beings if it has not been suppressed or destroyed by mistreatment. Stimulation by problem situations also occurs naturally in normal persons. Finally, the learner must perceive the facilitative conditions in the teacher, and here, also, individuals who have not been mistreated, deceived, conned, or turned off will be open to and recognize these conditions.

". . . The real teacher does not know everything and does not pretend to. He or she can admit mistakes. The teacher manifests prizing, acceptance, and trust by really listening to the student, without evaluating her or him, and by responding to what the student says—to the attitudes and feelings expressed as well as the content. Listening also evidences the attempt to understand, and responding attempts to communicate understanding. Teaching becomes a real, spontaneous, personal encounter with students.

"The teacher also facilitates learning by building upon real problems in the lives and culture of students, by providing many easily accessible resources (including his or her own knowledge), by developing contracts with students through which they can develop their own learning programs, by providing programmed instruction units, by small group sessions and discussions or projects, by inquiry learning, by simulation learning, and by encounter-group sessions." (pp. 330–31)

Obviously, there are differences and commonalities among the five approaches reviewed. Ironically, one of the strong commonalities is that all propose views about the processes of learning and teaching that public schools have yet to adopt on any large scale.

MODELS OF TEACHING

Joyce and Weil (1980) take another approach to synthesizing ideas about instruction. They propose a framework for grouping twenty-three separate (but not mutually exclusive) teaching approaches or "models" into four categories. Each approach is seen as having "much to say about the kinds of realities admitted to the classroom and the kinds of life-views likely to be generated as teacher and learner work together" (p. 1).

The four categories are (1) information-processing models, (2) personal models, (3) social interaction models, and (4) behavioral models. Joyce and Weil's description of these categories and the models grouped under each are summarized here.

Information-processing models. These approaches are oriented toward human capacity for processing information and how individuals can improve their ability to acquire information. Information processing refers to the handling of stimuli from the environment—including organizing data, sensing problems, generating concepts and solutions, and using verbal and nonverbal symbols. Although the emphasis is on concepts and information related to academic subjects, most of the models in this category "are also concerned about social relationships and the development of an integrated, functioning self" (p. 9). They choose to accomplish such goals, however, through development of intellectual processes.

Seven models are grouped under this category: (1) concept attainment, (2) inductive thinking, (3) inquiry training, (4) advance organizers, (5) memory model, (6) cognitive growth, and (7) biological science inquiry model.

Personal models. These approaches are oriented toward the individual and the development of selfhood (the capacity to function as an integrated personality). They focus on how individuals construct and organize their unique reality. Some give considerable stress to emotional life. In this context, a "focus on helping individuals to develop a productive relationship with their environments and to view themselves as capable persons is also expected to result in richer interpersonal relations and a more effective information-processing capability" (p. 10).

Four models are included in this category: (1) nondirective teaching, (2) synectics, (3) awareness training, and (4) the classroom meeting model (mental health through group process).

Social interaction models. These approaches are oriented toward an individual's relationships with others or with society in general. They emphasize the processes by which reality is socially negotiated. Along with stressing social relations, there is also concern for cognitive and personal development.

Six models are included in this category: (1) group investigation (democratic processes as a source), (2) role playing (studying social behavior and values), (3) jurisprudential inquiry (clarifying public issues), (4) laboratory training (T-group model), (5) social simulation, and (6) social inquiry.

Behavioral models. These approaches are oriented toward the processes by which human behavior is shaped and reinforced. The focus is on changing the visible behavior of the learner rather than unobservable behavior and underlying psychological structure. Among the specific behaviors emphasized are basic academics and social skills. Common to behavioral models is an emphasis on breaking learning tasks into a series of small, sequenced behaviors.

Six models are included in this category: (1) contingency management, (2) self-control through operant methods, (3) training model, (4) stress reduction, (5) desensitization, and (6) assertiveness training.

Joyce and Weil stress the view that

"We teach by creating environments for children. . . .

"We believe the strength in education resides in the intelligent use of [the] powerful variety of approaches—matching them to different goals and adapting them to the student's styles and characteristics. Competence in teaching stems from the capacity to reach out to differing children and to create a rich and multidimensional environment for them. Curriculum planners need to design learning centers and curricula that offer children a variety of educational alternatives. . . . The existing models of teaching are one basis for the repertoire of alternative approaches that teachers, curriculum makers, and designers of materials can use to help diverse learners reach a variety of goals. . . .

"We believe the world of education should be a pluralistic one—that children and adults alike should have a 'cafeteria of alternatives' to stimulate their growth and nurture both their unique potential and their capacity to make common cause in the rejuvenation of our troubled society." (pp. xxiii–iv)

SPECIAL TOPIC REFERENCES

If you want to look at some of the original sources mentioned, see the following.

BRUNER, J. S. (1966). *Toward a theory of instruction.* Cambridge, Mass.: Harvard University Press.

FURTH, H. G., & WACHS, H. (1974). *Thinking goes to school: Piaget's theory in practice.* New York: Oxford.

JOYCE, B., & WEIL, M. (1980). *Models of teaching,* 2nd ed. New York: Prentice-Hall.

MEICHENBAUM, D. (1977). *Cognitive-behavior modification: An integrative approach.* New York: Plenum.

MONTESSORI, M. (1964). *The Montessori Method,* trans. Anne E. George. New York: Schocken. (First published in Italian in 1909 and in English in 1912.)

PATTERSON, C. H. (1977). *Foundations for a theory of instruction and educational psychology.* New York: Harper & Row.

ROGERS, C. R. (1969). *Freedom to learn.* Columbus, Ohio: Merrill.

SKINNER, B. F. (1968). *The technology of teaching.* Englewood Cliffs, N.J.: Prentice-Hall.

Reading *I*

To the Rescue

So you want to help! That's a nice attitude, but it can sometimes lead to trouble—especially if you aren't aware of the interpersonal dynamics that can arise in helping relationships. Several concerns have been discussed in the psychotherapy literature. One that almost everyone has experienced has been described as a "rescue" (Karpman, 1968).

A *rescue* is helping gone astray. Rescues encompass a cycle of negative interpersonal transactions that too commonly arise when one person sets out to intervene in another's life in order to help the person.

Think about a time when someone you know told you about a problem she or he was having. Because the person seemed not to know how to handle the problem, you offered some suggestions. For each idea you offered, the person had an excuse for why it wouldn't work. After a while, you started to feel frustrated and maybe even a bit angry at the person. You may have thought or said to the individual, "You don't really want to solve this problem; you just want to complain about it."

In rescue terms, you tried to help, but the person didn't work with you to solve the problem. The individual's failure to try may have frustrated you, and you felt angry and wanted to tell the person off. And that may only have been the beginning of a prolonged series of unpleasant interpersonal transactions related to the situation.

If you were ever in such a situation, you certainly experienced the price a person pays for assuming the role of rescuer. Of course, you know you didn't mean to become involved in a negative set of transactions. You wanted to help, but you didn't realize fast enough that the individual with the problem wasn't about to work with you in order to solve it. And you didn't know what to do when things started going wrong with the process.

If you can't remember a time you were the rescuer, you may recall a time when someone tried to rescue you. Perhaps your parents, a teacher, or a good friend made the mistake of trying to help you when or in ways you didn't want to be helped. The person probably thought she or he was acting in your best interests, but it only made you feel upset—perhaps increased your anxiety, frustration, anger, and maybe even made you feel rather inadequate.

Rescue cycles occur frequently between teachers and students and parents and their children. Well-intentioned efforts to help usually begin to go astray because someone tries to help at a time, in a way, or toward an end the person to be helped doesn't experience as positive.

Let's take the example of a teacher, Ms. Benevolent, and one of her students, Jack. Ms. Benevolent is a new teacher who has just begun to work with a group of students with learning problems. She sees her students, Jack included, as handicapped individuals, and she wants so much to help them.

Unfortunately, Jack doesn't want to be helped at the moment. And when he doesn't want to be helped, Jack is not mobilized to work on solving his problems. Indeed, efforts to intervene often make him feel negative toward his teacher and even toward himself. For example, he may feel anger toward Ms. Benevolent and feel guilty and incompetent because of not working to solve his learning problem. Ironically, not only doesn't he see the teacher as a helper, he also feels victimized by her. In response to these feelings, he behaves in a self-protective and defensive manner. Sometimes he even assumes the stance of being a helpless victim. ("How can you expect me to do that? Don't you know I have a learning handicap?")

Because Jack continues to respond passively or in ways the teacher views as inappropriate, eventually she becomes upset and starts to react to him in nonhelpful and sometimes provocative ways. She may even have a tendency to subtly persecute Jack for not being appreciative of all her efforts to help him. ("You're just lazy." "If your attitude doesn't improve, I'm going to have to call your parents.")

The more the teacher pushes Jack to act differently and attacks him for acting (and feeling) as he does, the more likely he is to feel victimized. However, sooner or later he is likely to become angry enough about being victimized that he reacts and counterattacks. That is, if he can, he shifts from the role of victim to the role of persecutor.

When interveners who see themselves as benevolent helpers are attacked, they may tend to feel victimized. Indeed, the experience of having been unsuccessful in helping may be sufficient to make some interveners feel this way. As Jack shifts to a persecuting role, Ms. Benevolent adopts a victim role. ("After all I've done for you, how can you treat me this way?" "All I'm trying to do is help you.")

Of course, interveners are unlikely to remain victims for very long if they can help it. If they do, "burn out" may well occur.

Sometimes, after the fighting stops, the parties make up, and the intervener starts to see the other person's behavior as part of the individual's problems and tries once more to help. However, if great care is not taken, this just begins the whole cycle again.

How can the cycle be avoided or broken? As we have stressed in Chapter 9, one of the essential ingredients in a good helping relationship is a person who wants to be helped. Thus, it is necessary to be sure that the person is ready and willing to pursue the type of help that is being offered.

If the person is not ready and willing, interveners are left with only a few options. For one, the intervener can choose to give up trying to help. Or if it is essential that the individual be *forced* to do something about the problem, the intervener can adopt a socialization strategy. Or effort can be made to explore with the individual whether he or she wants to think about accepting some help. In effect, this last approach involves trying to establish motivational readiness (as discussed in Chapters 8 and 9).

Fernald's Techniques in Their Motivational Context

Near the beginning of her classic volume *Remedial Techniques in Basic School Subjects* (1943), Grace Fernald states:

> "Too often in present-day methods of teaching writing and spelling, voluntary activity is so limited from the start that even those children who have no special difficulty in learning do not like to write. The child may be required to sit in a certain position, conform to specific ways of making the details of his letters, and spell his words correctly. When finally he does all these things, he may be allowed to express an idea in written form. Usually, some adult will tell him what idea he should be *eager to express*. The result is that the little child who was bursting with ideas he wanted to put in writing has lost them in the formalities of learning to write and spell and at the same time has been negatively conditioned toward these activities." (p. 13)

As is clear from this statement, Fernald was concerned with far more than the "tracing" method, or VAKT techniques, that textbook writers tend to stress in reviewing her work. She was concerned with the learner's thoughts and feelings related to school activities and learning. VAKT techniques were to be used in a motivational context.

> "Throughout the remedial work, projects suitable to the child's age and connected with his interests are made the basis of his writing and later of his reading. . . . The topics he chooses to write about depend upon his interests and aptitudes." (p. 94)

We do not mean to suggest that Fernald was unconcerned with other factors in the learning process. She obviously believed that the learning problems of some individuals were caused by defects in visual or auditory modalities and that "the hand-kinesthetic method . . . serves to build up an adequate apperceptive background, which makes it possible for the child to use effectively such sensory cues as he has" (p. 32). However, she always stressed that her techniques for teaching included much more than the "hand-kinesthetic method." In particular, she was interested in procedures by which each individual "not only learns rapidly but develops a positive emotional conditioning" (p. 13).

In keeping with the innovative spirit of Fernald's pioneering work, the staff at the Fernald Laboratory and Clinic at UCLA continues to explore new directions in dealing with learning problems. We have been especially interested in systematic ways to address motivational considerations. One aspect of this work involves delineating the motivational context for what has become known as the Fernald Method or Techniques.

MOTIVATIONAL CONSIDERATIONS

In all our efforts to develop a motivational context for instruction, a major focus has been on three overlapping phases of motivation in learning and performance: (1) motivational readiness for instruction, (2) maintaining motivation during instruction, and (3) continued independent interest in the area for which instruction is provided. That is, during phase 1, the focus is on creating and enhancing motivational readiness for instruction. Phase 2 involves efforts to maintain and increase motivation during instruction. Phase 3 is concerned with ensuring that instruction doesn't undermine *intrinsic* motivation and that long-term intrinsic motivation is enhanced.

Throughout all three phases, the emphasis is on (a) clarifying intrinsic reasons for pursuing learning activities and overcoming problems, (b) providing meaningful opportunities for learners to make personal and active choices from among a variety of options, and (c) involving learners in evaluating how well their intrinsic objectives are being met.

Phase 1: Motivational Readiness for Instruction

There is little need to point out that all individuals learn. It is also evident that an individual may not have the ability or interest to learn certain things at a given time. What is not so obvious to many people is the fact that an individual may have the ability and may want to learn something but may not be psychologically ready to accept instruction.

Students who misbehave at school clearly may be disturbed or hyperactive or have a variety of other pathological conditions. However, some misbehavior seems primarily to be a reaction to *demands* that students learn things they aren't interested in learning and to *required* participation in instructional activities when students don't want to be taught.

The first step in working with students who react against teacher and parental pressure is that of finding ways to establish readiness for instruction by reducing avoidance and increasing approach tendencies. This involves

- eliminating or at least minimizing transactions that lead to avoidance, such as activities students tend to see as coercive and aversive, and
- establishing procedures that increase student options and choices in terms of learning content, outcomes, and processes

That is, the emphasis is on evolving a personalized learning environment. The program should be one in which instruction is not forced on students, many valued learning opportunities are presented, and help is offered and available at all times to aid students as they pursue desired learning outcomes.

The first aspect of establishing readiness for instruction, then, is to create a stimulating learning environment in which instruction is provided only *after* a student indicates that it is wanted. When instruction is sought, the emphasis shifts to the creation of a positive attitude or "set" toward teaching processes and immediate outcomes. The intent is to convey to each student how well the program matches her or his current interests and capabilities.

In the Fernald Method, the focus on motivational readiness for instruction begins with the teacher clarifying that there is no intention of forcing the student to learn anything. This is particularly important for students who are reacting against teachers and instruction. In such cases, the initial focus is on exploring many topics and possible areas for learning until the student identifies an area of interest. Then, efforts are made to introduce a variety of independent learning activities in the area. The teacher remains interested and available to help at any time the learner requests assistance but does not intervene, as long as the student is not disruptive.

The objective is to allow the individual to rediscover that there are intrinsic reasons for working with a teacher. In addition, as students have the opportunity to explore a wide range of learning interests and identify areas for self-improvement, they generally decide they need to improve basic reading, writing, and arithmetic skills. (What makes such skills *basic* is the fact that one finds the skills are necessary for pursuing so many interests and future goals.)

When students no longer resist instruction and when all those with learning problems are ready to accept instruction, there remains the matter of maximizing motivational readiness. They need to be introduced to each instructional procedure in ways that maximize their expectations of success and their valuing of the opportunity to be taught. Fernald introduced students to the "hand-kinesthetic" method as follows:

"We start by telling the child that we have a new way of learning words, which we want him to try. We explain . . . that many bright people have had the same difficulty he has had in learning to read and have learned easily by this new method, which is really just as good as any other way. We let him select any word he wants to learn, regardless of length, and teach it to him by the method" (p. 33)

Thus, in introducing the method, she stressed the newness and novelty of the approach, tried to present it as special in a positive sense, and had the student sample the process under fairly optimal circumstances, with emphasis on student choice. She then moved on quickly to embed the method in what she called "story writing" and "special projects"; today these strategies are widely known as language experience and discovery approaches.

Fernald's efforts to provide a stimulating context for instruction reflected her concern with motivation. In this connection, over the years, we have continued to find that the best strategy usually is to introduce the tracing method and other remedial techniques within the context of a student's current in-

terests. That is, we offer it as an aid to students as they pursue some chosen activity, such as personally identified writing activity (a story, poem, or newspaper article) or some discovery-oriented project of personal interest. Thus, rather than being limited by a specific technique's power to mobilize a student's interest, we are able to capitalize on a wide range of substantive and popular activities and topics in efforts to facilitate motivational readiness.

Phase 2: Maintaining Motivation During Instruction

Maintaining appropriate motivation depends on a student's continuing perception of instruction as a positive means to valued ends. The optimal situation for maintaining such motivation seems to be one in which

- a broad range of learner-valued content, outcome, and procedural options are available
- the learner is able to experience a high degree of self-determination in specifying learning content, outcomes, and processes
- support and guidance are varied in keeping with the learner's perceived needs
- the learner experiences a sense of satisfaction and competence from what is learned.

This means, for example, that the learner (1) has chosen a personally meaningful context for learning skills, (2) has identified which skills (e.g., dealing with words, punctuation, facts, ideas) and how many will become the focus of instruction, and (3) has helped develop ways to structure and evaluate learning so that the activity results in feelings of personal satisfaction and increased competence.

With the Fernald Method, learners are provided opportunities to explore a wide range of options in story writing and special projects. Given a state of motivational readiness, they choose from what is offered or create their own context for learning. In either case, they draw on their own experiences and learn within a context that is personally meaningful and interesting. In addition, each student is encouraged to state what he or she wants to learn and practice each day.

For example, students are to specify whether they want to spend time improving vocabulary (reading or spelling), the mechanics of English, handwriting, etc. In doing so, they are encouraged to choose the specific words or skills to be learned and to specify the amount they want to learn at any given time.

Special care is taken not to underestimate the learner's range of interests and capability. As Fernald stated in discussing the learning of reading and writing vocabulary:

". . . remedial work is started by discovering some technique whereby the individual can learn to write any word he wishes to use. . . . The child is much more interested in writing and reading fairly difficult material that is on the level of his understanding than simpler material which is below his mental age level. In fact, the child who has never been able to read or write anything takes delight in learning difficult words. Our records show that these longer, more difficult words are actually easier to recognize on later presentations after the child has written them, than easier, shorter ones." (p. 44)

The steps devised by Fernald and evolved over the years (described in a subsequent section) provide a framework for working out novel and personalized learning and practice activity. They demonstrate ways to provide structure (support and guidance) and feedback to maximize the type of learning and feelings of satisfaction and increased competence that are prerequisites to maintaining what is learned.

The steps used for instructional purposes are designed to match the learner's motivation and capability. The steps for ongoing practice, review, and reteaching are designed to provide motivated practice. And motivated practice, of course, is necessary for maintaining what is learned and seems to be a necessary, if insufficient, prerequisite for generalization of learning.

Phase 3: Motivation After Instruction

If motivational concerns are properly attended to during instruction, the learner will continue to be interested in the area studied and have a positive attitude about the skills learned. Thus, the previous considerations are major determinants of later directions for learning (including maintenance and generalization). Given positive antecedent conditions, three ongoing conditions are necessary for continued and expanded use of what has been learned. These are

- *opportunities* to use what has been learned
- continuing *desire* to use and expand on what has been learned
- continuing *self-determination* and *supportive structure*, when necessary, related to learning and performance

Opportunities for use may take several forms. For example, there can be free time at school to read, write, pursue projects, and so forth. There also can be structured enrichment activities at school and in the home and neighborhood designed to provide creative and exciting learning opportunities that are not tied to developmental and remedial objectives.

The desire to expand on what has been learned is a likely product of the learner's continued perception of personal choice and self-efficacy and the learner's feelings of self-determination and competence. Such perceptions and feelings are most likely to occur when an individual experiences control over fundamental decisions in the area of learning and has support and guidance as needed to prevent too much failure.

We have not stressed the use of extrinsic rewards and punishment as a way to establish, maintain, or enhance motivation. We know that the on-task behavior of many individuals can be increased to some degree through the systematic use of external reinforcers. However, we are also aware that such procedures can be counterproductive in establishing and maintaining the type of long-term behavior that is needed by most individuals if they are to meaningfully overcome their problems. Although Fernald did not specifically discuss this topic, the methods she developed avoid overreliance on extrinsics. It is likely she understood that overemphasis on extrinsics often is incompatible with maintaining and enhancing people's internal push to overcome their problems and their understanding that learning is something one does for oneself—not for others. Analyses of the procedures she developed show how much she tried to capitalize on student's personal interests, curiosity, and basic desires to feel competent and self-determining.

In summary, in the teacher's use of the Fernald Method or Techniques, the following motivational considerations apply:

1. Motivational readiness for instruction, which involves

   - avoiding coercion
   - establishing valued options and choices
   - establishing positive "set" with regard to expectations of success and valued opportunities (processes and outcomes)

2. Maintaining motivation during instruction, which involves

   - the learner's valuing of the available content, outcome, and procedural options
   - the learner's perceptions of self-determination
   - support and guidance in keeping with the learner's perceived needs
   - feedback that stresses feelings of personal satisfaction, self-determination, and competence

3. Motivation after instruction, which results from

   - all of 1 and 2
   - continued opportunities for learning and performance
   - the learner's continued desire to use and expand on learning
   - continued self-determination and supportive structure as needed

SUMMARY OF FERNALD TECHNIQUES: STAGES AND STEPS

Over the years, we have amplified Fernald's ideas to capitalize on contemporary thinking about how to develop, maintain, and enhance student motivation. Thus, the description that follows represents an amalgamation of Fernald's pioneering activity with recent thinking about motivation.

Fernald's original work and our current efforts, of course, deal with a full range of school subjects and basic skills. For purposes of illustration, however, the emphasis here is limited to one facet of instruction designed to improve reading.

In working with severe learning problems, Fernald found it useful to begin with methods that involved a multisensory or tracing approach for learning words. From this beginning stage, she moved systematically to procedures used widely in teaching anyone to improve vocabulary. In all, she delineated four overlapping stages through which she took individuals with reading problems.

All the stages are similar in that each new word to be learned is identified by the student, usually in the context of intrinsically motivated activity. That is, at any of the stages, words the student does not know are discovered as the individual reads and writes while pursuing a self-determined activity. The student is told to let the teacher know when he or she encounters an unknown word while reading or when a word is needed for a written product. No effort is made to teach the words at this point; they are simply read to or written for the student. This is done to avoid disrupting the student's flow, enjoyment, and satisfaction in reading and writing. By agreement, a temporary record is made of those words the student wants to consider learning. (Obviously, the same type of strategy can be used to assess and plan instruction for a wide range of other skill deficiencies, e.g., deficiencies in punctuation, capitalization, grammar.)

The stages also are similar because they all call for simultaneously looking at (visualizing) and saying (vocalizing) the word that is being learned and because they prescribe immediate and subsequent practice and review.

The stages *differ* as follows:

Stage 1: Visual-auditory-kinesthetic-tactile— tracing words the teacher has written on tracing slips

Stage 2: Visual-auditory—no tracing but continued use of tracing slips with teacher-written words, then making the transition to teacher-written words on flashcards.

Stage 3: Visual-auditory—use of words-in-print rather than teacher-written words

Stage 4: Independent learning—use of reference material, generalization, inference and other analytic and synthesizing skills to learn new words

Although Fernald specified four stages, these stages blend one into the other. Essentially, they form a continuum ranging from the extreme remedial strategy of stage 1 to the very general educational approaches used in stage 4.

The steps in each stage are described in the following sections.

Stage 1

This stage is used with students who are motivationally ready for instruction and who are manifesting severe problems learning to read. There are seven basic steps:

1. At an appropriate time, the teacher sits down beside the student to facilitate the learning of new words.

   Note: The point of sitting next to the student is to convey committed interest and readiness to spend time helping, as well as to communicate a desire to minimize psychological distance and authoritarian transactions.

2. The student looks over the list of words she or he has indicated an interest in mastering and chooses those to be worked on that day, including the order in which the words are to be learned.

3. With the student watching and listening, the teacher simultaneously says the first word aloud and writes it on a 4 × 11-in. tracing slip using a black crayon (see Box J–1).

   Notes:
   Black crayon is used because it produces a clear, dark, and *textured* stimulus.

   Newsprint is used for tracing slips because it is relatively inexpensive.

   In saying the word, the teacher reads it slowly and distinctly but without distorting it.

In writing the word, the teacher uses large, neat, and well-formed letters to produce an oversized model that the student can easily trace and emulate.

Unless the student can only print, cursive writing (script) is used because words written in script present a flowing, unbroken unit.

For record keeping, the tracing slip can be dated in one corner.

4. The student takes the slip and, looking carefully at the word, says it aloud several times.

5. Next, using the hand that she or he writes with, the student traces the word with the index or index and middle finger—maintaining good finger contact and flowing motion and saying the word clearly as it is traced. As a guideline, tracing and saying the word three times seems effective. But, like other similar matters, how many times the word is traced usually is best left for the student to decide.

Notes:
For Fernald, the point of this step was to ensure that the student experienced simultaneous visual, auditory, kinesthetic, and tactile cues related to the word as a whole unit.

However, even if the student doesn't need multisensory cues and a whole word approach, this step has a number of nice motivational features. For example, it represents a novel strategy and one that the student has not already failed at; it tends to capture a student's attention; it involves the student in active learning and practice.

6. After tracing and saying the word, the student turns the slip over and writes the word on the back, again saying it as it is written. If it is written incorrectly, what has been written is immediately blacked out (with the crayon) to limit confusion.

Then, the student repeats steps 5 and 6 until the word is written correctly on the back of the slip or until the student decides not to bother with the word for now (see Box J–1).

7. Newly learned words are practiced on subsequent days and reviewed periodically. (See the discussion of practice and review at the end of this summary of stages and steps.)

Stage 2

Following the student's lead, the teacher can gradually phase out tracing from the learning process. Tracing slips are still used at the outset of stage 2. However, 3 × 5-in. flashcards are introduced as soon as the student indicates interest and the ability to use them effectively. Thus, for the student who is motivationally and developmentally ready to streamline the process, the steps will be as follows:

1–4. These steps remain the same. When the student moves to flashcards, the main change is that the words are written by the teacher with a pen or pencil that leaves a dark imprint.

5. The student learns the word by looking at it (in a concentrated way) and saying it several times.

6–7. These steps remain the same. Of course, when students have trouble with a particular word, they may want to try the tracing procedures when they repeat step 5.

Stage 3

Again following the student's lead, the teacher can make a transition from stage 2 to 3. However, to do so, the student must not only be able to learn well using stage 2 but also must have learned how to look up words in a dictionary or other resource.

Box J–1

Tracing Slip

Front

(Reduced to half size—originals are 4 × 11 in.)

Back

Incorrectly
written word
blacked out

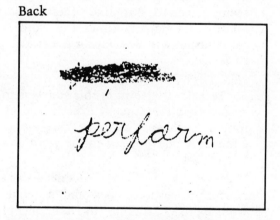

In stage 3, the individual sees a word-in-print that he or she wants to learn or looks up a desired word in a dictionary or comparable reference resource. Fernald stressed that, by this stage, the students she worked with wanted to do a lot more reading, and she provided opportunities for them "to read as much as and whatever" they wished (p. 51).

At this stage, the student uses the follow-ing self-initiated steps, asking for help from the teacher only when necessary:

1. The student learns the word by looking at it (in a concentrated way) and saying it several times.

2. The word is written by the student on a 3 × 5-in. card using immediate recall rather than copying it. That is, the original source is put away and, as in other

stages, the word is said as it is written from memory.

3. The word is checked against the original printed source. If it is incorrectly reproduced, it is crossed out and steps 1 and 2 are repeated (or the tracing method is used) until the word is written correctly or until the student decides not to bother with the word for now.

4. Newly learned words are practiced on subsequent days and reviewed periodically (as discussed in the next section).

Stage 4

Fernald described stage 4 as involving the ability to recognize new words from their similarity to words or parts of words already learned. From her clinical work, she found that

"Soon after the child is able to learn from the printed word, he begins to generalize and to make new words from their resemblance to words he already knows. If the case is handled skillfully enough, the child is now eager to read." (p. 51)

At stage 4, students usually are reading at least at the fourth-grade level and have the capability to use analytic and synthesizing skills in reading new words. Equally important at this stage is a positive attitude toward reading. Subsequent improvements in vocabulary, comprehension, speed, and fluency will occur only if the student likes reading enough to do a great deal more than is involved in daily school instruction.

Subsequent Practice and Review Steps

The importance of spaced (distributed) practice and review is widely acknowledged. Often ignored by teachers and parents, however, is the importance of finding ways to increase the *motivational* aspects of practice

activities. When practice activities in reading instruction are dull and boring, the minimal level of reading skill proficiency that is demanded may be acquired, but a dislike for reading may also be acquired. Thus, a student may learn several hundred new words but may never become a good reader because he or she never voluntarily spends time reading.

Fernald devised several strategies for spaced, short-term, motivated practice and review. The essence of these strategies is seen in the "storywriting" approach. Fernald noted:

"Some children begin their writing with stories about their pets, their families, and other personal matters. Several of our cases with marked artistic ability started with sketches and paintings of things about which they later wrote. Most of the children liked to represent any subject diagrammatically. Sometimes children made elaborate diagrams of things that interested them. Their first writing consisted of the labeling of the parts of the diagram." (p. 94)

Students interested in writing stories use this as a primary context in which to identify new words to learn. Some words are learned to improve reading vocabulary, and some may be taken as spelling words. With regard to reading, a student often finds the story he or she has written to be a most interesting and accessible subsequent reading activity. It can be especially exciting when the product is reproduced in print (e.g., typed).

Fernald capitalized on the motivational features of storywriting not only as a means of identifying skills to be learned but as a context for motivated practice. The following practice and review steps have been evolved:

1. With the story written and new words chosen and learned (using one of the four stages described before), the stu-

dent files the words in an alphabetical file for future reference. (Depending on the stage, either a 3 × 5-in. index card file box or one designed to handle tracing slips is used.)

2. The story is readied for typing. This preparation involves some basic editing and underlining of the words the student has chosen to learn (see Box J–2).

    Note: Since the student is encouraged to write freely and only a few new skills are focused on at any time, stories inevitably reflect skill deficiencies. Therefore, the teacher edits the story to the extent of correcting basic punctuation, capitalization, and grammar errors. This is done so that what is subsequently read by the student is a reasonably good model but still is the student's own words. (The student should be consulted about how much editing is done and whether the teacher is to do it alone or with the student's involvement.)

3. The story is typed, usually within twenty-four hours, and returned to the student as a reading activity (see Box J–3).

    Note: Two typed copies are made—one for the student to take home if desired, the other for practice and review. In no special order, the underlined words are typed in a vertical list down the left side of the page under the typed story.

4. The practice and review copy of the story and the original handwritten product are placed in a folder facing each other so that the student can refer to both.

5. The student reads the typed story to the teacher. Any word that is not recognized is read to the student—unless the student has shown both motivational and developmental readiness to figure out words.

6. After reading the story, the student reads the list of chosen words typed beneath the story. A mark is placed after each word to indicate whether it was read correctly or incorrectly, e.g., a "+" for correct, a "0" for incorrect. (Preferably the record keeping is done by the student.)

7. The next day, if the student has written another story, the process is repeated with the new story and word list. Whether there is a new story or not, the student again reads the list from the previous story. A second mark (e.g., + or 0) is recorded.

8. The process of reading the separate words listed is repeated until a predetermined criterion is met. The criterion established over the years at the Fernald Laboratory and Clinic is three consecutive correct responses.

9. If a word is read incorrectly, the student is encouraged to pull the word from the word file and relearn it.

    Note: If the word is particularly troublesome, the student may choose to put it aside and spend the time more productively.

10. Periodic reviews (e.g., weekly, bimonthly) of all recently learned words can take a variety of forms. To maintain and enhance a student's motivation for such reviews, a variety of word games have been evolved. In addition, progress can be charted by the student in a variety of ways, e.g., tallies, graphs.

Similar approaches have been worked out to provide motivated practice and review for learning words encountered in books and other reading material and for learning to spell. Furthermore, the same emphasis on motivated learning and practice can be found in Fernald's approaches to improving reading comprehension and speed and a wide range of other basic skills.

Box J–2

Original Story

Movie

Danse is good to learn, I'd to go on stage and to p prefor. I worl like to dance with Barishnikov. I like to dance with him, because he in famouse.

As written

(Writing reduced in size by 50%)

As edited by teacher

Movie

Dance is good to learn, I'd to go on stage and to p perfor. I would like to dance with Barishnikov. I like to dance with him, because he is famous.

Box J–3

Typed Story

Marva

1-4-85

Dance

Dance is good to learn. I'd like to go on stage and *perform*. I would like to dance with Barishnikov. I like to dance with him *because* he is *famous*.

⅕	⅙	⅑	⅒	1/11	
+	O	+	+	+	
O	O	dro	pped		
+	+	+			
+	+	+			

CONCLUDING COMMENTS

Fernald stressed that the process of helping individuals with reading (and other) problems requires systematic and diligent effort on the part of both the learner and the teacher. Usually, all parties begin the process with great enthusiasm, and significant success is common in the early stages. However, for a variety of reasons, the process may be cut short. Fernald lamented that in too many cases "the work is stopped at a stage when the individual still reads new material slowly and, if left to his own devices, word by word." (p. 55)

One reason for the frequent failure to overcome learning problems to the degree possible is that the motivational components of the learning process are not appropriately addressed. The methods attributed to Fernald, as well as all other remedial approaches, can be used in ways that maximize or undermine learner motivation. We suggest that in many cases, remedial procedures are ineffective because motivational considerations have not been planned systematically. And when remedial procedures are effective, the positive results may be primarily due to motivational factors. Clearly, the motivational impact and context of remedial practices is a matter deserving greater discussion and research.

Reading *K*

Guidelines for Serving the LD Adult

In a fall 1981 article in the *Learning Disability Quarterly*, Richard Gray set out to provide some structure to previous discussions and descriptions of programs for LD adults. The result was twenty-five planning suggestions dealing with (1) general principles, (2) descriptions and definitions, (3) assessment and content, (4) service delivery, and (5) research.

The twenty-five points are listed here by category. For a discussion of each, see the original article.

GENERAL PRINCIPLES

1. Program options must be available to the LD adult.
2. The LD adult should be treated as a client.
3. Learning disabled individuals, like nondisabled individuals, must be considered lifelong learners.

DESCRIPTIONS AND DEFINITIONS

4. As often as possible in the literature, we need to describe LD adult individuals rather than describing composites or characteristics frequently associated with the learning disabled.
5. Learning disabilities professionals must provide the leadership necessary to establish identification criteria for determining service eligibility and insuring consistent, manageable research.
6. Criteria should involve "severe" discrepancy between ability and performance.

ASSESSMENT AND CONTENT

7. Content of diagnostic and assessment devices and of educational services should be specific to life needs. The appropriateness of assessment procedures directed toward psychological processes and abilities thought to be prerequisite for meaningful learning should be carefully evaluated.
8. Assessment and intervention should be directly related to adult life goals.
9. LD professionals need to identify existing assessment devices which provide reliable and valid information about the adult in relation to his/her various environments.
10. New devices should be constructed which assess the individual's level of competence in relation to (a) expected competencies in his/her various environments and (b) the modifications necessary and/or possible in those environments.
11. Developmental and remedial instruction in basic skills should be made available to those who wish such training and for whom such programs are appropriate.
12. Our views of appropriate content for adult services should be expanded beyond traditional literacy requirements and vocational training.
13. Compensation should be a major focus of the content of our services to LD adults.
14. We must actively involve the LD adult in content decisions, but we cannot limit ourselves to that input.

DELIVERY OF SERVICES

15. We should make existing formal educa-

tional institutions accessible to the LD adult.

16. Faculty members of formal educational institutions should be encouraged to accept some of the challenge and responsibility for making their content accessible to the LD adult.

17. We should expand our repertoire of models for meeting needs beyond formal education to include informal and nonformal models.

18. Services should include training of individuals in the LD adult's various environments.

19. LD professionals should initiate and encourage cooperative efforts with other professionals interested in adult, life-long, and community education.

20. Counseling services should be available to LD adults.

21. Services for LD adults should include advocacy.

22. One individual should be available to act as finder and orchestrator for the LD adult.

23. Existing services, such as vocational rehabilitation, must become responsive to the needs of the LD adult.

RESEARCH

24. Descriptions of specific programs, case studies, and $N = 1$ studies should continue to be included in the literature.

25. Systematic, data-based research is needed to examine the LD adult's needs from his/her own perspective, from the perspective of the service provider, and from the perspective of the adult's environments.

In concluding, Gray stresses that

"Professionals in the field of learning disabilities have an obligation to direct the planning of services for LD adults and to serve as their advocates. With that responsibility comes the opportunity to build (nearly from scratch) an innovative and responsive system which recognizes new content, new technology, and new and varied 'classrooms.'" (p. 433)

Reading *L*

Ethical Concerns About Negative Effects

A variety of ethical concerns confront professionals in the LD field. Of particular concern are negative effects that can arise from diagnostic, treatment, and evaluation practices.

What negative effects? Among many others, there are

- mistaken diagnoses
- misprescriptions
- invasions of privacy
- self-fulfilling prophecies
- stigmatization of individuals
- overdependency on professionals

Just because a practice has a negative effect, of course, is not usually an adequate reason for not using it. Many medications you use, for example, have side effects, but if you think they will help you more than hurt you, you use them. Most practitioners arrive at conclusions about whether a practice is ethical in just this way. If they think it is more helpful than harmful, it is seen as ethical.

But what makes a practice more helpful than harmful? This question reflects a basic problem in trying to resolve ethical concerns about practices in the LD field. There is no easy answer to the question. If there

were, there would be far less controversy over what is and isn't ethical.

Although there is no simple answer, there are better ways to think about the matter than relying primarily on experience and intuition. Major concepts and principles provide an important foundation for thinking through ethical dilemmas. The following brief presentation may help clarify what we mean. (For more in-depth discussion, see the special topic references provided at the end of this selection.) Three topics are discussed: (1) costs vs. benefits, (2) fairness, and (3) consent.

COSTS VS. BENEFITS

Professional practices are designed to provide benefits. Such benefits can be acquired only at a cost, in several senses of the term.

Should we place a student in a special classroom? Should an individual be given remediation? Medication? Will the treatment correct the youngster's problem? If so, will the benefits justify the financial expense, discomfort, stigmatization, and other potential negative effects individuals may experience upon being labeled and treated as different from others?

Clearly, costs and benefits encompass more than financial considerations and often are not readily quantified. Besides finances, the costs and benefits most frequently discussed are psychological and physical effects, particularly those having to do with identification and subsequent interventions.

Unfortunately, the sparsity of data on effectiveness and negative effects makes it difficult to specify benefits and costs, let alone determine net gains or losses. Reviewers find the validity of reported studies limited and inconsistent. As a result, the claim of positive benefits for LD children often is more hope than fact. Thus, efforts to resolve ethical dilemmas by considering costs-benefits for the individual must decide how heavily to weigh potential—but unproved—positive and negative effects.

From another perspective, it has been suggested that cost-benefits also should be analyzed with reference to the societal biases reflected in certain intervention practices. For example, children whose backgrounds differ from the dominant culture may be classified and treated as deficient primarily because their values and norms, and thus their actions and performance, are different from those of the dominant culture. In such situations, whether intentional or not, beneficial practices seem to have the effect of colluding with biases against certain subgroups.

The point is that ethical (and legal) perspectives can no longer remain oriented only to individuals. Concern over the use of IQ testing with minority students is a recent dramatic illustration of this point. Litigants have argued that minority populations have been inappropriately served by most IQ tests and labeling (e.g., in California, *Diana* v. *State Board of Education*, 1970; *Larry P. v. Riles*, 1972). Court cases have stressed that intelligence testing should be "culture fair," including use of the individual's "home language," and that tests alone should not be used to classify students. Such litigation highlights the concern that the benefits of some identification practices for any individual may be considerably less than the costs to a particular subgroup of the society. In particular, there is concern about practices that may perpetuate racial injustices in the form of additional discrimination, stigmatization, and restriction of educational opportunities. What all this highlights is that harmful effects can go beyond individuals; the cost-benefit for subgroups also must be considered.

A broader ethical perspective focuses on the overall negative effect professional practices can have on the entire culture. Some writers warn of a general loss of people's ability to cope with their problems. As a result of mystification about professional practices, people in modern societies are manifesting an ever increasing, distressing, and unnecessary overdependence on professionals. With psychoeducational problems, this is illustrated by the large number of parents and students who simply accept labels, such as *learning disabilities* and *emotional disturbance*, and related special interventions with little or no question or understanding. Thus, the suggestion has been made that professionals must judge the ethics of their activities not only in terms of the impact on an individual and on subgroups but also with regard to the impact on the entire culture.

Balancing costs against benefits is important, but the complexity of determining that costs outweigh benefits makes the application of this notion difficult. Even when the principle can be used effectively, it is still only one of the ethical guidelines to be considered. For instance, decisions that overemphasize utility (costs vs. benefits) at the expense of equity and justice (fairness) have been especially criticized.

FAIRNESS

Recent legal emphasis on "rights to treatment" and "right of all children to an education" also has highlighted the moral obligation to ensure that services are allocated fairly. If someone has a psychological or educational problem, it seems only fair that they be helped. In providing help, interveners are expected to be just and fair. The problem is—How do we decide what is fair?

The matter of fairness involves such questions as, Fair for whom? Fair according to whom? Fair using what criteria and what procedures for applying the criteria? Obviously what is fair for the society may not be fair for an individual; what is fair for one person may cause an inequity for another. To provide special services for one group's problems raises the taxes of all citizens. To deny such services is unfair and harmful to those who need the help.

Making fair decisions about who should get what services and resources and about how rules should be applied involves principles of distributive justice. For example, should each person be (1) given an equal share of available resources? (2) provided for according to individual need? (3) served according to his or her societal contributions? or (4) given services on the basis of having earned them (merit)? Obviously, such principles can conflict with each other. Moreover, any may be weighted more heavily than another, depending on the social philosophy of the decision maker.[1]

Those practitioners who see themselves as helping professionals tend toward an emphasis on individual need. That is, they tend to believe fairness means that those with problems should be given special aid. Indeed, the duty to serve those in need is seen as an ethical reason *for* classifying or labeling children.

Decisions based on the fairness principle often call for unequal allocation and affirmative action with regard to who gets the resources and how rules are applied. Thus, although they are intended to be just and fair, such decisions can be quite controversial, especially when resources are scarce.

There are always conflicting views as to which of many needs should be assigned highest priority. Are programs for the gifted more important than programs for students with learning disabilities? Should school athletic teams be funded at higher levels than vocational programs?

On a more individual level, parents, teachers, psychologists, and other practitioners consistently are confronted with the problem of applying rules differentially. For example, should different consequences be applied for the same offense when the children involved differ in terms of problems, age, competence, and so forth?

Some persons try to simplify matters by not making distinctions and treating everyone alike. It was said of Coach Vince Lombardi that he treated all his players the same—like dogs! We recall many instances in which teachers of problem populations have insisted on enforcing rules without regard to a particular student's social and emotional problems. They usually argued that it was unfair to other students if the same rule was not applied in the same way to everyone. In general, however, although a "no exceptions" approach represents a simple solution, it ignores the possibility that such a nonpersonalized approach may make a child's problem worse and thus be unjust.

CONSENT

In a society that values fairness and personal liberty, consent is a very important concept. Such a society has a strong commitment to ensuring personal autonomy for everyone.

Children and individuals with problems often are treated in ways that diminish their autonomy. This occurs because of assumptions about their relative lack of competence and wisdom. Even when they are treated autonomously, their decisions may not be respected.

The idea that autonomy should be respected has made consent not only a legal but also a major moral concern. The legal

---

[1]For example: "*Egalitarian* theories emphasize equal access to the goods in life that every rational person desires; *Marxist* theories emphasize need; *Libertarian* theories emphasize contribution and merit; and *Utili-* tarian theories emphasize a mixed used of such criteria so that public and private utility are maximized" (Beauchamp and Childress, 1979, p. 173).

and moral mechanism for maintaining autonomy usually is designated "informed consent." Six major functions served by the consent mechanism are the promotion of individual autonomy, the protection of clients or subjects, the avoidance of fraud and duress, the promotion of rational decisions, the encouragement of self-scrutiny by professionals, and the involvement of the public in promoting autonomy as a general social value and in controlling professional practices and research (Capron, 1974).

The desirability of such outcomes seems evident. The problems and issues involved in appropriately eliciting consent have to do with such matters as, When is consent needed? When is it justified for one person to offer consent for another? Who decides when consent is needed and when one person can represent another? What information must be given in eliciting consent? How can anyone be certain that consent has been voluntarily given? Each of these questions raises significant dilemmas for professionals.

To highlight major concerns associated with the concept of consent, we focus on (1) competence and paternalism as they affect decisions about when consent must be elicited and from whom and (2) the nature of relevant information and voluntary consent.

The question of competence and the problem of paternalism. Competence in the context of consent refers to the ability to understand, e.g., the ability to receive and process information, make decisions, and choose from among alternatives. Criteria for deciding about the adequacy of these abilities are difficult to specify. Usually, very general criteria are established, such as age and mental status.

Children and those diagnosed as mentally retarded, autistic, or psychotic usually are seen as incompetent in a legal sense and in need of surrogates (parents, guardians, and courts) to give consent. However, the basis

for deciding what constitutes competence and when others should act remains controversial. The example of children's consent illustrates just how difficult the problem is. At what age should it be necessary to ask a child's consent before involving the child in a psychological or educational intervention (including testing)? With regard to certain school assessment activity, the legal answer is that no individual consent is needed from either parents or child during the age period when attendance is compelled by the state. With regard to special psychological testing, special class placement, and therapeutic treatments, the common answer is that only the parents' consent is needed, and in some cases, not even their consent is sought.

The question of competence is strongly related to the problem of paternalism. It comes as no surprise that professionals, parents, government agents, and many others in society have opinions as to what is good for children. Such opinions backed by the power to impose them may lead to excessive paternalism.

For example, the professional who tests a youngster who does not want to be tested is confronted with this problem. It is a paternalistic act whenever a child is made to undergo unwanted assessment, even though the activity is viewed as in the child's "best interests." Whether stated or not, when such actions are taken, the child's autonomy is made less important than the possible harm to the child or others if the child is not assessed or the possible benefits to be gained if the child is assessed.

Relevant information and voluntary consent. Whenever consent is to be elicited, relevant information must be provided and decisions must be made voluntarily. Relevant information must be provided in an understandable manner—a requirement that is difficult to meet when complex psychoeducational practices are used. Cultural and language differences also may be barriers in making information understandable.

Providing relevant information does not guarantee that consent is given voluntarily. In many situations, consent is given because people feel they have no meaningful alternative. For example, children in special school programs and their parents may consent to additional assessment (therapy, medication, and so forth) because of fear that if they refuse they may be asked to leave the program.

When is voluntary consent needed? In addition to legal and ethical guidelines, voluntary consent is needed whenever the intent is to establish a helping relationship. Power relationships and situations in which influence is relied upon to elicit compliance do not involve the consent of participants. In contrast, helping relationships are based on voluntary consent. Thus, by definition, the obtaining of informed and voluntary consent defines whether the intent of an intervention is social control or helping.

A related question is, When may consent be waived? The answer to this question seems clearest when a problem is extremely threatening or an intervention is extremely unthreatening. For instance, persons who are seen as immediately dangerous to others or as unable to protect or care for themselves generally are accepted as likely candidates for waivers of consent.

Activities that are common to everyday living, such as much of the assessment and evaluation activity that permeates all our lives, provide another example. But they usually are not understood in terms of waived consent. They are, however, instances of *de facto* waived consent.

Although ethical concerns about waived consent are most likely to be raised in cases of extreme problems and dramatic interventions, consent that is waived in a *de facto*

manner perhaps ought to be of equal concern. Many commonplace activities, such as routine achievement, intelligence, and interest testing in schools, can have life-shaping impact and are likely to have an effect on a large segment of the population. Moreover, in instances in which consent is ignored, coercion is involved and needs to be justified.

SPECIAL TOPIC REFERENCES

Should you be interested in further information about costs, benefits, fairness, consent, the ethics of coercion, and other *ethical considerations*, see the following.

ADELMAN, H. S., & TAYLOR, L. (1983). *Learning disabilities in perspective*. Glenview, Ill.: Scott, Foresman.

AMERICAN PSYCHOLOGICAL ASSOCIATION (1981). Ethical principles of psychologists. *American Psychologist, 36,* 633–38.

BEAUCHAMP, T. L., & CHILDRESS, J. F. (1979). *Principles of biomedical ethics.* New York: Oxford University Press.

CAPRON, A. (1974). Informed consent in catastrophic disease and treatment. *University of Pennsylvania Law Review, 123,* 364–76.

COUNCIL FOR EXCEPTIONAL CHILDREN (1983). Code of ethics and standards for professional practice. *Exceptional Children, 50,* 205–209.

DIVISION FOR CHILDREN WITH LEARNING DISABILITIES (1978). *Code of ethics and competencies for teachers of learning disabled children and youth.* Kansas City, Kan.: Council for Learning Disabilities.

FEINBERG, J. *Social philosophy.* Englewood Cliffs, N.J.: Prentice-Hall.

ILLICH, I. (1976). *Medical nemesis.* New York: Pantheon Books.

ROBINSON, D. N. (1974). Harm, offense, and nuisance: Some first steps in the establishment of an ethics of treatment. *American Psychologist, 29,* 233–38.

Reading *M*

Toward Services with an Informed Consumer Orientation

"What is dyslexia?" "How do I tell if my child has a perceptual-motor dysfunction?" "Where can I have my child tested, tutored, etc.?"

These and many similar questions are on the minds of those who come into contact with the LD field. People want and deserve the best information available about such matters.

To demonstrate a range of model services to meet the need for information and referral to services, the Fernald Laboratory and Clinic at UCLA has developed among its package of services (1) a community resource helpline, (2) a community resource referral system, and (3) an initial assessment and consultation program (see Box M–1). Each is described briefly here.

A HELPLINE FOR LEARNING PROBLEMS

Highly visible helplines provide one means not only for informing but also for protecting the general public. The specific intent of Fernald's Learning Problems Community Resource Line is to clarify, guide, and demystify by providing the type of general information that can be given readily over the phone during a brief conversation. The service is for anyone experiencing a problem learning (at any age), anyone concerned about a friend or family member, and anyone who has a question about labels, tests, and remedial programs.

The program is staffed and implemented as follows:

Between 9 A.M. and noon, Monday through Friday, Fernald staff members or university students-in-training are available to receive calls from anyone with a question about learning problems. If the question cannot be answered readily, expert resources are checked (e.g., library, other professionals); then the person is called back, or the caller is referred to a resource who is better equipped to answer the particular question.

Each person answering the phone has been trained to provide basic information of the type previous callers have sought. Students whose experience in the field is not extensive have ready access to a staff member for consultation when complex questions are raised. In addition, there is a catalogue of major resources for referral (i.e., the Community Resource System, described next).

To advertise the availability of the helpline, fliers are sent to schools and social service agencies and posted on bulletin boards in libraries, markets, etc. Announcements also are aired as public service features on radio and television and in newspapers.

The data gathered to date support current impressions about who calls and why. For example, mothers are most frequently involved in seeking help for their child, males are most likely to be the focus of concern, and reading has been the problem most frequently mentioned.

The staff has observed that a major benefit of the learning problem helpline has been to make it easier for consumers to find help and to encourage its earlier pursuit than otherwise might have been the case.

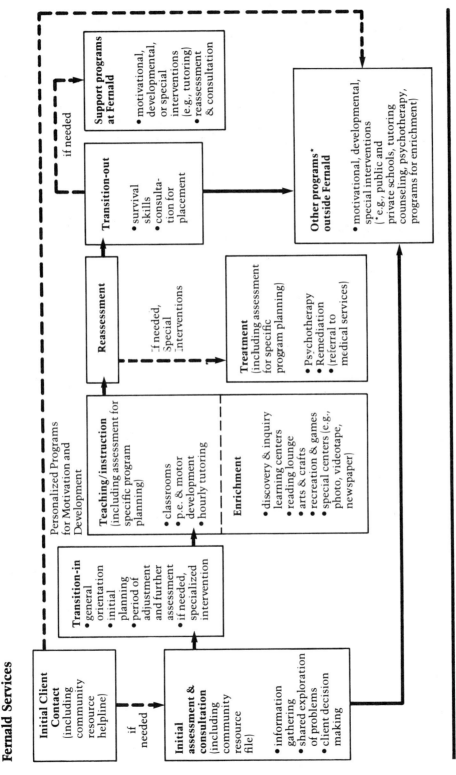

Box M–1

Fernald Services

COMMUNITY RESOURCE SYSTEMS: BEYOND "OLD BOY" REFERRAL NETWORKS

Referral practices tend to be taken for granted. Perhaps the most common practice remains that of the professional referral network, e.g., clients seeking referrals are given the names of one to three resources by a referral source. These names are seldom random choices. They tend to represent resources that the referrer has learned about through personal relationships (e.g., friends, colleagues), direct observation (e.g., brief visits), or through secondary sources (e.g., directories, brochures).

After an initial period of uncertainty and discomfort with their ability to match clients with services, most referrers begin to feel increasingly confident about their recommendations. This occurs despite the fact that there is little or no systematic evaluative information available on existing services; in particular, consumer feedback is virtually nonexistent.

In general, it is widely assumed that referrers do have adequate and objective information and that prevailing referral practices do result in satisfactory referrals. Unfortunately, these assumptions often are untrue.

The appropriateness of a referral depends not on the referrer's perspective and preferences but on the match between the recommended service and the practical and psychological requirements of the client, e.g., financial costs, geographical location, program characteristics. Thus, even if professional referral networks could (and they can't) adequately and objectively evaluate and ensure the quality of services to which they refer, they would still be confronted with the complex problem of determining that the service-client match will be a good one.

As a general approach, all Fernald services are based on the view that the more they re-flect consumer-oriented considerations, the greater the likelihood of appropriate decisions. For referrals to be consumer oriented, it is necessary to begin by clarifying consumer service needs (including the nature and scope of the problem as perceived by the client and the key characteristics of the services desired) and by clarifying the range of relevant options and basic information about each (e.g., cost, location, program rationale and features, and where feasible, previous consumer evaluations).

Then, to aid the consumer in reviewing potential services, the options and information should be presented in an organized and comprehensible manner. To facilitate decision making, it is useful to help explore the pros and cons of the most feasible alternatives and to identify several promising possibilities. To encourage consumer self-protection, it is helpful to outline basic evaluative questions that consumers can ask of potential service providers before contracting for services.

In sum, in developing a consumer-oriented community resource system at Fernald, the intent has been twofold: (1) to provide consumers with ready access to information on relevant services and (2) to minimize abuses in referral practices. At the same time, the hope has been that the positive side effects of such an approach will prove to be a higher degree of client self-reliance in problem solving, decision making, and consumer awareness.

The system's six components are as follows:

1. Standardized information. Potential referral resources are actively sought and invited to become entries in the system. Each is asked to fill out a standard form to provide summary information for easy reference and comparison with other services. The information encompasses characteristics of clients served (type of problems, age, sex), general type of services offered and fees, brief statements regarding specific characteristics of the services (e.g., particular philosophical and/or theoretical orientation), and an indication of who to contact to initiate services. These sheets are dated and categorized in loose-leaf binder notebooks.

Separate books are kept for major geographical areas in the community. Each book is organized to distinguish types of services, i.e., tutoring, school programs, assessment and consultation, counseling and psychotherapy, medical services, full-service facilities, other services such as vocational training and recreation facilities serving problem populations, etc. There is considerable cross-referencing (e.g., to multiple-service facilities).

2. Primary source material. Each service is asked to send all relevant descriptions and information (e.g., brochures, articles). These are dated, placed in sturdy plastic folders, and filed alphabetically in file cabinets.

Information on each service is periodically updated.

3. Published directories. Several of the many available commercial directories also are provided. These are meant primarily for reference to services not yet catalogued in the system and to those outside Fernald's geographical area.

4. System use information. This material explains the intent of the system and details steps for using each component. In brief, system users are directed to the binder notebooks, and it is suggested they first look at and compare services closest to home. Once they have identified several possible resources, the next step is to look at the additional filed information on each.

Then they are ready to make direct contact. In doing so, they are encouraged to review the consumer-protection guidelines provided. It is stressed that none of the services in the file has been evaluated by outside agencies, and thus, their presence in the file is not to be viewed as an endorsement.

Because all efforts to catalogue resources are limited, a list has been included of the type of general referral resources available in most communities (e.g., social welfare agencies, community mental health agencies, libraries, colleges, school coordinators, etc.). Clients who are unable to find what they need in Fernald's resource file can proceed to contact these other referral resources. The information about general referral sources can be especially useful to consumers who live in distant communities.

5. Consumer protection guidelines. Handouts, brief abstracts of articles, and references to consumer information material are prominently displayed. The handouts emphasize the types of questions a consumer might ask of a prospective service provider, e.g., about specific training and background of the individual who will actually provide the service, possible hidden costs, service benefits and risks of activities to be experienced, and so forth. The focus is on points such as those stressed by consumer advocates (see Chapter 14).

6. Consumer feedback. Currently, the main feedback emphasis is on the system itself. Users are encouraged to fill out suggestion cards describing ways in which the system might be improved. At a later date, data will be gathered on consumer evaluations of services used.

Over the years, clients have been found to vary considerably in their readiness (in terms of motivation and skills) to use the system. Some, of course, need little or no assistance. Others simply require a brief description by the facility's receptionist. A few need help at each step. This latter group are likely candidates for Fernald's Initial Assessment and Consultation program.

INITIAL ASSESSMENT
AND CONSULTATION

The increasing criticism of psychological and educational assessment and consultation services has underscored the need for new approaches. The focus of initial assessment and consultation is on *general* decisions about the types of services needed (e.g., special schooling, tutoring, psychotherapy) rather than on *detailed* decisions about intervention steps (e.g., specific programming prescriptions).

Although most professional assessment and consultation can be seen as a form of problem solving, such problem solving may or may not be an activity professionals *share* with clients. The process developed at Fernald is meant to be one of shared or guided problem solving because the objective is to help consumers (e.g., students and parents together) arrive at their own decisions rather than passively adopting the professional's recommendations and referrals.

A consumer-oriented, guided problem-solving approach eliminates a number of problems encountered in prevailing approaches. The service costs about a tenth of what other assessment and consultation services charge; it avoids making "expert" and detailed prescriptions that go beyond the validity of assessment procedures; and it avoids referrals based on "old boy" networks by incorporating the type of community resource referral system already described.

As with all assessment involved in decision making, the assessment aspect of the program has three major facets: (1) a rationale that determines what is assessed, (2) "measurement" or data gathering (in the form of analyses of records, observations, personal descriptions and perspectives, tests when needed, etc.), and (3) judgments of the meaning of what has been "measured."

The consultation aspect also has three major facets: (1) a rationale that determines the focus of consultation activity, (2) exploration of relevant information (including "expert" information), and (3) decision making by the consumers.

The specific procedures include

- initial screening, usually via a phone conversation;

- filling out of questionnaires by each concerned party (e.g., parents and child) regarding his or her perception of the cause of the referral problem and its correction;

- gathering records and reports from other professionals or agencies in those cases in which the consumers agree that it might be useful;

- analyzing—with the contribution of all interested parties—of questionnaires, reports, and records to determine whether there is a need to correct problems or verify their indications;

- brief, highly circumscribed testing, if necessary and desired by consumers;

- holding group conference(s) with immediately concerned parties to analyze problem(s) and in the process to determine whether other information is needed to complete the analysis;

- if needed, additional brief and specific information gathering through testing, teaching, or counseling;

- holding group conference(s) with the immediately concerned parties (1) to arrive at an agreement about how the problem will be understood for purposes of generating alternatives, (2) to generate, evaluate, and make decisions about alternatives to be pursued, (3) to formulate plans for pursuing alternatives and for any support needed; and

- follow-up via telephone or conference to evaluate the success of each pursued alternative and determine satisfaction with the process.

Problem analysis and decision making can be accomplished in one session. However, if additional assessment data are needed, one or two assessment sessions and a subsequent conference are planned.

Because of the degree to which some people have come to overrely on experts for diagnoses and prescriptions, a few individuals have been found to be a bit frustrated when they encounter an approach such as the one just described. They expect and believe that professionals should give a battery of tests that will provide definitive answers, and they want decisions made for them. They are convinced they cannot make good

decisions for themselves. These individuals may well reflect the negative side effects of professional practices that mystify consumers and make them feel totally dependent on professionals.

For more about these programs, see

ADELMAN, H. S., & TAYLOR, L. (1984). A helpline for learning problems. *Journal of Learning Disabilities.* 17, 237–239.

ADELMAN, H. S., & TAYLOR, L. (1979). Initial psychological assessment and related consultation. *Learning Disability Quarterly, 2,* 52–64.

ADELMAN, H. S., & TAYLOR, L. (1984). Helping clients find referrals. *Remedial and Special Education, 5,* 44–45.

ADELMAN, H. S., & TAYLOR, L. (1983). *Learning disabilities in perspective.* Glenview, Ill.: Scott, Foresman.

Areas of Professional Competence

Throughout the 1970s, there was a rapidly escalating interest in competency-based training for education professionals. Lists after lists of "competencies" were generated.

The good aspects of the trend were the focus on areas in which professionals should develop competence and on the *minimal levels of competence* in each area necessary for on-the-job success (Adelman, 1974). This view of competency-based training generally has been contrasted with training approaches that stress specific numbers of courses, units, and hours as a basis for professional certification. From the perspective of such a contrast, the competency-based idea can be seen as an extremely promising way to improve professional training.

Unfortunately, the trend toward competency-based professional training has taken on a narrow, behaviorist orientation. Rather than clarifying a broad range of knowledge, skills, and attitudes that professionals need to properly plan, implement, and evaluate interventions and programs, the emphasis has become one of formulating highly specific lists of behavioral and criterion-referenced objectives. This simplistic approach has led to a great deal of activity but has essentially ignored many important theoretical and practical questions about what is involved in preparing professionals.

With regard to LD professionals, in 1978,

CLD (the Council for Learning Disabilities, then called the Division for Children with Learning Disabilities) set forth a list of "competencies for teachers of learning disabled children and youth." Eleven major areas of competence were itemized; oral language, reading, written expression, spelling, mathematics, cognition, behavioral management, counseling and consulting, career/vocational education, educational operations, and historical-theoretical perspectives.

Because the CLD formulation represents a somewhat official statement that has been widely publicized and circulated, it can be viewed as encompassing a public view of what LD professionals are supposed to know and be able to do. In many ways, it is extremely comprehensive, quite idealistic, and certainly controversial. At the same time, it does suffer from some of the limitations seen in most lists of competencies.

Newcomer (1982) reports an official study (authorized by CLD) of the eleven competency areas. The study was "designed to measure the manner in which inservice professionals evaluated themselves in each competency area." Specifically, it reports that

"Two hundred and sixty-one professionals in learning disabilities rated their proficiency. . . . The evaluations included ratings of real competence, i.e., skills used on their jobs, and ideal competence, i.e., skills participants considered important for being able to function at maximum efficiency. The respondents were divided into subgroups based upon nine demographic conditions: Service Model, Teaching Level, Years of Teaching Experience, School Type, Years in Special Education, Degree, Location, Sex, and Age. Results revealed that reading was the most important competency area and that the majority of professionals felt most proficient in reading skills. At the other extreme, competence in cognition and career/vocational education was not viewed as particularly important. Other areas such as mathematics, written language, and oral language were regarded as important, but specific groups of professionals believed they were not fully competent in certain aspects of those areas. Other results suggested that teachers benefit from experience and academic degrees, and that they have little interest in research or professional organizations. Educational diagnosticians and supervisors believed that they had better training than other personnel; itinerant teachers viewed themselves as less competent than others in many areas." (p. 241)

The eleven areas of competence and the items listed for each are reproduced below:

ORAL LANGUAGE

General Information

The teacher:

1. understands association learning, linguistically oriented, and cognitive theories of language
2. understands the physical, social, and psychological correlates of oral language
3. understands the normal sequence for language development, e.g., prelinguistic stage, single-word stage
4. is familiar with theories which involve the relationship between language and thought
5. understands the components of language structure, i.e., phonology, semantics, morphology, and syntax, as well as the interrelationships among them
6. understands the processes involved in the development of the sound system (phonology)
7. is familiar with the patterns of phonological errors in child production
8. is familiar with theories of semantic development
9. understands the normal sequence of vocabulary development
10. understands types of semantic deficiency which limit communication
11. is familiar with theories of syntactic development
12. understands the sequence of normal syntactic development
13. understands phrase structure grammar and transformational grammar
14. understands problems related to syntactic deficits
15. understands the clinical syndromes associated with speech and language pathology, e.g., aphasia, apraxia
16. is familiar with general approaches to the remediation or correction of speech and language problems
17. understands the socio/cultural influence on speech and language problems
18. is familiar with research sources pertaining to oral language development and problems

Assessment

1. can administer and interpret standardized language tests in the areas of phonology, semantics, morphology, and syntax
2. can develop, use, and interpret informal assessment instruments in the areas of phonology, semantics, morphology, and syntax
3. can analyze a spontaneous speech sample for phonological, syntactic and semantic components
4. can diagnose the language impairment associated with the conditions of aphasia, hearing impairment, mental retardation, severe emotional disturbance, cerebral palsy, and brain injury
5. can assess levels of ideation and use of context words, function words, linguistic forms, melody patterns, and articulation in total production
6. can differentiate between speakers of non-standard English dialects and language disordered children

Instruction

1. can select appropriate commercially available developmental materials and programs
2. can plan and implement a remedial language program which is specifically designed for individualized use and which interrelates all areas of language comprehension and production
   a. can use knowledge of language development to plan a remedial program
   b. can sequence programs in step-wise fashion from easy to difficult
   c. can use comprehended forms as a base for eliciting production
   d. can use linguistic forms in varied context
   e. can incorporate high interest and environmentally relevant material
   f. can set realistic goals
   g. can record progress systematically
3. can modify commercial materials and programs for use with mildly handicapped children
4. can use informal language stimulation techniques
5. can implement English as a second language program for bilingual or dialect speaking children
6. can plan and implement developmental instructional programs for language delayed children

READING

General Knowledge

Developmental Reading

The teacher:

1. understands basic theories related to the field of reading

2. understands how these theories influence the teaching strategies and the materials used in reading instruction
3. understands the physical, psychological, and environmental correlates of reading
4. understands the skills related to reading readiness
5. understands the sequence of skills leading to the development of the mature reader
6. understands the components, focus, and approaches associated with developmental reading programs
7. understands the relationship of developmental reading instruction to corrective and remedial reading instruction

Specialized Reading Instruction

1. Corrective Reading
   a. understands that corrective reading instruction is used as a system for planning and delivering classroom instruction to students who experience minor deficiencies in the elements of developmental reading
   b. understands the type of student who will benefit from such instruction
   c. understands systems that may be used to implement such instruction in the regular classroom, on an itinerant basis, or in a self-contained classroom.
2. Remedial Reading
   a. understands that remedial reading instruction is used as a system for delivering intensive individualized instruction to students who have major reading problems in word recognition skills, including:
      (1) context analysis
      (2) sight words
      (3) phonic analysis
      (4) structural analysis
      (5) dictionary analysis
      (6) specialized vocabulary

c. understands various approaches to reading comprehension; these include:
   (1) skills (locating main idea, inference, etc.)
   (2) taxonomy of skills
   (3) imagery
   (4) models
   (5) correlational
   (6) factor analytic
   (7) readability
d. understands comprehension skills, including:
   (1) vocabulary
   (2) semantics
   (3) syntax
   (4) imagery
   (5) specific comprehension skills (locating the main idea, following a sequence, inference, noting detail, etc.)
   (6) critical reading skills
   (7) meaning in phrases, thought units, sentences, paragraphs, and discourse
e. understands the skills in reading fluency and reading rate involving both oral and silent reading
f. understands the interrelationship of reading skills development to other content areas, e.g., written and oral language, spelling, listening
g. understands the skills associated with problems in structure and syntax
h. understands the skills associated with problems in reading technical or content specific information

Assessment

Screening

1. has knowledge of appropriate instruments and techniques for general screening for reading

2. can administer and interpret such instruments and techniques
3. can identify those students for whom additional assessment and diagnostic evaluations are needed

Evaluation

1. has knowledge of the appropriate instruments and techniques for specific assessment of the student's level of reading achievement and the areas that warrant specific attention
2. can administer and interpret such instruments and techniques

Diagnosis

1. can select and administer formal and informal diagnostic instruments for those specific skills related to reading
2. can interpret diagnostic data to specify problems in reading
3. can use the formal and informal data to plan for appropriate reading instruction and intervention programs

Formative/Summative

1. can develop and use tests to monitor students' ongoing and final level of mastery

Instruction

Corrective Reading

1. can plan and implement instruction for minor problems associated with gaps or deficiencies in the developmental reading process
2. can use materials to teach the developmental and corrective reading process, e.g., basal reading programs, sight word

and phrase cards, specific skill developmental materials

Remedial Reading

1. can plan and implement intensive individualized reading instruction in the skill areas associated with remedial reading
2. can use special approaches related to intensive reading instruction
3. can use materials, approaches, and techniques that have application to specific types of reading problems
4. can plan and deliver instruction that will accommodate the development of reading skills in the content areas
5. can deliver instruction in the development of reading skills associated with problems in technical or content specific areas
6. can identify and secure the services of additional appropriate professional resources to meet specific needs
7. can design and deliver an individualized reading program to the student which assures appropriate progress, alterations, goal achievement, etc.
8. can work with others involved in the student's educational program to assure that instruction in reading is integrated into the whole curriculum and that appropriate progress is assured

WRITTEN EXPRESSION

General Knowledge

The teacher:

1. recognizes written expression as a method of conveying ideas or meanings
2. understands the components of writing

readiness, e.g., eye-hand coordination, left to right progression, adequate oral and reading vocabulary skill, knowledge of syntax
3. understands the interrelation of creative writing skills with reading, spelling, and oral language
4. differentiates between penmanship and creative writing
5. understands the mechanical aspects of written expression, e.g., punctuation, capitalization, spelling
6. understands the importance of sentence and paragraph writing
7. understands the chronology and sequence of development for written expression skills from 1st grade through 12th grade
8. understands the physical, social, and psychological correlates of written expression

Assessment

1. can administer and interpret standardized achievement tests of written expression
2. can administer and analyze diagnostic tests of creative writing
3. can use standardized measures of handwriting skill
4. can develop and use informal measures of student's written expression ability
   a. secure written sample
   b. error analysis—mechanics
   c. analysis of sentence and paragraph organization
   d. analysis of quality of content, e.g., ideas conveyed, conclusions drawn, appropriate use of words
   e. analysis of grammar, i.e., verb usage, pronouns, modifiers, etc.
   f. analysis of possible causes of errors, e.g., carelessness, haste, lack of knowledge

Instruction

1. can plan and implement an instructional program incorporating the basic components for writing
   a. purpose of composition
   b. arrangement of ideas
   c. compare and contrast skills
   d. organization of ideas
   e. types of prose, e.g., narrative, descriptive, expository, argumentation as well as poetry
2. can plan and implement a program which teaches handwriting, both manuscript and cursive
3. can plan and implement a program which teaches the mechanical skills required in written expression, e.g., capitalization, punctuation, spelling, penmanship
4. can plan and implement writing tasks utilizing varied formats, e.g., letter, note, report
5. can teach proofreading and evaluation skills including: narrowing content, ordering ideas, focusing to convey important information, personalization through appropriate novel vocabulary and taking responsibility for content accuracy
6. can coordinate written expression instruction with other content areas, e.g., reading, spelling
7. can plan and implement remedial programs in general language skills such as vocabulary development, reading comprehension, morphological usage

SPELLING

General Knowledge

The teacher:

1. understands the nature and rules of English orthography

2. understands different theories of teaching spelling
3. understands research related to the different spelling theories
4. understands various models of spelling behavior
5. is familiar with at least one scope and sequence of spelling skills
6. understands the importance of teaching spelling as part of a total language arts curriculum
7. has knowledge of basic core of spelling words used in children's and adults' writing

Assessment

1. can administer and interpret the spelling sections of standardized achievement tests
2. can administer and interpret standardized diagnostic spelling tests
3. can administer and interpret informal and/or criterion referenced spelling assessment instruments
4. can construct and administer an Informal Spelling Inventory (ISI)
5. can conduct an error analysis from a written sample of a student's work or from the results of a student's performance on a standardized achievement or spelling test
6. can determine which factors are affecting spelling performance, e.g., motivation, sensory deficit, language deficit, etc.
7. can determine which type of spelling techniques can be used most economically with the student

Instruction

1. can teach spelling skills using a planned sequence of activities
2. understands various approaches to teaching spelling

3. can utilize and, when necessary, modify various commercial basal and remedial spelling programs
4. can use different procedures to monitor progress in the acquisition of spelling skill, e.g., charting, precision teaching, etc.
5. can apply inferences and generalizations from research to teaching spelling
6. can integrate spelling as a naturalistic part of the total language arts program

MATHEMATICS

General Knowledge

Number Theory

The teacher:

1. understands all the concepts involved in numeration and counting
2. understands the concept of place value
3. understands the concepts and operations involved in converting from one base to another
4. understands both the Arabic and Roman numeral systems
5. understands the associative, commutative, and distributive properties of whole numbers
6. understands the concept of prime and composite numbers
7. can identify and explain common symbols used in mathematics
8. understands set theory

Addition and Subtraction

1. understands the computational process involved in adding and subtracting whole numbers
2. understands the concept of regrouping as it relates to addition and subtraction

3. knows the terms related to the operations involved in an addition and subtraction problem, e.g., addends, minuend, etc.

Multiplication and Division

1. understands the computational process involved in solving multiplication and division problems
2. knows the terms related to the operations of multiplication and division problems, e.g., quotient, divisor

Fractions, Decimals, and Percentage

1. understands all the operations involved in adding, subtracting, multiplying, and dividing fractions, decimal numbers, and numbers expressed as percentages
2. understands all the processes involved in converting a number from one form to another, e.g., a fraction to a decimal, a decimal to a percent, etc.

Geometry

1. understands simple common plane geometric figures, e.g., square, circle, triangle, and understands the processes used in determining perimeter and area of these figures
2. understands common solid geometric figures, e.g., cube, sphere, and understands the process used in determining the area and volume of each

Measurement

1. understands all the concepts involved in measurement of: time, linear planes, weight, liquids, and temperature
2. understands the metric system
3. understands the concepts and processes

involved in constructing simple charts and graphs

Money

1. understands the U.S. monetary system

Verbal Problem Solving

1. understands the variables that contribute to difficulty in verbal problem solving, e.g., reading level, level of syntactic complexity, distractors, etc.

Assessment

1. can administer and interpret the mathematical portion of standardized group achievement tests
2. can administer and interpret the mathematical portion of individual standardized achievement tests
3. can administer and interpret standardized diagnostic tests
4. can take a scope and sequence in each mathematical area and develop and administer an evaluation instrument that is based upon it
5. is familiar with several procedures which can be used to assess a student's attitude toward mathematics
6. is familiar with methods for conducting error analysis
7. is familiar with procedures used for determining a student's verbal problem solving ability

Instruction

1. can teach a specific mathematical skill by developing and following a planned sequence of activities
2. can evaluate, utilize, and/or adapt commercial mathematical programs and materials

3. can use appropriately and effectively a variety of manipulative mathematical materials, e.g., number line, counting blocks, cuisenaire rods, to teach a specific skill
4. is familiar with different conceptual and theoretical approaches to mathematics instuction
5. is familiar with non-traditional ways of teaching algorithms, e.g., "tractenberg" methods of addition, "equal addition method" for subtracting
6. can teach practical application of math concepts, e.g., liquid measurement as it relates to cooking, linear measurement as it relates to carpentry, time as it relates to the student's daily schedule

COGNITION

General Knowledge

Nature of Thought

The teacher:

1. understands various theories regarding thought and process of thinking
2. can compare various theories with respect to explanation of observed behavior

Piagetian Theories

1. understands the implications of a stage theory such as Piaget's and can compare it with age theories
2. understands the mechanisms for acquiring knowledge at each stage, e.g., sensorimotor, preoperational, concrete operations, formal operations
3. can predict differences in behavior using Piaget stages for exceptional learners

4. can compare Piagetian and psychometric approaches to intelligence

Association Theory

1. understands the implications of association theory and can analyze learning situations into stimulus and response components
2. can distinguish the roles of contiguity, mediation, and reinforcement in association learning
3. can apply association theory to concept formation tasks considering the variables making up concepts
   a. attributes and salience of attributes
   b. complexity in number of dimensions
   c. class concepts
   d. preferred dimensions
   e. abstractness
4. can analyze learning tasks of various types in terms of association theory
5. can explain and predict differences in learners as a function of
   a. general ability or intelligence differences
   b. age differences
   c. motivational differences
   d. cognitive style differences
   e. sensory capacities

Information Processing Theories

1. understands the implications of information processing theory as a model of human intelligence
2. can describe methods of solving problems, such as means-ends analyses and algorithms or heuristics
3 . can apply the above techniques to children's learning problems

Gestalt Theories

1. understands theories which view learning wholistically and can analyze

   a. discovery learning
   b. perceptual arousal
   c. creative or original responses
2. can describe several methods or types of learning
   a. insight problems
   b. search problems
   c. functional fixedness

Theories of Intelligence

1. understands Q-factor theory intelligence, "g" and special abilities
2. understands the Guilford factor-analytic models of intelligence
3. can explain differences in behavior of learners using these two theories

Assessment

Formal

1. can administer and interpret standardized tests of intelligence
2. can interpret results of intelligence tests administered by other personnel

Informal

1. can devise tasks which reveal children's skills at problem solving, inferential thinking, and concept development

Instruction

General

1. can incorporate information regarding cognitive development into general instructional programming
2. can teach conceptual skills such as: deductive and inductive reasoning, problem solving skills, inferential

reasoning, logical thought, categorization and classification skills

BEHAVIORAL MANAGEMENT

General Knowledge

The teacher:

1. understands general theoretical positions related to
   a. theories of learning
   b. theories of personality and psychopathology
   c. child development (normal and atypical)
2. understands the relationship between academic and social/emotional expectations and classroom behavior problems
3. understands varied approaches to altering behavior

Assessment

1. can define target behaviors
2. can apply knowledge of normal and atypical development to behavioral assessment
3. can obtain general and specific information by interpreting students' permanent records
4. can obtain general and specific information through observation
5. can use observational techniques such as
   a. automatic recording
   b. analysis of permanent products
   c. observational recording, e.g., anecdotal recording, event recording, time sampling
6. can obtain information through interviewing techniques
7. can obtain general and specific information through the use of behavioral checklists and inventories
8. can devise and use a teacher-made behavioral checklist
9. can obtain general and specific information through interactional analysis
10. can use and interpret interactional techniques such as sociometrics, Dyadic Interaction Analysis, and ecological assessment
11. can obtain general and specific information by analyzing the physical environment
12. can obtain general information through the use of standardized tests
13. can obtain general information from reports of testing and observations, written by ancillary professional personnel
14. can utilize assessment information obtained from personality measures
15. can record behavioral information in an accurate, systematic manner
16. can identify patterns in the environment by noting specific behaviors, antecedent events and consequences
17. can organize behavioral information into testable hypotheses
18. can accurately report behavioral information in a written report
19. can identify those behavior problems which can be managed within the classroom and those that should be referred to ancillary professionals

Intervention Strategies

1. can use remedial instructional procedures to modify behavior
2. can apply behavior modification programs appropriately
3. can counsel children with emotional problems
4. can apply milieu therapy techniques in immediate classroom situations and over extended period of time
5. can apply rational/cognitive therapeutic strategies
6. understands and can apply projective and media-oriented therapies such as

art, music, and play therapies, puppetry, and role playing

7. can plan cooperatively with professionals trained in implementing various therapies

8. can use affective curricular materials

COUNSELING AND CONSULTING

Consulting with Teachers and Administrators

The teacher:

1. must have knowledge about working with exceptional children in school settings involving handicapped and non-handicapped students

2. is able to establish lines of communication with regular educators and school administrators

3. is able to establish and maintain rapport with teachers and principals in order that he/she can exert influence and consequently function as a change agent on behalf of handicapped students

4. is able to determine the philosophy of a school relative to management, administrative policies and operational procedures, and be capable of maintaining behavior which is consistent with such policies and procedures

5. is able to effectively utilize resources and consulting skills to complete consultation tasks with teachers and/or principals

6. can employ effective interviewing skills

7. can determine needed and available human and non-human resources at the building and district level applicable to staff development activities

8. can provide interpretation for teachers pertaining to research, evaluative reports and ongoing programs of learning disabled students

9. can detect instructional problems being encountered by teachers and students

10. can employ varied staff development techniques, e.g., schedule individual conferences, demonstrate teaching skills, arrange for teachers to visit other classrooms, disseminate information

11. can interpret expressed and observed staff needs to appropriate administrators

12. can provide regular educators with useful information about mainstreamed learning disabled children

13. can provide regular educators with usable and realistic teaching suggestions for mainstreamed learning disabled children

14. can use tact and courtesy in reorganizing and overcoming regular educator's resistances to programming for exceptional children

Consulting and Counseling with Parents

1. can establish and maintain rapport with parents

2. can develop and maintain channels of communication with parents with regard to their child's social, physical, and academic progress

3. can effectively conduct parent conferences

4. can develop and supervise instructional and/or management programs using parents as intervention agents

5. can plan and conduct effective and efficient parent meetings

6. can understand and follow proper due process proceedings with regard to assessment, placement and programming for a student

7. can involve parents in a meaningful

way in the development of the student's Individualized Education Program

8. can assist parents in developing realistic expectations for their child and/or adolescent in academic and occupational areas

9. can direct parents to community and governmental agencies, volunteer and non-profit groups and parent organizations which provide supportive services to learning disabled students

Consulting and Counseling with Children

1. can establish and maintain rapport with children

2. can involve children in educational decision making

3. can act as child advocate and insure each child's optimal education in a least restrictive environment

4. can use counseling techniques to help children overcome specific problems in the classroom

CAREER/VOCATIONAL EDUCATION

General Knowledge

Knowledge of Individual Characteristics

The teacher:

1. is aware that each individual has unique patterns of abilities and limitations which affect career/vocational decisions

2. is aware that each individual has unique attitudes, interests and values which affect career/vocational decisions

Knowledge of Career and Occupational Opportunities

1. has comprehensive knowledge of a wide variety of occupational families

2. knows the abilities required in specific vocations or occupational families

3. knows the baseline interpersonal and functional skills which are required for vocational success

4. has a reasonable understanding of the technological, economic and social forces which influence current and future employment opportunities

5. can relate knowledge of specific vocational requirements to each individual's abilities, interests, and values

6. is familiar with resources which provide current information about career opportunity

7. is familiar with resources which provide students with direct experience in various vocations

8. is familiar with the content covered on the General Education Development Test

Assessment

1. can administer and interpret standardized vocational/career interest and aptitude tests

2. can make informal assessments of vocational/career interests through observation and interview skills

3. can coordinate information obtained through a comprehensive assessment of intellectual, scholastic, physical and social abilities with interests and attitude surveys to develop realistic vocational options for each child

Instruction

1. will provide information pertaining to a variety of career opportunities

2. will provide opportunities for students to make onsite observations of various occupations
3. will relate career/vocational instruction to child's physical, mental, social and scholastic level of development
4. will encourage group exploration and discussion of various career/vocational opportunities
5. will counsel individuals to help them make realistic vocational decisions based on their abilities and interests
6. will help students understand and develop the specific skills necessary for career entry, e.g., typing, filing
7. will teach practical job-securing skills when necessary, e.g., interview behavior, completion of job application forms
8. will teach self-help skills which affect employment opportunities, e.g., grooming, appropriate dress, use of handkerchief instead of sleeve
9. will teach daily living skills which affect career decisions, e.g., budgeting of money, best use of time, importance of rest and nutrition
10. will teach family management skills, e.g., family planning and child rearing, food selection and preparation, purchasing decisions
11. will provide opportunities to practice cooperative interaction with others in simulated or real work situations
12. will provide opportunities for the development of effective leadership skills
13. will relate successful employment to acceptance of responsibility for own behavior
14. will relate successful employment to feelings of personal satisfaction about accomplishments
15. will help students develop the skills needed to pass the General Education Development Test

EDUCATIONAL OPERATIONS

Assessment

The teacher:

1. is able to establish rapport during assessment
2. has knowledge of normal and atypical development patterns and can relate this knowledge to assessment
3. can determine the nature of the information to be supplied by assessment
4. can assess students' interest areas, motivational levels and responsibilities to particular avenues of instruction
5. understands the concepts of reliability and validity and can identify these items in instruments
6. can select appropriate tests and measures in each instructional area after weighing the purpose of the assessment, information provided in test manuals, and evaluation and research data provided in the literature
7. can devise informal devices when formal instruments are not available or appropriate
8. can develop a scope and sequence of specific academic and/or social skills
9. can task analyze behaviors and skills
10. can logically sequence an assessment battery for maximum effectiveness and efficiency
11. can modify assessment devices and procedures as necessary
12. can organize testable hypotheses from assessment results
13. can present a written report of assessment results
14. can conduct on-going formative evaluations of students' progress
15. can utilize on-going formative evaluations to effect appropriate changes,

goals, and objectives for students in teaching methods and/or in instructional materials

Materials

1. can determine student needs to be met by curricula
2. can use resources such as computer retrieval systems to locate and secure commercial programs and materials
3. can perform static evaluations of curricular materials
4. can select commercial materials whose objectives match the students' diagnosed needs
5. can select the appropriate content and/or level of material to meet students' diagnosed needs
6. can determine areas of materials and other resources which require adaptation and revision
7. can produce own material when necessary
8. can design and/or select devices appropriate for dynamic (or process) evaluation of material effectiveness
9. can communicate the results of materials efficacy studies

Audio/Visual

1. can identify and select A/V media appropriate for stated instructional objectives
2. can operate various media equipment, e.g., filmstrip projector, dry-mount press

Environment

1. can identify variables which influence learning in the school and classroom environment
2. can arrange the school environment to maximize teaching efforts and enhance learning, e.g., seating arrangements, interest centers
3. can select the educational placement which best meets each child's specific needs

Instruction

1. can plan and implement a sequential remedial program for a student
2. can establish long and short term goals in each academic area
3. can write behavioral objectives for each goal
4. can plan and sequence activities which will accomplish each objective
5. can teach skills by following a planned sequence of activities
6. can develop lesson plans using various formats
7. can secure appropriate instructional materials for the planned activities
8. can develop a scope and sequence in each academic area, i.e., spelling, written expression, etc.
9. can manage each student's individualized education plan to assure appropriate progress, goal achievement, etc.
10. can plan integrated programs with regular educators for mainstreamed students
11. can incorporate both formative and summative evaluation into the diagnostic teaching process
12. can incorporate multidisciplinary data into instructional programming
13. can formulate recommendations to maximize the student's education in the regular class setting
14. can deliver an individualized education program on a tutorial one-to-one basis as well as in a group setting
15. can make constructive use of teacher

aids and volunteer assistants in planning and implementing instructional programs

Research

1. can critically evaluate research data presented in journals and other publications
2. can plan and implement research projects
3. can report research results in publications or oral presentations

HISTORICAL-THEORETICAL PERSPECTIVES

History of Learning Disabilities

The teacher:

1. can identify early contributors to the field of learning disabilities
2. can trace the historical development of the field of learning disabilities
3. can explain various philosophical positions that have influenced thinking in the field of learning disabilities and

identify persons associated with each philosophical position
4. can explain the major court decisions that have impacted the field of learning disabilities
5. can explain federal legislation that has had an effect on the field of learning disabilities
6. can explain state legislation pertaining to learning disabilities

Program Models

1. can explain pertinent program models employed in delivering services to learning disabled children
2. can explain various roles that learning disability personnel can have
3. can explain various instructional arrangements used with learning disabled children

Professional Organizations

1. is aware of various professional organizations in learning disabilities
2. belongs to and participates in the structure and organization of professional organizations in learning disabilities

Perspectives

One of the joys of reading occurs when you find a bit of wisdom or a provocative statement that seems so good you want to cherish and share it with as many other people as will listen. Over the years, we have gathered bits and pieces to share with students in our class on learning disabilities. A few of our favorites are offered here.

On Education and Teaching

Alfred Adler is said to have defined education as "the process of transferring the notes of the teacher to the notebook of the pupil without passing through the head of either."

Einstein is said to have quipped: "Education is *what's left* when you have forgotten everything you learned in school."

"I suppose teachers have always been intuitively aware of the fact that when they change their method of teaching, certain children who have appeared to be slow learners or even nonlearners become outstanding achievers." (Torrance, 1965, p. 253)

Anatole France wrote: "The whole art of teaching is only the art of awakening the natural curiosity of young minds for the purpose of satisfying it afterwards." (1890, p. 178)

"School is not easy and it is not for the most part very much fun, but then, if you are very lucky, you may find a teacher. Three real teachers in a lifetime is the very best of luck.

My first was a science and math teacher in high school, my second a professor of creative writing at Stanford and my third was my friend and partner, Ed Rickets.

"I have come to believe that a great teacher is a great artist and that there are as few as there are any other great artists. It might even be the greatest of the arts since the medium is the human mind and spirit.

"My three had these things in common— They all loved what they were doing. They did not tell—they catalyzed a burning desire to know. Under their influence, the horizons sprung wide and fear went away and the unknown became knowable. But most important of all, the truth, that dangerous stuff, became beautiful and very precious." (John Steinbeck, 1955, p. 7)

Half in jest, someone (we can't recall who) said to us: "If schools had to teach children to speak, we'd have as many speech problems as there are reading problems."

On Children

"Children . . . do much of their learning in great bursts of passion and enthusiasm. Except for those physical skills which can't be learned any other way, children rarely learn on the slow, steady schedules that schools make for them. They are more likely to be insatiably curious for a while about some particular interest, and to read, write, talk, and ask questions about it for hours a day and for days on end. Then suddenly they may drop that interest and turn to something completely different or even for a while seem to have no interest at all. This usually means that for the time being they have all the information on that subject that they can digest, and need to explore the world in a different way, or perhaps simply get a firmer grip on what they already know." (John Holt, 1983, p. 288)

Bemoaning the tendency for adults to interpret a child's behavior in adult terms, David Nyberg suggests: "It is to this malady that we owe most of the incredible variety of ways a child can 'fail' at something. A child knows that he makes mistakes and blunders but they *become* other things to do, they change things around and point to new things, and they are just as intriguing (maybe more so) as straightaway accomplishments. Adults see activities from a success-failure view of things. A child lives more with an interesting-uninteresting view of things. Remember?" (1971, p. 166)

"To a grown up person who is too absorbed in his own affairs to take an interest in children's affairs, children doubtless seem unreasonably engrossed in their own affairs." (John Dewey, 1966, p. 44)

On Changing Things

Ulric Neisser notes that "changing the individual while leaving the world alone is a dubious proposition." (1976, p. 183)

"Having partial answers does not mean that we are helpless, nor does it keep us from attempting to put what we do know into practical application; it does mean we must be aware of the limitations of our knowledge, of where fact leaves off and belief begins." (Stevenson, 1972, p. 1)

Abraham Maslow warned: "If the only tool you have is a hammer, you tend to treat everything as if it were a nail."

Do not follow where the path may lead. Go, instead where there is no path and leave a trail. (Anonymous)

"The pessimist says that a 12-ounce glass containing 6 ounces of drink is half empty—the optimist calls it half full. I won't say what I think the pessimist could say about research and practice in special education at this point, but I think the optimist could say that we have a wonderful opportunity to start all over!" (Scriven, 1981, p. 10)

And, finally, in the immortal words of whoever said it first, if you are going to try to change things for the better, "Illegitimati non carborundum!" Translation: "Don't let the bastards grind you down!"

REFERENCES

This is a listing of references that are cited only by author and date within each chapter. Additional references are listed with full citations within many chapters and at their end. To find the page on which these additional references are cited, look up author names in the index.

ADELMAN, H. S. (1971). The not so specific learning disability population. *Exceptional Children, 8,* 114–20.

ADELMAN, H. S. (1972). The special task of special education. *Academic Therapy, 7,* 323–26.

ADELMAN, H. S. (1974). *Competency-based training in education: A conceptual view.* Monograph published by ERIC (ED 090207). Washington, D.C.: U.S. Dept. of Education.

ADELMAN, H. S. (1978). The expert trap. *Journal of Learning Disabilities, 11,* 10–12.

ADELMAN, H. S. (1978). The concept of intrinsic motivation: Implications for practice and research with the learning disabled. *Learning Disability Quarterly, 1,* 43–54.

ADELMAN, H. S., & COMPAS, B. (1977). Stimulant drugs and learning problems. *Journal of Special Education, 11,* 377–416.

ADELMAN, H. S., KASER-BOYD, N., & TAYLOR, L. (1984). Children's participation in consent for psychotherapy and their subsequent response to treatment. *Journal of Clinical Child Psychology, 13,* 170–78.

ADELMAN, H. S., & TAYLOR, L. (1983). *Learning disabilities in perspective.* Glenview, Ill.: Scott, Foresman.

ADELMAN, H. S., & TAYLOR, L. (1983). Enhancing motivation for overcoming learning and behavior problems. *Journal of Learning Disabilities, 16,* 384–92.

ADELMAN, H. S., & TAYLOR, L. (1984). Ethical concerns and identification of psychoeducational problems. *Journal of Clinical Child Psychology, 13,* 16–23.

ADELMAN, H. S., & TAYLOR, L. (1985). Toward integrating intervention theory, research, and practice. In S. I. Pfeiffer (Ed.), *Clinical child psychology: An introduction to theory, research, and practice.* New York: Grune & Stratton.

ADELMAN, H. S., & TAYLOR, L. (1985). Fundamental concerns facing the learning disabilities field: A survey looking to the future. *Journal of Learning Disabilities.*

ALBERTO, P. A., & TROUTMAN, A. C. (1982). *Applied behavioral analysis for teachers: Influencing student performance.* Columbus, Ohio: Merrill.

ALTMAN, I. (1975). *The environment and social behavior.* Monterey, Calif.: Brooks-Cole.

AMERICAN PSYCHOLOGICAL ASSOCIATION (1968). Psychology as a profession. *American Psychologist, 23,* 195–200.

AMERICAN PSYCHOLOGICAL ASSOCIATION (1981). Ethical principles of psychologists. *American Psychologist, 36,* 633–38.

AMES, L. B. (1983). Learning disability: Truth or trap? *Journal of Learning Disabilities, 16,* 19–21.

ARTER, J. A. & JENKINS, J. R. (1979). Differential diagnosis-prescriptive teaching: A critical appraisal. *Review of Educational Research, 49,* 517–55.

AUSUBEL, N. (Ed.) (1948). Applied psychology. In *A Treasury of Jewish Folklore.* New York: Crown.

AYRES, A. J. (1965). Patterns of perceptual-motor dysfunction in children: A factor analytic study. *Perceptual and Motor Skills, 20,* 235–368.

AYRES, A. J. (1969). Deficits in sensory integration in educationally handicapped children. *Journal of Learning Disabilities, 2,* 160–68.

AYRES, A. J. (1978). Learning disabilities and the vestibular system. *Journal of Learning Disabilities, 11,* 18–29.

BANDURA, A. (1978). The self system in reciprocal determinism. *American Psychologist, 33,* 344–58.

BARKLEY, R. A. (1977). A review of stimulant drug research with hyperkinetic children. *Journal of Child Psychology and Psychiatry, 18,* 137–65.

BARSCH, R. (1967). *Achieving perceptual-motor efficiency: A space-oriented approach to learning.* Seattle: Special Child Publications.

BAUM, S., & KIRSCHENBAUM, R. (1984). Recognizing special talents in learning disabled students. *Teaching Exceptional Children, 16,* 92–98.

BAUMRIND, D. (1978). Reciprocal rights and responsibilities in parent-child relations. *Journal of Social Issues, 34,* 179–96.

BEAUCHAMP, T. L., & CHILDRESS, J. F. (1979). *Principles of biomedical ethics.* New York: Oxford University Press.

BENDER, L. (1947). Childhood schizophrenia: Clinical study of one hundred schizophrenic children. *American Journal of Orthopsychiatry, 17,* 40–55.

BENJAMIN, H. (1949). *The cultivation of idiosyncracy.* Cambridge, Mass.: Harvard University Press.

BERNE, E. (1964). *Games people play: The psychology of human relationships.* New York: Grove Press.

BIJOU, S. W., & BAER, D. M. (Eds.) (1967). *Child development: Readings in experimental analysis.* Englewood Cliffs, N.J.: Prentice-Hall.

BIKLEN, D. (1978). Consent as a cornerstone concept. In J. Mearig & Associates (Ed.), *Working for children: Ethical issues beyond professional guidelines.* San Francisco: Jossey-Bass.

BIKLEN, D. (1985). Mainstreaming: From compliance to quality. *Journal of Learning Disabilities, 18,* 58–61.

BLATT, B. (1972). Public policy and the education of children with special needs. *Exceptional Children, 38,* 537–45.

BLOOM, B. S., ENGLEHART, M. D., FURST, E. J., HILL, W. H., & KRATHWOHL, D. R. (1956). *Taxonomy of educational objectives: Handbook I: Cognitive domain.* New York: McKay.

BREHM, S. S., & BREHM, J. W. (1981). *Psychological reactance: A theory of freedom and control.* New York: Academic Press.

BRUNER, J. S. (1966). *Toward a theory of instruction.* Cambridge, Mass.: Belknap Press.

BRYAN, J., & BRYAN, T. (1984). The social life of the learning disabled youngster. In J. D. McKinney & L. Feagans (Eds.), *Current topics in learning disabilities, Vol. 1.* Norwood, N.J.: Ablex Publishing Co.

BRYAN, T., PEARL, R., DONAHUE, M., BRYAN, J., & PFLAUM, S. (1983). The Chicago Institute for the Study of Learning Disabilities. *Exceptional Education Quarterly, 4,* 1–22.

BURTON, W. H. (1962). *The guidance of learning activities.* New York: Appleton-Century-Crofts.

CHASE, S. (1956). *Guides to straight thinking.* New York: Harper & Brothers.

CLD RESEARCH COMMITTEE (1983). Minimum standards for the description of subjects in learning disabilities research reports. Draft provided by D. D. Smith, committee chair.

CLEMENTS, S. D. (1966). *Minimal brain dysfunction in children: Terminology and identification. Phase one of a three-phase project.* NINDS Monograph No. 3. U.S. Public Health Service Publication No. 1415. Washington, D.C.: U.S. GPO.

COLEMAN, J. C., & SANDHU, M. (1967). A descriptive relational study of 364 children referred to a university clinic for learning disorders. *Psychological Reports, 20,* 1091–1105.

COLLETTI, L. (1979). Relationship between pregnancy and birth complications and the later development of learning disabilities. *Journal of Learning Disabilities, 12,* 25–29.

COMENIUS, J. S. (1632). *The great didactic,* translated into English and edited by M. W. Kentinge. New York: Russell & Russell.

CONNOR, F. P. (1983). Improving school instruction for learning disabled children: The Teachers College Institute. *Exceptional Education Quarterly, 4,* 23–44.

CORDONI, B. K., O'DONNELL, J. P., RAMANIAH, N. V., KURTZ, J., & ROSENSHEIN, K. (1981). Wechsler adult intelligence score patterns for learning disabled young adults. *Journal of Learning Disabilities, 14,* 404–407.

CRATTY, B. J. (1967). *Developmental sequences of perceptual-motor tasks.* Freeport, N.Y.: Educational Activities.

CRONBACH, L. J. (1970). Essentials of psychological testing, 3rd ed. New York: Harper & Row.

CRUICKSHANK, W. M. (1983). Straight is the bamboo tree. *Journal of Learning Disabilities, 16,* 191–97.

CRUICKSHANK, W. M., BENTZEN, F. A., RATZEBURG, F. H., & TANNHAUSER, M. T. (1961). *A teaching method for brain-injured and hyperactive children.* Syracuse, N.Y.: Syracuse University Press.

CURTIS, B. A., JACOBSON, S., & MARCUS, E. M. (1972). *An introduction to the neurosciences.* Philadelphia: Saunders.

DALBY, J. T. (1979). Deficit or delay: Neuropsychological models of developmental dyslexia. *Journal of Special Education, 13,* 239–64.

DARROW, H. F., & VAN ALLEN, R. (1961). *Independent activities for creative learning.* New York: Teachers College Press.

DECI, E. L. (1975). *Intrinsic motivation.* New York: Plenum.

DECI, E. L. (1980). *The psychology of self-determination.* Lexington, Mass.: Lexington Books.

DELACATO, C. H. (1959). *The treatment and prevention of reading problems: The neurological approach.* Springfield, Ill.: Charles C. Thomas.

DELACATO, C. H. (1959). *Neurological organization and reading.* Springfield, Ill.: Charles C. Thomas.

DENCKLA, M. B., LEMAY, M., & CHAPMAN, C. A. (1985). Few CT scan abnormalities found even in neurologically impaired LD children. *Journal of Learning Disabilities, 18,* 132–135.

DESHLER, D. D., SCHUMAKER, J. B., & LENZ, B. K. (1984). Academic and cognitive interventions for LD adolescents: Part I. *Journal of Learning Disabilities, 17,* 108–117.

DESHLER, D. D., SCHUMAKER, J. B., LENZ, B. K., & ELLIS, E. (1984). Academic and cognitive interventions for LD adolescents: Part II. *Journal of Learning Disabilities, 17,* 170–79.

DEWEY, J. (1889). *Lectures in the philosophy of education.* R. D. Archambault (Ed.). New York: Random House.

DEWEY, J. (1938). *Experience and education.* New York: Collier Books.

DEWEY, J. (1966). *Lectures in the philosophy of education, 1899.* R. D. Archambault, (Ed.). New York: Random House.

DIANA V. STATE BOARD OF EDUCATION, No. C-70-37 (N.D. Calif. 1970).

DOUGLAS, V. I. (1972). Stop, look, and listen: The problem of sustained attention and impulse control in hyperactive and normal children. *Canadian Journal of Behavior Science, 4,* 259–81.

DUDLEY-MARLING, C. (1985). Perceptions of the usefulness of the IEP by teachers of learning disabilities and emotionally disturbed children. *Psychology in the Schools, 22,* 65–67.

DUNN, L. (1968). Special education for the mildly retarded—Is much of it justifiable? *Exceptional Children, 35,* 5–22.

DYKMAN, R. A., ACKERMAN, P. T., HOLCOMB, P. J., & BOUDREAU, A. Y. (1983). Physiological manifestations of learning disability. *Journal of Learning Disabilities, 16,* 46–53.

ENGLEMANN, S., & BRUNER, E. (1969). *Distar reading I and II: An instructional system.* Chicago: Science Research Associates.

FEDERAL REGISTER (1977). U.S. Office of Education. Education of handicapped children. *Federal Register, 42,* 65082-85.

FERNALD, G. (1943). *Remedial techniques in basic school subjects.* New York: McGraw-Hill.

FISHER, H. K. (1967). What is special education? *Special Education in Canada, 41,* 9–16.

FORNESS, S. R., SINCLAIR, E., & GUTHRIE, D. (1983). Learning disability discrepancy formulas: Their use in actual practice. *Learning Disability Quarterly, 6,* 107–114.

FRANCE, A. (1890). *The crime of Sylvestre Bonnard.* Translated by L. Hearn. New York: Harper & Brothers.

FRANK, J. D. (1961). *Persuasion and healing.* Baltimore: Johns Hopkins Press.

FROSTIG, M., & HORNE, D. (1964). *The Frostig program for the development of visual perception: Teacher's guide.* Chicago: Follett.

FROSTIG, M., LEFEVER, D., & WHITTLESEY, J. (1961). A developmental test of visual perception for evaluating normal and neurologically handicapped children. *Perceptual and Motor Skills, 12,* 383–94.

FROSTIG, M., MASLOW, P., LEFEVER, D., & WHITTLESEY, J. (1964). *The Marianne Frostig developmental test of visual perception: 1963 standardization.* Palo Alto, Calif.: Consulting Psychologists Press.

FROSTIG, M., & MASLOW, P. (1973). *Learning problems in the classroom.* New York: Grune & Stratton.

GADDES, W. H. (1985). *Learning disabilities and brain function: A neuropsychological approach,* 2nd edition. New York: Springer-Verlag.

GADOW, K. D. (1981). Prevalence of drug treatment for hyperactivity and other childhood behavior disorders. In K. D. Gadow & J. Loney (Eds.), *Psychological aspects of drug treatment for hyperactivity.* Boulder, Colo.: Westview Press.

GADOW, K. D. (1983). Effects of stimulant drugs on academic performance in hyperactive and learning disabled children. *Journal of Learning Disabilities, 16,* 290–99.

GAGNÉ, R. M. (Ed.) (1967). *Learning and individual differences.* Columbus, Ohio: Merrill Publishing Co.

GARRETT, H. E. (1954). Statistics in psychology and education. New York: Longmans Green.

GETMAN, G. N. (1965). The visuomotor complex in the acquisition of learning skills. In J. Hellmuth (Ed.), *Learning disorders,* Vol. 1. Seattle: Special Child Publications.

GOLDSTEIN, D., & MYERS, B. (1980). Cognitive lag and group differences in intelligence. *Child Study Journal, 10,* 119–32.

GOLDSTEIN, H., ARKELL, C., ASHCROFT, S. C., HURLEY, O. L., & LILLY, M. S. (1975). Schools. In N. Hobbs (Ed.), *Issues in the classification of children,* Vol. 2, San Francisco: Jossey-Bass.

GOLDSTEIN, K. (1936). The modifications of behavior consequent to cerebral lesions. *Psychiatric Quarterly, 10,* 586–610.

GOLDSTEIN, K. (1939). *The organism.* New York: American Book.

GOODLAD, J. I. (1984). *A place called school.* New York: McGraw-Hill.

GRACEY, C. A., AZZARA, C. V., & REINHERZ, H. (1984). Screening revisited: A survey of U.S. requirements. *Journal of Special Education, 18,* 101–107.

GRADEN, J. L., CASEY, A., & CHRISTENSEN, S. L. (1985). Implementing a prereferral intervention system: Part I. The model. *Exceptional Children. 51,* 377–384.

GRANT, W. V., & LUND, C. G. (1977). *Digest of educational statistics: 1976 edition.* National Center for Education Statistics No. 77-401. Washington, D.C.: U.S. GPO.

GRAY, R. A. (1981). Services for the LD adult: A working paper. *Learning Disability Quarterly, 4,* 426–434.

GUILFORD, J. P. (1956). *Fundamental statistics in Psychology.* New York: McGraw-Hill.

HACKETT, M. G. (1971). *Criterion reading: Individualized learning management system.* Westminister, Md.: Random House.

HALL, J., & GALLAGHER, J. J. (1984). Minimum competency testing and the learning disabled student. In J. D. McKinney & L. Feagans (Eds.), *Current topics in learning disabilities, Vol. 1.* Norwood, N.J.: Ablex Publishing Co.

HALLAHAN, D. P., HALL, R. J., IANNA, S. O., KNEEDLER, R. D., LLOYD, J. W., LOPER, A. B., & REEVE, R. E. (1983). Summary of research findings at the University of Virginia Learning Disabilities Institute. *Exceptional Education Quarterly, 4,* 95–114.

HALLAHAN, D. P., & KAUFFMAN, J. M. (1977). Labels, categories, behaviors: ED, LD, and EMR reconsidered. *Journal of Special Education, 11,* 139–49.

HAMMILL, D. D., GOODMAN, L., & WIEDERHOLT, J. L. (1974). Visual-motor processes: What success have we had in training them? *The Reading Teacher, 27,* 469–78.

HAMMILL, D. D., LEIGH, J. E., McNUTT, G., & LARSEN, S. C. (1981). A new definition of learning disabilities. *Learning Disability Quarterly, 4,* 336–42.

HARACKIEWICZ, J. M., SANSONE, C., & MANDERLINK, G. (1985). Competence, achievement orientation, and intrinsic motivation: A process analysis. *Journal of Personality and Social Psychology, 48,* 493–508.

HARBER, J. (1981). Learning disability research: How far have we progressed? *Learning Disability Quarterly, 4,* 372–82.

HARING, N. G., & PHILLIPS, E. L. (1962). *Analysis and modification of classroom behavior.* Englewood Cliffs, N.J.: Prentice-Hall.

HARING, N. G., & WHELAN, R. J. (1965). Experimental methods in education and management. In N. J. Long, W. C. Morse, & R. G. Newman (Eds.), *Conflict in the classroom.* Belmont, Calif.: Wadsworth.

HARRINGTON, T. F. (1982). *Handbook for career planning for special needs students.* Rockville, Md.: Aspen Publications.

HEWETT, F. M. (1968). *The emotionally disturbed child in the classroom.* Boston: Allyn & Bacon.

HEWETT, F. M., & TAYLOR, F. D. (1980). *The emotionally disturbed child in the classroom: The orchestration of success,* 2nd ed. Boston: Allyn & Bacon.

HOBBS, N. (1975). *The future of children: Categories, labels, and their consequences.* San Francisco: Jossey-Bass.

HOLT, J. (1964). *How children fail.* New York: Pitman Publishing.

HOLT, J. (1983). *How children learn,* rev. ed. New York: Delacorte Press.

HORN, W. F., O'DONNELL, J. P., & VITULANO, L. A. (1983). Long-term follow-up studies of learning-disabled persons. *Journal of Learning Disabilities, 16,* 542–55.

ILLICH, I. (1976). *Medical nemesis.* New York: Pantheon Books.

IVARIE, J., HOGUE, D., & BRULLE, A. (1984). An investigation of mainstream teacher time spent with students labeled as learning disabled. *Exceptional Children, 51,* 142–49.

JOHNSON, D., & MYKLEBUST, H. R. (1967). *Learning disabilities: Educational principles and practices.* New York: Grune & Stratton.

JONES, E. E., & NISBETT, R. (1971). The actor and observer: Divergent perceptions of the causes of behavior. In E. E. Jones, D. E. Kanouse, H. H. Kelley, R. E. Nisbett, S. Valens, & B. Weiner, *Attribution: Perceiving the causes of behavior.* Morristown, N.J.: General Learning Press.

JOYCE, B., & WEIL, M. (1980). *Models of teaching,* 2nd ed. New York: Prentice-Hall.

KANFER, F. H., & GOLDSTEIN, A. P. (1980). *Helping people change: A textbook of methods,* 2nd ed. New York: Pergamon Press.

KARPMAN, S. (1968). Script drama analysis. *Transactional Analysis Bulletin, 7,* 39–43.

KAUFMAN, A. S. (1979). *Intelligent testing with the WISC-R.* New York: John Wiley.

KAUFMAN, A. S. (1981). The WISC-R and learning disabilities assessment: State of the art. *Journal of Learning Disabilities, 14,* 520–26.

KAVALE, K., & NYE, C. (1981). Identification criteria for learning disabilities: A survey of the research literature. *Learning Disability Quarterly, 4,* 383–88.

KAZDIN, A. E. (1984). *Behavior modification in applied settings.* Homewood, Ill.: Dorsey Press.

KEOGH, B. (1983). A lesson from Gestalt psychology. *Exceptional Education Quarterly, 4,* 115–27.

KEOGH, B. K., & PELLAND, M. (1985). Vision training revisited. *Journal of Learning Disabilities, 18,* 228–236.

KEPHART, N. C. (1960). *The slow learner in the classroom.* Columbus, Ohio: Merrill. (2nd ed. 1971).

KEPHART, N. C., & STRAUSS, A. A. (1940). A clinical factor influencing variations in I.Q. *American Journal of Orthopsychiatry, 10,* 345–50.

KIBLER, R. J., BARKER, L. L., & MILES, D. T. (1970). *Behavior objectives and instruction.* Boston: Allyn & Bacon.

KINSBOURNE, M., & CAPLIN, P. (1979). *Children's learning and attention problems.* Boston: Little, Brown.

KIRK, S. A. (1962). *Educating exceptional children.* Boston: Houghton-Mifflin.

KIRK, S. A., & GALLAGHER, J. (1979). *Educating exceptional children,* 3rd ed. Boston: Houghton-Mifflin.

KIRK, S. A., & KIRK, W. D. (1983). On defining learning disabilities. *Journal of Learning Disabilities, 16,* 20–21.

KIRK, S. A., MCCARTHY, J. J., & KIRK, W. D. (1961). *Illinois test of psycholinguistic abilities.* Urbana: University of Illinois Press. (rev. ed. 1968)

KOESTNER, R., RYAN, R. M., BERNIERI, F., & HOLT, K. (1984). Setting limits on children's behavior: The differential effects of controlling vs. informational styles on intrinsic motivation and creativity. *Journal of Personality, 52,* 242–248.

KOPPITZ, E. (1973). Special class pupils with learning disabilities: A five year follow-up study. *Academic Therapy, 13,* 133–40.

KRATHWOHL, D. R., BLOOM, B. S., & MASIA, B. B. (1964). *Taxonomy of educational objectives: Handbook II: Affective domain.* New York: McKay.

LARRY P. V. RILES, 343 F Supp. 1306 (N.D. Calif. 1972).

LENNARD, H., EPSTEIN, L. J., BERNSTEIN, A., & RANSOM, D. C. (1970). Hazards implicit in prescribing psychoactive drugs. *Science, 169,* 438–41.

LEPPER, M. R., & GREENE, D. (1978). *The hidden costs of reward.* Hillsdale, N.J.: Erlbaum Press.

LERNER, J. W. (1976). *Children with learning disabilities,* 2nd ed. Boston: Houghton-Mifflin.

LEVINE, R. J. (1975). *The nature and definition of informed consent in various research settings.* Washington, D.C.: National Commission for the Protection of Human Subjects.

LINDSAY, G. A., & WEDELL, K. (1982). The early identification of educationally "at risk" children revisited. *Journal of Learning Disabilities, 15*, 212–17.

LINDSLEY, O. R. (1964). Direct measurement and prothesis of retarded behavior. *Journal of Education, 147*, 62–81.

LISCIO, M. A. (Ed.) (1985). *A guide to colleges for learning disabled students.* Orlando, Fla.: Academic Press.

LOVITT, T. C. (1975a). Applied behavior analysis and learning disabilities—Part I: Characteristics of ABA, general recommendations, and methodological limitations. *Journal of Learning Disabilities, 8*, 432–43.

LOVITT, T. C. (1975b). Applied behavior analysis and learning disabilities—Part II: Specific research recommendations and suggestions for practitioners. *Journal of Learning Disabilities, 8*, 504–18.

MCCANN, S. K., SEMMELL, M. I., & NEVIN, A. (1985). Reverse mainstreaming: Nonhandicapped students in special education classrooms. *Remedial and Special Education, 6*, 13–19.

MCGRATH, J. H. (1972). *Planning systems for school executives: The unity of theory and practice.* Scranton, Pa.: Intext Educational Publishers.

MCKINNEY, J. D., & FEAGANS, L. (Eds.) (1984). *Current topics in learning disabilities, Vol. 1.* Norwood, N.J.: Ablex Publishing Co.

MCMURRIN, S. M. (1963). Introduction. In J. D. Koerner, *The mis-education of American teachers.* Boston: Houghton-Mifflin.

MAHONEY, M. J. (1974). *Cognition and behavior modification.* Cambridge, Mass.: Ballinger Publishing Co.

MANGRUM, C. T., & STRICHART, S. S. (1983). College possibilities for the learning disabled: Part one. *Learning Disabilities, 2*, 57–68.

MANGRUM, C. T., & STRICHART, S. S. (1983). College possibilities for the learning disabled: Part two. *Learning Disabilities, 2*, 69–81.

MANGRUM, C. T., & STRICHART, S. S. (Eds.) (1985). *College and the learning disabled student: A guide to program selection, development, and implementation.* Orlando, Fla.: Grune & Stratton.

MANN, L., DAVIS, C., BOYER, C., METZ, C., & WOLFORD, B. (1983). LD or not LD, that was the question. *Journal of Learning Disabilities, 16*, 14–17.

MASSENZIO, S. (1983). Legal resource networks for parents and individuals with special needs. *Exceptional Children, 50*, 273–75.

MEANS, R. K. (1968). *Methodology in education.* Columbus, Ohio: Merrill.

MEICHENBAUM, D. (1977). *Cognitive-behavior modi*

fication: An integrative approach. New York: Plenum.

MELTON, G. B. (1983). Children's competence to consent: A problem in law and social science. In G. B. Melton, G. P. Koocher, & M. J. Saks (Eds.), *Children's competence to consent.* New York: Plenum.

MERCER, C. D., HUGHES, C., & MERCER, A. R. (1975). Learning disabilities definitions used by state education departments. *Learning Disability Quarterly, 8*, 45–55.

MEYEN, E. L. (Ed.) (1971). *Proceedings—The Missouri conference on the categorical/non-categorical issue in special education.* Columbia, Mo.: University of Missouri Press.

MEYEN, E. L. (1976). *Instructional based appraisal system.* Bellevue, Wash.: Edmark Associates.

MEYEN, E. L. (1982). *Exceptional children and youth,* 2nd ed. Denver: Love Publishing Co.

MILLER, A. (1981). Conceptual matching models and interactional research in education. *Review of Educational Research, 51*, 33–84.

MILLER, S. R., & SCHLOSS, P. J. (1982). *Career-vocational education for handicapped youth.* Rockville, Md.: Aspen.

MIRKIN, P., MARSTON, D., & DENO, S. L. (1982). Direct and repeated measurement of academic skills: An alternative to traditional screening, referral, and identification of learning disabled students. Research Report No. 75. Minneapolis: University of Minnesota, Institute for Research on Learning Disabilities.

MOOS, R. H. (1979). *Evaluating educational environments.* San Francisco: Jossey-Bass.

MORRISON, G. M., MACMILLAN, D. L., & KAVALE, K. (1985). System identification of learning disabled children: Implications for research sampling. *Learning Disability Quarterly, 8*, 2–10.

MYKLEBUST, H. R. (1954). *Auditory disorders in children.* New York: Grune & Stratton.

MYKLEBUST, H. R. (1968). Learning disabilities: Definition and overview. In H. R. Myklebust (Ed.), *Progress in learning disabilities.* New York: Grune & Stratton.

NEISSER, U. (1976). *Cognition and reality: Principles and implications of cognitive psychology.* San Francisco: W. H. Freeman & Co.

NEWCOMER, P. L. (1982). Competencies for professionals in learning disabilities. *Learning Disability Quarterly, 5*, 241–52.

NUNNALLY, J. C. (1978). *Psychometric theory,* 2nd ed. New York: McGraw-Hill.

NYBERG, D. (1971). *Tough and tender learning.* Palo Alto, Calif.: National Press Books.

ORTON, S. T. (1937). *Reading, writing, and speech problems in children.* New York: Norton.

PAIS, A. (1982). *'Subtle is the Lord': The science and the life of Albert Einstein.* New York: Oxford University Press.

PASAMINICK, B., & KNOBLOCK, H. (1973). The epidemiology of reproductive causality. In S. Sapir & A. Nitzburg (Eds.), *Children with learning problems: Readings in a development-interaction approach.* New York: Brunner/Mazel Publishing.

PERLMUTER, L. C., & MONTY, R. A. (Eds.) (1979). *Choice and perceived control.* Hillsdale, N.J.: Erlbaum Associates.

PHIPPS, P. M. (1982). The merging categories: Appropriate education or administrative convenience? *Journal of Learning Disabilities, 15,* 153–54.

PIHL, R. O. (1975). Learning disabilities: Intervention programs in the schools. In H. R. Myklebust (Ed.), *Progress in learning disabilities,* Vol. 3. New York: Grune & Stratton.

PERLMUTTER, B. F., & PARUS, M. V. (1983). Identifying children with learning disabilities: A comparison of diagnostic procedures across school districts. *Learning Disability Quarterly, 6,* 321–28.

POPHAM, W. J., EISNER, E. W., SULLIVAN, H. J., & TYLER, L. L. (1969). *Instructional objectives.* AERA Monograph Series on Curriculum Evaluation. Chicago: Rand McNally.

QUAY, H. (1968). The facets of educational exceptionality: A conceptual model for assessment, grouping, and instruction. *Exceptional Children, 35,* 25–32.

RABINOVITZ, R. D. (1959). Reading and learning disabilities. In S. Arieti (Ed.), *American handbook of psychiatry,* Vol. 1. New York: Basic Books.

REAGAN, N. (1983). Message from Mrs. Reagan. *Their World.* New York: Foundation for Children with Learning Disabilities.

REGER, R., SCHROEDER, W., & USCHOLD, D. (1968). *Special education: Children with learning problems.* New York: Oxford University Press.

RISLEY, T. R., & BAER, D. M. (1973). Operant behavior modification: The deliberate development of behavior. In B. M. Caldwell & N. N. Ricciuti (Eds.), *Review of child development research,* Vol. 3. Chicago: University of Chicago Press.

ROBERSON, S. D., KEITH, T. Z., & PAGE, E. B. (1983). Now who aspires to teach? *Educational Researcher, 12,* 13–21.

ROGERS, C. (1977). *On personal power: Inner strength and its revolutionary impact.* New York: Delacorte Press.

ROSS, A. O. (1985). To form a more perfect union. *Behavior Therapy, 16,* 195–204.

RUBIN, R., & BALOW, B. (1971). Learning and behavior disorders: A longitudinal study. *Exceptional Children, 38,* 293–99.

RUBLE, D. N., & BOGGIANO, A. K. (1980). Optimizing motivation in an achievement context. In B. Keogh (Ed.), *Advances in special education: Basic constructs and theoretical orientations.* Greenwich Conn.: JAI Press.

SABATINO, D. A. (1981). Elementary and middle school services and program delivery. In D. A. Sabatino, T. L. Miller, & C. R. Schmidt (Eds.), *Learning disabilities: Systematizing teaching and service delivery.* Rockville, Md.: Aspen.

SALVIA, J., & YSSELDYKE, J. E. (1981). *Assessment in special and remedial education,* 2nd ed. Boston: Houghton-Mifflin.

SARASON, S. B. (1982) *The culture of the school and the problem of change,* 2nd ed. Boston: Allyn & Bacon.

SCHAIN, R. J. (1972). *Neurology of childhood learning disorders.* Baltimore: Williams & Wilkins.

SCHEFFELIN, M. M., RAGSDALE, D., & MARTINEZ, J. (1985). Program evaluation in special education: From policy to practice in California. *Journal of Learning Disabilities, 18,* 87–88.

SCHRAG, P., & DIVOKY, D. (1975). *The myth of the hyperactive child and other means of child control.* New York: Pantheon Books.

SCHUMAKER, J. B., DESHLER, D. D., ALLEY, G. R., & WARNER, M. M. (1983). Toward the development of an intervention model for learning disabled adolescents: The University of Kansas Institute. *Exceptional Education Quarterly, 4,* 45–74.

SCHWARTZ, L., OSTEROFF, A., BRUCKER, H., & SCHWARTZ, R. (Eds.) (1972). *Innovative non-categorical and interrelated projects in the education of the handicapped.* Tallahassee, Fla.: Florida State University Press.

SCHWORM, R. (1976). Models in special education: Considerations and cautions. *Journal of Special Education, 10,* 179–86.

SCRIVEN, M. (1981). Comments on Gene Glass. Paper presented at the Wingspread Working Conference of Social Policy and Educational Leaders to Develop Strategies for Special Education in the 1980's, Racine, Wisc.

SENF, G. M. (1981). Issues surrounding diagnosis of learning disabilities: Child handicap versus failure of child-school interaction. In T. R. Kratochwill (Ed.), *Advances in school psychology,* Vol. 1. Hillsdale, N.J.: Erlbaum Associates.

SHAYWITZ, S., COHEN, D., & SHAYWITZ, B. (1978). The biochemical basis of minimal brain dysfunction. *Journal of Pediatrics, 92,* 179–87.

SHEPARD, L. A., & SMITH, M. L. (1983). An evaluation of the identification of learning disabled students in Colorado. *Learning Disability Quarterly, 6,* 115–27.

SIEBEN, R. L. (1977). Controversial medical treatments of learning disabilities. *Academic Therapy, 13,* 133–48.

SILBERMAN, C. E. (1970). *Crisis in the classroom: The remaking of American education.* New York: Vintage Books.

SKAGER, R. W., & WEINBERG, C. (1971). Fundamentals of educational research: An introductory approach. Glenview, Il.: Scott, Foresman.

SKINNER, B. F. (1974). *About behaviorism.* New York: Alfred A. Knopf.

SMITH, C. R. (1983). *Learning disabilities: The interaction of learner, task, and setting.* Boston: Little, Brown.

SMITH, S. D., & PENNINGTON, B. F. (1983). Genetic influences on learning disabilities I: Clinical genetics. *Learning Disabilities, 2,* 31–42.

SNART, F. (1985). Cognitive-processing approaches to the assessment of remediation of learning problems. An interview with J. P. Das and Rewven Feuerstein. *Journal of Psychoeducational Assessment, 3,* 1–14.

SPARKS, R., & RICHARDSON, S. O. (1981). Multicategorical/cross-categorical classrooms for learning disabled children. *Journal of Learning Disabilities, 14,* 60–61.

SPREEN, O. (1982). Adult outcome of reading disorders. In R. N. Malatesha & P. G. Aaron (Eds.), *Reading disorders: Varieties and treatments.* New York: Academic Press.

STAKE, R. E. (1967). The countenance of educational evaluation. *Teachers College Record, 68,* 523–40.

STAKE, R. E. (1976). *Evaluating educational programs: The need and the response.* Paris: Organization for Economic Cooperation and Development.

STEINBECK, J. (1955). Like captured fireflies. *California Teachers Association Journal, 51,* 7.

STEPHENS, T. M. (1977). *Teaching skills to children with learning and behavior disorders.* Columbus, Ohio: Merrill.

STEPHENS, T. M. (1985). Personal behavior and professional ethics: Implications for special educators. *Journal of Learning Disabilities, 18,* 187–192.

STEVENSON, H. W. (1972). *Children's learning.* New York: Appleton-Century-Crofts.

STINSON, M. (1984). Research on motivation in educational settings: Implications for hearing-impaired students. *Journal of Special Education, 18,* 177–98.

STRAUSS, A. A. (1943). Diagnosis and education of the cripple-brained, deficient child. *Journal of Exceptional Children, 9,* 163–68.

STRAUSS, A. A., & KEPHART, N. C. (1955). *Psychopathology and education of the brain-injured child,* Vol. 2: *Progress in theory and clinic.* New York: Grune & Stratton.

STRAUSS, A. A., & LEHTINEN, L. E. (1947). *Psychopathology and education of the brain-injured child.* New York: Grune & Stratton.

STRICHART, S. S., & GOTTLIEB, J. (1981). Learning disabilities at the crossroads. In J. Gottlieb & S. S. Strichart (Eds.), *Developmental theory and research in learning disabilities.* Baltimore: University Park Press.

STRUPP, H. H., & HADLEY, S. M. (1977). A tripartite model for mental health and therapeutic outcomes with special reference to negative effects in psychotherapy. *American Psychologist, 32,* 187–96.

SWIFT, C., & LEWIS, R. B. (1985). Leisure preferences of elementary-aged learning disabled boys. *Research in Special Education, 6,* 37–42.

TAYLOR, H. G., & FLETCHER, J. (1983). Biological foundations of "specific developmental disorders": Methods, findings, and future directions. *Journal of Clinical Child Psychology: 12,* 46–65.

TAYLOR, L., ADELMAN, H. S., & KASER-BOYD, N. (1984). Attitudes toward involving minors in decisions. *Professional Psychology, 15,* 436–49.

TAYLOR, L., ADELMAN, H. S., & KASER-BOYD, N. (1985). Minors' attitudes and competence toward participation in psychoeducational decisions. *Professional Psychology, 16,* 226–235.

TEYLER, T. J. (1978). The brain sciences. In J. S. Chall & A. F. Mirsky (Eds.), *Education and the brain.* Chicago: National Society for the Study of Education.

THORNDIKE, R. L., & HAGEN, E. P. (1977). *Measurement and evaluation,* 2nd ed. New York: Wiley.

THURLOW, M., & YSSELDYKE, J. (1979). Currect assessment and decision making practices in model programs for learning disabled students. *Learning Disability Quarterly, 2,* 15–24.

TINDAL, G. (1985). Investigating the effectiveness of special education. *Journal of Learning Disabilities, 18,* 101–112.

TORGESEN, J. K., & LICHT, B. G. (1984). The learning disabled child as an inactive learner: Retrospect and prospects. In J. D. McKinney & L. Feagans (Eds.), *Current topics in learning disabilities,* Vol. 1. Norwood, N.J.: Ablex Publishing Co.

TORRANCE, E. P. (1965). Different ways of learning for different kinds of children. In E. P. Torrance & R. D. Strom (Eds.), *Mental health and achievement:*

Increasing potential and reducing school dropout. New York: Wiley.

TUCKER, J., STEVENS, L. J., & YSSELDYKE, J. E. (1983). Learning disabilities: The experts speak out. *Journal of Learning Disabilities, 16,* 6–14.

TURNBULL, A. P., & SCHULTZ, J. B. (1979). *Mainstreaming handicapped students: A guide for the classroom teacher.* Boston: Allyn & Bacon.

VAN DUYNE, H. J., GARGIULO, R., & ALLEN, J. A. (1980). A survey of Illinois preschool screening programs. *Illinois Council for Exceptional Children Quarterly, 29,* 11–16.

WASSERSTROM, R. (1975). Lawyers as professionals: Some moral issues. *Human Rights, 5,* 1–24.

WEDELL, K. (1970). Diagnosing learning disabilities: A sequential strategy. *Journal of Learning Disabilities, 3,* 311–17.

WEINER, B. A. (1979). A theory of motivation for some classroom experiences. *Journal of Educational Psychology, 71,* 3–25.

WEINER, B. A. (1980). *Human motivation.* New York: Holt, Reinhart & Winston.

WEINTRAUB, F. J., ABESON., A., BALLARD, J., & LA VOR, M. L. (Eds.) (1976). *Public policy and the education of exceptional children.* Reston, Va.: The Council for Exceptional Children.

WEITHORN, L. A. (1983). Involving children in decisions affecting their own welfare: Guidelines for professionals. In G. B. Melton, G. P. Koocher, & M. J. Saks (Eds.), *Children's competence to consent.* New York: Plenum Press.

WENDER, P. H. (1976). Hypothesis for possible biochemical basis of minimal brain dysfunction. In R. M. Knights & D. J. Bakker (Eds.), *The neuropsychology of learning disorders: Theoretical approaches.* Baltimore: University Park Press.

WERNER, H., & STRAUSS, A. A. (1940). Causal factors in low performance. *American Journal of Mental Deficiency, 45,* 213–18.

WERNER, H., & STRAUSS, A. A. (1941). Pathology as figure-background relation in the child. *Journal of Abnormal and Social Psychology, 36,* 236–48.

WHALEN, C. K., & HENKER, B. (1976). Psychostimulants and children: A review and analysis. *Psychological Bulletin, 83,* 1113–30.

WHELAN, R. J. (1966). The relevance of behavior modification procedures for teachers of emotionally disturbed children. In P. Knoblock (Ed.), *Intervention approaches in educating emotionally disturbed children.* Syracuse, N.Y.: Syracuse University Press.

WINKLER, A., DIXON, J. F., & PARKER, J. B. (1970). Brain function in problem children and controls: Psychometric, neurological, and electroencephalographic comparisons. *American Journal of Psychiatry, 125,* 94–105.

WISSINK, J. F., KASS, C. E., & FERRELL, W. R. (1975). A Bayesian approach to the identification of children with learning disabilities. *Journal of Learning Disabilities, 8,* 158–66.

WOLPE, J. (1958). *Psychotherapy by reciprocal inhibition.* Stanford, Calif.: Stanford University Press.

WORTHORN, B. R., & SANDERS, J. R. (1973). *Educational evaluation: Theory and practice.* Worthington, Ohio: Charles E. Jones.

YSSELDYKE, J. E., & ALGOZZINE, B. (1982). *Critical issues in special and remedial education.* Boston: Houghton-Mifflin.

YSSELDYKE, J. E., & MIRKIN, P. K. (1981). The use of assessment information to plan instructional interventions: A review of the research. In C. Reynolds & T. Gutkin (Eds.), *A handbook for school psychology.* New York: Wiley.

YSSELDYKE, J., THURLOW, M., GRADEN, J., WESSON, C., ALGOZZINE, B., & DENO, S. (1983). Generalizations from five years of research on assessment and decision making: The University of Minnesota Institute. *Exceptional Education Quarterly, 4,* 75–93.

Name Index

Subject Index

A

Academic Therapy Publications, 74, 227
Accommodating individual differences, 97, 98, 100, 127, 140, 170, 268–270, 275
Accountability, 180, 184, 186, 191, 213–215
Achievement age (AA), 58
Achievement-intelligence discrepancy, 7, 12, 54–58. *See also* Discrepancy formula
Achievement tests, 3, 7, 60, 78, 247
ACLD. *See* Association for Children and Adults with Learning Disabilities
Adolescents
  and LD, 10, 25, 26, 65, 91, 100
  rights of, 64
  service options for, 59, 75
  See also Career education; College programs for LD
Adults
  and LD, 10, 22, 25, 32, 91, 100, 217, 299–300
  National Network of Learning Disabled Adults, 225
  postsecondary careers and education, 22, 25, 201, 224, 323–324
  service options for, 59, 75
American Psychological Association, 211, 213
American Speech-Language-Hearing Association (ASHA), 7
Anoxia (oxygen deprivation), 29, 32, 38
Aphasia, 8, 23

Applied behavioral analysis, 20, 73, 74–76, 280–281. *See also* precision teaching
Aptitude-treatment interaction (ATI). *See* Match
Assessment, 26, 51, 52–59, 66, 83 (fig.), 196–199, 237–244
  of achievement. *See* Achievement tests
  bias in, 66, 79, 94, 251, 302
  and classification, 44, 83, 94
  and consultation, 93–94
  and decisions, 79, 88, 92, 94–95
  of environment, 55
  errors of, 12, 14, 46–48, 55, 76, 82, 99–100, 121, 199, 204, 247–248, 301
  ethical concerns of. *See* Ethical concerns
  improving, 87–94, 102
  of motivation, 137, 163
  negative effects of. *See* Negative effects
  and neurological signs, 3, 6, 43–46, 49
  neuropsychological, 10, 11, 44–46, 49, 70, 198
  norms used in, 245, 249–251
  orientations to, 51, 77–82, 86
  of person-environment interaction, 55
  purposes and functions of, 56–59, 62–63, 77–82, 83 (fig.)
  reassessment. *See* Reassessment
  reliability of, 80, 245–246
  sequential approaches to, 88–89, 93–94, 100, 102, 121, 199
  standards used in, 188, 245, 249–251

tests and other procedures in, 51, 60–61, 77, 78, 80, 81, 82, 198, 199, 237, 238–241 (tab.), 304, 310
  test profiles and patterns in, 60–61
  in treatment planning, 60, 70, 75, 77–82, 83, 88, 93, 94
  validity and validity problems of, 56–57, 60–61, 63, 78, 80, 82, 197, 213, 237, 245, 246–249
  See also Diagnosis; Evaluation; Placement; Planning for intervention; Screening; specific tests by name
Association of Children and Adults with Learning Disabilities (ACLD), 7, 8, 10–11, 22, 215, 225
Attention deficit disorder, 169
Attention problems, 6, 12, 26, 34, 38, 42, 48, 72, 169
Attitudes, and learning, 97, 104, 105, 111, 115, 122, 138
Attribution, 26
  bias in, 54
  tendencies, 54, 141–142

B

Backlash, 85, 207
Basic psychological processes, 7, 9, 10, 59, 70–72, 117
Basic skills, 72–74, 97, 100, 126–128, 141–144, 146, 172
Beery-Buktenica Developmental Test of Motor Integration, 78
Behavioral analysis. *See* Applied behavioral analysis